*The Revival
of Learning*

JOHN ADDINGTON SYMONDS

The Revival
of Learning

At tibi fortassis, si, quod mens sperat et optat,
Es post me victura diu, meliora supersunt
Secula; non omnes veniet lethaeus in annos
Iste sopor; poterunt, discussis forte tenebris,
Ad purum priscumque jubar remeare nepotes.
Tunc Helicona novâ revirentem stirpe videbis,
Tunc lauros frondere sacras; tunc alta resurgent
Ingenia atque animi dociles, quibus ardor honesti
Pieridum studii veterem geminabit amorem.
                    PETRARCHAE *Africa, lib. ix*

CAPRICORN BOOKS
G. P. PUTNAM'S SONS   New York

CAPRICORN EDITION, 1960

The Revival of Learning is Volume II of
Symonds' RENAISSANCE IN ITALY

Library of Congress Catalog Card
Number: 60-6632

MANUFACTURED IN THE UNITED STATES OF AMERICA

PREFACE

——◦•◦——

THIS VOLUME on the 'Revival of Learning' follows that on the 'Age of the Despots,' published in 1875, and precedes that on the 'Fine Arts,' which is now also offered to the public. In dealing with the 'Revival of Learning' and the 'Fine Arts,' I have tried to remember that I had not so much to write again the history of these subjects, as to treat their relation to the 'Renaissance in Italy.' In other words, I have regarded each section of my theme as subordinate to the general culture of a great historical period. The volume on 'Italian Literature,' still in contemplation, is intended to complete the work.

While handling the theme of the Italian Renaissance, I have selected such points, and emphasised such details, as I felt to be important for the biography of a nation at the most brilliant epoch of its intellectual activity. The historian of culture sacrifices much that the historian of politics will judge essential, and calls attention to matters that the general reader may sometimes find

[1] To the original edition of this volume.

superfluous. He must submit to bear the reproach of having done at once too little and too much. He must be content to traverse at one time well-worn ground, and at another to engage in dry or abstruse inquiries. He must not shrink from seeming to affect the fame of a compiler; nor, unless his powers be of the highest, can he hope altogether to avoid repetitions wearisome alike to reader and to writer. His main object is to paint the portrait of national genius identical through all varieties of manifestation; and in proportion as he has preserved this point of view with firmness, he may hope to have succeeded.

For the History of the Revival of Learning I have had continual recourse to Tiraboschi's 'Storia della Letteratura Italiana.' That work is still the basis of all researches bearing on the subject. I owe besides particular obligations to Vespasiano's 'Vite di Uomini Illustri,' to Comparetti's 'Virgilio nel Medio Evo,' to Rosmini's 'Vita di Filelfo,' 'Vita di Vittorino da Feltre,' and 'Vita di Guarino da Verona,' to Shepherd's 'Life of Poggio Bracciolini,' to Dennistoun's 'Dukes of Urbino,' to Schultze's 'Gemistos Plethon,' to Didot's 'Alde Manuce,' to Von Reumont's 'Lorenzo de' Medici,' to Burckhardt's 'Cultur der Renaissance in Italien,' to Voigt's 'Wiederbelebung des classischen Alterthums,' and to Gregorovius's 'Geschichte der Stadt Rom.' To Voigt and Burckhardt, having perforce traversed the same ground that they have done, I feel that I have been in a special sense indebted. At the same time I have made it my invariable practice, as the notes to this volume will show, to found my own opinions on the study of original

sources. To mention in detail all the editions of the
works of humanists and scholars I have consulted, would
be superfluous.

To me it has been a labour of love to record even the
bare names of those Italian worthies who recovered for
us in the fourteenth and fifteenth centuries ' the everlasting consolations ' of the Greek and Latin classics.
The thought that I was tracing the history of an
achievement fruitful of the weightiest results for modern
civilisation has sustained me in a task that has been
sometimes tedious. The collective greatness of the
Revival has reconciled my mind to many trivialities of
detail. The prosaic minutiæ of obscure biographies and
long-forgotten literary labours have been glorified by
what appears to me the poetry and the romance of the
whole theme. It lies not in my province or my power
to offer my readers any adequate apology for such defects
as my own want of skill in exposition, or the difficulty
of transfiguring with vital light and heat a subject so
remote from present interests, may have occasioned. I
must leave this volume in their hands, hoping that some
at least may be animated by the same feeling of gratitude toward those past workers in the field of learning
which has supported me.

CLIFTON : *March* 1877.

CONTENTS

CHAPTER I

THE MEN OF THE RENAISSANCE

CHAPTER II

FIRST PERIOD OF HUMANISM

CHAPTER IV

SECOND PERIOD OF HUMANISM

CHAPTER V

SECOND PERIOD OF HUMANISM

CHAPTER VI

THIRD PERIOD OF HUMANISM

CHAPTER VII

FOURTH PERIOD OF HUMANISM

CHAPTER VIII

LATIN POETRY

CHAPTER IX

CONCLUSION

RENAISSANCE IN ITALY

CHAPTER I

THE MEN OF THE RENAISSANCE

Formation of Conscious Personality in Italy—Aristocracy of Intellect—
Self-culture as an Aim—Want of National Architecture—Want of
National Drama—Eminence of Sculpture and Painting—Peculiar
Capacity for Literature—Scholarship—Men of Many-sided Genius—
Their Relation to the Age—Conflict between Mediæval Tradition
and Humanism—Petrarch—The Meaning of the Revival begun by
him—Cosmopolitan Philosophy—Toleration—An Intellectual Em-
pire—Worldliness—Confusion of Impulses and Inspirations—
Copernicus and Columbus—Christianity and the Classics—Italian
Incapacity for Religious Reformation—Free Thought takes the form
of License—Harmonies attempted between Christianity and Antique
Philosophy—Florentine Academy—Physical Qualities of the Italians
—Portraits of Two Periods—Physical Exercises—Determination of
the Race to Scholarship—Ancient Memories of Rome—The Cult of
Antiquity—Desire of Fame—Fame to be found in Literature—The
Cult of Intellect—The Cult of Character—Preoccupation with
Personal Details—Biography—Ideal Sketches—Posthumous Glory—
Enthusiasm for Erudition—Piero de' Pazzi—Florence and Athens
—Paganism—Real Value of Italian Humanism—Pico on the Dignity
of Man.

THE conditions, political, social, moral, and religious, described
in the first volume of this work, produced among the Italians
a type of character nowhere else observable in Europe. This
character, highly self-conscious and mentally mature, was
needed for the intellectual movement of the Renaissance.
Italy had proved herself incapable of forming an united

nation, or of securing the principle of federal coherence; of maintaining a powerful military system, or of holding her own against the French and Spaniards. For these defects her Communes and her Despots, the Papacy and the kingdom of Naples, the theories of the mediæval doctrinaires and the enthusiasm of the humanists, were alike responsible; though the larger share belongs to Rome, resolutely hostile to the monarchical principle, and zealous, by espousing the Guelf faction, to maintain the discord of the nation. At the same time the very causes of political disunion were favourable to the intellectual growth of the Italians. Each State, whether republican or despotic, had, during the last years of the Middle Ages, formed a mixed society of nobles, merchants, and artisans, enclosed within the circuit of the city walls, and strongly marked by the peculiar complexion of their native place. Every town was a centre of activity and industry, eagerly competing with its neighbours, proud of its local characteristics, anxious to confer distinction on citizens who rose to eminence by genius or practical ability. Party strife in the republics, while it disturbed their internal repose, sharpened the intellect and strengthened the personality of the burghers. Exile and proscription, the common climax of civic warfare, made them still more self-determined and self-reliant by driving each man back upon his own resources. The despots, again, through the illegal tenure of their authority, were forced to the utmost possible development of individual character: since all their fortunes depended on their qualities as men. The plots and counterplots of subjects eager for a change of government, and of neighbours anxious to encroach upon their territory, kept the atmosphere of their Courts in a continual state of agitation. One type of ability was fostered by the diplomatic relations of the several cities, yielding employment to a multitude of secretaries and ambassadors; another by the system of

Condottiere warfare, offering a brilliant career to ambitious adventurers. In all departments open to a man of talent birth was of less importance than natural gifts ; for the social barriers and grades of feudalism had either never existed in Italy, or had been shaken and confounded during the struggles of the twelfth and thirteenth centuries. The ranks of the tyrants were filled with sons of Popes and captains risen from the proletariat. The ruling class in the republics consisted of men self-made by commerce ; and here the name at least of Popolo was sovereign. It followed that men were universally rated at what they proved themselves to be; and thus an aristocracy of genius and character grew up in Italy at a period when the rest of Europe presented but rare specimens of individuals emergent from the common herd. As in ancient Greece, the nation was of less importance than the city, and within the city personal ability carried overwhelming weight. The Italian history of the Renaissance resumes itself in the biography of men greater than their race, of mental despots, who absorbed its forces in themselves.

The intellectual and moral milieu created by multitudes of self-centred, cultivated personalities was necessary for the evolution of that spirit of intelligence, subtle, penetrative, and elastic, that formed the motive force of the Renaissance. The work achieved by Italy for the world in that age was less the work of a nation than that of men of power, less the collective and spontaneous triumph of a puissant people than the aggregate of individual efforts animated by one soul of free activity, a common striving after fame. This is noticeable at the very outset. The Italians had no national Epic : their Divine Comedy is the poem of the individual man. Petrarch erects self-culture to the rank of an ideal, and proposes to move the world from the standpoint of his study, darting his spirit's light through all the void circumference, and making thought a power.

The success and the failure of the Italians are alike referable to their political subdivisions, and to this strong development of their personality. We have already seen how they fell short of national unity and of military greatness. Even in the realm of art and literature the same conditions were potent. Some of the chief productions of humanity seem to require the co-operation of whole peoples working sympathetically to a common end. Foremost among these are architecture and the drama. The most splendid triumphs of modern architecture in the French and English Gothic were achieved by the half-unconscious striving of the national genius through several centuries. The names of the builders of the cathedrals are unknown : the cathedrals themselves bear less the stamp of individual thought than of popular instinct ; their fame belongs to the race that made them, to the spirit of the times that gave them birth. It is not in architecture, therefore, that we expect the Italians, divided into small and rival States, and distinguished by salient subjectivity, to show their strength. Men like Niccola Pisano, Arnolfo del Cambio, Alberti, Brunelleschi, and Bramante were gifted with an individuality too paramount for the creation of more than mighty experiments in architecture. They bowed to no tradition, but followed the dictates of their own inventive impulse, selecting the types that suited them, and dealing freely with the forms they found around them. Instead of seeking to carry on toward its accomplishment a style, not made, but felt and comprehended by their genius, they were eager to produce new and characteristic masterpieces—signs and symbols of their own peculiar quality of mind. Italy is full of splendid but imperfect monuments of personal ability, works of beauty displaying no unbroken genealogy of unknown craftsmen, but attesting the skill of famous artists.

For the practical architect her palaces and churches may, for this reason, be less instructive and less attractive than the public buildings of France. Yet for the student of national and personal characteristics, who loves to trace the physiognomy of a people in its edifices, to discover the mind of the artist in his work, their interest is unrivalled. In each city the specific *genius loci* meets us face to face : from each town-hall or cathedral the soul of a great man leans forth to greet our own. These advantages compensate for frequent extravagances, for audacities savouring of ignorance, and for awkwardness in the adoption and modification of incongruous styles. Moreover, it must always be remembered that in Italy the architect could not forget the monuments of Roman and Byzantine art around him. Classic models had to be suited to the requirements of modern life and Christian ritual; and when the Germans brought their Gothic from beyond the Alps, it suffered from its adaptation to a southern climate. The result was that Italy arrived at no great national tradition in architecture, and that free scope was offered to the whims and freaks of individual designers. When at length, at the end of the sixteenth century, the Italians attained to uniformity of taste, it was by the sacrifice of their originality. The pedantry of the classical revival did more harm to architecture than to letters, and pseudo-Roman purism superseded the genial caprices of the previous centuries.

If architecture may be said to have suffered in Italy from the supremacy of local characteristics and personal genius, overruling tradition and thwarting the evolution of a national style, the case was quite different with the other arts. Painting and sculpture demand the highest independence in the artist, and are susceptible of a far more many-sided treatment than architecture. They cannot be the common product of a people, but require the conscious application of a special ability to the task of translating thought and feeling into form. As painters, the Italians hold the first rank among civilised nations of the modern and the ancient world ; and their inferiority as sculptors to the Greeks is mainly due to their mastery over painting, the essentially romantic art. The sensibilities of the new age craved a more emotional and agitated expression than is proper to sculpture. As early as the days of Ghiberti and Donatello it became clear that the Italian sculptors were following the methods of the sister art in their designs, while Michael Angelo alone had force enough to make marble the vehicle of thoughts that properly belong to painting or to music. The converse probably held good with the Greeks. What remains of their work in fresco and mosaic seems to show that they were satisfied with groups and figures modelled upon bas-reliefs and statues ; just as the Florentines carved pictures, with architecture and landscape, in stone. More need not here be said upon this topic, since the achievements of the Italians in painting and in sculpture will form a main part of my history.

As regards literature, the subdivision of Italy into numerous small States and the energetic self-assertion of the individual were distinctly favourable. Though the want of a great public, such as can alone be found in the capital of a free, united nation, may be reckoned among the many reasons which prevented the Italians from developing the drama, yet the rivalry of town with town and of burgher with burgher, Court life with its varied opportunities for the display of talent, and municipal life with its restless competition in commerce and public affairs, encouraged the activity of students, historians, statisticians, critics, and poets. Culture, in the highest and widest sense of the word, was what Renaissance Italy obtained and gave to Europe ; and this culture implies a full-formed personality in the men who seek it. It was the highly perfected individuality of the

Italians that made them first emerge from mediæval bondage and become the apostles of humanism for the modern world. It may be regretted that their force was expended upon the diffusion of learning and the purification of style, instead of being concentrated on the creation of national masterpieces. We seek in vain for Dante's equal among the poets of the Renaissance. The 'Orlando Furioso' is but a poor second to the 'Divina Commedia;' and all those works of scholarship, which seemed to our ancestors the *ne plus ultra* of refinement, are now relegated to the lumber-room of erudition that has been superseded, or of literary ingenuity that has lost its point. Now that the boon of culture, so hardly won by the students of the fifteenth and sixteenth centuries, has become the common heritage of Europe, it is not always easy to explain the mental grandeur of the Italians in that age. Yet we should fail to recognise their merit, if we did not comprehend that, precisely by this absorption of their genius in the task of the Revival, they conferred the most enduring benefits upon humanity. What the modern world would have been, if the Italian nation had not devoted its energies to the restoration of liberal learning, cannot even be imagined. The history of that devotion will form the principal subject of my present volume.

The comprehensive and many-sided natures, frequent in Renaissance Italy, were specially adapted for the dissemination of the new spirit. The appearance of such men as Leo Battista Alberti, Lionardo da Vinci, Lorenzo de' Medici, Brunelleschi and Buonarroti, Poliziano and Pico della Mirandola, upon the stage of the Renaissance is not the least fascinating of its phenomena. We can only find their parallels by returning to the age of Pericles. But the problem for the Florentines differed from that which the Athenians had before them. In Greece, the morning-land of civilisation, men of genius, each perfect in his own capacity, were needed.

Standards had to be created for the future guidance of the world in all the realms of art and thought. We are therefore less struck with the versatility than with the concentration of Pheidias, Pindar, Sophocles, Socrates. Italy, on the other hand, had for her task the reabsorption of a bygone culture. It was her vocation to resuscitate antiquity, to gather up afresh the products of the classic past, and so to blend them with the mediæval spirit as to generate what is specifically modern. It was indispensable that the men by whom this work was accomplished should be no less distinguished for largeness of intelligence, variety of acquirements, quickness of sympathy, and sensitive susceptibility, than for the complete development of some one faculty. The great characters of the Greek age were what Hegel calls plastic, penetrated through and through with a specific quality. Those of the Italian age were comprehensive and encyclopædic; the intensity of their force in any one sphere is less remarkable than its suitableness to all. They were of a nature to synthesise, interpret, reproduce, and mould afresh—like Mr. Browning's Cleon, with the addition of the consciousness of young and potent energy within them. It consequently happens that, except in the sphere of the Fine Arts, we are tempted to underrate the heroes of the Renaissance. The impression they leave upon our minds at any one point is slight in comparison with the estimate we form of them when we consider each man as a whole. Nor can we point to monumental and colossal works in proof of their creative faculty.

The biographies of universal geniuses like Leo Battista Alberti or Lionardi da Vinci, so multiform in their capacity and so creative in their intuitions, prompt us to ask what is the connection between the spirit of an age and the men in whom it is incorporated. Not without reason are we forced to personify the Renaissance as something external to its greatest characters. There is an intellectual strength outside them in the century, a heritage of power prepared for them at birth. The atmosphere in which they breathe is so charged with mental vitality that the least stirring of their special energy brings them into relation with forces mightier than are the property of single natures. In feebler periods of retrospect and criticism we can but wonder at the combination of faculties so varied, and at miracles so easily accomplished. These times of clairvoyance and of intellectual magnetism, when individuals of genius appear to move like vibrios in a life-sustaining fluid specially adapted to their needs, are rare in the history of the world ; nor has our science yet arrived at analysing their causes. They are not on that account the less real. To explain them by the hypothesis of a *Weltgeist,* the collective spirit of humanity proceeding in its evolution through successive phases, and making its advance from stage to stage by alternations of energy and repose, is simply to restore, in other terms, a mystery that finds its final and efficient cause in God.[1]

Gifted with the powerful individuality I am attempting to describe, the men of the Renaissance received their earliest education in the religion of the Middle Ages, their second in the schools of Greece and Rome. It was the many-sided struggle of personal character with time-honoured tradition on the one hand, and with new ideals on the other, that lent so much of inconsistency and contradiction to their aims. Dante remained within the pale of mediæval thoughts, and gave them full poetical expression. To him, in a truer sense than to any other poet, belongs the double glory of immortalising in verse the centuries behind him, while he inaugurated the new age.

---

[1] The analogy of the individual might be quoted. We are aware within ourselves of times when thought is fertile and insight clear, times of conception and projection, followed by seasons of slow digestion, assimilation, and formation, when the creative faculty stagnates, and the whole force of the intellect is absorbed in mastering through years what it took minutes to divine.

The ' Vita Nuova ' and the ' Divina Commedia ' are modern,
in so far as the one is the first complete analysis of personal
emotion, and the other is the epic of the soul conceived as
concrete personality.   But the form and colour, the material
and structure, the warp of thought and the woof of fancy, are
not modern.   Petrarch opens a new era.   He is not satisfied
with the body of mediæval beliefs and intellectual conceptions.
Antiquity presents a more fascinating ideal to his spirit, and
he feels the subjectivity within him strong enough to assimilate what suits it in the present and the past.   The Revival
of Learning, begun by Petrarch, was no mere renewal of
interest in classic literature.   It was the emancipation of
the reason in a race of men, intolerant of control, ready to
criticise accepted canons of conduct, enthusiastic in admiration
of antique liberty, freshly awakened to the sense of beauty,
and anxious above all things to secure for themselves free
scope in spheres outside the region of authority.   Men so
vigorous and independent felt the joy of exploration.   There
was no problem they feared to face, no formula they were
not eager to recast according to their new convictions.   This
liberty of judgment did not of necessity lead to lawlessness ;
nor in any case did it produce that insurgence against Catholic
orthodoxy which marked the German Reformation.   Yet it
lent a characteristic quality to thought and action.   Men
were, and dared to be, themselves for good or evil without
too much regard for what their neighbours thought of them.
At the same time they were tolerant.   The culture of the
Renaissance implied a philosophical acceptance of variety in
fashion, faith, and conduct ; and this toleration was no doubt
one reason why Italian scepticism took the form of cynicism,
not of religious revolution.   Contact with Islam in the south
and east, diplomatic relations with the Turks, familiarity with
the mixed races of Spain, and commerce with the nations of
the north, had widened the sympathies of the Italians, and

taught them to regard humanity as one large family. The liberal spirits of the Renaissance might have quoted Marcus Aurelius with slight alteration : ' I will not say, dear City of St. Peter, but, dear City of Man ! ' And just as their moral and religious sensibilities were blunted, so patriotism with them ceased to be an instinct. Instead of patriotism, the Italians were inflamed with the zeal of cosmopolitan culture.

In proportion as Italy lost year by year the hope of becoming an united nation, in proportion as the military instincts died in her, and the political instincts were extinguished by despotism, in precisely the same ratio did she evermore acquire a deeper sense of her intellectual vocation. What was world-embracing in the spirit of the mediæval Church passed by transmutation into the humanism of the fifteenth century. As though aware of the hopelessness of being Italians in the same sense as the natives of Spain were Spaniards, or the natives of France were Frenchmen, the giants of the Renaissance did their utmost to efface their nationality in order that they might the more effectually restore the cosmopolitan ideal of the human family. To this end both artists and scholars, the depositaries of the real Italian greatness at this epoch, laboured ; the artists by creating an ideal of beauty with a message and a meaning for all Europe, the scholars by recovering for Europe the burghership of Greek and Roman civilisation. In spite of the invasions and convulsions that ruined Italy between the years 1494 and 1527, the painters and the humanists proceeded with their task, as though the fate of Italy concerned them not, as though the destinies of the modern world depended on their activity. After Venice had been desolated by the armies of the League of Cambray, Aldus Manutius presented the peace-gift of Plato to the foes of his adopted city ; and when the Lutherans broke into Parmegiano's workshop at Rome, even they were awed by the tranquil

majesty of the Virgin on his easel. Stories like these remind
us that Renaissance Italy met her doom of servitude and
degradation in the spirit of ancient Hellas, repeating as they
do the tales told of Archimedes in his study, and of Paulus
Æmilius face to face with the Zeus of Pheidias.

As patriotism gave way to cosmopolitan enthusiasm, and
toleration took the place of earnestness, in like manner the
conflict of mediæval tradition with revived Paganism in the
minds of these self-reliant men, trained to indulgence by their
large commerce with the world, and familiarised with impiety
by the ever-present pageant of an anti-Christian Church, led,
as I have hinted, to recklessness and worldly vices, rather
than to reformed religion. Contented with themselves and
their surroundings, they felt none of the unsatisfied cravings
after the infinite, none of the mysterious intuitions and ascetic
raptures, the self-abasements and transfigurations, stigmata
and beatific visions, of the Middle Ages. The plenitude of
life within them seemed to justify their instincts and their
impulses, however varied and discordant these might be.
The sonorous current of the world around them drowned the
voice of conscience, the suggestion of religious scruples.   It
is only thus we can explain to ourselves the attitude of such
men as Sixtus and Alexander, serenely vicious in extreme old
age.   The gratification of their egotism was so complete as to
exclude self-judgment by the rules and standards they profes-
sionally applied ; their personality was too exacting to admit
of hesitation when their instincts were concerned ; in common
with their age they had lost sight of all but mundane aims
and interests.   Three aphorisms, severally attributed to three
representative Italians, may be quoted in illustration of these
remarks.   ' You follow infinite objects ; I follow the finite ;'
said Cosimo de' Medici ; ' you place your ladders in the
heavens ; I on earth, that I may not seek so high or fall so
low.'   ' If we are not ourselves pious,' said Julius II., ' why

should we prevent other people from being so?' 'Let us enjoy the Papacy,' said Leo X., 'now that God has given it to us.'

It was only under the influence of some external terror—a plague, a desolating war, an imminent peril to the nation—that the religious sense, deadened by worldliness and selfish philosophy, made itself felt. At such seasons whole cities rushed headlong into fierce revivalism, while men of violent or profligate lives saw visions, and betook themselves to penance. Cellini's Memoirs are, on this point, a valuable mirror of the age in which he lived. It is clear that his ecstasies of devotion in the dungeons of S. Angelo were as sincere as the fiery impulses he obeyed with so much complacency. Passionate and worldly as men of Cellini's stamp might be, they could not shake off the associations that bound them to the past. The energy of their intense individuality took turn by turn the form and colour of ascetic piety and Pagan sensuality; and at times these strong contrasts of emotion seemed bordering upon insanity. Ungovernable natures, swayed by no fixed principle, and bent on moulding the world of thought afresh to suit their own desires, became the puppets of astrological superstition, the playthings of mad lust. Much that appears unaccountable and contradictory in the Renaissance may be referred to this imperfect blending of ecclesiastical tradition and idealised Paganism in natures potent enough to be original and wilful, but not yet tamed from semi-savagery into acquiescence by experience. Experience came to the Italians in servitude beneath the heel of Spain.

The confusion of influences, classical and mediæval, Christian and Pagan, in that age is not the least extraordinary of its phenomena. Even the new thoughts that illuminated the minds of great discoverers, seemed to them like reflections from antiquity; and while they were opening fresh worlds, their hearts were turned toward the Holy Land of the Crusades. Columbus and Copernicus, the two men who did more than any others to revolutionise the mental attitude of humanity, appealed to their contemporaries on the strength of texts from Aristotle and Philolaus. Conscious that the guesses of the Greek cosmographers had stimulated in themselves that curiosity whereby they made the motion of the earth a certainty, and found a way across the waves to a new continent, these mighty spirits forgot how slight in reality was their debt to the inert speculators of the classic age. The truth was that in them throbbed a force of enterprise and conquering discovery, a spirit of exploration resolute and hardy, denied to the ancients.

How far this new and fruitful temper of the modern mind was due to Christianity, is a problem for the deepest speculation. The conception of a God who had made no part of His world in vain, of a Christ who had bought with His blood the whole seed of Adam, and who imposed the preaching of the faith upon His followers as a duty, wrought powerfully on Columbus. The Crusades, again, had familiarised the nations with distant objects and ideal quests; while chivalry was essentially antagonistic to positive and selfish aims. The spirit of mankind had marched a long stage during the Middle Ages. It was not possible now to conceive of God as a tranquil thinking upon thought, with Aristotle. There was no Augustus to set arbitrary limits to the empire of the world in the interest of a conquering nation, or to make the two words *orbs* and *urbs* synonymous. When Strabo hazarded the opinion that there might be populous islands in the other hemisphere, he added, with the sublime indifference of a Roman, 'But these speculations have nothing in common with practical geography; and if such islands exist, they cannot support peoples of like origin with us.' Such language was impossible for a man educated in the Christian faith, and imbued with the instincts of romanticism. Therefore, though the study of Strabo and Ptolemy at Pavia impressed Columbus with the certainty of the new route across the ocean, he owed the courage that sustained him to the conviction that God was leading him to a great end. 'When I first undertook to start for the discovery of the Indies,' he says in his will, 'I intended to beg the King and Queen to devote the whole of the money that might be drawn from these realms to Jerusalem.' The religious yearning of the mediæval pilgrim added fervour to the conviction of the student, who, by reasoning on antique texts, guessed the greatest secret of which the world has record. At the same time there was something more in Columbus than either antiquity or mediævalism could provide. The modern spirit is distinct from both; and though, in the Renaissance, creation wore the garb of imitation, and the new forces used the organs they were destined to outlive and destroy, yet we must allow to native personality the lion's share in such achievement as that of Columbus. It is the variety of spiritual elements in combination and solution, which he illustrates, that makes the psychology of the Renaissance at once so fascinating and so difficult to analyse.

While so much liberty of thought prevailed in Italy, it may be wondered why the Renaissance, eminently fertile in the domains of art and culture, bore but meagre fruit in those of religion and philosophy. The German Reformation was the Renaissance of Christianity; and in this the Italians had no share, though it should be remembered that, without their previous labours in the field of scholarship, the band who led the Reformation could hardly have given that high intellectual character to the movement which made it a new starting-point in the history of the reason. To expect from Italy the ethical regeneration of the modern world would be

to misapprehend her true vocation ; art and erudition were
sufficient to engage her spiritual energies. The Church,
again, though by no means adverse to laxity in morals, was
jealous of heterodoxy. So long as freethinkers confined
their audacity to such matters as form the topic of Poggio's
' Facetiæ,' Beccadelli's ' Hermaphroditus,' or La Casa's
' Capitolo del Forno,' the Roman Curia looked on and smiled
approvingly. The most obscene books to be found in any
literature escaped the Papal censure, and Aretino, notorious
for ribaldry, aspired not wholly without reason to the scarlet
of a cardinal. But even in the fifteenth century the taint
of heresy was dangerous, and this peril was magnified when
the Lutheran schism had roused the Papacy to a sense of
its position. Under the patronage, therefore, of ecclesiastics,
in the depraved atmosphere of Rome, the free thought of
the Italians turned to licentiousness ; this suited the temper
of the people, fascinated by Paganism and little inclined to
raise debate upon matters of no practical utility. Those
who reflected on religious topics kept their own counsel.
How purely political were the views of profound thinkers in
Italy upon all Church questions may be gathered from the
observations of Guicciardini and Machiavelli ; how little the
most earnest antagonist of ungodly ecclesiastics dreamed of
disturbing the Catholic Church system is clear in the biography of Savonarola.[1] The first satire of Ariosto may be
indicated as an epitome of the opinions entertained by sound
and liberal intellects in Italy upon the relation of Papal
Rome to the nation. There is not a trace in it of Teutonic
revolt against authority, of pious yearning for a purer faith.
The standpoint of the critic, though solid and sincere, is
worldly.

True to culture as their main preoccupation, the Italian

[1] See Vol. I., *Age of Despots*, pp. 239, 350-356, 415-420, where I have
endeavoured to treat these topics more at length.

thinkers sought to philosophise faith by bringing Christianity into harmony with antique speculation, and forming for themselves a theism that should embrace the systems of the Platonists and Stoics, the Hebrew Cabbala and the Sermon on the Mount. There is much that strikes us as both crude and pedantic, at the same time infantine and pompous, in the systems elaborated by those pioneers of modern eclecticism. They lack the vigorous simplicity that gave its force to Luther's intuition, the sublime unity of Spinoza's deductions. The dross of erudition mingles with the pure gold of personal conviction; while Pagan phrases, ill suited to express Christian notions, lend an air of unreality to the sincerest efforts after rational theology. The Platonic Academy of Florence was the centre of this search after the faith of culture, whereof the real merit was originality, and the true force lay in the conviction that humanity is one and indivisible. Its apostles were Pico della Mirandola and Ficino. It found lyrical expression in verses like the following, translated by me from the Greek hexameters of Poliziano :—

O Father, Lord enthroned on gold, that dwellest in high heaven,
O King of all things, deathless God, Thou Pan supreme, celestial !
That seest all, and movest all, and all with might sustainest,
Older than oldest time, of all first, last, and without ending !
The firmament of blessed souls, of stars the heavenly splendour,
The giant sun himself, the moon that in her circle shineth,
And streams and fountains, earth and sea, are things of Thy creating.
Thou givest life to all ; all these Thou with Thy Spirit fillest.
The powers of earth and powers of heaven, and they in pain infernal
Who pine below the roots of earth, all these obey Thy bidding.
Behold, I call upon Thee now, Thy creature on earth dwelling,
Poor, short of life, O God, of clay a mean unworthy mortal,
Repenting sorely of my sins, and tears of sorrow shedding.
O God, immortal Father, hear ! I cry to Thee ; be gracious,
And from my breast of this vain world the soul-enslaving passion,
The demon's wiles, the wilful lust, that damns the impious, banish !
Wash throughly all my heart with Thy pure Spirit's rain abundant,
That I may love Thee, Lord, alone, Thee, King of kings, for ever.

This is but a poor substitute for the Lord's Prayer. Hell
and purgatory are out of place in its theism. χρυσόθρονος
and αἴθερι ναίων are tawdry epithets for Our Father which
art in heaven.' Yet it is precisely in these contradictions
and confusions that we trace the sincerity of the Renaissance
spirit, seeking to fuse together the vitality of the old faith
and the forms of novel culture, worshipping a Deity created
in the image of its own mind, composite and incoherent.

Physically, the Italians of the Renaissance were equal to
any task they chose to set themselves. No mistake is greater
than to suppose that, because the summer climate of Italy
is hotter than our own, therefore her children must be
languid, pleasure-loving, and relaxed. Twelve months spent
in Tuscany would suffice to dissipate illusions about the
enervating Italian air, even if the history of ancient Rome
were not a proof that the hardiest race of combatants and
conquerors the world has ever seen were nurtured between
Soracte and the sea. After the downfall of the Empire, what
remained of native vigour in the Latin cities found a refuge
in the lagoons of Venice and other natural strongholds.
Walled towns in general retained a Roman population. The
primitive Italic races still existed in the valleys of the Apennines, while the Ligurians held the Genoese Riviera; nor
were the Etruscans extinct in Tuscany. It is true that Rome
had fused these races into a people using the same language.
Yet the ethnologist will hardly allow that the differences
noticeable between the several districts of Italy were not
connected with original varieties of stock. To the people, as
Rome had made it, fresh blood was added by the Goths,
Lombards, and Germans descending from the North. Greeks,
Arabs, Normans, and, in course of time, Franks influenced
the South. During the Middle Ages a new and mighty breed
of men sprang into being by the combination of these diverse
elements, each district deriving specific quality from the vary-

ing proportions in which the chief constituents were mingled. It is noticeable that where the Roman-Etruscan blood was purest probably from mixture, in the valley of the Arno, the modern Italian genius found its home. Florence and her sister cities formed the language and the arts of Italy. To this race, in conjunction with the natives of Lombardy and Central Italy, was committed the civilisation of Europe in the fifteenth century. It was only south of Rome, where the brutalising traditions of the Roman *latifundia* had never yielded to the burgh-creating impulse of the Middle Ages, that the Italians were unfit for their great duty. On these southern states the Empire of the East, Saracen marauders and Norman conquerors, the French and the Spanish dynasties, had successively exercised a pernicious influence; nor did the imperial policy of Frederick II. remain long enough in operation to effect a radical improvement in the people. Even at Naples culture was always an exotic. Elsewhere throughout the peninsula the Italians of the new age were a noble nation, gifted with physical, emotional, and mental faculties in splendid harmony. In some districts, notably in Florence, circumstance and climate had been singularly favourable to the production of such glorious human beings as the world has rarely seen. Beauty of person, strength of body, and civility of manners were combined in the men of that favoured region with intellectual endowments of the highest order : nor were these gifts of nature confined to a caste apart ; the whole population formed an aristocracy of genius.

In order to comprehend the greatness of this Italian type in the Renaissance, it is only needful to study the picture galleries of Florence or of Venice with special attention to the portraits they contain. When we compare those senators and sages with the subjects of Dürer's and of Cranach's art, we feel the physical superiority of the Italians. In like manner a comparison of the men of the fifteenth century with those of the sixteenth shows how much of that physical grandeur had been lost. It is easy to wander astray while weaving subtle theories on this path of criticism. Yet it cannot be a mere accident that Vandyck's portrait of the Cardinal de' Bentivogli in the Pitti Palace differs as it does from that of the Cardinal Ippolito de' Medici by Pontormo or by Titian. The Medici is an Italian of the Renaissance, with his imperious originality and defiance of convention. He has refused to be portrayed as an ecclesiastic. Titian has painted him in Hungarian costume of dark red velvet, moustached, and sworded like a soldier; in Pontormo's picture he wears a suit of mail, and rests his left hand on a large white hound. The Bentivoglio is an Italian of the type produced by the Counter-Reformation. His delicate lace ruffs, the coquetry of his scarlet robes, and the fine keen cut of his diplomatic features betray a new spirit.[1] Surely the physical qualities of a race change with the changes in their thought and feeling. The beauty of Tasso is more feminine and melancholy than that of Ariosto, in whom the liberal genius of the Renaissance was yet alive. Among the scowling swordsmen of the seventeenth century you cannot find a face like Giorgione's Gattamelata;[2] the nobles who bear themselves so proudly on the canvases of Vandyck at Genoa lack the urbanity of Raphael's Castiglione; Moroni's black-robed students are more pinched and withered than the Pico of the Uffizzi. It will not do to strain such points. It is enough to suggest them. What remains, however, for certain is that the Italians of the fifteenth century—and among these must

[1] It would be easy to multiply these contrasts, comprising, for example, the Cardinals Inghirami and Bibbiena and the Leo of Raphael with the Farnesi portraits at Modena or the grave faces of Moroni's patrons at Bergamo.

[2] Portrait in the Uffizzi, ascribed to Giorgione, but more probably by some pupil of Mantegna.

be included those who lived through the first half of the sixteenth—had physical force and character corresponding to their robust individuality. Until quite late in the Renaissance so much survived of feudal customs even in Italy that riding, the handling of the lance and sword, and all athletic exercises formed a part of education no less indispensable than mental training. Great cities had open places set apart for tournaments and games; in Tuscan burghs the *palio* was run on feast days, and May mornings saw the prentice lads of Florence tilting beneath the smiles of girls who danced at nightfall on the square of Santa Trinità. Bloody battles in the streets were frequent. The least provocation caused a man to draw his dagger. Combats *a steccato chiuso* were among the pastimes to which a Pope might lend his countenance. Skill in swordsmanship was therefore a necessity. For the rest, we learn from Castiglione that the perfect gentleman was bound to be an accomplished dancer, a bold rider, a skilled wrestler, a swift runner, to shoot well at the mark, to hurl the javelin and the quoit with grace, and to play at tennis and *pallone*. In addition he ought to affect some one athletic exercise in such perfection as to beat professors of the same on their own ground. Cesare Borgia took pride in felling an ox at a single blow, and exhibited his marksman's cunning by shooting condemned criminals in a courtyard of the Vatican.

That such men should have devoted their energies to intellectual culture at a time when English nobles could barely read or write, and when the chivalry of France regarded learning with disdain, was a proof of their rich natural endowments. Nor was the determination of the race to scholarship in any sense an accident. Throughout the length and breadth of Italy, memories of ancient greatness spurred her children on to emulation. Ghosts of Roman patriots and poets seemed hovering round their graves, and calling on posterity to give them life again. If we cannot bring back Greece and Rome, at least let us make Florence a second Athens, and restore the Muses to Ausonian vales. That was the cry. It was while gazing on the ruins of Rome that Villani felt impelled to write his chronicle. Pavia honoured Boethius like a saint. Mantua struck coins with the head of Virgil, and Naples pointed out his tomb. Padua boasted of Livy, and Como of the Plinies. 'Sulmona,' cried Boccaccio, 'mourns because she holds not Ovid's dust; and Parma is glad that Cassius rests within her walls.' Such reverence for the great men of antiquity endured throughout the Middle Ages, creating myths that swayed the fancy, and forming in the popular consciousness a presentiment of the approaching age. There is something pathetic in the survival of old Roman titles, in the freak of the legend-making imagination that gave to Orlando the style of Roman senator, in the outburst of enthusiasm for Rienzi when he called himself Tribunus Populi Romani. With the Renaissance itself this affection for the past became a passion. Pius II. amnestied the people of Arpino because they were fellow-citizens of Cicero. Alfonso of Naples received as a most precious gift from Venice a bone supposed to be the leg of Livy. All the patricians of Italy invented classical pedigrees; and even Paul II., because he was called Barbo, claimed descent from the Ahenobarbi. Such instances might be multiplied indefinitely. It is, however, more to the purpose here to notice that in Italy this adoration of the antique world was common to all classes; not students alone, but the people at large regarded the dead grandeur of the classic age as their especial heritage. To resuscitate that buried glory, and to reunite themselves with the past, was the earnest aim of the Italians as a nation. A conviction prevailed that the modern world could never be so radiant as the old. This found its expression in the saying that Rome's chief orna-

ments were her ruins; in the belief that Julia's corpse, discovered in the Appian Way, surpassed all living maidens;
in Matarazzo's observation that Astorre Baglioni's body
was worthy of an ancient Roman. In their admiration for
antiquity, scholars were blind to the specific glories of the
modern genius. Lionardo Bruni, for example, exclaimed
that 'the ancient Greeks by far excelled us Italians in
humanity and gentleness of heart.' Yet what Greek poem
can be compared for tenderness with Dante's ' Vita Nuova,'
with the 'Canzoniere' of Petrarch, or with the tale of Griselda
in Boccaccio? *Gentilezza di cuore* was the most characteristic product of chivalry, and the fourth Æneid is the only
classic masterpiece of pure romantic pathos. This humility
of discipleship was not, however, strong enough to check
emulation. On the contrary, the yearning towards antiquity
acted like a potent stimulus on personal endeavour, generating
an acute desire for fame, a burning aspiration to be numbered
with the mighty men of old. When Virgil introduced Dante
to the company of Homer and his peers, the rank of *sesto tra
cotanto senno* rewarded him for all his labour in the rhyme
that made him thin through half a lifetime. Petrarch, who
exceeded Dante in the thirst for literary honour, turned from
the men of his generation to converse in long epistles with
the buried saints of Latin culture. For men of less ambition it was enough to feel that they could raise their souls
through study to communion with the stately spirits of
antiquity, passing like Machiavelli from trivial affairs into
their closet, where they donned their reading robes and shook
hands across the centuries with Cicero or Livy. It was the
universal object of the humanists to gain a consciousness of
self distinguished from the vulgar herd, and to achieve this
by joining the great company of bards and sages, whose glory
could not perish.

Whoever felt within himself the stirring of the spirit under

any form, sought earnestly for fame ; and in this way a new
social atmosphere, unknown to the nations of the Middle
Ages, was formed in Italy. A large and liberal acceptance,
recognising ability of all kinds, irrespective of rank or piety
or martial prowess, displaced the narrower judgments of
the Church and feudalism. Giotto, the peasant's son, ranked
higher in esteem than Cimabue, the Florentine citizen,
because his work of art was worthier. Petrarch had his
place in no official capacity, but as an honoured equal, at
the marriage feasts of princes. Poliziano corresponded with
kings, promising immortality as a more than regal favour.
Pomponius Lætus could afford to repel the advances of the
Sanseverini, feeling that erudition ranked him higher than
his princely kinsmen. It was not wealth or policy alone
that raised the Medici among the Despots so far above the
Baglioni of Perugia or the Petrucci of Siena. They owed
this distinction rather to their comprehension of the craving
of their age for culture. Thus though birth commanded
respect for its own sake, a new standard of eminence had
been established, and personal merit was the passport which
carried the meanest into the most illustrious company. Men
of all conditions and all qualifications met upon the common
ground of intellectual intercourse. The subjects they discussed may be gathered from the introductions to Firenzuola's novels, from Bembo's 'Asolani' and Castiglione's
'Cortegiano,' from Guicciardini's 'Dialogue on Florence,' or
from the 'Camaldolese Discourses' of Landino. Society of
this kind existed nowhere else in Europe. To Italy belongs
the proud priority of having invented the art of polite conversation, and anticipated the French *salon* after an original
and urbane fashion of her own.

Under these conditions a genuine cultus of intellect
sprang up in Italy. Princes and people shared a common
impulse to worship the mental superiority of men who had

no claim to notice but their genius. It was in the spirit of this hero-worship that the terrible Gismondo Pandolfo Malatesta transferred to Rimini the bones of Pletho, and wrote his impassioned epitaph upon the sarcophagus outside Alberti's church. The biographies of the humanists abound in stories of singular honours paid to men of parts, not only by princes who rejoiced in their society, but also by cities receiving them with public acclamation. And, as it often happens that a parody reveals the nature of the art it travesties, such light is thrown upon our subject by the vile Pietro Aretino, who, because he was a man of talent and unscrupulous in its employment, held kings and potentates beneath his satyr's hoof. It is not, however, needful to go thus far afield for instances. Some lines of our own poet Webster exactly describe the Catholicity of the Renaissance, which first obtained in Italy for men of marked abilities, and after-wards to some extent prevailed at large in Europe :—

> Virtue is ever sowing of her seeds :
> In the trenches for the soldier ; in the wakeful study
> For the scholar ; in the furrows of the sea
> For men of our profession : of all which
> Arise and spring up honour.

The virtue here described bears the Italian sense of *virtù*, the Latin *virtus*, the Greek ἀρετή, that which makes a man. It might display itself in a thousand ways ; but all alike brought honour, and honour every man was bound to seek. The standard whereby the Italians judged this virtue was æsthetical rather than moral. They were too dazzled by brilliant achievement to test it in the crucible of ethics. This is the true key to Machiavelli's critique of Castruccio Castracane, Gianpaolo Baglioni, Cesare Borgia, and Piero Soderini. In common with his race, he was fascinated by character, and attached undue importance to the force that made men seek success even through crime.

The thirst for glory and the worship of ability stimulated the Italians, earlier than any other nation, to commemorate what seemed to them noteworthy in their own lives and in those of their contemporaries. Dante, within the pale of mediævalism, led the way in both of these directions. His ' Vita Nuova ' is a chapter of autobiography restrained within the limits of consummate art. His portraits of S. Francis and S. Dominic (not to mention other medallions and cameos of predecessors or contemporaries—Farinata, for example, or Boniface VIII.) record the special qualities whereby those heroes of the faith were distinguished from the herd of men around them. Boccaccio's ' Life of Dante ' is a further step in the direction of purely modern biography. Then follow the collections of Filippo Villani, Giovanni Cavalcanti, Vespasiano, Platina, Decembrio, Beccadelli, Caracciolo, and Paolo Giovio. Vasari's ' Lives of the Painters ' are unique in their attempt to embrace within a single work whatever struck their author as most characteristic in the career of one particular class of men. For historical precision the portraits composed by Machiavelli, Guicciardini, Varchi, Pitti, and many of the minor annalists leave nothing to be desired. Such autobiographies as those of Petrarch, Cellini, Cardano, and Cornaro are models in their kind ; whether their object were simply self-glorification, or whether a scientific and didactic purpose underlay the chronicle of a lifetime, the result is equally vivid and interesting. Hero-worship prompted Gian Francesco Pico to compose the ' Life of Savonarola,' and Condivi to write that of Michael Angelo. Scorn and hatred impelled Platina to transmit the outline of Paul II. to posterity in a caricature, the irony of which is so restrained that it might pass for sincerity. Machiavelli's ' Biography of Castruccio ' is a political romance indited with a philosophical intention. What motive, beyond admiration, produced the anonymous ' Memoir of Alberti,' so terse in its portraiture, so

tranquil in style, we do not know; but this too, like Prendi-
lacqua's 'Life of Vittorino da Feltre,' is a masterpiece of
natural delineation. For these biographies the works of
Plutarch and Suetonius served no doubt as models. Yet this
does not make the preoccupation of the Italians with the
phenomena of personality the less remarkable.

Another phase of the same impulse led to special treatises
upon ideal characters. The picture of the perfect householder
was drawn by Alberti, that of the courtier by Castiglione, that
of the prince by Machiavelli. Da Vinci discoursed upon the
physical proportions of the human form. Firenzuola and
Luigini analysed the beauty of women; Piccolomini undertook to describe the manners of a well-bred lady; and La
Casa laid down rules for polite behaviour in society. The
names of treatises of this description might easily be multiplied. Enough, however, has been said to show the tendency
of the Italian intellect to occupy itself with salient qualities,
whether exhibited in individuals or idealised and abstracted
by the reflective fancy. The whole of this literature implies
an intense self-consciousness in the nation, an ardent interest
in men as men, because of the specific virtue to be found in
each. The spirit, therefore, in which these authors of the
Renaissance approached their task was wholly different from
that which induced the mediæval annalist to register the
miracles of saints, to chronicle the princes of some dynasty
or the abbots of a convent. Nor had it much in common
with the mythologising enthusiasm of romantic poets. The
desire for edification and the fire of fancy had yielded to an
impulse more strictly scientific, to a curiosity more positive.

The attention directed in literature and social intercourse
upon great men implied a corresponding thirst for posthumous
glory as a subjective quality of the Renaissance character.
To perpetuate a name and fame was the most fervent passion,
shared alike by artists and princes, by men of letters and by

generals. It was not enough for a man to show forth the vigour that was in him, or to win the applause of his contemporaries. He must go beyond and wrest something permanent for himself from the ideal world that will survive our transient endeavours. When Alfonso the Magnanimous employed Fazio to compose his chronicle, when Francesco Sforza paid Filelfo for his verses by the dozen, when Cosimo de' Medici regretted that he had not spent more wealth on building, when Bartolommeo Colleoni decreed the erection of his chapel at Bergamo, and his statue on the public square of Venice, these men, so different in all things else, were striving, each after his own fashion, to buy an immortality his own achievements in the field or Senate might not win. Dante, here as elsewhere the first to utter the word of the modern age, has given expression to this thirst for lasting recollection in his lines about the planet Mercury : [1]—

> Questa picciola stella si correda
> De' buoni spirti, che son stati attivi,
> Perchè onore e fama gli succeda.

At the same time Dante, imbued with the mystic spirit of the Middle Ages, felt an antagonism between worldly ambition and the ideal of the Christian life. There are other passages, where fame is mentioned by him as a fleeting breath, a flower that blooms and fades.[2] In truth, the passionate desire for glory was part of the Renaissance worldliness, caught from communion with the classic past, and connected with that vivid apprehension of human life which gave its vigour to an age of reawakened impulses and positive ambitions. This world was so much with them, so much to them, that these men would not lose their grasp of it in death, or willingly exchange it for a paradise of hopes beyond.

The enthusiasm for antiquity coloured this desire for

[1] *Paradiso*, vi. 112.   [2] Notably *Purg.* xi. 100-117.

fame by forcing on the Italians the conviction that in culture was the real title to eternity. How could they have entered into the spiritual kingdom of the Greeks and Romans, if it had not been for MSS. and works of art? It became the fashion, therefore, to seek immortality through literature. The study of the classics was not then confined to men of a peculiar bent. On all alike, even on women, there weighed the one belief that to be a scholar was the surest way of saving something from the wreck that is the doom of human deeds.[1] Only at rare intervals, and in rare natures of the type of Michael Angelo, did the Christian ideal resume its sway. Tired with the radiance of art or learning, they turned to the Cross of Christ, and laid their secular achievements down as vain and worthless. The time, however, had not yet come when a disgust of culture and an exhaustion of the intellect should make asceticism and monastic ecstasy acceptable once more. That belonged to the age of Spanish tyranny, and what is called the Counter-Reformation. For the real Renaissance Leo's memorable *imprimatur*, granted to the editors of Tacitus, struck the true key-note; while Sappho's solemn lines of warning to a friend careless of literature might be paraphrased to speak the feeling of Poliziano :—

> Lo, thou shalt die,
> And lie
> Dumb in the silent tomb ;
> Nor of thy name
> Shall there be any fame
> In ages yet to be or years to come :
> For of the rose
> That on Pieria blows
> Thou hast no share ;
> But in sad Hades' house,
> Unknown, inglorious,
> Mid the dim shades that wander there,
> Shalt thou flit forth and haunt the filmy air.

---

[1] A curious echo of this Italian conviction may be traced in Fletcher's *Elder Brother*.

These words found no uncertain echo in Renaissance Italy, where lads with long dark hair and liquid eyes left their loves to listen to a pedant's lectures, where Niccolo de' Niccoli wooed Piero de' Pazzi from a life of pleasure by the promise of a spiritual kingdom in the world of books. Piero was 'a man born with thy face and throat, Lyric Apollo!' His only object was to enjoy—*darsi buon tempo*, as the phrase of Florence hath it. Yet these words of the student: 'Seeing thou art the son of such a man, and of comely person, it is a shame thou dost not give thyself to learn Latin, the which would be unto thee a great ornament; and if thou dost not learn it, thou wilt be nought esteemed; the flower of youth once passed, thou wilt find thyself without virtue'—these words carried such weight, and sank so deeply into the young man's heart, that, smitten with the love of learning, he forsook his boon companions, engaged Pontano as house-tutor at a salary of one hundred golden florins, and spent his leisure time in learning Livy and the 'Æneid' by heart.[1] What he sought he gained; his name is still recorded, now that not only the bloom of youth, but life itself has passed away, and he has slept for nearly four centuries in Florentine earth. Yet we, no less wearied of erudition than Faust was, when he held the cup of laudanum in his hand and heard the Easter voices singing, may well ask ourselves what Piero carried with him to the grave more than Sardanapalus, over whom the Greeks inscribed their bitter epitaphs. Disenchanted and disillusioned as we are by those four centuries of learning, the musical lament of

[1] Vespasiano, *Vita di Piero de' Pazzi*. Compare the beautiful letter of Æneas Sylvius Piccolomini to his nephew (*Ep. Lib.* i. 4). He reminds the young man that fair as youth is, and delightful as are the pleasures of the May of life, learning is more fair and knowledge more delightful. 'Non enim Lucifer aut Hesperus tam pulcher est quam sapientia quæ studiis acquiritur litterarum.'

Dido and the stately periods of Latin prose are little better, considered as spiritual sustenance, to us than the husks that the swine did eat. How can we picture to ourselves the conditions of an age when scholarship was an evangel, forcing the Levis of Florence by the persuasion of its irresistible beauty to forsake the tables of the money-changers, tempting young men of great possessions to sell all and give to the Muses, making of Lucrezia Borgia herself the Magdalen of polite literature ? Fortunately for the civilisation of the modern world, the men of the Renaissance, untroubled by a surfeit of knowledge, made none of these reflections. It was an age of sincere faith in the goodness and the glory of the intellect revealed by art and letters. When we read Vespasiano's account of the grey-haired Niccolo accosting the young Pazzi on the steps of the Bargello, our mind turns instinctively to an earlier dayspring of the reason in ancient Greece ; we think of the charm exercised by Socrates over Critias and Alcibiades : and had an Aristophanes appeared in Italy, we fancy how he might have criticised this seduction of the youth from citizenship and arms to tranquil contemplations and the cosmopolitan interests of culture.

It is not without real reason that these Hellenic parallels confront us in the study of Italian Renaissance. Florence borrowed her light from Athens, as the moon shines with rays reflected from the sun. The Revival was the silver age of that old golden age of Greece. In a literal, not a merely metaphorical sense, the fifteenth century witnessed a new birth of the classic spirit. And what, let us ask ourselves, since here at last is the burning point of our inquiry, what was the true note of this spirit, in so far as its recovery concerned the Italian race ? Superficial observers will speak of the Paganism of the Renaissance, its unblushing license, its worldliness, its self-satisfied sensuality, as though that were all, as though these qualities were not inherent in human

nature, ready at any moment to emerge when the strain of
nobler enthusiasm is relaxed, or the self-preservative instincts
of society are enfeebled.   There is indeed a truth in this rough
and ready answer, which requires to be stated on the threshold.   The contact of the modern with the ancient world did
encourage a profligate and godless mode of living in men who
preferred Petronius to S. Paul, and yearned less after Galilee
than Corinth.   The humanists were distinguished even above
the Roman clergy for open disorder in their lives.   They
developed filthy speaking as a special branch of rhetoric, and
professed the science of recondite and obsolete obscenity.   It
was just this fashion of the learned classes that made Erasmus
mistrust the importation of scholarship into the North.   'One
scruple still besets my mind,' he wrote, 'lest under the cloak
of revived literature Paganism should strive to raise its head,
there being among Christians men who, while they recognise
the name of Christ, breathe in their hearts the spirit of the
Gentiles.'   Christianity, especially in Italy, where the spectacle of the Holy See inspired disgust, had been prostituted to
the vilest service by the Church.[1]   Faith was associated with
folly, superstition, ignorance, intolerance, and cruelty.   The
manners of the clergy were in flagrant discord with the
Gospel, and Antichrist found fitter incarnation in Roderigo
Borgia than in Nero.   While the essence of religion was thus
sacrificed by its professors, there appeared upon the horizon
of the modern world, like some bright blazing star, the ideal
of that Pagan civilisation against which in its decadence the
ascendant force of Christianity had striven.   It was not unnatural that a reaction in favour of Paganism, now that the
Church had been found wanting, should ensue, or that the
passions of humanity should justify their self-indulgence by
appealing to the precedents of Greece and Rome.   Good and

---

[1] It is enough to refer to Luther's *Table Talk* upon the state of
Rome in Leo's reign.

bad were mingled in the classical tradition. Vices, loathsome enough in a Pope who had instituted the censure of the press, seemed venial when combined with the manliness of Hadrian or the refined charm of Catullus. Sin itself lost half its evil coming from the new-found Holy Land of culture. Still this so-called Paganism of the Renaissance, real as it was, had but a superficial connection with classical studies. The corruption of the Church and the political degeneracy of the commonwealths had quite as much to do with it as the return to heathen standards. Nor could the Renaissance have been the great world-historical era it truly was, if such demoralisation had been a part and parcel of its essence. Crimes and vices are not the hotbed of arts and literature : lustful priests and cruel despots were not necessary to the painting of Raphael or the poetry of Ariosto. The faults of the Italians in the age of the Renaissance were neither productive of their high achievements, nor conversely were they generated by the motion of the intellect toward antique forms of culture. The historian notes synchronisms, whereof he is not bound to prove the interdependence, and between which he may feel there is no causal link.

It does not, moreover, appear that the demoralisation of Italian society, however this may have been brought about, produced either physical or intellectual degeneration in the people. Commercial prosperity, indeed, had rendered them inferior in brute strength to their semi-barbarous neighbours ; while the cosmopolitan interests of culture had destroyed the energy of national instincts. But it would be wrong to charge their neopaganism alone with results whereof the causes were so complex.

Meanwhile, what gave its deep importance to the classical revival, was the emancipation of the reason, consequent upon the discovery that the best gifts of the spirit had been enjoyed by the nations of antiquity. An ideal of existence distinct

from that imposed upon the Middle Ages by the Church, was
revealed in all its secular attractiveness. Fresh value was
given to the desires and aims, enjoyments and activities of
man, considered as a noble member of the universal life, and
not as a diseased excrescence on the world he helped to
spoil. Instead of the cloistral service of the 'Imitatio Christi,'
that conception of communion, through knowledge, with God
manifested in His works and in the soul of man, which forms
the indestructible religion of science and the reason, was
already generated. The intellect, after lying spell-bound
during a long night, when thoughts were as dreams and
movement as somnambulism, resumed its activity, interro-
gated nature, and enjoyed the pleasures of unimpeded energy.
Without ceasing to be Christians (for the moral principles
of Christianity are the inalienable possession of the human
race), the men of the Revival dared once again to exercise
their thought as boldly as the Greeks and Romans had done
before them. More than this, they were now able, as it were,
by the resuscitation of a lost faculty, to do so freely and clear-
sightedly. The touch upon them of the classic spirit was like
the finger of a deity giving life to the dead.

That more and nobler use was not made of the new
light which dawned upon the world in the Revival; that the
humanists abandoned the high standpoint of Petrarch for a
lower and more literary level; that society assimilated the
Hedonism more readily than the Stoicism of the ancients;
that scholars occupied themselves with the form rather than
the matter of the classics; that all these shortcomings in
their several degrees prevented the Italians from leading the
intellectual movement of the sixteenth century in religion and
philosophy, as they had previously led the mind of Europe in
discovery and literature—is deeply to be lamented by those
who are jealous for their honour. For the rest, no words can
be found more worthy to express their high conception of

man, regarded as a free yet responsible personality, sent into
the world to mould his own nature, and by this power of self-
determination severed from both brutes and angels, than the
following passage from Pico della Mirandola's ' Oration on the
Dignity of Man.'   It combines antique liberty of thought with
Christian faith in a style distinctive of the Renaissance at its
best; nor is its note of mediæval cosmology uncharacteristic
of an age that divined as yet more than it firmly grasped the
realities of modern science.   Here, if anywhere, may be hailed
the Epiphany of the modern spirit, contraposing God and
man in a relation inconceivable to the ancients, unapprehended in its fulness by the Middle Ages.   ' Then the Supreme
Maker decreed that unto Man, on whom He could bestow
nought singular, should belong in common whatsoever had
been given to His other creatures.   Therefore He took man,
made in His own individual image, and having placed him in
the centre of the world, spake to him thus : " Neither a fixed
abode, nor a form in thine own likeness, nor any gift peculiar
to thyself alone, have we given thee, O Adam, in order that
what abode, what likeness, what gifts thou shalt choose, may
be thine to have and to possess.   The nature allotted to all
other creatures, within laws appointed by ourselves, restrains
them.   Thou, restrained by no narrow bounds, according to
thy own free will, in whose power I have placed thee, shalt
define thy nature for thyself.   I have set thee midmost the
world, that thence thou mightest the more conveniently
survey whatsoever is in the world.   Nor have we made thee
either heavenly or earthly, mortal or immortal, to the end
that thou, being, as it were, thy own free maker and moulder,
shouldst fashion thyself in what form may like thee best.
Thou shalt have power to decline unto the lower or brute
creatures.   Thou shalt have power to be reborn unto the
higher, or divine, according to the sentence of thy intellect."

Thus to Man, at his birth, the Father gave seeds of all variety and germs of every form of life.'

Out of thoughts like these, if Italy could only have been free, if her society could have been uncorrupted, if her Church could have returned to the essential truths of Christianity, might have sprung, as from a seed, the noblest growth of human science. But *dis aliter visum est*. The prologue to this history of culture—the long account taken of selfish tyrants, vicious clergy, and incapable republics, in my 'Age of the Despots'—is intended to make it clear why the conditions under which the Revival began in Italy rendered its accomplishment imperfect.

CHAPTER II

FIRST PERIOD OF HUMANISM

Importance of the Revival of Learning—Mediæval Romance—The Legend of Faustus—Its Value for the Renaissance—The Devotion of Italy to Study—Italian Predisposition for this Labour—Scholarship in the Dark Ages—Double Attitude assumed by the Church—Piety for Virgil—Meagre Acquaintance with the Latin Classics—No Greek Learning—The Spiritual Conditions of the Middle Ages adverse to Pure Literature—Italy no exception to the rest of Europe—Dante and Petrarch—Definition of Humanism—Petrarch's Conception of it—His Æsthetical Temperament—His Cult for Cicero, Zeal in collecting Manuscripts, Sense of the Importance of Greek Studies—Warfare against Pedantry and Superstition—Ideal of Poetry and Rhetoric—Critique of Jurists and Schoolmen—S. Augustine—Petrarch's Vanity—Thirst for Fame—Discord between his Life and his Profession—His Literary Temperament—Visionary Patriotism—His Influence—His Successors—Boccaccio and Greek Studies—Translation of Homer—Philosophy of Literature—Sensuousness of Boccaccio's Inspiration—Giovanni da Ravenna—The Wandering Professor—His Pupils in Latin Scholarship—Luigi Marsigli—The Convent of S. Spirito—Humanism in Politics—Coluccio de' Salutati—Gasparino da Barzizza—Improved Style in Letter-writing—Revival of Greek Learning—Manuel Chrysoloras—His Pupils—Lionardo Bruni—Value of Greek for the Renaissance.

I HAVE already observed that it would be inaccurate to identify the whole movement of the Renaissance with the process whereby the European nations recovered and appropriated the masterpieces of Greek and Latin literature. At the same time this reconquest of the classic world of thought was by far the most important achievement of the fifteenth and sixteenth centuries. It absorbed nearly the whole mental energy of the Italians, and determined in a great measure the quality of all their intellectual production in the period I have undertaken to illustrate. Through their activity in the field of scholarship the proper starting-point was given to the modern intellect. The revelation of what men were and what they wrought under the influence of other faiths and other impulses, in distant ages with a different ideal for their aim, not only widened the narrow horizon of the Middle Ages, but it also restored self-confidence to the reason of humanity. Research and criticism began to take the place of scholastic speculation. Positive knowledge was substituted for the intuitive guesses of idealists and dreamers. The interests of this world received their due share of attention, and the *litteræ humaniores* of the student usurped upon the *divinarum rerum cognitio* of theologians.

All through the Middle Ages uneasy and imperfect memories of Greece and Rome had haunted Europe. Alexander, the great conqueror; Hector, the noble knight and lover; Helen, who set Troy town on fire ; Virgil, the magician ; Dame Venus lingering about the hill of Hörsel—these phantoms, whereof the positive historic truth was lost, remained to sway the soul and stimulate desire in myth and saga. Deprived of actual knowledge, imagination transformed what it remembered of the classic age into romance. The fascination exercised by these dreams of a half-forgotten past over the mediæval fancy expressed itself in the legend of Doctor Faustus. That legend tells us what the men upon the eve of the Revival longed for, and what they dreaded, when they turned their minds towards the past. The secret of enjoyment and the source of strength possessed by the ancients, allured them ; but they believed that they could only recover this lost treasure by the suicide of their soul. So great was the temptation that Faustus paid the price. After imbibing all the knowledge of his age, he sold himself to the Devil, in order that his thirst for experience might be quenched, his grasp upon the world be strengthened, and the ennui of his inactivity be soothed. His first use of this dearly-bought power was to make blind Homer sing to him. Amphion tunes his harp in concert with Mephistopheles. Alexander rises from the dead at his behest, with all his legionaries ; and Helen is given to him for a bride. Faustus is therefore a parable of the impotent yearnings of the spirit in the Middle Ages—its passionate aspiration, its conscience-stricken desire, its fettered curiosity amid the cramping limits of imperfect knowledge and irrational dogmatism. That for which Faustus sold his soul, the freedom he acquired by magic, the sense of beauty he gratified through visions, the knowledge he gained by interrogation of demons, was yielded to the world without price at the time of the Renaissance. Homer, no longer by the intervention of a fiend, but by the labour of the scholar, sang to the new age. The pomp of the empires of the old world was restored in the pages of historians. The indestructible beauty of Greek art, whereof Helen was an emblem, became, through the discovery of classic poetry and sculpture the possession of the modern world. Mediævalism took this Helen to wife, and their offspring, the Euphorion of Goethe's drama, is the spirit of the modern world. But how was this effected ? By long and toilsome study, by the accumulation of MSS., by the acquisition of dead languages, by the solitary labour of grammarians, by the lectures of itinerant professors, by the scribe, by the printing press, by the self-devotion of magnificent Italy to erudition. In this way the Renaissance realised the dream of the Middle Ages, and the genius of the Italians wrought by solid toil what the myth-making imagination of the Germans had projected in a poem.

It is impossible to exaggerate the benefit conferred upon Europe by the Italians at this epoch. The culture of the classics had to be reappropriated before the movement of the modern mind could begin : before the nations could start upon a new career of progress, the chasm between the old and new world had to be bridged over. This task of reappropriation the Italians undertook alone, and achieved at the sacrifice of their literary independence and their political freedom. The history of Renaissance literature in Italy is the history of a national genius deviating from the course of self-development into the channels of scholarship and antiquarian research. The language created by Dante as a thing of power, polished by Petrarch as a thing of beauty, trained by Boccaccio as the instrument of melodious prose, was abandoned even by the Tuscans in the fifteenth century for revived Latin and newly-discovered Greek. Patent acquisition took the place of proud inventiveness; laborious imitation of classical authors suppressed originality of style. The force of mind which in the fourteenth century had produced a 'Divine Comedy' and a 'Decameron,' in the fifteenth was expended upon the interpretation of codices, the settlement of texts, the translation of Greek books into Latin, the study of antiquities, the composition of commentaries, encyclopædias, dictionaries, ephemerides. While we regret this change from creative to acquisitive literature, we must bear in mind that those scholars who ought to have been poets accomplished nothing less than the civilisation, or, to use their own phrase, the humanisation, of the modern world.[1] At the critical moment when the Eastern Empire was being shattered by the Turks, and when the other European nations were as yet unfit for culture, Italy saved the arts and sciences of Greece and Rome, and interpreted the spirit of the classics. Devoting herself to what appears the slavish work of compilation and collection, she transmitted an inestimable treasure to the human race; and though for a time the beautiful Italian tongue was superseded by a jargon of dead languages, yet the literature of the

[1] Poliziano, Pontano, Sannazzaro, and Bembo divided their powers between scholarship and poetry, to the injury of the latter.

Renaissance yielded in the end the poetry of Ariosto, the political philosophy of Machiavelli, the histories of Guicciardini and Varchi. Meanwhile the whole of Europe had received the staple of its intellectual education.

It is necessary to repeat the observation that this absorption of energy in the task of scholarship was no less natural to the Italians than necessary for the world at large. The Italians were not a new nation like the Franks and Germans. Nothing is more remarkable in the mediæval history of Italy than the sense, shared alike by poets and jurists, by the leaders of popular insurrections and the moulders of philosophic thought, that the centre of national vitality existed in the Roman Empire. It was this determination to look backward rather than forward, to trust the past rather than the present, that neutralised the forces of the Lombard League, and prevented the communes from asserting their independence face to face with foreigners who claimed to be the representatives of Cæsar. The Italians, unlike any other European people, sacrificed the reality of political freedom for the idea of majesty and glory, to be recovered by the restitution of the Empire. Guelf and Ghibelline coincided in this delusion, that Rome, whether Papal or Imperial, was destined still to place the old Italic stock upon the throne of civilised humanity. When the three great authors of the thirteenth century appeared, each in turn cast his eyes to ancient Rome as the true source of national greatness. The language of modern Italy was known to be a scion of the Latin speech, and the Italians called themselves *Latini*. The attempt to conform their literature to the Roman type was therefore felt to be but a return to its true standard ; the ' Æneid ' of Virgil was their *Nibelungen-Lied*. Thus the humanistic enthusiasm of the fifteenth century assumed an almost patriotic character. In it, moreover, the doctrine that had ruled the Middle Ages, interrupting political cohesion without acquiring the consistency of fact, attained at last its proper sphere of development. The ideal of Dante in the ' De Monarchiâ ' had proved a baseless dream ; no emperor was destined to take his seat in Rome and sway the world. But the ideal of Petrarch was realised ; the scholars, animated by his impulse, reacquired the birthright of culture which belonged of old to Italy, and made her empress of the intellect for Europe. Not political but spiritual supremacy was the real heritage of these new Romans.

As an introduction to the history of the Revival, and in order that the work to be performed by the Italian students may be accurately measured, it will be necessary to touch briefly upon the state of scholarship during the dark ages. To underrate the achievement of that period, especially in logic, theology, and law, is only too easy, seeing that a new direction was given to the mind of Europe by the Renaissance, and that we have moved continuously on other lines to other objects since the opening of the fifteenth century. Mediæval thought was both acute and strenuous in its own region of activity. What it lacked was material outside the speculative sphere to feed upon. Culture, in our sense of the word, did not exist, and the intellect was forced to deal subtly with a very limited class of conceptions.

Long before the fall of the Roman Empire it became clear that both fine arts and literature were gradually de-clining. Sculpture in the age of Constantine had lost dis-tinction of style ; and though the practice of verse survived as a rhetorical exercise, no works of original genius were pro-duced. Ausonius and Claudian, just before the division of the Empire and the irruption of the barbarian races, uttered the last swan's note of classic poetry. Meanwhile true taste and criticism were extinct.[1] The Church, while battling with

[1] For the low state of criticism, even in a good age, see Aulus Gellius, lib. xiv. cap. vi. He describes the lecture of a rhetor, *quispiam*

Paganism, recognised her deadliest foes in literature. Not only were the Greek and Latin masterpieces the stronghold of a mythology that had to be erased from the popular mind ; not only was their morality antagonistic to the principles of Christian ethics : in addition to these grounds for hatred and mistrust, the classics idealised a form of human life which the new faith regarded as worthless. What was culture in comparison with the salvation of the soul ? Why should time be spent upon the dreams of poets, when every minute might be well employed in pondering the precepts of the Gospels ? What was the use of making this life refined and agreeable by study, when it formed but an insignificant prelude to an eternity wherein mere mundane learning would be valueless ? Why raise questions about man's condition on this earth, when the creeds had to be defined and expounded, when the nature of God and the relation of the human soul to its Creator had to be established ? It was easy to pass from this state of mind to the belief that learning in itself was impious.[1] 'Let us shun the lying fables of the poets,' cries Gregory of Tours, 'and forego the wisdom of sages at enmity with God, lest we incur the doom of endless death by sentence of our Lord.' Even Augustine deplored his time spent in reading Virgil, weeping over Dido's death by love, when all the while he was himself both morally and spiritually dead. Alcuin regretted that in his boyhood he had preferred Virgil to the legends of the Saints, and stigmatised the eloquence of the Latin writers by the epithet of wanton. Such phrases as *poetarum figmenta, gentilium figmenta sive deliramenta* (the fictions or mad ravings of Pagan

linguæ Latinæ literator, on a passage in the seventh Æneid. The man's explanation of the word *bidentes* proves an almost more than mediæval puerility and ignorance.

[1] Most of the following quotations will be found in Comparetti, *Virgilio nel Medio Evo*, vol. i., a work of sound scholarship and refined taste upon the place of Virgil in the Middle Ages.

poets) are commonly employed by Christian authors of the
Lives of Saints, in order to mark the inferiority of Virgil and
Ovid to their own more edifying compositions. Relying on
their spiritual pretensions, the monkish scribes gloried in
ignorance and paraded want of grammar as a sign of grace.
'I warn the curious reader,' writes a certain Wolfhard in the
'Life of S. Walpurgis,' 'not to mind the mass of barbarisms
in this little work; I bid him ponder what he finds upon
these pages, and seek the pearl within the dung-heap.'
Gregory the Great goes further, and defies the pedantry of
pedagogues. 'The place of prepositions and the cases of the
nouns I utterly despise, since I deem it unfit to confine the
words of the celestial oracle within the rules of Donatus.'
'Let philosophers and impure scholars of Donatus,' writes a
fanatic of Cordova, 'ply their windy problems with the bark-
ing of dogs, the grunting of swine, snarling with skinned
throat and teeth ; let the foaming and bespittled grammarians
belch, while we remain evangelical servants of Christ, true
followers of rustic teachers.' Thus the opposition of the
Church to Paganism, the conviction that Christianity was
alien to culture, and the absorption of intellectual interest
in theological questions contributed to destroy what had
remained of sound scholarship in the last years of the Empire.
The task of the Church, moreover, in the Middle Ages was
not so much to keep learning alive as to moralise the savage
races who held Europe at their pleasure. Pure Latinity,
even if it could have been instilled into the nations of the
North, was of less moment than elementary discipline in
manners and religion. It must not be forgotten that the
literature of ancient Rome was artificial in its best days, confined to a select few, and dependent on the capital for its
support. After the dismemberment of the Empire the whole
of Europe was thrown open to the action of spiritual powers
who had to use unlettered barbarians for their ministers and

missionaries. To submit this vast field to classic culture at
the same time that Christianity was being propagated, would
have been beyond the strength of the Church, even had she
chosen to undertake this task, and had the vital forces of
antiquity not been exhausted.

At this point an inevitable reaction, illustrating the com-
promise thrust upon the Church by her peculiar position,
made itself apparent. In proportion as the dangers of
Paganism decreased, the clergy, on whom devolved the double
duty of civilising as well as moralising society, began to feel
the need of arresting the advance of ignorance. Knowledge
of Latin was required for ecclesiastical uses, for the interpretation of Scripture, for the study of the Fathers, and for the
establishment of a common language among many divers
nationalities. A middle course between the fanaticism which
regarded classical literature as worthless and impure, and the
worldliness that might have been encouraged by enthusiasm
for the ancients, had therefore to be steered. Grammar was
taught in the schools, and where grammar was taught, it was
impossible to exclude Virgil and some other Latin authors.
A conflict in the monkish mind was the unavoidable consequence. Since the classics alone communicated sound learning, the study of them formed a necessary part of education ;
and yet these authors were unbaptized Pagans, doomed to
everlasting death because of their impiety and immorality.
Poets who had hitherto been regarded as deadly foes, were
now accepted as auxiliaries in the battle of the Church against
barbarism. While copying the elegies of Ovid, the compas-
sionate scribe sought to place them in a favourable light, and
to render them edifying at the cost of contradicting their
plain meaning.[1] Virgil was credited with allegorical signifi-

---

[1] *Hoc est quod pueri tangar amore minus*, for example, was altered
into *Hoc est quod pueri tangar amore nihil* ; for *lusisset amores* was
substituted *dampnasset amores*, and so forth.

cance ; and the strong sympathy he roused in those who felt
the beauty of his style, produced a belief that, if not quite, he
was almost a Christian. The piety and pity for Virgil as a
gentle soul who had just missed the salvation offered by
Christ, found expression in the service for S. Paul's Day used
at Mantua : [1]—

> Ad Maronis mausoleum
> Ductus, fudit super eum
>   Piæ rorem lacrymæ ;
> Quem te, inquit, reddidissem
> Si te vivum invenissem,
>   Poetarum maxime !

Meanwhile the utter confusion consequent upon the
downfall of the Roman Empire and the irruption of the
Germanic races was causing, by the mere brute force of circumstance, a gradual extinction of scholarship too powerful
to be arrested. The teaching of grammar for ecclesiastical
purposes was insufficient to check the influence of many
causes leading to this overthrow of learning. It was impossible to communicate more than a mere tincture of knowledge
to students separated from the classical tradition, for whom
the antecedent history of Rome was a dead letter. The
meaning of Latin words derived from the Greek was lost.
Smaragdus, a grammarian, mistook *Eunuchus Comœdia* and
Orestes Tragœdia, mentioned by Donatus, for the names of
authors. Remigius of Auxerre explained *poema* by *positio*,
and *emblema* by *habundantia*. Homer and Virgil were supposed to have been friends and contemporaries, while the

---

[1] The hymn quoted above in the text refers to a legend of S. Paul
having visited the tomb of Virgil at Naples :—

> ' When to Maro's tomb they brought him
> Tender grief and pity wrought him
>   To bedew the stone with tears ;
> What a saint I might have crowned thee,
> Had I only living found thee,
>   Poet first and without peers ! '

Latin epitome of the 'Iliad,' bearing the name of Pindar, was fathered on the Theban lyrist. Theological notions, grotesque and childish beyond description, found their way into etymology and grammar. The three persons of the Trinity were discovered in the verb, and mystic numbers in the parts of speech. Thus analytical studies like that of language came to be regarded as an open field for the exercise of the mythologising fancy ; and etymology was reduced to a system of ingenious punning. *Voluntas* and *voluptas* were distinguished, for example, as pertaining to the nature of *Deus* and *diabolus* respectively ; and, in order to make the list complete, *volumtas* was invented as an attribute of *homo*. It is clear that on this path of verbal quibbling the intellect had lost tact, taste, and common sense together.

When the minds of the learned were possessed by these absurdities to the exclusion of sound method, we cannot wonder that antiquity survived but as a strange and shadowy dream in popular imagination. Virgil, the only classic who retained distinct and living personality, passed from poet to philosopher, from philosopher to Sibyl, from Sibyl to magician, by successive stages of transmutation, as the truth about him grew more dim and the faculty to apprehend him weakened. Forming the staple of education in the schools of the grammarians, and metamorphosed by the vulgar consciousness into a wizard,[1] he waited on the extreme verge of the dark ages to take Dante by the hand, and lead him, as the type of human reason, through the realms of Hell and Purgatory.

With regard to the actual knowledge of Latin literature possessed in the Middle Ages, it may be said in brief that Virgil was continually studied, and that a certain familiarity with Ovid, Lucan, Horace, Juvenal, and Statius was never

---

[1] The common use of the word *grammarie* for occult science in our ballads illustrates this phase of popular opinion. So does the legend of Friar Bacon. See Thoms, *Early English Prose Romances*.

lost. Among the prose-writers, portions of Cicero were used in education; but the compilations of Boethius, Priscian, Donatus, and Cassiodorus were more widely used. In the twelfth century the study of Roman law was revived, and the scholastic habit of thought found scope for subtlety in the discussion of cases and composition of glosses. The general knowledge and intellectual sympathy required for comprehension of the genuine classics were, however, wanting; and thus it happened that their place was taken by epitomes and abstracts, and by the formal digests of the Western Empire in its decadence. This lifeless literature was better suited to the meagre intellectual conditions of the Middle Ages than the masterpieces of the Augustan and Silver periods.

Of Greek there was absolutely no tradition left.[1] When the names of Greek poets or philosophers are cited by mediæval authors, it is at second hand from Latin sources; and the Aristotelian logic of the schoolmen came through Latin translations made by Jews from Arabian MSS. Occasionally it might happen that a Western scholar acquired Greek at Constantinople or in the south of Italy, where it was spoken; but this did not imply Hellenic culture, nor did such knowledge form a part and parcel of his erudition. Greek was hardly less lost to Europe then than Sanskrit in the first half of the eighteenth century.

The meagreness of mediæval learning was, however, a less serious obstacle to culture than the habit of mind, partly engendered by Christianity and partly idiosyncratic to the new races, which prevented students from appreciating the true spirit of the classics. While mysticism and allegory ruled supreme, the clearly-defined humanity of the Greeks and Romans could not fail to be misapprehended. The little that was known of them reached students through a hazy and dis-

[1] Didot, in his *Life of Aldus*, tries to make out that Greek learning survived in Ireland longer than elsewhere.

torting medium. Poems like Virgil's fourth Eclogue were prized for what the author had not meant when he was writing them; while his real interests were utterly neglected. Against this mental misconception, this original obliquity of vision, this radical lie in the intellect, the restorers of learning had to fight at least as energetically as against brute ignorance and dulness. It was not enough to multiply books and to discover codices; they had to teach men how to read them, to explain their inspiration, to defend them against prejudice, to protect them from false methods of interpretation. To purge the mind of fancy and fable, to prove that poetry apart from its supposed prophetic meaning was delightful for its own sake, and that the history of the antique nations, in spite of Paganism, could be used for profit and instruction, was the first step to be taken by these pioneers of modern culture. They had, in short, to create a new mental sensibility by establishing the truth that pure literature directly contributes to the dignity and happiness of human beings. The achievement of this revolution in thought was the great performance of the Italians in the fourteenth and fifteenth centuries.

During the dark ages Italy had in no sense enjoyed superiority of culture over the rest of Europe. On the contrary, the first abortive attempt at a revival of learning was due to Charlemagne at Aix, the second to the Emperor Frederick in Apulia and Sicily; and while the Romance nations had lost the classical tradition, it was still to some extent preserved by the Moslem dynasties. The more we study the history of mediæval learning, the more we recognise the debt of civilised humanity to the Arabs for their conservation and transmission of Greek thought in altered form to Europe. Yet, though the Italians came comparatively late into the field, their action was decisive. Neither Charlemagne nor Frederick, neither the philosophy of the Arabian sages nor the precocious literature of Provence, succeeded in effect-

ing for the education of the modern intellect that which
Dante and Petrarch performed—the one by the production of
a monumental work of art in poetry, the other by the com·
munication of a new enthusiasm for antiquity to students.

Dante does not belong in any strict sense to the history of
the Revival of Learning. The 'Divine Comedy' closes the
Middle Ages and preserves their spirit. It stands before the
vestibule of modern literature like a solitary mountain at the
entrance of a country rich in all varieties of landscape. In
order to become acquainted with its grandeur, we must leave
the fields and forests that we know, ascend the heights, and
use ourselves to an austerer climate. In spite of this isolation,
Dante's influence was powerful upon succeeding generations.
The modern mind first found in him its scope, and recognised
its freedom ; first dared and did what placed it on a level with
antiquity in art. Many ideas, moreover, destined to play an
important part in the coming age, received from him their
germinal expression. It may thus be truly said that Dante
initiated the movement of the modern intellect in its entirety,
though he did not lead the Revival considered as a separate
moment in this evolution. That service was reserved for
Petrarch.

There are spots upon the central watershed of Europe
where, in the stillness of a summer afternoon, the traveller
may listen to the murmurs of two streams—the one hurrying
down to form the Rhine, the other to contribute to the Danube
or the Po. Born within hearing of each other's voices, and
nourished by the self-same clouds that rest upon the crags
around them, they are henceforth destined to an ever-widening
separation. While the one sweeps onward to the Northern seas,
the other will reach the shores of Italy or Greece and mingle
with the Mediterranean. To these two streamlets we might
compare Dante and Petrarch, both of whom sprang from
Florence, both of whom were nurtured in the learning of the

schools and in the lore of chivalrous love. Yet how different was their mission ! Petrarch marks the rising of that great river of intellectual energy which flowed southward to recover the culture of the ancient world. The current of Dante's genius took the contrary direction. Borne upon its mighty flood, we visit the lands and cities of the Middle Ages, floating toward infinities divined and made the heritage of human nature by the mediæval spirit.

In speaking of Petrarch here, it is necessary to concentrate attention upon his claims to be considered as the apostle of scholarship, the inaugurator of the humanistic impulse of the fifteenth century. We have nothing to do with his Italian poetry. The *Rime* dedicated to Madonna Laura have eclipsed the fame of the Latin epic, philosophical discourses, epistles, orations, invectives, and dissertations, which made Petrarch the Voltaire of his own age, and on which he thought his immortality would rest. Yet it is with these latter products of his genius, not with the *Canzoniere*, that we are now concerned ; nor can it be too emphatically asserted that his originality was even more eminently displayed in the revelation of humanism to the modern world than in the verses that impressed their character upon Italian literature. To have foreseen a whole new phase of European culture, to have interpreted its spirit, and determined by his own activity the course it should pursue, is in truth a higher title to fame than the composition of even the most perfect sonnets. The artist, however, has this advantage over the pioneer of intellectual progress, that his delicate creations are indestructible, and that his work cannot be merged in that of a continuator. Therefore Petrarch lives and will live in the memory of millions as the poet of Laura, while only students know how much the world owes to his humanistic ardour.

As I cannot dispense with the word Humanism in this portion of my work, it may be well to fix the sense I shall attach to it.[1] The essence of humanism consisted in a new and vital perception of the dignity of man as a rational being apart from theological determinations, and in the further perception that classic literature alone displayed human nature in the plenitude of intellectual and moral freedom. It was partly a reaction against ecclesiastical despotism, partly an attempt to find the point of unity for all that had been thought and done by man, within the mind restored to consciousness of its own sovereign faculty. Hence the single-hearted devotion to the literature of Greece and Rome that marks the whole Renaissance era. Hence the watchword of that age, the *Litteræ Humaniores*. Hence the passion for antiquity, possessing thoughtful men, and substituting a new authority for the traditions of the Church. Hence the so-called Paganism of centuries bent upon absorbing and assimilating a spirit no less life-giving from their point of view than Christianity itself. Hence the persistent effort of philosophers to find the meeting-point of two divergent inspirations. Hence, too, the ultimate antagonism between the humanists, or professors of the new wisdom, and those uncompromising Christians who, like S. Paul, preferred to remain fools for Christ's sake.

Humanism in this, the widest, sense of the word was possessed by Petrarch intuitively. It belonged to his nature as much as music to Mozart ; so that he seemed sent into the world to raise, by the pure exercise of innate faculties, a standard for succeeding workers. Physically and æsthetically, by the fineness of his ear for verbal harmonies, and by the exquisiteness of his sensibilities, he was fitted to divine what

---

[1] The word Humanism has a German sound, and is in fact modern. Yet the generic phrase *umanità* for humanistic culture, and the name *umanista* for a professor of humane studies, are both pure Italian. Ariosto, in his seventh satire, line 25, writes—

'Senza quel vizio son pochi umanisti.'

it took centuries to verify. While still a boy, long before he could grasp the meaning of classical Latin, he used to read the prose of Cicero aloud, delighting in the sonorous cadence and balanced periods of the master's style.[1] Nor were the moral qualities of industry and perseverance, needed to supplement these natural gifts, defective. In his maturity he spared no pains to collect the manuscripts of Cicero, sometimes transcribing them with his own hand, sometimes employing copyists, sending and journeying to distant parts of Europe where he heard a fragment of his favourite author might be found.[2] His greatest literary disappointment was the loss of a treatise by Cicero on Glory, a theme exceedingly significant for the Renaissance, which he lent to his tutor Convennevole, and which the old man pawned.[3] Though he could not read Greek, he welcomed with profoundest reverence the codices of Homer and Plato sent to him from Constantinople, and exhorted Boccaccio to dedicate his genius to the translation of the sovran poet into Latin.[4] In this suscepti-

---

[1] See the interesting letter to Luca di Penna, *De Libris Ciceronis*, p. 946, and compare *De Ignorantiâ sui ipsius*, &c. p. 1044. These references, as well as those which follow under the general sign *Ibid.*, are made to the edition of Petrarch's collected works, Basle, 1581.

[2] *Ibid.* p. 948. Cf. the fine letter on the duty of collecting and pre serving codices (*Fam. Epist.* lib. iii. 18, p. 619). 'Aurum, argentum, gemmæ, purpurea vestis, marmorea domus, cultus ager, pictæ tabulæ, phaleratus sonipes, cæteraque id genus mutam habent et superficiariam voluptatem : libri medullitus delectant, colloquuntur, consulunt, et vivâ quâdam nobis atque argutâ familiaritate junguntur.'

[3] *De Libris Ciceronis*, p. 949. Cf. his *Epistle to Varro* for an account of a lost MS. of that author. *Ibid.* p. 708.

[4] *Ibid.* p. 948. Cf. *De Ignorantiâ*, pp. 1053, 1054. See, too, the letter to Nicolaus Syocerus of Constantinople, *Epist. Var.* xx. p. 998, thanking him for the Homer and the Plato, in which Petrarch gives an account of his slender Greek studies. 'Homerus tuus apud me mutus, immo vero ego apud illum surdus sum. Gaudeo tamen vel aspectu solo, et sæpe illum amplexus et suspirans dico. . . . Plato philosophorum princeps . . . . nunc tandem tuo munere Philosophorum principi Poetarum princeps asserit. Quis tantis non gaudeat et glorietur hospi-

bility to the melodies of rhetorical prose, in this special cult of Cicero, in the passion for collecting manuscripts, and in the intuition that the future of scholarship depended upon the resuscitation of Greek studies, Petrarch initiated the four most important momenta of the classical Renaissance. He, again, was the first to understand the value of public libraries;[1] the first to accumulate coins and inscriptions, as the sources of accurate historical information; the first to preach the duty of preserving ancient monuments. It would seem as though, by the instinct of genius, he foresaw the future for at least three centuries, and comprehended the highest uses whereof scholarship is capable.

So far the outside only of Petrarch's instinct for humanism has been touched. How fully he possessed its large and liberal spirit is shown by the untiring war he carried on against formalism, tradition, pedantry, and superstition. Whatever might impede the free play of the intellect aroused his bitterest hatred. Against the narrow views of scholastic theologians, against the futile preoccupations of the Middle-Age materialists, against the lawyers and physicians and astrologers in vogue, he declared inexorable hostility.[2] These

tibus? . . . . Græcos spectare, et si nihil aliud, certe juvat.' The letter urging Boccaccio to translate Homer—'an tuo studio, meâ impensâ fieri possit, ut Homerus integer bibliothecæ huic, ubi pridem Græcus habitat, tandem Latinus accedat'—will be found *Ep. Rer. Sen.* lib. iii. 5, p. 775. In another letter, *Ep. Rer. Sen.* lib. vi. 2, p. 807, he thanks Boccaccio for the Latin version.

[1] *De Remediis utriusque Fortunæ*, p. 43. A plea for public as against private collections of useful books. 'Multos in vinculis tenes,' &c.

[2] See the four books of Invectives, *Contra Medicum quendam*, and the treatise *De sui ipsius et aliorum Ignorantiâ.* Page 1038 of the last dissertation contains a curious list of frivolous questions discussed by the Averrhoists. Cf. the letter on the decadence of true learning, *Ep. Var.* 31, p. 1020; the letter to a friend exhorting him to combat Averrhoism, *Epist. sine titulo*, 18, p. 731; two letters on physicians *Epist. Rerum Senilium*, lib. xii. 1 and 2, pp. 897-914; a letter to Fran-

men, by their puerilities and falsities, obstructed the natural
action of the mind; therefore Petrarch attacked them. At
the same time he recognised the liberators of the reason by a
kind of tact. Though he could not interpret the sixteen dialogues of Plato he possessed in Greek, he perceived intuitively
that Plato, as opposed to Aristotle, would become the saint
of liberal philosophy, surveyed by him as in a Pisgah-view.
His enthusiasm for Cicero and Virgil was twofold; in both
respects he proved how capable he was of moulding the taste
and directing the mental force of his successors. As an
artist, he discerned in their style the harmonies of sound and
the proprieties of diction, whereby Latin might once again
become the language of fine thoughts and delicate emotions.
As a champion of intellectual independence, he saw that,
studying their large discourse of all things which the reason
and imagination can appropriate, the thinkers of the modern
age might shake off scholastic fetters, and enter into the
inheritance of spiritual freedom. Poetry and rhetoric he
regarded not merely as the fine arts of literature, but as two
chief instruments whereby the man of genius arrives at self-
expression, perpetuates the qualities of his own soul, and
impresses his character upon the age. Since this realisation
of the individual in a high and puissant work of art appeared
to him the noblest aim of man on earth, it followed that the
inspired speech of the poet and the eloquence of the orator
became for Petrarch the summit of ambition, the two-peaked
Parnassus he struggled through his lifetime to ascend.[1]

cesco Bruno on the lies of the astrologers, *Epist. Rer. Sen.* lib. i. 6,
p. 747; a letter to Boccaccio on the same theme, *Epist. Rer. Sen.*
lib. iii. 1, p. 765; another on physicians to Boccaccio, *Epist. Rer. Sen.*
lib. v. 4, p. 796. Cf. the Critique of Alchemy, *De Remediis utriusque
Fortunæ,* p. 93.

[1] In comparing the orator and the poet, Petrarch gives the palm to
the former. He thought the perfect rhetorician, capable of expressing
sound philosophy with clearness, was rarer than the poet. See *De
Remediis utriusque Fortunæ,* lib. ii. dial. 102, p. 192.

The ideal was literary; but literature implied for Petrarch more than words and phrases. It was not enough to make melodious verse, or to move an audience with well-sounding periods. The hexameters of the epic and the paragraphs of the oration had to contain solid thought, to be the genuine outcome of the poet's or the rhetorician's soul. The writer was bound to be a preacher, to discover truth, and make the truths he found agreeable to the world.[1] His life, moreover, ought to be in perfect harmony with all he sought to teach.[2] Upon the purity of his enthusiasm, the sincerity of his inspiration, depended the future well-being of the world for which he laboured.[3] Thus for this one man at least the art of letters was a priesthood ; and the earnestness of his vocation made him fit to be the master of succeeding ages. It is not easy for us to appreciate the boldness and sincerity of these conceptions. Many of them, since the days of Petrarch, have been overstrained and made ridiculous by false pretensions. Besides, the whole point of view has been appropriated; and men invariably undervalue what they feel they cannot lose. It is only by comparing Petrarch's own philosophy of literature with the dulness of the schoolmen in their decadence, and with the stylistic shallowness of subsequent scholars, that we come to comprehend how luminous and novel was the thesis he supported.

Having thus conceived of literature, Petrarch obtained a standard for estimating the barren culture of his century. He taxed the disputations of the doctors with lifeless repeti-

[1] See, among other passages, *Inv. contra Medicum*, lib. i. p. 1092. 'Poetæ studium est veritatem veram pulchris velaminibus adornare.' Cf. p. 905, the paragraph beginning 'Officium est ejus fingere,' &c.

[2] See the preface to the *Epistolæ Familiares*, p. 570. 'Scribendi enim mihi vivendique unus (ut auguror) finis erit.'

[3] For his lofty conception of poetry see the two letters to Boccaccio and Benvenuto da Imola, pp. 740, 941. *Epist. Rerum Senilium*, lib. i. 4, lib. xiv. 11.

tion and unmeaning verbiage. Schoolman after schoolman
had been occupied with formal trifles. The erudition of the
jurist and the theologian revealed nothing fruitful for the
heart or intellect; and everything was valueless that did not
come straight from a man's soul, speaking to the soul of one
who heard him. At the same time he read the Fathers and
the Scriptures in a new light. Augustine, some few of whose
sentences had been used as links in the catena of dogmatic
orthodoxy, seemed to Petrarch no longer a mere master of
theology, but a man conversing with him across the chasm of
eight centuries. In the ' Confessions,' ' running over with a
fount of tears,' the poet of Vaucluse divined a kindred nature;
one who used exalted eloquence for the expression of vital
thoughts and passionate emotions; one, moreover, who had
reached the height of human happiness in union with God.[1]
Not less real was the grasp he laid upon the prophets and
apostles of the Bible. All words that bore a message to his
heart were words of authority and power. The *ipse dixit* of
an Aristotle or a Seraphic doctor had for him no weight,
unless it came home to him as a man.[2] Even Cicero and
Seneca, the saints of philosophical antiquity, he dared to
criticise for practising less wisdom than they preached.[3]

While regarding Petrarch as the first and, in some respects,
the greatest of the humanists, we are bound to recognise the
faults as well as the good qualities he shared with them. To

[1] The references to Augustine as a ' divine genius,' equal to Cicero in
eloquence, superior to the classics in his knowledge of Christ, are too
frequent for citation. See, however, *Fam. Epist.* lib. ii. 9, p. 601; the
letter to Boccaccio, *Variarum*, 22, p. 1001; and *Fam. Epist.* lib. iv. 9,
p. 635. The phrase describing the *Confessions*, quoted in my text, is
from Petrarch's letter to his brother Gerard, *Epist. Var.* 27, p. 1012,
' Scatentes lachrymis Confessionum libros.'

[2] ' Sum sectarum negligens, veri appetens.' *Epist. Rer. Sen.* lib. i.
5, p. 745. ' Nam apud Horatium Flaccum, nullius jurare in verba
magistri, puer valde didiceram.' *Epist. Fam.* lib. iv. 10, p. 637.

[3] See the letters addressed to Cicero and Seneca, pp. 705, 706.

dwell on these in detail would be a thankless task, were it not for the conviction that his personality impressed itself too strongly on the fourteenth century to escape our criticism. We cannot afford to leave even the foibles of the man who gave a pattern to his generation unstudied. Foremost among these may be reckoned his vanity, his eagerness to grasp the poet's crown, his appetite for flattery, his restless change from place to place in search of new admirers, his self-complacent garrulity. This vanity was perhaps inseparable from the position he assumed upon the threshold of the modern world. It was hardly possible that the prophet of a new phase of culture should not look down with contempt upon the uneducated masses, and believe that learning raised a man into a demigod. Study of the classics taught him to despise his age and yearn for immortality ; but the assurance of the honours that he sought, could only come to him upon the lips of his contemporaries. In conflict with the dulness and the darkness of preceding centuries, he felt the need of a new motive, unrecognised by the Church and banished from the cloister. That motive was the thirst for fame, the craving to make his personality eternal in the minds of men. Meanwhile he was alone in a dim wilderness of transitory interests and sordid aims, where human life was shadowy, and where, when death arrived, there would remain no memory of what had been. The gloom of this present in contrast with the glory of the past he studied, and the glory of the future he desired, confirmed his egotism. His name and fame depended on his self-assertion. To achieve renown by writing, to wrest for himself even in his lifetime a firm place among the immortals, became his feverish spur to action. He was conscious how deep a hold the passion for celebrity had taken on his nature ; and not unfrequently he speaks of it as a disease.[1]

[1] ' Ægritudo ' is a phrase that constantly recurs in his epistles to

The Christian within him wrestled vigorously with the renascent Pagan. Religion taught him to renounce what ambition prompted him to grasp. Yet he continued to deceive
himself. While penning dissertations on the worthlessness
of praise and the futility of fame, he trimmed his sails to
catch the breeze of popular applause; and as his reputation
widened, his desires grew ever stronger. The last years of
his life were spent in writing epistles to the great men of the
past, in whom alone he recognised his equals, and to posterity,
in whom he hoped to meet at last with judges worthy
of him.

This almost morbid vanity, peculiar to Petrarch's temperament and encouraged by the circumstances of his life,
introduced a division between his practice and his profession.
He was never tired of praising solitude, and many years of
his manhood he spent in actual retirement at Vaucluse.[1]
Yet he only loved seclusion as a contrast to the society of
Courts, and would have been most miserable if the world,
taking him at his own estimate, had left him in peace. No
one wrote more eloquently about equal friendship, or professed
a stronger zeal for candid criticism. Yet he admitted few but
professed admirers to his intimacy, and regarded his literary
antagonists as personal detractors. The same sensitive egotism led him to depreciate the fame of Dante, in whom he
cannot but have recognised a poet in the highest sense
superior to himself.[2] Again, while he complained of celebrity
as an obstacle to studious employment, he showed the most
acute interest when the details of his life were called in ques-

indicate a restless, craving habit of the soul. See, too, the whole second
book of the *De Contemptu Mundi*.

[1] See the treatise *De Vitâ Solitariâ*, pp. 223–292, and the letters on
' Vaucluse,' pp. 691–697.

[2] See the discussion of this point in Baldelli's *Vita del Boccaccio*,
pp. 130–135.

tion.[1] Nothing, if we took his philosophic treatises for record, would have pleased him better than to live unnoticed. His letters make it manifest that he believed the eyes of the whole world were fixed upon him, and that he courted this attention of the public with a greedy appetite.

These qualities and contradictions mark Petrarch as a man of letters, not of action. He belonged essentially to the *genus irritabile vatum*, for whom the sphere of thoughts expressed on paper is more vivid than the world of facts. We may trace a corresponding weakness in his chief enthusiasms. Unable to distinguish between the realities of existence and the dreamland of his study, he hailed in Rienzi the restorer of old Rome, while he stigmatised his friends the Colonnesi as barbarian intruders.[2] The Rome he read of in the pages of Livy, seemed to the imagination of this visionary still alive and powerful; nor did he feel the absurdity of addressing the mediæval rabble of the Romans in phrases high-flown for a Gracchus.[3] While he courted the intimacy of the Correggi, and lived as a house-guest with the Visconti, he denounced these princes as tyrants, and appealed to the Emperor to take the reins and bring all Italy beneath his yoke.[4] Herein, it may be urged, Petrarch did but share a delusion common to his age. This is true ; but the point to notice is the contradiction between his theories and the habits of his life. He was not a partisan on the Ghibelline side, but a believer in impossible ideals. His patriotism was no less

[1] Compare the chapter in the dissertation *De Remediis* on troublesome notoriety, p. 177, with the letter on his reception at Arezzo, p. 918, the letter to Nerius Morandus on the false news of his death, p. 776, and the letter to Boccaccio on his detractors, p. 749.

[2] See the *Epistles to Rienzi*, pp. 677, 535.

[3] Epistle to the Roman people, beginning 'Apud te invictissime domitorque terrarum popule meus,' p. 712.

[4] Epistle to Charles IV., *De Pacificandâ Italiâ*, p. 531. This contradiction struck even his most ardent admirers with painful surprise. See Boccaccio quoted in Baldelli's *Life*, p. 115.

literary than his temperament. The same tendency to measure all things by a student's standard made him exaggerate mere verbal eloquence. Words, according to his view, were power. Cicero held the highest place in his esteem, because his declamation was most copious. Aristotle, in spite of his profound philosophy, was censured for his lack of rhetoric.[1] Throughout the studied works of Petrarch we can trace this vice of a stylistic ideal. Though he never writes without ome solid germ of thought, he loves *to* play with phrases, producing an effect of unreality, and seeming emulous of casuistical adroitness.[2]

The foregoing analysis was necessary because Petrarch became, as it were, a model for his followers in the field of scholarship. Italian humanism never lost the powerful impress of his genius, and the value of his influence can only be appreciated when the time arrives for summing up the total achievement of the Revival.[3] It remains to be regretted that the weaknesses of his character, his personal pretension and literary idealism, were more easily imitated than his strength. Petrarch's egotism differed widely from the insolent conceit of Filelfo and the pedantic boasts of Alciato. Nor did his enthusiasm for antiquity degenerate, like theirs, into a mere uncritical and servile worship. His humanism was both loftier and larger. He never forgot that Christianity was an advance upon Paganism, and that the accomplished man of letters must acquire the culture of the ancients without losing the virtues or sacrificing the hopes of a Christian. If only the humanists of the Renaissance could have preserved this point of view intact, they would have avoided the worst

[1] *Rerum memorandarum*, lib. ii. p. 415.
[2] This is particularly noticeable in the miscellaneous collection of essays called *De Remediis utriusque Fortunæ*, where opposite views on a wide variety of topics are expressed with great dexterity.
[3] See the last chapter of this volume.

evils of the age, and have secured a nobler liberation of the modern reason. Petrarch created for himself a creed compounded of Roman Stoicism and Christian doctrine, adapting the precepts of the Gospels and the teaching of the Fathers, together with the ethics of Cicero and Seneca, to his own needs. Herein he showed the freedom of his genius, and led the way for the most brilliant thinkers of the coming centuries. The fault of his successors was a tendency to recede from this high vantage-ground, to accept the customary creed with cynical facility, while they inclined in secret to a laxity adopted from their study of the classics. By separating himself from tradition, without displaying an arrogant spirit of revolt against authority, Petrarch established the principle that men must guide their own souls by the double lights of culture and of conscience. His followers were too ready to make culture all in all, and lost thereby the opportunity of grounding a rational philosophy of life upon a solid basis for the modern world. Petrarch made it his sincere aim to be both morally and intellectually his highest self ; and if he often failed in practice—if he succumbed to carnal frailty while he praised sobriety—if he sought for notoriety while professing indifference to fame—if he mistook dreams for realities and words for facts—still the ideal he proposed to himself and eloquently preached to his contemporaries, was a new and lofty one. After the lapse of five centuries, few as yet have passed beyond it. Even Goethe, for example, can claim no superiority of humanism above Petrarch, except by right of his participation in the scientific spirit.

We are therefore justified in hailing Petrarch as the Columbus of a new spiritual hemisphere, the discoverer of modern culture. That he knew no Greek, that his Latin verse was lifeless and his prose style far from pure, that his contributions to history and ethics have been superseded, and that his epistles are now only read by antiquaries, cannot impair his claim to this title. From him the inspiration needed to quicken curiosity and stimulate a zeal for knowledge proceeded. But for his intervention in the fourteenth century, it is possible that the Revival of Learning, and all that it implies, might have been delayed until too late. Petrarch died in 1374. The Greek Empire was destroyed in 1453. Between those dates Italy recovered the Greek classics ; but whether the Italians would have undertaken this labour if no Petrarch had preached the attractiveness of liberal studies, or if no school of disciples had been formed by him in Florence, remains more than doubtful. We are brought thus to recognise in him one of those heroes concerning whose relation to the spirit of the ages Hegel has discoursed in his ' Philosophy of History.' Petrarch, by anticipating the tendencies of the Revival, created the intellectual milieu required for its evolution.[1] Yet we are not therefore justified in saying that he was not himself the product of already existing spiritual forces in his century. The vast influence he immediately exercised, while Dante, though gifted with a far more powerful individuality, remained comparatively inoperative, proves that the age was specially prepared to receive his inspiration.

What remains to be said about the first period of Italian humanism is almost wholly concerned with men who either immediately or indirectly felt the influence of Petrarch's genius.[2] His shadow stretches over the whole age. Incited by his brilliant renown, Boccaccio, while still a young man, began to read the classical authors, bemoaning the years he had wasted in commerce and the study of the law to please his father. From what the poet of the ' Decameron ' has himself told us about the origin of his literary enthusiasm, it

[1] The lines from the *Africa* used as a motto for this volume are a prophecy of the Renaissance.

[2] It is very significant of Petrarch's influence that his contemporaries ranked him higher, even as a sonnet-writer, than Dante. See *Coluccio de' Salutati's Letters*, part ii. p. 57.

appears that Petrarch's example was decisive in determining his course. There is, however, another tale, reported by his fellow-citizen Villani, so characteristic of the age that to omit it in this place would be to sacrifice one of the most attractive legends in the history of literature.[1] 'After wandering through many lands, now here, now there, for a long space of time, when he had reached at last his twenty-eighth year, Boccaccio, at his father's bidding, took up his abode at Naples in the Pergola. There it chanced one day that he walked forth alone for pleasure, and came to the place where Virgil's dust lies buried. At the sight of this sepulchre, he fell into long musing admiration of the man whose bones it covered, brooding with meditative soul upon the poet's fame, until his thoughts found vent in lamentations over his own envious fortunes, whereby he was compelled against his will to give himself to things of commerce that he loathed. A sudden love of the Pierian Muses smote his heart, and turning homeward, he abandoned trade, devoting himself with fervent study to poetry; wherein very shortly, aided alike by his noble genius and his burning desire, he made marvellous progress. This when his father noted, and perceived the heavenly inspiration was more powerful within his son than the paternal will, he at last consented to his studies, and helped him as best he could, although at first he tried to make him turn his talents to the canon law.'

The hero-worship of Boccaccio, not only for the august Virgil, but also for Dante, the master of his youth and the idol of his mature age, is the most amiable trait in a character which, by its geniality and sweetness, cannot fail to win affection.[2] When circumstances brought him into personal

[1] Filippo Villani, *Vite d' Uomini Illustri Fiorentini*, Firenze, 1826, p. 9.

[2] With his own hand Boccaccio transcribed the *Divine Comedy*, and sent the MS. to Petrarch, who in his reply wrote thus:—'Inseris nominatim hanc hujus officii tui escusationem, quod tibi adolescentulo

relations with Petrarch, he transferred the whole homage of his ardent soul to the only man alive who seemed to him a fit inheritor of ancient fame.[1]   Petrarch became the director of his conscience, the master of his studies, the moulder of his thoughts upon the weightiest matters of literary philosophy. The friendship established between the poet of Vaucluse and the lover of Fiammetta lasted through more than twenty years, and was only broken by the death of the former. Throughout this long space of time Boccaccio retained the attitude of a humble scholar, while in his published works, the 'Genealogia Deorum' and the 'Comento sopra i Primi Sedici Capitoli dell' "Inferno" di Dante,' he uniformly spoke of Petrarch as his father and his teacher, the wonder of the century, a heavenly poet better fitted to be numbered with the giants of the past than with the pygmies of a barren age. The fame enjoyed by Petrarch, the honours showered upon him by kings and princes, his own vanity, and even the discrepancies between his habits and his theories, produced no bitterness in Boccaccio's more modest nature.   It was enough for the pupil to use his talents for the propagation of his master's views ; and thus the influence of Petrarch was communicated to Florence, where Boccaccio continued to reside.[2]

primus studiorum dux, prima fax fuerit.'   Baldelli, p. 133.   The enthusiasm of Boccaccio for Dante contrasts favourably with Petrarch's grudging egotism.

[1] Boccaccio was present at Naples when Petrarch disputed before King Robert for his title to the poet's crown (*Gen. Deor.* xiv. 22); but he first became intimate with him as a friend during Petrarch's visit to Florence in 1350.

[2] Salutato, writing to Francesco da Brossano, describes his conversations with Boccaccio thus :—'Nihil aliud quam de Francisco (*i.e.* Petrarcha) conferebamus.   In cujus laudationem adeo libenter sermones usurpabat, ut nihil avidius nihilque copiosius enarraret.   Et eo magis quia tali orationis generi me prospiciebat intentum.   Sufficiebat enim nobis Petrarcha solus, et omni posteritati sufficiet in moralitate sermonis, in eloquentiæ soliditate atque dulcedine, in lepore prosarum et in concinnitate metrorum.'   *Epist. Fam.* p. 45.

In obedience to Petrarch's advice, Boccaccio in middle
life applied himself to learning Greek. Petrarch had never
acquired a real knowledge of the language, though he received
a few lessons at Avignon from Barlaam, a Calabrian, who
had settled in Byzantium, and who sought to advance his
fortunes in Italy and Greece by alternate acts of apostasy,
and afterwards at Venice from Leontius Pilatus.[1] The opportunities of Greek study enjoyed by Boccaccio were also very
meagre, and his mastery of the idiom was superficial. Yet
he advanced considerably beyond the point reached by any of
his predecessors, so that he deserves to be named as the first
Grecian of the modern world. Leontius Pilatus, a Southern
Italian and a pupil of Barlaam, who, like his teacher, had
removed to Byzantium and renounced the Latin faith, arrived
at Venice on his way to Avignon in 1360. Boccaccio induced
him to visit Florence, received him into his own house, and
caused him to be appointed Greek Professor in the University.
Then he set himself to work in earnest on the text of Homer.
The ignorance of the teacher was, however, scarcely less than
that of his pupil. While Leontius possessed a fair knowledge of Byzantine Greek, his command of Latin was very
limited, and his natural stupidity was only equalled by his
impudent pretensions. Of classical usages he seems to have
known nothing. The imbecility of his master could scarcely
have escaped the notice of Boccaccio. Indeed, both he and
Petrarch have described Leontius as a sordid cynic with a
filthy beard and tangled hair, morose in his temper and disgusting in his personal habits, who concealed a bovine ignorance beneath a lion's hide of ostentation. It was, however,
necessary to make the best of him; for Greek in Northern
Italy could nowhere else be gained, and Boccaccio had not
thought, it seems, of journeying to Byzantium in search of

[1] *Epist. Rer. Sen.*, lib. xi. 9, p. 887; lib. vi. 1, p. 806; lib. v. 4,
p. 801.

what he wanted.[1] Boccaccio, accordingly, drank the muddy stream of pseudo-learning and lies that flowed from this man's lips, with insatiable avidity. The nonsense administered to him by way of satisfying his thirst for knowledge may best be understood from the following etymologies. Ἀχιλλεύς was derived from ἀ and χιλός, 'without fodder.'[2] The names of the Muses gave rise to these extraordinary explanations :[3]— Melpomene is derived from *Melempio comene*, which signifies *facente stare la meditazione* ; Thalia is the same as *Tithonlia* or *pognente cosa che germini*; Polyhymnia, through *Polium neemen*, is the same as *cosa che faccia molta memoria* ; Erato becomes *Euruncomenon* or *trovatore del simile*, and Terpsichore is described as *dilettante ammaestramento*.

Such was the bathos reached by erudition in Byzantium. Yet Boccaccio made what use he could of his contemptible materials. At the dictation of Leontius he wrote out the 'Iliad' and 'Odyssey' in Latin ; and this was the first translation made of Homer for modern readers. The manuscript, despatched to Petrarch, was, as we have seen already, greeted with enthusiasm.[4] This moment in the history of scholarship is so memorable that I may be excused for borrowing

---

[1] Petrarch's letter to Ugone di San Severino, *Epist. Rer. Sen.* lib. xi. 9, p. 887, deserves to be read, since it proves that Italian scholars despaired at this time of gaining Greek learning from Constantinople. They were rather inclined to seek it in Calabria. 'Græciam, ut olim ditissimam, sic nunc omnis longe inopem disciplinæ . . . quod desperat apud Græcos, non diffidit apud Calabros inveniri posse.'

[2] *De Gen. Deor.* xv. 6, 7.

[3] *Comento sopra Dante, Opp. Volg.* vol. x. p. 127. After allowing for the difficulty of writing Greek, pronounced by an Italian, in Italian letters, and also for the errors of the copyist and printer, it is clear that a Greek scholar who thought Melpomene was one 'who gives fixity to meditation,' Thalia one 'who plants the capacity of growth,' Polyhymnia she 'who strengthens and expands memory,' Erato 'the discoverer of similarity,' and Terpsichore 'delightful instruction,' was on a comically wrong track.

[4] See above, p. 53, note 4.

Baldelli's extract from an ancient copy of Boccaccio's autograph.[1]   Lycaon addresses his last prayer to Achilles :—

> Genu deprecor te Achilles : tu autem venerare et me miserere.
> Vada Servus.   Jove genite venerabilis.
> Penes enim te primo gustavi Cereris farinam,
> Die illo, quando me cepisti in bene facto viridario ;
> Et me transtulisti procul ferens patreque amicisque
> Lemnon ad gloriosam.   Hecatombium autem honorem inveni,
> Nunc autem læsus ter tot ferens.   Dies autem mihi est
> Hæc duodecima, quando ad Ilion veni
> Multa passus.   Nunc iterum me in tuis manibus posuit
> Fatum destructibile.   Debeo odio esse Jovi patri,
> Qui me tibi iterum dedit, medio cuique, me mater
> Genuit Lathoi, filia Altai senis.

Only by keeping firmly in mind that such men as Petrarch
and Boccaccio, the two chief masters of Italian literature,
prized this wretched stuff as an inestimable treasure, can we
justly conceive how utterly Greek had been lost, and what an
effort it required to restore it to the modern world.

Indefatigable industry was Boccaccio's great merit as a
student.   He transcribed the whole of Terence with his own
hands, and showed a real sense of the advantage to be gained
by a critical comparison of texts.   In his mythological, geographical, and historical collections he bequeathed to posterity
a curious mass of miscellaneous knowledge, forming, as it were,
the first dictionaries of biography and antiquity for modern
scholars.[2]   Far from sharing the originality of Petrarch's
humanistic ideal, he remained at best a laborious chronicler
of facts and anecdotes.   The author of the ' Decameron,' so
richly gifted with humour, pathos, and poetic fancy, when he
wrapped his student's robe around him, became a painstaking
pioneer of antiquarian research.

---

[1] *Vita del Boccaccio*, p. 264.   The autograph was probably burned
with other books of Boccaccio, and some of the unintelligible passages
in the above quotation may be due to the ignorance of the copyist.

[2] *De Genealogiâ Deorum ; De Casibus Virorum ac Feminarum
Illustrium ; De Claris Muliebribus; De Montibus, Silvis, Fontibus*, &c.

One very important part of Petrarch's programme was eloquently supported by Boccaccio. The fourteenth and fifteenth books of the 'Genealogia Deorum' form what may be termed the first defence of poesy, composed in honour of his own art by a poet of the modern world. In them Boccaccio expounds a theory already sketched in outline by Petrarch. We have seen that the worst obstacle to humanistic culture lay, not so much in ignorance, as in misconceptions based upon prejudice and scruple. The notion of fine literature as an elevating and purifying influence had been lost. To restore it was the object of these earliest humanists. By poetry, contends Boccaccio, we must understand whatever of weighty in argument, deep in doctrine, and vivid in imagination the man of genius may produce with conscious art in prose and verse. Poetry is instruction conveyed through allegory and fiction. Theology itself, he reasons, is a form of poetry; even the Holy Ghost may be called a Poet, inasmuch as He used the vehicle of symbol in the visions of the prophets and the Revelation of S. John.[1] To such strained arguments was the apostle of culture driven in order to persuade his hearers, and to drag literature from the Avernus of mediæval neglect. We must not, however, imagine that Boccaccio was himself superior to a point of view so puerile. Allegory appeared to him a necessary condition of art: only a madman could deny the hidden meaning of the 'Georgics' and the 'Æneid;'[2] while the verses of Dante and of Petrarch owed their value to the Christian mysteries they shrouded. The poet, according to this mediæval philosophy of literature, was a sage and teacher

---

[1] 'La teologia e la poesia quasi una cosa si possono dire . . . la teologia niuna altra cosa è che una poesia d' Iddio.' *Vita di Dante*, p. 59. Cf. *Comento sopra Dante*, loc. cit. p. 45. The explanation of the Muses referred to above is governed by the same determination to find philosophy in poetry.

[2] See Petrarch's letter 'De quibusdam fictionibus Virgilii.' *Ep. Rer. Sen.* lib. iv. 4, p. 785.

wrapping up his august meanings in delightful fictions.[1]
Though the common herd despised him as a liar and a false-
hood-fabricator, he was, in truth, a prophet uttering his dark
speech in parables.   How foolish, therefore, reasons the
apologist, are the enemies of poetry—sophistical dialecticians
and avaricious jurists, who have never trodden the Phœbean
hill, and who scorn the springs of Helicon because they do
not flow with gold ! Far worse is the condition of those
monks and hypocrites who accuse the divine art of immorality
and grossness, instead of reading between the lines and seeking the sense conveyed to the understanding under veils of
allegory.   Truly, proceeds Boccaccio, we do well to shun the
errors of Pagans ; nor can it be denied that poets of antiquity
have written verse abhorrent to the Christian spirit. But,
Jesus Christ be praised, the faith has triumphed. Strong in
the doctrines of the Gospel and the Church, the student may
safely approach the masterpieces of classic literature without
fearing the seductions of the Siren.

This argument, forming the gist of the 'Apology for Poetry'
in the ' Genealogia Deorum,' is repeated in the ' Comment upon
Dante.' It is doubly interesting, both as showing the popular
opinion of poetry and the prejudices Boccaccio thought it
needful to attack, and also as containing a full exposition of
the allegorising theories with which humanism started. For
some time after Boccaccio's death the paragraphs condensed
above supplied the champions of culture with weapons to be
used against their ecclesiastical and scholastic antagonists ;
nor was it until humanism had triumphed, that the allegorical
interpretation of the ancients was finally abandoned.

Independently of his contributions to learning, Boccaccio
occupies a prominent place in the history of the Revival through
the new spirit he introduced into the vulgar literature. He

[1] See the privilege granted to Petrarch by the Roman senator in
1343, *Petr. Opp.* tom. iii p. 6.

was the first who frankly sought to justify the pleasures of
the carnal life, whose temperament, unburdened by asceticism,
found a congenial element in amorous legends of antiquity.
The romances of Boccaccio, with their beautiful gardens and
sunny skies, fair women and luxurious lovers, formed a
transition from the chivalry of the early Italian poets to the
sensuality of Beccadelli and Pontano. He prepared the nation
for literary and artistic Paganism by unconsciously divesting
thought and feeling of their spiritual elevation. Dante had
made the whole world one in Christ. Petrarch put humanity
to school in the lecture-room of Roman sages and in the
councils of the Church. A terrestrial paradise of sensual
delight, where all things were desirable and delicate, contented
the poet of the ‘Fiammetta’ and ‘Filostrato.’ To the beatific
vision of the ‘Divine Comedy,’ to the ‘Trionfo della Morte,’
succeeded the ‘Visione Amorosa ’—a review of human life, in
which Boccaccio begins by invoking Dame Venus and ends
with earthly love, *Il Sior di tutta pace*.

The name given to Boccaccio by contemporaries,
Giovanni della Tranquillità, sufficiently indicates his peaceful
temperament. He was, in fact, the scholar, working in his
study, and contributing to the erudition of his age by writings.
Another of Petrarch's disciples, Giovanni Malpaghino, called
from his birthplace Giovanni da Ravenna, exercised a more
active personal influence over the destinies of scholarship.
While still a youth he had been employed by Petrarch as
secretary and amanuensis. His general ability, clear handwriting, and enthusiasm for learning first recommended him
to the poet, who made use of him for copying manuscripts
and arranging his familiar letters. In the course of this
work John of Ravenna became himself a learned man,
acquiring a finer sense of Latinity than was possessed by any
other scholar of his time. Something, too, of the sacred fire
he caught from Petrarch, so that in his manhood the very

faults of his nature became instrumental in diffusing throughout Italy the passion for antiquity. He could not long content himself with being even Petrarch's scribe. Irresistible restlessness impelled him to seek adventures in the outer world, to mix with men and gain the glory he was always reading of. Petrarch, incapable of comprehending that any honour was greater than that of being his satellite, treated this ambitious pupil like a wilful child. A quarrel ensued. Giovanni left his benefactor's house and went forth to try his fortunes. Without repeating the vicissitudes of his career in detail, it is enough to mention that want and misery soon drove him back to Petrarch ; that once more the vagrant impulse came upon him, and that for a season he filled the post of chancellor in the little principality of Carrara.[1] The one thing, however, which he could not endure, was the routine of fixed employment. Therefore we find that he abandoned the Court of the Malaspini, and betook himself to the more congenial work of a wandering professor. His prodigious memory, by enabling him to retain, word for word, the text of authors he had read, proved of invaluable service to him in this career. His passionate poetic temper made him apt to raise enthusiasm in young souls for literary studies. Giovanni da Ravenna was in fact the first of those vagabond humanists with whom we shall be occupied in the next chapters, and of whom Filelfo was the most illustrious example. Florence, Padua, Venice, and many other cities of Italy received the Latinist, whose reputation now increased with every year. In each of these towns in succession he lectured upon Cicero and the Roman poets, pouring forth the knowledge he had acquired in Petrarch's study, and transmitting to his audience the inspiration he had received from

---

[1] De Sade, in his *Memoirs of Petrarch*, gives an interesting account of this romantic episode in his life. See too Petrarch, *Epist. Rer. Sen.* lib. v. 6 and 7, pp. 802–806.

his master. The school thus formed was compared a
century later to the Trojan horse, whence issued a band of
heroes destined to possess the capital of classic learning. As
a writer, he produced little that is worth more than a passing
notice. His real merit consisted, as Lionardo Bruni witnessed, in his faculty of arousing a passion for pure literature,
and especially for the study of Cicero. Among his most
illustrious pupils may be mentioned Francesco Barbaro, Palla
degli Strozzi, Roberto de' Rossi, Francesco Filelfo, Carlo
Marsuppini, Poggio Bracciolini, Lionardo Bruni, Guarino da
Verona, Vittorino da Feltre, Ambrogio Traversari, Ognibene
da Vicenza, and Pier Paolo Vergerio. This list, as will
appear from the sequel of my work, includes nearly all those
scholars who devoted their energies to erudition at Venice,
Florence, Rome, Mantua, Ferrara, and Perugia in the fifteenth
century. Giovanni da Ravenna deserves, therefore, to be
honoured as the link between the age of Petrarch and the age
of Poggio, as the vessel chosen for communicating the sacred
fire of humanism to the Courts and Republics of Italy. None
but a wanderer, *vagus quidam*, as Petrarch, half in scorn and
half in sorrow, called his protégé, could so effectually have
carried on the work of propagation.[1]

The name of the next student claiming our attention as a
disciple of Petrarch, brings us once more back to Florence.
Luigi Marsigli was a monk of the Augustine Order of
S. Spirito. Petrarch, noticing his distinguished abilities, had
exhorted him to make a special study of theology, and to enter
the lists as a champion of Christianity against the Averrhoists.[2]
Under the name of Averrhoists in the fourteenth century were
ranged all freethinkers who questioned the fundamental
doctrines of the Church, doubted the immortality of the soul,
and employed their ingenuity in a dialectic at least as trivial

---

[1] *Epist. Rer. Sen.* lib. xiv. 14, p. 942.
[2] *Epist. sine titulo*, xviii. p. 732.

as that of the schoolmen, but directed to a very different end.[1] Petrarch disliked their want of liberal culture as much as he abhorred their affectation of impiety. The stupid materialism they professed, their gross flippancy, and the idle pretence of natural science upon which they piqued themselves, were regarded by him as so many obstacles to his own ideal of humanism. He only saw in them another set of scholastic wranglers, worse than the theologians, inasmuch as they had cast off Christ. Against Averrhoes, 'the raging hound who barked at all things sacred and Divine,' Petrarch therefore sought to stimulate the young Marsigli. Marsigli, however, while he shared Petrarch's respect for humane culture, seems to have sympathised with the audacity and freedom of his proposed antagonists. The Convent of S. Spirito became under his influence the centre of a learned society, who met there regularly for disputations. The theme chosen for discussion was posted up upon the wall of the debating-room, metaphysical and ethical subjects forming the most frequent matter of inquiry.[2] Among the members of the circle who sharpened their wits in this species of dialectic, we find Coluccio de' Salutati, Roberto de' Rossi, Niccolo de' Niccoli, and Giannozzo Manetti. The influence of Marsigli in forming their character was undoubtedly powerful. Poggio, in his funeral oration upon Niccolo de' Niccoli, tells us that 'the house of Marsigli was frequented by distinguished youths, who set themselves to imitate his life and habits; it was, moreover, the resort of the best and noblest burghers of this city, who flowed together from all quarters to him as to some oracle of more than human wisdom.'[3] His intellectual

---

[1] See the exhaustive work of Renan, *Averroès et l'Averroïsme.*

[2] See Manetti's *Life,* Mur. xx. col. 531. Other references will be found in Vespasiano's *Lives.* Boccaccio's library was preserved in this convent.

[3] *Poggii Opera,* p. 271.

acuteness, solid erudition, and winning eloquence were displayed in moral disquisitions upon Virgil, Cicero, and Seneca. In this way he had the merit of combining the dialectic method and the bold spirit of the Averrhoists with the sound learning and polite culture of the newly-discovered humanities. The Convent of S. Spirito has to be mentioned as the first of those many private academies to which the free thought and the scholarship of Italy were afterwards destined to owe so much.

It is my object in this chapter to show how humanistic scholarship, starting from Petrarch, penetrated every department of study, and began to permeate the intellectual life of the Italians. We have now to notice its intrusion into the sphere of politics. Petrarch died in 1374, Boccaccio in 1375. The latter date is also that of Coluccio de' Salutati's entrance upon the duties of Florentine Chancellor. Salutato, the friend of Boccaccio and the disciple of Marsigli, the professed worshipper of Petrarch and the translator of Dante into Latin verse, was destined to exercise an important influence in his own department as a stylist. Before he was called to act as secretary to the Signory of Florence in his forty-sixth year, he had already acquired the learning and imbibed the spirit of his age. He was known as a diligent collector of manuscripts and promoter of Greek studies, as a writer on mythology and morals, as an orator and miscellaneous author.[1] His talents had now to be concentrated on the weightier business of the

---

[1] Salutato's familiar letters, *Lini Coluci Pieri Salutati Epistolarum Pars Secunda, Florentiæ*, MDCCXXXXI., are a valuable source of information respecting scholarship at the close of the fourteenth century. See especially his letter to Benvenuto da Imola on the death of Petrarch (p. 32), his letter to the same about Petrarch's *Africa* (p. 41), another letter about the preservation of the *Africa* (p. 79), a letter to Petrarch's nephew Francesco da Brossano on the death of Boccaccio (p. 44), and a letter to a certain Comes Magnificus on the literary and philosophical genius of Petrarch (p. 49).

Florentine Republic ; but his study of antiquity caused him
to conceive his duties and the political relations of the State
he served, in a new light.   During the wars carried on with
Gregory XI. and the Visconti, his pen was never idle.   For
the first time he introduced into public documents the gravity
of style and melody of phrase he had learned in the school
of classic rhetoricians.   The effect produced by this literary
statesman, as elegant in authorship as he was subtle in the
conduct of affairs, can only be estimated at its proper value
when we remember that the Italians were now ripe to receive
the influence of rhetoric, and only too ready to attribute
weight to verbal ingenuity.   Gian Galeazzo Visconti is said
to have declared that Salutato had done him more harm
by his style than a troop of paid mercenaries.[1]   The epistles,
despatches, protocols, and manifestoes composed by their
Chancellor for the Florentine priors, were distributed throughout Italy.   Read and copied by the secretaries of other states,
they formed the models of a new State eloquence.[2]   Elegant
Latinity became a necessary condition of public documents,
and Ciceronian phrases were henceforth reckoned among the
indispensable engines of a diplomatic armoury.   Offices of
trust in the Papal Curia, the courts of the Despots, and the
chanceries of the republics were thus thrown open to profes-

[1] 'Galeacius Mediolanensium Princeps crebro auditus est dicere non
tam sibi mille Florentinorum equites quam Colucii scripta nocere.' *Pii
Secundi Europæ Commentarii,* p. 454.

[2] 'Costui fu de' migliori dittatori di pistole al mondo, perocchè
molti quando ne potevano avere, ne toglieano copie; sì piaceano a tutti
gl' intendenti : e nelle corte di Re e di signori del mondo, e anchora de'
cherici era di lui in questa arte maggiore fama che di alcuno altro uomo.'
From the Chronicle of Luca da Scarparia. These epistles were collected
and printed by Josephus Rigaccius, Bibliopola Florentinus Celeberrimus,
in 1741. Among the letters written for the Signory of Florence, that of
congratulation to Gian Galeazzo Visconti on his murder of Bernabo
(p. 16), that to the French Cardinals (p. 18), to Sir John Hawkwood, or
Domino Joanni Aucud (p. 107), to the Marquis of Moravia (p. 110), and
to the Romans (p. 141) deserve to be read.

sional humanists. In the next age we shall find that neither
princes, popes, nor priors could do without the services of
trained stylists.

While concentrating attention upon this chief contribution
of Salutato to Italian scholarship, I must not omit to notice,
however briefly, the patronage he exercised at Florence.
Both Poggio Bracciolini and Lionardo Bruni owed their
advancement to his interest.[1] Giacomo da Scarparia, the
first Florentine who visited Byzantium with a view to learning Greek, received from him the warmest encouragement,
together with a commission for the purchase of manuscripts.
To his activity in concert with Palla degli Strozzi was due the
establishment of a Greek chair in the University of Florence.
Nor was this zeal confined to the living. He composed the
Lives of Dante, Petrarch, and Boccaccio, translated a portion
of the ' Divine Comedy ' into Latin for its wider circulation
through the learned world, and caused the ' Africa ' of Petrarch
to be published.[2] When the illustrious Chancellor died, in the
year 1406, at the age of seventy-six, he was honoured with a
public funeral ; the poet's crown was placed upon his brow, a
panegyrical oration was recited, and a monument was erected
to him in the Duomo.[3]

[1] See the letter of Lionardo Bruni, quoted in *Lini Coluci Pieri
Salutati Epistolæ*, p. xv. Coluccio's own letter recommending Lionardo
to Innocent VII., ib. p. 5, and his numerous familiar letters to Poggio,
ib. pp. 13, 173, &c.

[2] ' Certe cogitabam revidere librum, et si quid, ut scribis, vel ab-
sonum, vel contra metrorum regulam intolerabile deprehendissem,
curiosius elimare et sicut Naso finxit in Æneida, singulos libros paucis
versiculis quasi in argumenti formam brevissime resumere, et exinde
pluribus sumptis exemplis, et per me ipsum correctis et diligenter revisis,
unum ad Bononiense gymnasium, unum Parisiis, unum in Angliam cum
meâ epistolâ de libri laudibus destinare, et unum in Florentiâ ponere in
loco celebri,' &c. *Epistolæ*, part ii. p. 80.

[3] Among the other *laureati* who filled the post of Florentine Chancellor may be mentioned Dante's tutor, Brunetto Latini, Lionardo Bruni,

What Salutato accomplished for the style of public documents, Gasparino da Barzizza effected for familiar correspondence.　After teaching during several years at Venice and Padua, he was summoned to Milan in 1418 by Filippo Maria Visconti, who ordered him to open a school in that capital. Gasparino made a special study of Cicero's Letters, and caused his pupils to imitate them as closely as possible, forming in this way an art of fluent letter-writing known afterwards as the *ars familiariter scribendi*.　Epistolography in general, considered as a branch of elegant literature, occupied all the scholars of the Renaissance, and had the advantage of establishing a link of union between learned men in different parts of Italy.　We therefore recognise in Gasparino the initiator, after Petrarch, of a highly important branch of Italian culture.　This, when it reached maturity, culminated in the affectations of the Ciceronian purists.　It must be understood that neither Salutato nor Gasparino attained to real polish or freedom of style.　Compared even with the Latinity of Poggio, theirs is heavy and uncouth ; while that of Poggio seems barbarous by the side of Poliziano's, and Poliziano in turn yields the palm of mere correctness to Bembo.　It was only by degrees that the taste of the Italians formed itself, and that facility was acquired in writing a lost language.　The fact that mediæval Latin was still used in legal documents, in conversation, in the offices of the Church, and in the theological works which formed the staple of all libraries, impeded the recovery of a classic style.　When the Italians had finally learned how to polish prose, it was easy to hand on the art to other nations ; while to sneer at their pedantry, as Erasmus did, was no matter of great difficulty.　By that time their scrupulous and anxious preoccupation with purity of phrase threatened danger to the interests of liberal learning.

Carlo Marsuppini, Poggio Bracciolini, and Benedetto Accolti, of whom more hereafter.

Hitherto, with the exception only of Boccaccio's Greek studies, I have had to trace the rise of Latin letters and to call particular attention to the cult of Cicero in Italy. It is now necessary to mention the advent of a man who played a part in the revival of learning only second to that of Petrarch. Manuel Chrysoloras, a Byzantine of noble birth, came to Italy during the Pontificate of Boniface IX., charged by the Emperor Palæologus with the mission of attempting to arm the states of Christendom against the Turk. Like all the Greeks who visited Western Europe, Chrysoloras first alighted in Venice ; but the Republic of the Lagoons neither understood the secret nor felt the need of retaining these birds of passage. After a few months they almost invariably passed on to Florence—the real centre of the intellectual life of Italy. As soon as it was known that Chrysoloras, who enjoyed the fame of being the most accomplished and eloquent Hellenist of his age, had arrived with his companion, Demetrios Kydonios, in Venice, two noble Florentines, Roberto de' Rossi and Giacomo d'Angelo da Scarparia, set forth to visit him. The residence of the Greek ambassadors in Italy on this occasion was but brief ; they found that, politically, they could effect nothing. But Giacomo da Scarparia journeyed in their society to Byzantium ; while Roberto de' Rossi returned to Florence, full of the impression which the erudite philosophers had left upon him. The report he made to his fellow-citizens awoke a passionate desire in Palla degli Strozzi and Niccolo de' Niccoli to bring Chrysoloras in person to Florence. Their urgent appeals to the Signory resulted in an invitation whereby Chrysoloras in 1396 was induced to fill the Greek chair in the university. A yearly stipend of 150 golden florins, raised afterwards to 250, was voted for his maintenance. This engagement secured the future of Greek erudition in Europe. The merit of having brought the affair to a successful issue belongs principally to Palla degli Strozzi, of whom Vespasiano

wrote : ' There being in Florence exceeding good knowledge
of Latin letters, but of Greek none, he resolved that this
defect should be remedied, and therefore did all he could to
make Manuel Grisolora visit Italy, using all his influence
thereto and paying a large portion of the expense incurred.' [1]
We must not, however, omit the share which Coluccio Salutato,[2] by his influence with the Signory, and Niccolo de'
Niccoli, by the interest he exerted with the Uffiziali dello
Studio, may also claim.   Among the audience of this the first
true teacher of Greek at Florence were numbered Palla degli
Strozzi, Roberto de' Rossi, Poggio Bracciolini, Lionardo Bruni,
Francesco Barbaro, Giannozzo Manetti, Carlo Marsuppini, and
Ambrogio Traversari—some of them young men of eighteen,
others old and grey-haired, nearly all of them the scholars
in Latinity of Giovanni da Ravenna.   Nor was Florence the
only town to receive the learning of Chrysoloras.   He opened
schools at Rome, at Padua, at Milan, and at Venice ; so that
his influence as a wandering professor was at least equal to
that exercised by Giovanni da Ravenna.

The impulse communicated to the study of antiquity by
Chrysoloras, and the noble enthusiasm of his scholars for
pure literature, may best be understood from a passage in the
' Commentaries ' of Lionardo Bruni, whereof the following is
a compressed translation : [3]—'Letters at this period grew
mightily in Italy, seeing that the knowledge of Greek, inter-
mitted for seven centuries, revived. Chrysoloras of Byzantium,
a man of noble birth and well skilled in Greek literature,
brought to us Greek learning.   I at that time was following
the civil law, though not ill-versed in other studies ; for by
nature I loved learning with ardour, nor had I given slight

<hr />

[1] *Vite d' Uomini Illustri*, p. 271.
[2] Cf. the letter quoted by Voigt (p. 130) to Giacomo da Scarparia,
which shows Coluccio's enthusiasm for Greek.
[3] Mur. xix. 920.

pains to dialectic and to rhetoric. Therefore, at the coming of Chrysoloras, I was made to halt in my choice of lives, seeing that I held it wrong to desert law, and yet I reckoned it a crime to omit so great an occasion of learning the Greek literature; and oftentimes I reasoned with myself after this manner:—Can it be that thou, when thou mayest gaze on Homer, Plato, and Demosthenes, together with other poets, philosophers, and orators, concerning whom so great and so wonderful things are said, and mayest converse with them, and receive their admirable doctrine—can it be that thou wilt desert thyself and neglect the opportunity divinely offered thee? Through seven hundred years no one in all Italy has been master of Greek letters; and yet we acknowledge that all science is derived from them. Of civil law, indeed, there are in every city scores of doctors; but should this single and unique teacher of Greek be removed, thou wilt find no one to instruct thee. Conquered at last by these reasonings, I delivered myself over to Chrysoloras with such passion that what I had received from him by day in hours of waking, occupied my mind at night in hours of sleep.'

The earnestness of this paragraph is characteristic of the whole period. The scholars who assembled in the lecture-rooms of Chrysoloras, felt that the Greek texts, whereof he alone supplied the key, contained those elements of spiritual freedom and intellectual culture without which the civilisation of the modern world would be impossible. Nor were they mistaken in what was then a guess rather than a certainty. The study of Greek implied the birth of criticism, comparison, research. Systems based on ignorance and superstition were destined to give way before it. The study of Greek opened philosophical horizons far beyond the dream-world of the churchmen and the monks; it stimulated the germs of science, suggested new astronomical hypotheses, and indirectly led to the discovery of America. The study of Greek resuscitated a sense of the beautiful in art and literature. It subjected the creeds of Christianity, the language of the Gospels, the doctrine of S. Paul, to analysis, and commenced a new era for Biblical inquiry. If it be true, as a writer no less sober in his philosophy than eloquent in his language has lately asserted, that, 'except the blind forces of nature, nothing moves in this world which is not Greek in its origin,' we are justified in regarding the point of contact between the Greek teacher Chrysoloras and his Florentine pupils as one of the most momentous crises in the history of civilisation. Indirectly, the Italian intellect had hitherto felt Hellenic influence through Latin literature. It was now about to receive that influence immediately from actual study of the masterpieces of the Attic authors. The world was no longer to be kept in ignorance of those ' eternal consolations ' of the human race. No longer could the scribe omit Greek quotations from his Latin text with the dogged snarl of obtuse self-satisfaction—*Græca sunt, ergo non legenda*. The motto had rather to be changed into a cry of warning for ecclesiastical authority upon the verge of dissolution—*Græca sunt, ergo periculosa* : since the re-awakening faith in human reason, the reawakening belief in the dignity of man, the desire for beauty, the liberty, audacity, and passion of the Renaissance, received from Greek studies their strongest and most vital impulse.

CHAPTER III

FIRST PERIOD OF HUMANISM

HAVING so far traced the quickening of a new sense for antiquity among the Italians, it will be well at this point to consider the external resources of Humanism before continuing the history of the Revival in the fifteenth century. The condition of the universities, the state of the book trade before the invention of printing, and the discovery of manuscripts claim separate attention; nor may it be out of place to inquire what stimulus the enthusiasm for classical studies received from the ruins of Rome. A review of these topics will help to explain the circumstances under which the pioneers of culture had to labour, and the nature of the crusade they instituted against ignorance in every part of Europe.

The oldest and most frequented university in Italy, that of Bologna, is represented as having flourished in the twelfth century.[1] Its prosperity in early times depended greatly on the personal conduct of the principal professors, who, when they were not satisfied with their entertainment, were in the habit of seceding with their pupils to other cities. Thus high schools were opened from time to time in Modena, Reggio, and elsewhere by teachers who broke the oaths that bound them to reside in Bologna, and fixed their centre of education in a rival town. To make such temporary changes was not difficult in an age when what we have to call an university, consisted of masters and scholars, without college buildings, without libraries, without endowments, and without scientific apparatus. The technical name for such institutions seems to have been *studium scholarium*, Italianised into *studio* or *studio pubblico*.[2] Among the more permanent results of these secessions may be mentioned the establishment of the high school at Vicenza by translation from Bologna in 1204, and the opening of a school at Arezzo under similar circumstances in 1215 ; the great University of Padua first saw the light in consequence of political discords forcing the professors to quit Bologna for a season.[3]

The first half of the thirteenth century witnessed the foundation of these *studi* in considerable numbers. That of Vercelli was opened in 1228, the municipality providing two certified copyists for the convenience of students who might

---

[1] Tiraboschi, *Storia della Letteratura Italiana*, vol. iv. p. 42 *et seq.*, vol. v. p. 60 *et seq.* Large quarto, Modena, 1787.

[2] See Muratori, vol. viii. 15, 75, 372. Matteo Villani, lib. i. cap. 8.

[3] 'Hoc anno translatum est Studium Scholarium de Bononiâ Paluam.' Mur. viii. 372.

wish to purchase text-books.[1] In 1224 the Emperor Frederick II., to whom the south of Italy owed a precocious eminence in literature, established the University of Naples by an
Imperial diploma.[2] With a view to rendering it the chief seat
of learning in his dominions, he forbade the subjects of the
Regno to frequent other schools, and suppressed the University
of Bologna by letters general. Thereupon Bologna joined the
Lombard League, defied the emperor, and refused to close the
schools, which numbered at that period about ten thousand
students of various nationalities. In 1227 Frederick revoked
his edict, and Bologna remained thenceforward unmolested.
Political and internal vicissitudes, affecting all the Italian
universities at this period, interrupted the prosperity of that
of Naples. In the middle of the thirteenth century Salerno
proved a dangerous rival ; but when the House of Anjou was
established in the kingdom of the Sicilies, special privileges
were granted, restoring the high school of the capital to the
first rank. Charles I. created a separate court of jurisdiction
for its management. This consisted of a judge and three
assessors, one for the control of foreigners, another for the
subjects of the Regno, and the third for Italians from other
states.

In 1264 we find a public school in operation at Ferrara.
By its charter the professors were exempt from military service. The University of Piacenza came into existence a little
earlier. Innocent IV. established it in 1248, with privileges
similar to those of Paris and Bologna. An important group
of *studi pubblici* owed their origin to Papal or Imperial
charters in the first half of the fourteenth century. That of
Perugia was founded in 1307 by a Bull of Clement V. That

[1] They were called ‘ Exemplatores.’ See Tiraboschi, vol. iv. lib. i
cap. 2.

[2] Muratori, vii. p. 997. Amari, *Storia dei Mussulmani di Sicilia,*
vol. iii. p. 706.

of Rome dated from 1303, in which year Boniface VIII. gave
it a constitution by a special edict ; but the translation of the
Papal See to Avignon caused it to fall into premature decadence.   The University of Pisa had already existed for some
years, when it received a charter in 1343 from Clement VI.
That of Florence was first founded in 1321.[1]   In 1348 a place
for its public buildings was assigned between the Duomo and
the Palazzo Pubblico, on the site of what was afterwards
known as the Collegium Eugenianum.   A council of eight
burghers was appointed for its management, and a yearly sum
was set apart for its maintenance.   In 1349 Clement VI. gave
it the same privileges as the University of Bologna, while in
1364 it received an Imperial diploma from Charles IV.   The
same emperor granted charters to Siena in 1357, to Arezzo in
1356, and to Lucca in 1369.   In 1362 Galeazzo Visconti obtained a charter for his University of Pavia from Charles IV.,
with the privileges of Paris, Oxford, and Bologna.

It will be observed that the majority of the *studi pubblici*
obtained charters either from the Pope or the emperor, or
from both, less for the sake of any immediate benefit to be
derived from Papal or Imperial patronage, than because
supreme authority in Italy was still referred to one or other
of these heads.   It was a great object with each city to increase its wealth by attracting foreigners as residents, and to
retain the native youth within its precincts.   The municipali-
ties, therefore, accorded immunities from taxation and military
service to *bona fide* students, prohibited their burghers from
seeking rival places of learning, and in some cases allowed the
university authorities to exercise a special jurisdiction over
the motley multitude of scholars from all countries.   How
miscellaneous the concourse in some of the high schools used
to be, may be gathered from the reports extracted by Tiraboschi from their registers.   At Vicenza, for example, in 1209

---

[1] See Von Reumont, *Lorenzo de' Medici*, vol. i. p. 521.

we find the names of Bohemians, Poles, Frenchmen, Burg-
undians, Germans, and Spaniards, as well as of Italians of
divers towns. The rectors of this *studio* in 1205 included an
Englishman, a Provençal, a German, and a Cremonese. The
lists of illustrious students at Bologna between 1265 and 1294
show men of all the European nationalities, proving that the
foreigners attracted by the university must have formed no
inconsiderable element in the whole population.[1] This will
account for the prominent part played by the students from
time to time in the political history of Bologna.[2]

The importance attached by great cities to their universities
as a source of strength, may be gathered from the chapter in
Matteo Villani's Chronicle describing the foundation of the
studio pubblico in Florence.[3] He expressly mentions that
the Signory were induced to take this step in consequence of
the depopulation inflicted by the Black Death of 1348. By
drawing residents to Florence from other States, they hoped
to increase the number of the inhabitants, and to restore the
decayed fame and splendour of the commonwealth.[4] At the
same time they thought that serious studies might put an end
to the demoralisation produced in all classes by the plague.
With this object in view, they engaged the best teachers, and
did not hesitate to devote a yearly sum of 2,500 golden florins
to the maintenance of their high school. Bologna, which
owed even more than Florence to its university, is said to
have lavished as much as half of its revenue, about 20,000
ducats, on the pay of professors and other incidental expenses.
The actual cost incurred by cities through their schools cannot, however, be accurately estimated, since it varied from
year to year according to the engagements made with special

---

[1] In 1320 there were at least 15,000 students in Bologna.
[2] See Sismondi, vol. iii. p. 349.
[3] Lib. i. cap. 8.
[4] 'Volendo attrarre gente alla nostra città, e dilatarla in onore, e
dare materia a' suoi cittadini d' essere scienziati e virtudiosi.'

teachers. At Pavia, for example, in 1400, the university supported in Canon Law several eminent doctors, in Civil Law thirteen, in Medicine five, in Philosophy three, in Astrology one, in Greek one, and in Eloquence one.[1] Whether this staff was maintained after the lapse of another twenty years we do not know for certain.

The subjects taught in the high schools were Canon and Civil Law, Medicine, and Theology. These faculties, important for the professional education of the public, formed the staple of the academical curriculum. Chairs of Rhetoric, Philosophy, and Astronomy were added according to occasion, the last sometimes including the study of judicial astrology. If we inquire how the humanists or professors of classic literature were related to the universities, we find that, at first at any rate, they always occupied a second rank. The permanent teaching remained in the hands of jurists, who enjoyed life engagements at a high rate of pay, while the Latinists and Grecians could only aspire to the temporary occupation of the Chair of Rhetoric, with salaries considerably lower than those of lawyers or physicians. The cause of this inferiority is easily explained. It was natural that important and remunerative branches of learning like law and medicine should attract a greater number of students than pure literature, and that their professors should be better paid than the teachers of eloquence. Padua, Bologna, and Pavia in particular retained their legal speciality throughout the period of the Renaissance, and remained but little open to humanistic influences. At Padua we find from Sanudo's Diary [2] that an eminent jurist received a stipend of 1,000 ducats. A Doctor of Medicine at the same university, in 1491, received a similar stipend, together with the right of private practice. At

[1] Cf. Corio, p. 290. He gives the names of the professors who attended at the funeral of Gian Galeazzo Visconti.
[2] Mur. xxii. 000.

Bologna the famous jurist Abbas Siculus (Niccolo de' Tudeschi) drew 800 scudi yearly ; at Padua Giovanni da Imola in 1406, and Paolo da Castro in 1430, drew a sum of 600 ducats.[1] About the same time (1453) Lauro Quirino, who professed rhetoric at Padua, was paid at the rate of only forty ducats yearly, while Lorenzo Valla, at Pavia, filled the Chair of Eloquence with an annual stipend of fifty sequins. The disparity between the remuneration of jurists and that of humanists was not so great at all the universities. Florence in especial formed a notable exception. From the date of its commencement the Florentine *studio* was partial to literature ; and it is worth remarking that when Lorenzo de' Medici transferred the high school to Pisa, he retained at Florence the professors of the liberal sciences and *belles-lettres*. The great reputation of eminent rhetoricians, again, often secured for them temporary engagements at a high rate. Thus we gather from Rosmini's ' Life of Filelfo ' that this humanist received from Venice the offer of 500 sequins yearly as remuneration for his professorial services. Bologna proposed an annual stipend of 450 sequins when he undertook to lecture upon eloquence and moral philosophy. At Florence his income amounted to 350 golden florins, secured for three years, and subsequently raised to 450. With Siena he stipulated for 350 golden florins for two years. At Milan his Chair of Eloquence was endowed with 500 golden florins, and this salary was afterwards increased to 700. Nicholas V. offered him an annual income of 600 ducats if he would devote himself to the translation of Greek books into Latin, while Sixtus IV. tried to bring him to Rome by proposing 600 Roman florins as the stipend of the Chair of Rhetoric.

The fact, however, remains that while the special study of antiquity preoccupied the minds of the Italians, and attracted all the finer intellects among the youth ambitious

[1] See Voigt, p. 447.

of distinction, its professors never succeeded in taking complete possession of the universities. Their position there was
always that of wandering stars and resident aliens. This
accounts in some measure for the bitter hostility and arrogant
scorn which they displayed against the teachers of theology
and law and medicine. The real home of the humanists was
in the Courts of princes, the palaces of the cultivated burghers,
the Roman Curia, and the chanceries of the republics. As
secretaries, house tutors, readers, Court poets, historiographers,
public orators, and companions they were indispensable.
We shall therefore find that the private academies formed
by the literati and their patrons, the schools of princes established at Mantua and Ferrara, and the residences of great
nobles play a more important part in the history of humanism
than do the universities. At the same time the spirit of the
new culture diffused by the humanists so thoroughly permeated the whole intellectual activity of the Italians, that in
course of time the special studies of the high schools assumed
a more literary and liberal form. The classics then supplied
the starting-point for juristic and medical disquisitions.
Poliziano was seen lecturing upon the Pandects of Justinian,
while Pomponazzi made the Chair of Philosophy at Padua
subservient to the exposition of materialism. This triumph
of humanism, like its triumph in the Church, was effected
less by immediate working on the universities than by a
gradual and indirect determination of the whole race towards
the study of antiquity.

In picturing to ourselves the method pursued by the
humanists in the instruction of their classes, we must divest
our minds of all associations with the practice of modern
professors. Very few of the students whom the master saw
before him, possessed more than meagre portions of the text
of Virgil or of Cicero ; they had no notes, grammars, lexicons,
or dictionaries of antiquities and mythology, to help them.

It was therefore necessary for the lecturer to dictate quotations, to repeat parallel passages at full length, to explain
geographical and historical allusions, to analyse the structure
of sentences in detail, to provide copious illustrations of
grammatical usage, to trace the stages by which a word
acquired its meaning in a special context, to command a full
vocabulary of synonyms, to give rules for orthography, and to
have the whole Pantheon at his fingers' ends. In addition to
this, he was expected to comment upon the meaning of his
author, to interpret his philosophy, to point out the beauties
of his style, to introduce appropriate moral disquisition on his
doctrine, to sketch his biography, and to give some account
of his relation to the history of his country and to his predecessors in the field of letters. In short, the professor of
rhetoric had to be a grammarian, a philologer, an historian, a
stylist, and a sage in one. He was obliged to pretend at least
to an encyclopædic knowledge of the classics, and to retain
whole volumes in his memory. All these requirements, which
seem to have been satisfied by such men as Filelfo and Poliziano, made the profession of eloquence—for so the varied
subject matter of humanism was often called—a very different
business from that which occupies a lecturer of the present
century. Scores of students, old and young, with nothing
but pen and paper on the desks before them, sat patiently
recording what the lecturer said. At the end of his discourses
on the ' Georgics ' or the ' Verrines,' each of them carried away
a compendious volume, containing a transcript of the author's
text, together with a miscellaneous mass of notes, critical,
explanatory, ethical, æsthetical, historical, and biographical.
In other words, a book had been dictated, and as many scores
of copies as there were attentive pupils had been made.[1] The

---

[1] Many of the earliest printed editions of the Latin poets give an
exact notion of what such lectures must have been. The text is embedded in an all-embracing commentary.

language used was Latin. No dialect of Italian could have been intelligible to the students of different nationalities who crowded the lecture-rooms. The elementary education in grammar requisite for following a professorial course of lectures had been previously provided by the teachers of the Latin schools, which depended for maintenance partly on the State[1] and partly on private enterprise. The Church does not seem to have undertaken the management of these primary boys' schools.

Since this was the nature of academical instruction in the humanities before the age of printing, it followed that the professor had a direct interest in frequently shifting his scene of operations. More than a certain number of such books as I have just attempted to describe could not be carried in his head. After he had dictated his work on the ' Georgics ' at Florence, he was naturally anxious to move to Milan and to do the same. A new audience gave new value to his lectures, and another edition, as it were, of his book was put in circulation. In the correspondence which passed between professors and the rectors of the high schools previously to an engagement, we sometimes find that the former undertake to explain particular authors during their proposed residence. On these authors they had no doubt bestowed the best years of their lives, making them the vehicle for all the miscellaneous learning they possessed, and grounding their fame upon the beauty, clearness, and copiousness of their exposition.[2]

Having described the conditions under which professorial teaching was conducted in the fifteenth century, it is now of some importance to form a notion of the state of the book market and the diffusion of MSS. before the invention of

---

[1] Cf. Villani's Statistics of Florence, and Corio's of Milan.

[2] For humorous but vivid pictures of a professor's lecture-room, see the macaronic poems of Odassi and Fossa quoted by me in vol. v. of this work.

printing. Difficult as it is to speak with accuracy on these topics, some facts must be collected, seeing that the high price and comparative rarity of books contributed in a very important degree to determine the character of the instruction provided by the humanists.

Scarcity of books was at first a chief impediment to the study of antiquity. Popes and princes and even great religious institutions possessed far fewer books than many farmers of the present age. The library belonging to the Cathedral Church of S. Martino at Lucca in the ninth century contained only nineteen volumes of abridgments from ecclesiastical commentaries. The Cathedral of Novara in 1212 could boast copies of Boethius, Priscian, the 'Code of Justinian,' the 'Decretals,' and the 'Etymology' of Isidorus, besides a Bible and some devotional treatises.[1] This slender stock passed for great riches. Each of the precious volumes in such a collection was an epitome of mediæval art. Its pages were composed of fine vellum adorned with pictures.[2] The initial letters displayed elaborate flourishes and exquisitely illuminated groups of figures. The scribe took pains to render his caligraphy perfect, and to ornament the margins with crimson, gold, and blue. Then he handed the parchment sheets to the binder, who encased them in rich settings of velvet or carved ivory and wood, embossed with gold and precious stones. The edges were gilt and stamped with patterns. The clasps were of wrought silver, chased with niello. The price of such masterpieces was enormous. Borso d' Este, in 1464, gave eight gold ducats to Gherardo Ghislieri of Bologna for an illuminated Lancellotto, and in 1469 he bought a Josephus and Quintus Curtius for forty ducats.[3] His great Bible in two

[1] See Cantù, *Storia della Letteratura Italiana*, p. 105, note.
[2] 'Hodie Scriptores non sunt Scriptores sed Pictores,' quoted by Tiraboschi, vol. iv. lib. i. cap. 4.
[3] See Cantù, loc. cit. p. 104.

volumes is said to have cost 1,375 sequins. Rinaldo degli
Albizzi notes in his Memoirs that he paid eleven golden florins
for a Bible at Arezzo in 1406. Of these MSS. the greater
part were manufactured in the cloisters, and it was here too
that the martyrdom of ancient authors took place. Lucretius
and Livy gave place to chronicles, antiphonaries, and homilies.
Parchment was extremely dear, and the scrolls which nobody
could read might be scraped and washed. Accordingly, the
copyist erased the learning of the ancients, and filled the fair
blank space he gained with litanies. At the same time it is
but just to the monks to add that palimpsests have occasionally been found in which ecclesiastical works have yielded
place to copies of the Latin poets used in elementary education.[1]

Another obstacle to the diffusion of learning was the
incompetence of the copyists. It is true that at the great
universities *stationarii*, who supplied the text-books in use to
students, were certified and subjected to the control of special
censors called *peciarii*. Yet their number was not large, and
when they quitted the routine to which they were accustomed
their incapacity betrayed itself by numerous errors.[2] Petrarch's
invective against the professional copyists shows the depth
to which the art had sunk. ' Who,' he exclaims, ' will discover
a cure for the ignorance and vile sloth of these copyists, who
spoil everything and turn it to nonsense ? If Cicero, Livy,
and other illustrious ancients were to return to life, do you
think they would understand their own works ? There is no
check upon these copyists, selected without examination
or test of their capacity. Workmen, husbandmen, weavers,

[1] See Comparetti, vol. i. p. 114.
[2] In Milan, in the fourteenth century, when the population was
estimated at about 200,000, the town could boast of only fifty copyists.
Tirab. loc. cit. cap. 4.

artisans, are not indulged in the same liberty.' [1]   Coluccio
Salutato repeats the same complaint, averring that the copies
of Dante and Petrarch no more correspond to the originals
than bad statues to the men they pretend to represent.   At
the same time the copyists formed a necessary and flourishing
class of craftsmen. They were well paid. Ambrogio Traversari
told his friend Giustiniani in 1430 that he could recommend
him a good scribe at the pay of thirty golden florins a year
and his keep.   Under these circumstances it was usual for
even the most eminent scholars, like Petrarch, Boccaccio, and
Poggio, to make their own copies of MSS.   Niccolo de' Niccoli
transcribed nearly the whole of the codices that formed the
nucleus of the Library of the Mark. Sometimes they sold
them or made advantageous changes. Poggio, for example,
sold two volumes of S. Jerome's ' Letters ' to Lionello d' Este
for 100 golden florins.   Beccadelli bought a Livy from him for
120 golden florins, having parted with a farm to defray the
expense.   It is clear that the first step toward the revival of

---

[1] *De Remediis utriusque Fortunæ*, lib. i. dial. 43, p. 42. The passage
condensed above is so valuable for a right understanding of the humanistic feeling about manuscripts that I shall transcribe portions of the
original :—' Libri innumerabiles sunt mihi. Et errores innumeri, quidam
ab impiis, alii ab indoctis editi. Illi quidem religioni ac pietati et divinis
literis, hi naturæ ac justitiæ moribusque et liberalibus disciplinis seu
historiæ rerumque gestarum fidei, omnes autem vero adversi; inque
omnibus, et præsertim primis ubi majoribus agitur de rebus, et vera falsis
immixta sunt, perdifficilis ac periculosa discretio est . . . scriptorum
inscitiæ inertiæque, corrumpenti omnia miscentique . . . ignavissima
ætas hæc culinæ solicita, literarum negligens, et coquos examinans non
scriptores. Quisquis itaque pingere aliquid in membranis, manuque
calamum versare didicerit, scriptor habebitur, doctrinæ omnis ignarus,
expers ingenii, artis egens . . . nunc confusis exemplaribus et exemplis,
unum scribere polliciti, sic aliud scribunt ut quod ipse dictaveris, non
agnoscas . . . accedunt et scriptores nullâ frenati lege, nullo probati
examine, nullo judicio electi; non fabris, non agricolis, non textoribus,
non ulli fere artium tanta licentia est, cum sit in aliis leve periculum, in
hâc grave ; sine delectu tamen scribendum ruunt omnes, et cuncta vas-
tantibus certa sunt pretia.'

learning implied three things : first, the collection of MSS. wherever they could be saved from the indolence of the monks ; secondly, the formation of libraries for their preservation ; and, thirdly, the invention of an art whereby they might be mutiplied cheaply, conveniently, and accurately.

The labour involved in the collection of classical manuscripts had to be performed by a few enthusiastic scholars, who received no help from the universities and their academical scribes, and who met with no sympathy in the monasteries they were bent on ransacking. The new culture demanded wholly new machinery ; and new runners in the torch-race of civilisation sprang into existence. The high schools were contented with their summaries and glosses. The monks performed at best the work of earthworms, who unwittingly preserve fragments of Greek architecture from corrosion by heaping mounds of mould and rubbish round them. Meanwhile the humanists went forth with the instinct of explorers to release the captives and awake the dead. From the convent libraries of Italy, from the museums of Constantinople, from the abbeys of Germany and Switzerland and France, the slumbering spirits of the ancients had to be evoked. The chivalry of learning, banded together for this service, might be likened to Crusaders. As the Franks deemed themselves thrice blest if they returned with relics from Jerusalem, so these new Knights of the Holy Ghost, seeking not the sepulchre of a risen God, but the tombs wherein the genius of the ancient world awaited resurrection, felt holy transports when a brown, begrimed, and crabbed copy of some Greek or Latin author rewarded their patient quest. Days and nights they spent in carefully transcribing it, comparing their own MS. with the original, multiplying facsimiles, and sending them abroad with free hands to students who in their turn took copies, till the treasure-trove became the common property of all who could appreciate its value. This work of discovery began with Petrarch. I have already alluded to the journeys he undertook in the hope of collecting the lost MSS. of Cicero. It was carried on by Boccaccio. The account given by Benvenuto da Imola of Boccaccio's visit to Monte Cassino brings vividly before us both the ardour of these first explorers and the apathy of the Benedictines (who have sometimes been called the saviours of learning) with regard to the treasures of their own libraries : [1]—' With a view to the clearer understanding of this text (' Paradiso,' xxii. 74), I will relate what my revered teacher, Boccaccio of Certaldo, humorously told me. He said that when he was in Apulia, attracted by the celebrity of the convent, he paid a visit to Monte Cassino, whereof Dante speaks. Desirous of seeing the collection of books, which he understood to be a very choice one, he modestly asked a monk—for he was always most courteous in manners—to open the library, as a favour, for him. The monk answered stiffly, pointing to a steep staircase, " Go up ; it is open." Boccaccio went up gladly ; but he found that the place which held so great a treasure, was without or door or key. He entered, and saw grass sprouting on the windows, and all the books and benches thick with dust. In his astonishment he began to open and turn the leaves of first one tome and then another, and found many and divers volumes of ancient and foreign works. Some of them had lost several sheets ; others were snipped and pared all round the text, and mutilated in various ways. At length, lamenting that the toil and study of so many illustrious men should have passed into the hands of most abandoned wretches, he departed with tears and sighs. Coming to the cloister, he asked a monk whom he met, why those valuable books had been so disgracefully mangled. He answered that the monks, seeking to gain a few *soldi*, were in the habit of cutting off sheets and

---

[1] ' Commentary on the *Divine Comedy*,' ap. Muratori, *Antiq. Ital.* vol. i. p. 1296.

making psalters, which they sold to boys. The margins too
they manufactured into charms, and sold to women. So then,
O man of study, go to and rack your brains ; make books that
you may come to this ! '

What Italy contained of ancient codices soon saw the
light. The visit of Poggio Bracciolini to Constance (1414)
opened up for Italian scholars the stores that lay neglected in
transalpine monasteries. Poggio's office of Apostolic Secretary obliged him to attend the Council of Constance for the
purpose of framing reports and composing diplomatic documents. At the same time he had ample leisure on his hands,
and this he spent in exploring the libraries of Swiss and
Suabian convents. The treasures he unearthed at Reichenau,
Weingarten, and above all S. Gallen, restored to Italy many
lost masterpieces of Latin literature, and supplied students
with full texts of authors who had hitherto been known in
mutilated copies. The account he gave of his visit to S.
Gallen in a Latin letter to a friend is justly celebrated.[1] After
describing the wretched state in which the ' Institutions ' of
Quintilian had previously existed,[2] he proceeds as follows :—
' I verily believe that, if we had not come to the rescue, he
[Quintilian] must speedily have perished ; for it cannot be
imagined that a man magnificent, polished, elegant, urbane,
and witty could much longer have endured the squalor of the
prison-house in which I found him, the savagery of his jailers,
the forlorn filth of the place. He was indeed right sad to
look upon, and ragged, like a condemned criminal, with rough
beard and matted hair, protesting by his countenance and
garb against the injustice of his sentence. He seemed to be
stretching out his hands, calling upon the Romans, demanding

---

[1] Mur. xx. 160.
[2] Petrarch in 1350 found a bad copy at Florence. Poggio describes
it thus :—' Is vero apud nos antea, Italos dico, ita laceratus erat, ita
circumcisus culpâ, ut opinor, temporum, ut nulla forma, nullus habitus
hominis in eo recognosceretur.'

to be saved from so unmerited a doom. Hard indeed it was for him to bear, that he who had preserved the lives of many by his eloquence and aid, should now find no redresser of his wrongs, no saviour from the unjust punishment awaiting him. But as it often happens, to quote Terence, that what you dare not wish for comes to you by chance, so a good fortune for him, but far more for ourselves, led us, while wasting our time in idleness at Constance, to take a fancy for visiting the place where he was held in prison. The monastery of S. Gallen lies at the distance of some twenty miles from that city. Thither, then, partly for the sake of amusement and partly of finding books, whereof we heard there was a large collection in the convent, we directed our steps. In the middle of a well-stocked library, too large to catalogue at present, we discovered Quintilian, safe as yet and sound, though covered with dust and filthy with neglect and age. The books, you must know, were not housed according to their worth, but were lying in a most foul and obscure dungeon at the very bottom of a tower, a place into which condemned criminals would hardly have been thrust; and I am firmly persuaded that if anyone would but explore those *ergastula* of the barbarians wherein they incarcerate such men, we should meet with like good fortune in the case of many whose funeral orations have long ago been pronounced. Besides Quintilian, we exhumed the three first books and a half of the fourth book of the "Argonautica" of Flaccus, and the "Commentaries" of Asconius Pedianus upon eight orations of Cicero.' Poggio, immediately after this discovery, set himself to work at transcribing the Quintilian, a labour accomplished in the brief space of thirty-two days. The MS. was then despatched to Lionardo Bruni, who received it with ecstatic welcome, as appears from this congratulatory epistle addressed to Poggio :—

'The republic of letters has reason to rejoice not only in

the works you have discovered, but also in those you have still to find. What a glory for you it is to have brought to light by your exertions the writings of the most distinguished authors! Posterity will not forget that MSS. which were bewailed as lost beyond the possibility of restoration, have been recovered, thanks to you. As Camillus was called the second founder of Rome, so may you receive the title of the second author of the works you have restored to the world. Through you we now possess Quintilian entire; before we only boasted of the half of him, and that defective and corrupt in text. O precious acquisition! O unexpected joy! And shall I, then, in truth be able to read the whole of that Quintilian which, mutilated and deformed as it has hitherto appeared, has formed my solace? I conjure you send it me at once, that at least I may set eyes on it before I die.'

In addition to the authors named above, Poggio discovered and copied with his own hand MSS. of Lucretius and Columella. Silius Italicus, Manilius, and Vitruvius owed their resurrection to his industry. At Langres he found a copy of Cicero's oration for Cæcina; at Monte Cassino a MS. of Frontinus. Ammianus Marcellinus, Nonius Marcellus, Probus, Flavius Caper, and Eutyches are also to be ranked among the captives freed by him from slavery. In exploring foreign convents where he suspected that ancient authors might lie buried, he spared neither trouble nor expense. 'No severity of winter cold, no snow, no length of journey, no roughness of roads, prevented him from bringing the monuments of literature to light,' wrote Francesco Barbaro.[1] Nor did he recoil from theft, if theft seemed necessary to secure a precious codex. In a letter to Ambrogio Traversari he relates his negotiations with a monk for the fraudulent abduction of an Ammianus and a Livy from a convent library in Hersfeld.[2]

[1] Mur. xx. 169. Cf. the Elegy of Landino quoted in the notes to Roscoe's *Lorenzo*, p. 399.   [2] Voigt, p. 138.

Not unfrequently his most golden anticipations with regard to literary treasures were deceived, as when a Dane appeared at the Court of Martin V. bragging of a complete Livy to be found in a Cistercian convent near Röskilde. This man protested he had seen the MS., and described the characters in which it was written with some minuteness. At Poggio's instance the Cardinal Orsini sent off a special messenger to seek for this, which would have been the very phœnix of MSS. to the Latinists of that period, while Cosimo de' Medici put his agents at Lübeck to work for the same purpose. All their efforts were in vain, however. The Livy could not be discovered, and the Dane passed for a liar, in spite of the corroboration his story received from another traveller.[1] Poggio himself, who would willingly have ransacked Europe for a MS., was jealous of money spent on any other object. In his treatise ' De Infelicitate Principum ' he complains that ' these exalted personages [popes and princes] spend their days and their wealth in pleasure, in unworthy pursuits, in pestiferous and destructive wars. So great is their mental torpor that nothing can rouse them to search after the works of excellent writers, by whose wisdom and learning mankind are taught the way to true happiness.' This lamentation, written probably under the unfavourable impression produced upon his mind by the Papal Court, where as yet the spirit of humanism had hardly penetrated, must not be taken in any strict sense. Never was there a time in the world's history when money was spent more freely upon the collection and preservation of MSS., and when a more complete machinery was put in motion for the sake of securing literary treasures. Prince vied with prince, and eminent burgher with burgher, in buying books. The commercial correspondents of the Medici and other great Florentine houses, whose banks and discount offices extended over Europe and the Levant, were

---

[1] See Voigt, p. 139, for this story.

instructed to purchase relics of antiquity without regard for cost, and to forward them to Florence. The most acceptable present that could be sent to a king was a copy of a Roman historian. The best credentials which a young Greek arriving from Byzantium could use to gain the patronage of men like Palla degli Strozzi was a fragment of some ancient; the merchandise ensuring the largest profit to a speculator who had special knowledge in such matters was old parchment covered with crabbed characters.

The history of the foundation of libraries will form part of the next chapter. For the present it is requisite to mention some of Poggio's fellow workmen in the labour of collection. Among these a certain Nicholas of Treves, employed to receive monies due to the Papal Curia in Germany, deserves a place, seeing that in 1429 he sent the most complete extant copy of Plautus to Rome. Bartolommeo da Montepulciano, following the lead of Poggio, pursued investigations while at Constance, and discovered the lost writings of Vegetius and Pompeius Festus. In 1409 Lionardo Bruni chanced upon a good MS. of Cicero's letters at Pistoja, and about the year 1425 a magnificent capture of Cicero's rhetorical treatises was made at Lodi in the Duomo by Gherardo Landriani. The extant works of Tacitus, so ardently desired, were not collected earlier than the reign of Leo.

While Poggio was releasing the Latin authors from their northern prisons, and sending them to walk like princes through the Courts and capitals of Italy, three other scholars devoted no less energy to the collection of Greek MSS. Giovanni Aurispa, on his return from Byzantium in 1423, brought with him 238 codices, while Guarino of Verona and Francesco Filelfo both arrived in Italy heavily laden. There is an old story that Guarino lost a part of his cargo at sea, and landed with hair whitened by the grief this misfortune cost him. Considering the special advantages enjoyed by

these three scholars, who were pupils of the learned Manuel
Chrysoloras, and before whose eager curiosity the libraries of
Byzantium remained open through nearly half a century previous to the fall of the Greek Empire, we have good reason
to believe that the greater part of Attic and Alexandrian
literature known to the later Greeks was transferred to Italy.
The avidity shown by the Florentines for codices and copies,
the opportunities afforded by their mercantile connection with
Constantinople, and the obvious interest which the Court of
Byzantium at that crisis had in gratifying their taste for such
acquisitions, contribute to render it unlikely that any of the
more important and illustrious authors were destroyed in
the taking of the city by the Turk.[1] It is probable that causes
similar to those which slowly wrought the ruin of Latin
literature in the West—the apathy of an uncultured public,
the rancorous animosity of a superstitious clergy, and the
decay of students as a class—had long before the age of the
Renaissance ruined beyond the possibility of recovery those
masterpieces whereof we still deplore the loss.[2] The preservation of Neoplatonic and Patristic literature in comparative completeness, while so much that was more valuable
perished, may be ascribed to the theological content of these
writings.

[1] See the emphatic language about Palla degli Strozzi, Cosimo de'
Medici, and Niccolo de' Niccoli, in Vespasiano's *Lives*. Islam, more-
over, as is proved by Pletho's Life, was at that period more erudite than
Hellas.

[2] I have touched upon this subject elsewhere. See *Studies of Greek
Poets*, second series, pp. 304-307. In order to form a conception of the
utter decline of Byzantine learning after Photius, it is needful to read
the passages in Petrarch's letters, where even Calabria is compared
favourably with Constantinople. In a state of ignorance so absolute as
he describes, it is possible that treasures existed unknown to professed
students, and therefore undiscovered by Filelfo and his fellow-workers.
The testimony of Demetrius Chalcondylas, quoted by Didot, *Alde Manuce*,
p. xiv., goes to show that the Greeks attributed their losses in large
measure to the malice of the priests.

Not to render some account of the effect produced upon
the minds of scholars in the fourteenth and fifteenth centuries
by the sight of Roman ruins in decay, would be to omit an
important branch of the subject I have undertaken. Yet
this part of the inquiry leads us into a region somewhat
different from that hitherto traversed in the present chapter,
since it properly belongs to the history of enthusiasm. No
small portion of the motive impulse that determined the
Revival was derived from the admiration, curiosity, and awe
excited by the very stones of ancient Rome. During the
Middle Ages the right point of view for studying the architectural works of the Romans had been lost. History yielded
ever more and more to legend, until at last it was believed
that demons and magicians had suspended those gigantic
vaults in air. Telesmatic virtues were attributed to figures
carved on temple-fronts and friezes, while the great name
of Virgil attached itself to what remained unhurt of Latin
art in Rome and Naples.[1] The Rome of the *Mirabilia* was
supposed to be the handiwork of fiends constrained by poets
of the bygone age with spells of power to move hell from its
centre. This transference of interest from the real to the
fanciful, from the substantial to the visionary, was characteristic of the whole attitude assumed by the mind in the
Middle Ages. History, literature, and art alike submitted to
the alchemy of the imagination.[2] At the same time the very
grossness of these fables testified to the profound impression
produced by the ruins of the Eternal City, and to the haunting
magic of a memory surviving degradation and decay. When
the Anglo-Saxon pilgrims returned from Rome in the eighth
century, the fascination of the great works they had seen

---

[1] The details of Virgil's romance occupy the first half of Comparetti's
second volume on *Virgil in the Middle Ages.* For the English version
of this legend see Thoms.

[2] See above, pp. 38-49.

expressed itself in a memorable prophecy.[1] 'As long as the Coliseum stands, Rome shall stand; when the Coliseum falls, Rome will fall; when Rome falls, the world will fall.'

About the year 1300 a new historic sense appears to have arisen in Italy. Instead of dreams and legends, the positive facts of the past began to have once more their value. This change might be compared to the discovery we make upon the borderland of sleep and waking, when what we fancied was a figure draped in white by our bedside turns out to be the wall with moonlight shining on it. Giovanni Villani, when he gazed upon the baths and amphitheatres of Rome, was not moved to think of the fiends who raised them, but of the buried grandeur of the Roman commonwealth.[2] What Rome once was, Florence may one day become, was the reflection that impelled him to write the chronicle of his native town. Dante, who with Villani witnessed the Jubilee of 1300, cried that the very stones of Rome were sacred. 'Whoso robs her, or despoils her, with blasphemy of act offendeth God, who only for His own use made her holy.'[3] The city was to him the outward symbol and terrestrial station of that God-appointed Monarchy for ruling all the peoples of the earth in peace. His most enthusiastic speculations, as well as the practical policy set forth in his epistles, attached themselves to Rome as a reality; nor did he ever tire of bidding German emperors return and fix their throne upon the bank of Tiber. We know now that this idealism was a delusion, no less incapable of realisation than it was pernicious to the liberties of the Italians. It haunted the imagination of the race, however, until at last, as I have said above, the proper vent was found in humanism.

The same passion for Rome took different form in the mind of another and less noble patriot. It impelled Rienzi

---

[1] Gibbon, ch. lxxi.   [2] Vol. I., *Age of the Despots*, p. 200.
          [3] *Purg.* xxxiii. 58.

to conceive the plan of rehabilitating the Republic.   The Popes
were far away at Avignon.   The emperors seemed to have
forgotten Italy.   Yet Rome remained, and the mere name of
Rome was Empire.   Why should not the *Senatus Populusque
Romanus*, whose initials still survived in uncial letters upon
blocks of travertine and marble, be restored to place and
power ?   Wandering among those spacious vaults, and
lingering beneath the triumphal arches, where the marks of
chariot-wheels were traced upon the massive paved work of
the Roman ways, the young enthusiast conceived that even he
might live to be the Tribune of that people, born invincible,
and called by destiny to rule the world.   With what energy
he devoted himself to studying the histories of Livy, Sallust,
and Valerius Maximus ; how he strove to master the meaning of inscriptions found among the wrecks of Rome ; with
what eloquence he moved his fellow-citizens to sympathy—
are familiar matters not only to scholars, but to readers of
romance.   His vision of the restored Republic seemed for
a moment destined to become reality.   The Romans placed
the power of life and death, of revenues and armies, in the
hands of the seer, who had stirred them by his rhetoric.
Rienzi took rank among the potentates of Italy.   Even the
Papal Court acknowledged him.

   What followed proved the political incapacity of the new
dictator, his want of critical insight into the ideal he had set
before himself.   There is something both pathetic and ridiculous in the vanity displayed by this barber's son exalted to a
place among the princes.   Not satisfied with calling himself
Tribune and Knight, the style he affected in his correspondence
with Clement VI. ran as follows :—' Candidatus, Spiritus
Sancti Miles, Nicolaus Severus et Clemens, Liberator Urbis,
Zelator Italiæ, Amator Orbis, et Tribunus Augustus.'   Like
Icarus, he spread these waxen wings to the sun's noontide
blaze.   The same extravagant confusion of things sacred and

profane, classical and mediæval, marked the pageantry of his
State ceremonials in Rome. On August 15, 1347, in celebration of his election to the Tribunate, he assumed six crowns—
of ivy, myrtle, laurel, oak, olive, and gilt silver. His arms
were blazoned with the keys of Peter and the letters
S.P.Q.R. His senatorial sceptre was surmounted, not with
the eagle or the wolf of Romulus, but with a golden ball and
cross enclosing the relic of a saint. The poetic fancy could
not have suggested a more striking allegory to illustrate an
undiscriminating reverence for the Imperial and Pontifical
prestige of Rome, than was presented in this tragic farce of
actual history. Not in this way, by a mixture of Christian
and Pagan titles, by emblematic pomp, by heraldry and declamation, could the old Republic be brought to life again. The
very attempt to do so proved how far the mind of man,
awaking from the long sleep of the Middle Ages, was removed
from the severe simplicity that gave its strength to ancient
Rome. Along those giddy parapets of fame we watch Rienzi
walking through his months of glory like a somnambule
sustained by an internal dream. That he should fall was
inevitable. With him expired the Utopia of a Roman
commonwealth, to be from time to time revived as an
ineffectual fancy in the brains of a few visionaries.[1]

The relations of Petrarch to Rienzi offer matter for curious
reflection, while they illustrate the part played by the enthusiasm for ancient Rome in the early history of humanism.
Petrarch and Rienzi had been friends and correspondents
before the emergence of the latter into public notice ; and
when the Tribune seemed about to satisfy the dearest desire
of the poet's heart by re-establishing the Roman commonwealth, Petrarch addressed him with an animated letter of
congratulation and encouragement.[2] In his charmed eyes he

---

[1] Stefano Porcari, for example. See Vol. I., *Age of the Despots*, pp.
296, 302.   [2] *De Capessendâ Libertate, Hortatoria*, p. 535.

seemed a hero, *vir magnanimus*, worthy of the ancient world,
a new Romulus, a third Brutus, a Camillus. The Roman
burghers, that scum and sediment of countless races, bar-
barised by the lingering miseries of the Middle Ages, needed
nothing, it appeared, but words and wishes to make them
once again *cives Romani*, no longer clamorous for bread and
games, but ready to reconquer all their ancestors had lost.[1]
'Where,' cried Petrarch, 'can the empire of the world be
found, except in Rome? Who can dispute the Roman right?
What force can stand against the name of Romans?'
Neither the patriot nor the scholar discerned that the revival
they were destined to inaugurate was intellectual. Though
the spirit of the times refused a political Renaissance, refused
to Italy the maintenance of even such freedom as she then
possessed, far more refused a resuscitation of ancient Rome's
imperial sway, yet both Rienzi and Petrarch persisted in
believing that, because they glowed with fervour for the past,
because they could read inscriptions, because they expressed
their desires eloquently, the world's great age was certain to
begin anew. It was a capital fault of the Renaissance to
imagine that words could work wonders, that a rhetorician's
stylus might become the wand of Prospero. Seeming passed
for being in morals, politics, and all affairs of life. I have
already touched on this as a capital defect in Petrarch's
character; but it was a weakness inherent not only in him
and in the age he inaugurated, but one, moreover, that has
influenced the whole history of the Italians for evil. Sounding
phrases like the *barbaros expellere* of Julius II., like the
va fuori d' Italia of Garibaldian hymns, from time to time
have roused the nation to feverish enthusiasm, too soon succeeded by dejected apathy. When the inefficiency of Rienzi
was proved, all that remained for Petrarch was to warn and
scold.

[1] See Petrarch's *Epistle to the Roman People*, p. 712.

The interest excited in Petrarch by the sight of Rome's
ruins was important for his humanistic ideal.   They stirred
him as a moralist, an antiquarian, and a man who owed his
mental vigour to the past.   He tells how often he used to
climb above the huge vaults of the Baths of Diocletian in company with his friend Giovanni Colonna.[1]   Seated there among
the flowering shrubs and scented herbs that clothed decay
with loveliness, they held discourse concerning the great men
of old, and deplored the mutability of all things human.
Whatever the poet had read of Roman grandeur was brought
back to his mind with vivid meaning during his long solitary
walks.   He never doubted that he knew for certain where
Evander's palace stood, and where the cave of Cacus opened
on the Tiber.   The difficulties of modern antiquarian research
had not been yet suggested, and his fancy was free to map out
the topography of the seven hills as pleased him best.   Yet
he complained that nowhere was less known about Rome than
in Rome itself.[2]   This ignorance he judged the most fatal
obstacle to the resurrection of the city.[3]   The palaces where
dwelt those heroes of the past, had fallen into ruins; the
temples of the gods were desecrated ; the triumphal arches
were crumbling ; the very walls had yielded to decay.   None
of the Romans cared to arrest destruction ; they even robbed
the marble columns and entablatures in order to deck Naples
with the spoils.[4]   The last remnants of the city would soon,

[1] *Epist. Fam.* lib. ii. 14, p. 605; lib. vi. 2, p. 657.

[2] ' Qui enim hodie magis ignari rerum Romanarum sunt, quam
Romani Cives ? Invitus dico, nusquam minus Roma cognoscitur quam
Romæ.' *Epist. Fam.* lib. ii. 14, p. 658.

[3] ' Quis enim dubitare potest, quin illico surrectura sit si cœperit se
Roma cognoscere ? ' *Ibid.*

[4] ' Vi vel senio collapsa palatia, quæ quondam ingentes tenuere viri,
diruptos arcus triumphales . . . indignum de vestris marmoreis columnis, de liminibus templorum, ad quæ nuper ex toto orbe concursus devo-
tissimus fiebat, de imaginibus sepulchrorum, sub quibus patrum ves-
trorum venerabilis cinis erat, ut reliquas sileam, desidiosa Neapolis
adornatur.' *Ibid.* p. 536.

he exclaimed, be levelled with the ground. Time has been
unable to destroy them; but man was ruining what Time had
spared.[1]

There is no doubt that, shortly before the date of Petrarch's
visits to Rome, the city had suffered grievously in its monuments.   We know, for instance, that the best preserved of the
theatres, baths, and tombs formed the residences and fortresses
of nobles in the Middle Ages; and when we read that in 1258
the senator Brancaleone found it necessary to destroy one
hundred and forty of these fortified dwellings, we obtain a
standard for measuring the injury that must have ensued to
precious works of classic architecture.   The ruins, moreover,
as Petrarch hinted, had been used as quarries.   What was worse,
the burghers burned the marbles, rich, perhaps, with inscriptions and carved bas-reliefs, for lime.   We shall shortly see
what Poggio relates upon this topic.   For the present it will
suffice to quote an epigram of Pius II., written some time
after the revival of enthusiasm for antiquity :—

> Oblectat me, Roma, tuas spectare ruinas,
>   Ex cujus lapsu gloria prisca patet.
> Sed tuus hic populus muris defossa vetustis
>   Calcis in obsequium marmora dura coquit.
> Impia ter centum si sic gens egerit annos,
>   Nullum hic indicium nobilitatis erit.[2]

---

[1] 'Quanta quod integræ fuit olim gloria Romæ,
     Reliquiæ testantur adhuc, quas longior ætas
     Frangere non valuit, non vis, aut ira cruenti
     Hostis, ab egregiis franguntur civibus heu, heu.'
                                    Petr. *Epist. Metr.* lib. ii. p. 98.
[2] 'It delights me to contemplate thy ruins, Rome, the witness amid
desolation to thy pristine grandeur.   But thy people burn thy marbles
for lime, and three centuries of this sacrilege will destroy all sign of thy
nobleness.'   Compare a letter from Alberto degli Alberti to Giovanni
de' Medici, quoted by Fabroni, *Cosmi Vita*, Adnot. 86.   The real pride
of Rome was still her ruins.   Nicolo and Ugo da Este journeyed in 1396
to Rome, 'per vedere quelle magnificenze antiche che al presente si
possono vedere in Roma.'   Murat. xxiv. 815.

Poggio Bracciolini opens a new epoch in Roman topography. The ruins that had moved the superstitious wonder
of the Middle Ages, that had excited Rienzi to patriotic enthusiasm, and Petrarch to reflections on the instability of human
things, were now for the first time studied in a truly antiquarian spirit. Poggio read them like a book, comparing the
testimony they rendered with that of Livy, Vitruvius, and
Frontinus, and seeking to compile a catalogue of the existing
fragments of old Rome. The first section of his treatise
'De Varietate Fortunæ,' forms by far the most important source
of information we possess relating to the state of Rome in the
fifteenth century.[1] It appears that the Baths of Caracalla
and Diocletian could still boast of columns and marble incrus-
tations, but that within Poggio's own recollection the marbles
had been stripped from Cæcilia Metella's tomb, and the so-
called Temple of Concord had been pillaged.[2] Among the
ruins ascribed to the period of the Republic are mentioned a
bridge, an arch, a tomb, a temple, a building on the Capitol,
and the pyramid of Cestius.[3] Besides these, Poggio enume-
rates, as referable chiefly to the Imperial age, eleven temples,
seven *thermæ*, the Arches of Titus, Severus, and Constantine,
parts of the Arches of Trajan, Faustina, and Gallienus, the
Coliseum, the Theatres of Pompey and Marcellus, the Circus
Agonalis and Circus Maximus, the Columns of Trajan and
Antonine, the two horses ascribed to Pheidias and Praxiteles,

[1] My references are made to the Paris edition of 1723. The first
book is sometimes cited under the title of *Urbis Romæ Descriptio*.
[2] 'Juxta viam Appiam, ad secundum lapidem, integrum vidi sepul-
chrum L. Cæciliæ Metellæ, opus egregium, et id ipsum tot sæculis in-
tactum, ad calcem postea majori ex parte exterminatum' (p. 19).
'Capitolio contigua forum versus superest porticus ædis Concordiæ,
quam, cum primum ad urbem accessi, vidi fere integram, opere mar-
moreo admodum specioso; Romani postmodum, ad calcem ædem totam
et porticûs partem, disjectis columnis, sunt demoliti.' *Ibid.*
[3] Pp. 8, 9.

together with other marble statues, one bronze equestrian statue, and the mausoleums of Augustus and Hadrian.

We have to regret that Poggio's description was subservient and introductory to a rhetorical dissertation. Had he applied himself to the task of tabulating more minutely what he had observed, his work would have been infinitely precious to the archæologist. No one knew more about the Roman buildings than he did. No one felt the impression of their majesty in desolation more profoundly. The mighty city appeared to him, he said, like the corpse of a giant, like a queen in slavery. The sight of her magnificence, despoiled and shorn of ornaments as she had been, moved him daily to deeper admiration. It was his custom to lead strangers from point to point among the ruins, in order to enjoy the effect produced upon fresh minds by their stupendous evidence of strength and greatness in decay.

The pathos of this former empress of the world exposed to insult and indignity had not been first felt by Poggio. Petrarch described her as an aged matron with grey hair and pale cheeks, whose torn and sordid raiment ill accorded with the nobleness of her demeanour.[1] Fazio degli Uberti personified her as a majestic woman, wrapped around with rags, who pointed out to him the ruins of her city, ' to the end that he might understand how fair she was in years of old.' [2]

In this way a sentimental feeling for the relics of the past grew up and flourished side by side with the archæological interest they excited. The literature of the Renaissance abounds in matter that might be used in illustration of this remark,[3] while nothing was commoner in art than to paint for backgrounds broken arches and decayed buildings, 'whose

---

[1] *De Pacificandâ Italiâ, Ad Carolum Quartum*, p. 531.

[2] In the *Dittamondo*, about 1360.

[3] Such, for example, as Boccaccio's description of the ruins of Baiæ in the *Fiammetta*, Sannazzaro's lines on the ruins of Cumæ, Æneas Sylvius Piccolomini's notes on ancient sites in Italy.

ruins are even pitied.' The double impulse of romantic
sentiment and antiquarian curiosity, set going in this age of
the Revival, contributed no little to the development of
architecture, sculpture, and painting. In the section of my
work which deals with the fine arts in Italy will be found
the proper sequel to this subject. Meanwhile the history of
antiquarian research in Rome itself will be resumed in another chapter of this volume.

Among the representative men of the first period of the
Revival must be mentioned an enthusiast who devoted his
whole life to topographical studies and to the copying of
classical inscriptions. Ciriaco de' Pizzicolli was born about
1404 at Ancona, and from this town he took the name he
bears among the learned. Like many other pioneers of
erudition, he was educated for commerce, and had slender
opportunities for acquiring the dead languages in his youth.
His manhood was spent in restless journeying, at first undertaken for the purposes of trade, but afterwards for the
sole object of discovery. Smitten with the zeal for classical
antiquity, he made himself a tolerable Latin scholar, and
gained a fair knowledge of Greek. In the course of his long
wanderings he ransacked every part of Italy, Greece, and
the Greek islands, collecting medals, gems, and fragments of
sculpture, buying manuscripts, transcribing records, and
amassing a miscellaneous store of archæological information.
The enthusiasm that possessed him was so untempered by
sobriety that it excited the suspicion of contemporaries.
Some regarded him as a man of genuine learning; others
spoke of him as a flighty, boastful, and untrustworthy fanatic.[1]

[1] Filippo Maria Visconti is said to have denounced him as an impostor. Ambrogio Traversari mentions his coins and gems with mistrust. Poggio describes him as a conceited fellow with no claim to
erudition. On the other hand, he gained the confidence of Eugenius IV.,
and received the panegyrics of Filelfo, Barbaro, Bruni, and others.
See Tiraboschi, vol. vi. lib. i. cap. 5.

The mistakes he made in copying inscriptions depreciated the general value of his labours, while he was even accused of having passed off fabrications on the credulity of the public. The question of his alleged forgeries has been discussed at length by Tiraboschi.[1] To settle it at this distance of time is both unimportant and impossible. While we may well believe that Ciriac was a conceited enthusiast, accepting as genuine what he ought to have rejected, and interpreting according to his fancy rather than the letter of his text, his life retains real value for the student of the Revival. In him the curiosity of the new age reached its acme of expansiveness. The passion for discovery pursued him from shore to shore, and the vision of the past, to be reconquered by the energy of the present, haunted his imagination till the moment of his death. When asked what object he had set his heart upon in those perpetual journeyings, he answered, ' I go to awake the dead.' That word, the motto for the first age of the Revival, explains the fanaticism of Ciriac, and is a sufficient title to fame.

  [1] In the place just cited. The temptation, at this epoch of discovery, when criticism was at a low ebb, and curiosity was frantic, to pass off forgeries upon the learned world must have been very great. The most curious example of this literary deception is afforded by Annius of Viterbo, who, in 1498, published seventeen books of spurious histories, pretending to be the lost works of Manetho, Berosus, Fabius Pictor, Archilochus, Cato, &c. Whether he was himself an impostor or a dupe is doubtful. A few of his contemporaries denounced the histories as patent fabrications. The majority accepted them as genuine. Their worthlessness has long been undisputed. See Tiraboschi, vol. vi. lib. iii. cap. 1.

CHAPTER IV

SECOND PERIOD OF HUMANISM

THE great difficulty with which a critic desirous of rendering a succinct account of this phase of Italian culture has to deal, is the variety and complexity of the subject. It is easy to perceive the unity of the humanistic movement, and to regard the scholars of the fifteenth century as a literary community with well-defined relations to each other. Yet when we attempt to trace the growth of scholarship in all its branches, the peculiar conditions of political and social life in Italy present almost insuperable obstacles to any continuity of treatment. The republics, the principalities, and the Church have each their separate existence. Venice, Florence, Naples, Milan, Rome, Ferrara, form distinct and independent centres, imposing their own specialities upon the intellectual activity of citizens and aliens. The humanists, meanwhile, to some extent efface these local differences, spreading a network of common culture over cities and societies divided by all else but interest in learning. To these combinations and permutations, arising from the contact of the scholars with their patrons in the several States of Italy, is due the intricacy of the history of the Revival. The same men of eminence appear by turns in each of the chief Courts and commonwealths, passing with bewildering rapidity from north to south and back again, in one place demanding attention under one head of the subject, in another presenting new yet not less important topics for investigation. What Filippo Maria Visconti, for instance, required from Filelfo had but little in common with the claims made on him by Nicholas V., while his activity as a satirist and partisan at Florence differed from his labour as a lecturer at Siena. Again, the biography of each humanist to some extent involves that of all his contemporaries. The coteries of Rome are influenced by the cliques of Naples; the quarrels of Lorenzo Valla ramify into the squabbles of Guarino; political animosity combines with literary jealousy in the disputes of Poggio with Filelfo. While some of the most eminent professors remain stationary in their native or adopted towns, others move to and fro with the speed of comets. From time to time, at Rome or elsewhere, a patron rises, who assembles all the wandering stars around himself. His death disperses the group; or accidents rouse jealousy among them, and cause secessions from the circle. Then fresh combinations have to be considered. In no one city can we trace firm chronological progression, or discover the fixed local character which justifies our dividing the history of Italian painting by its schools. To avoid repetition, and to preserve an even current of narration amid so much that is shifting, is almost impossible.

Some method may be introduced by sketching briefly at the outset the principal periods through which the humanistic movement passed. Though to a certain extent arbitrary, these periods mark distinct moments in an evolution uniform in spite of its complexity.

The first, starting with Petrarch, and including the lives and labours of those men he personally influenced, has been traced in a preceding chapter. This was the age of inspiration and discovery, when the enthusiasm for antiquity was generated and the remnants of the classics were accumulated. The second may be described as the age of arrangement and translation. The first great libraries were founded in this period; the study of Greek was pursued in earnest, and the Greek authors were rendered into Latin. Round Cosimo de' Medici at Florence, Alfonso the Magnanimous at Naples, and Nicholas V. in Rome the leaders of the Renaissance at this time converge. The third is the age of academies. The literary republic, formed during the first and second periods, now gathers into coteries, whereof the Platonic Academy at Florence, that of Pontanus at Naples, that of Pomponius Lætus in Rome, and that of Aldus Manutius at Venice are the most important. Scholarship begins to exhibit a marked improvement in all that concerns style and taste. At the same time Italian erudition reaches its maximum in Poliziano. Externally this third period is distinguished by the rapid spread of printing and the consequent downfall of the humanists as a class. In the fourth period we notice a gradual decline of learning; æsthetic and stylistic scholarship begins to claim exclusive attention. This is the age of the purists, over whom Bembo exercises the sway of a dictator, while the Court of Leo X. furnishes the most brilliant assemblage of literati in Europe. Erudition, properly so called, is now upon the point of being transplanted beyond the Alps, and the Reviva of Learning closes for the historian of Italy.

Although the essential feature of this subject is variety, and though each city of Italy contributed its quota to the sum of culture, attention has now to be directed in a special sense on Florence. Nothing is more obvious to the student who has mastered the first difficulties caused by the intricacy of Italian history, than the fact that all the mental force of the nation was generated in Tuscany, and radiated thence, as from a centre of vital heat and light, over the rest of the peninsula. This is true of the fine arts no less than of Italian poetry, of the revival of learning as well as of the origin of science. From the republics of Tuscany, and from Florence in particular, proceeded the impulse and the energy which led to fruitful results in all of these departments. In proportion as Florence continued to absorb the neighbouring free States into herself, her intellectual pre-eminence became the more unquestionable. Arezzo, Volterra, Cortona, Montepulciano, Prato, and Pistoja were but rivulets feeding the stream of Florentine industry.

What caused this superiority of the Tuscans is a problem as difficult to solve as the similar problem with respect to Athens among the states of Greece. Something may no doubt be attributed to ethnology, and something to climate. Much, again, was due to the purity of a dialect which retained more of native energy and literary capacity, and which had suffered less from barbarian admixtures than the dialects of northern or of southern Italy. The conquest of the Lombards passed the Tuscans by, nor did feudal institutions take the same root in the valley of the Arno which they struck in the kingdom of Naples. The cities of Tuscany were therefore less exposed to foreign influences than the rest of Italy. While they pursued their course of internal growth in comparative tranquillity, they were better fitted for reviving the past glories of Latin civilisation upon its native soil. The free institutions of the Florentine commonwealth must also be taken into account.

In Florence, if anywhere in Italy, existed the conditions under which a republic of letters and of culture could be formed. The aristocracy of Naples indulged the semi-savage tastes of territorial *seigneurs* ; the nobles of Rome delighted in feats of arms and shared their wealth with retinues of *bravi* ; the great families of Umbria, Romagna, and the March followed the profession of *condottieri* ; the Lombards were down-trodden by their Despots and deprived of individual freedom ; the Genoese developed into little better than traders and sea-robbers ; the Sienese, divided by the factions of their *Monti*, had small leisure or common public feeling left for study. Florence meanwhile could boast a population of burghers noble by taste and culture, owing less to ancestry than to personal eminence, devoting their energies to civic ambition worthy of the Romans, and to mental activity which reminds us of the ancient Greeks. Between the people and this aristocracy of wealth and intellect there was at Florence no division like that which separated the Venetian *gentiluomini* from the *cittadini*. The so-called *nobili* and *popolani* did not, as in Venice, form a caste apart, bound to the service of a tyrannous state-system. The very mobility which proved the ultimate source of disruption and of ruin to the commonwealth, aided the intellectual development of Florence. Stagnation and oppression were alike unknown. Here, therefore, and here alone, was created a public capable instinctively of comprehending what is beautiful in art and humane in letters, a race of craftsmen and of scholars who knew that their labours could not fail to be appreciated, and a class of patrons who sought no better bestowal of their wealth than on those arts and sciences which dignify the life of man. The Florentines, moreover, as a nation, were animated with the strongest sense

of the greatness and the splendour of Florence. Like the
Athenians of old, they had no warmer passion than their love
for their city. However much we may deplore the rancorous
dissensions which from time to time split up the commonwealth into parties, the remorseless foreign policy which
destroyed Pisa, the political meanness of the Medici, and the
base egotism of the *ottimati*, the fact remains that, æsthetically and intellectually, Florence was 'a city glorious,' a
realised ideal of culture and humanity for all the rest of Italy,
and, through Italian influence in general, for modern Europe
and for us.

What makes the part played by Florence in the history of
learning the more remarkable is, that the chiefs of the political
factions were at the same time the leaders of intellectual progress. Rinaldo degli Albizzi and Cosimo de' Medici, while
opposed as antagonists in a duel to the death upon the stage
of the republic, vied with each other in the patronage they
extended to men of letters. Rinaldo was himself no mean
scholar; and he chose one of the greatest men of the age,
Tommaso da Sarzana, to be tutor to his children. Of Palla
degli Strozzi's services in the cause of Greek learning I have
already spoken in the second chapter of this volume. Beside
the invitation which he caused to be sent to Manuel Chrysoloras, he employed his wealth and influence in providing books
necessary for the prosecution of Hellenic studies. 'Messer
Palla,' says Vespasiano, 'sent to Greece for countless volumes,
all at his own cost. The " Cosmography " of Ptolemy, together
with the picture made to illustrate it, the " Lives " of Plutarch,
the works of Plato, and very many other writings of philosophers, he got from Constantinople. The " Politics " of Aristotle
were not in Italy until Messer Palla sent for them ; and when
Messer Lionardo of Arezzo translated them, he had the copy
from his hands.'[1] In the same spirit of practical generosity

[1] Vespasiano, p. 272.

Palla degli Strozzi devoted his leisure and his energies to the improvement of the *studio pubblico* at Florence, giving it that character of humane culture which it retained throughout the age of the Renaissance.[1] To him, again, belongs the glory of having first collected books for the express purpose of founding a public library. This project had occupied the mind of Petrarch, and its utility had been recognised by Coluccio de' Salutati,[2] but no one had as yet arisen to accomplish it. 'Being passionately fond of literature, Messer Palla always kept copyists in his own house and outside it, of the best who were in Florence, both for Greek and Latin books; and all the books he could find he purchased, on all subjects, being minded to found a most noble library in Santa Trinità, and to erect there a most beautiful building for the purpose. He wished that it should be open to the public, and he chose Santa Trinità because it was in the centre of Florence, a site of great convenience to everybody. His disasters supervened, and what he had designed he could not execute.'[3]

The calamities alluded to by Vespasiano may be briefly told. Palla degli Strozzi, better fitted by nature for study than for party warfare, was one of the richest of the merchant princes of Florence. In the *catasto* of 1427 his property was valued at one-fifth more than that returned by Giovanni, then the chief of the Medicean family; and the extraordinary tax (*gravezza*) imposed upon it reached the sum of 800 florins.[4] During the conflict for power carried on between the Albizzi and the Medici he strove to preserve a neutral attitude; but after Cosimo's return from exile, in 1434, the presence of so powerful and rich a leader in the State seemed dangerous to the Medicean party. It was their policy to annihilate all greatness but their own, and to reduce the Florentines to slavery by creating a body of dependents and allies whose

[1] Vespasiano, p. 273.
[2] See Voigt, p. 202.
[3] Vespasiano, p. 275.
[4] *Ibid.* p. 276.

interests should be bound up with their own supremacy.[1] Palla degli Strozzi was accordingly banished to Padua for ten years, nor, at the expiration of this period, was he suffered to return to Florence. He died in exile, separated from his children, who shared the same fate in other parts of Italy, while Florence lost the services of the most enlightened of her sons.[2] Amid the many tribulations of his latter years Palla continued to derive comfort from study. John Argyropoulos was his guest at Padua, where the collection of books and the cultivation of Greek learning went on with no less vigour than at Florence.

The work begun by Palla degli Strozzi at Florence was ably continued by his enemy Cosimo de' Medici. Though the historian cannot respect this man, whose mean and selfish ambition undermined the liberties of his native city, there is no doubt that he deserves the credit of a prudent and munificent Mæcenas. No Italian of his epoch combined zeal for learning and generosity in all that could advance the interests of arts and letters, more characteristically, with political corruption and cynical egotism. Early in life Cosimo entered his father's house of business, and developed a rare faculty for finance. This faculty he afterwards employed in the administration of the State, as well as in the augmentation of the riches of his family by trade. As he gained political importance, he made it his prime object to place out monies in the hands of needy citizens, and to involve the public affairs of Florence with his own commerce by means of loans and other expedients. He not only attached individuals by debts and obligations to his person, but he also rendered it difficult to control the State expenditure without regard to his private bank. Few men have better understood the value

[1] See Von Reumont, vol. i. pp. 147–153, for the cruel treatment of the Albizzi and other leading citizens.
[2] See Vespasiano, pp. 283–287.

of money in the acquisition of power, or the advantage of so using it that jealousy should not be roused by personal display. 'Envy,' he remarked, 'is a plant you must not water.' Accordingly, while he spent large sums on public works, he declined Brunelleschi's sumptuous project for a palace, on the score that such a dwelling was more fitted for a prince than a citizen. In his habits he was temperate and simple. Games of hazard he abhorred, and found his recreation in the company of learned men. Sometimes, but rarely, he played at chess. Contemporaries recorded how, like an ancient Roman, he rose early in the morning to prune his own pear trees and to plant his vines. In all things he preferred the reality to the display of power and riches. While wielding the supreme authority of Florence, he seemed intent upon the dull work of the counting-house. Other men were put forward in the execution of designs that he had planned ; and this policy of ruling the State by cat's-paws was followed so consistently, that at the end of his life his influence was threatened by the very instruments he had created. At the same time he exercised virtual despotism with a pitiless tenacity unsurpassed by the Visconti. The cruelty with which he pushed the Albizzi to their ruin, prolonged the exile of Palla degli Strozzi, reduced Giannozzo Manetti to beggary, and oppressed his rivals in general with forced loans—using taxation like a poignard, to quote a phrase from Guicciardini—is enough to show that only prudence caused him to refrain from violence.[1] A cold and calculating policy, far-sighted, covert, and secretive, governed all the measures he took for fastening his family on Florence. The result was that the roots of the Medici, while they seemed to take hold slowly, struck deep ; you might fancy they were

---

[1] Manetti's obligations to the commune were raised by arbitrary impositions to the enormous sum of 135,000 golden florins. He was broken in his trade and forced to live on charity in exile.

nowhere, just because they had left no part unpenetrated.
The Republic, like Gulliver in Liliput, was tied down by a
thousand threads, each almost imperceptible, but so varied in
quality and so subtly interwoven that to escape from the network was impossible.

Much of the influence acquired by Cosimo, and transmitted
to his descendants, was due to sympathy with the intellectual
movement of the age. He had received a solid education ;
and though he was not a Greek scholar, his mind was open
to the interests which in the fifteenth century absorbed
the Florentines. He collected manuscripts, gems, coins, and
inscriptions, employing the resources of his banking house
and engaging his commercial agents in this work. Painters
and sculptors, no less than scholars and copyists, found in
him a liberal patron. At the death of his son Piero the
treasures of the Casa Medici, not counting plate and costly
furniture, were valued at 30,000 golden florins.[1] The sums
of money spent by him in building were enormous. It was
reckoned that, one year with another, he disbursed from
15,000 to 18,000 golden florins annually in edifices for the
public use.[2] Of these the most important were the Convent
of S. Marco, which altogether cost about 70,000 florins ; S.
Lorenzo, which cost another 40,000 ; and the Abbey of Fiesole.
On his own palace he expended 60,000 florins, while the
building of his villas at Careggi and Cafaggiuolo implied a
further large expenditure. Not a shilling of this money was
wasted ; for while Cosimo avoided the reproach of personal
extravagance, he gave work to multitudes of labourers, who
received their wages regularly every Saturday at his office.
To this free use of wealth in the employment of artisans may
be ascribed the popularity of the Medici with the lower classes,
which was more than once so useful to them at a perilous
turn of fortune.

[1] See Von Reumont, vol. ii. p. 175.   [2] Vespasiano, p. 257.

Comprehending the conditions under which tyranny might be successfully practised in the fifteenth century, Cosimo attached great value to this generosity. He used, in later life, to regret that ' he had not begun to spend money upon public works ten years earlier than he did.' [1] Every costly building that bore his name, each library he opened to the public, and all the donations lavished upon scholars served the double purpose of cementing the despotism of his house and of gratifying his personal enthusiasm for culture. Superstition mingled with these motives of the tyrant and the dilettante. Knowing that much of his wealth had been ill-gotten, he besought the Pope, Eugenius, to indicate a proper way of restitution. Eugenius advised him to spend 10,000 florins on the Convent of S. Marco. Thereupon Cosimo laid out considerably more than four times that sum, adding the famous Marcian Library, and treating the new foundation of the Osservanza, one of the Pope's favourite crotchets, with more than princely liberality.[2]

Of his generosity to men of letters the most striking details are recorded. When Niccolo de' Niccoli ruined himself by buying books, Cosimo opened for him an unlimited credit with the Medicean bank. The cashiers received orders to honour the old scholar's drafts ; and in this way Niccolo drew 500 ducats for his private needs.[3] Tommaso Parentucelli was treated with no less magnificence. As Bishop of Bologna, soon after his patron Albergati's death, he found himself with very meagre revenues and no immediate prospect of preferment. Yet the expenses of his station were con-

---

[1] Vespasiano, p. 257.

[2] *Ibid.* p. 252. Cosimo ordered his clerks to honour all drafts presented with the signature of one of the chief brethren of the convent. ' Aveva ordinato al banco, che tutti i danari, che gli fussino tratti per polizza d' uno religioso de primi del convento, gli pagasse, e mettessegli a suo conto, e fussino che somma si volessino.'

[3] Vespasiano, pp. 264, 475.

siderable, and he had occasion to request a loan from the
Medici.   Cosimo issued a circular letter to his correspondents,
engaging them to supply Tommaso with what sums of money
he might want.[1]   When the Bishop of Bologna assumed the
tiara, with the name of Nicholas V., he rewarded Cosimo by
making him his banker; and the Jubilee bringing 100,000
ducats into the Papal treasury, the obligation was repaid a
hundredfold.[2]

The chief benefit conferred by Cosimo de' Medici on learning was the accumulation and the housing of large public
libraries.   During his exile (Oct. 3, 1433—Oct. 1, 1434) he
built the Library of S. Giorgio Maggiore at Venice, and after
his return to Florence he formed three separate collections of
MSS.   While the hall of the Library of S. Marco was in
process of construction, Niccolo de' Niccoli died, in 1437,
bequeathing his 800 MSS., valued at 6,000 golden florins, to
sixteen trustees.   Among these were Cosimo and Lorenzo de'
Medici, Ambrogio Traversari, Lionardo Bruni, Carlo Marsuppini, Poggio Bracciolini, Giannozzo Manetti, and Franco
Sacchetti.   At the same time the estate of Niccolo was com-
promised by heavy debts.   These debts Cosimo cancelled,
obtaining in exchange the right to dispose of the library.   In
1441 the hall of the convent was finished.   Four hundred of
Niccolo's MSS. were placed there, with this inscription upon
each : *Ex hereditate doctissimi viri Nicolai de Nicolis de
Florentiâ*.   Tommaso Parentucelli made a catalogue at
Cosimo's request, in which he not only noted the titles of
Niccoli's books, but also marked the names of others wanting
to complete the collection.   This catalogue afterwards served
as a guide to the founders of the libraries of Fiesole, Urbino,
and Pesaro, and was, says Vespasiano, indispensable to book-
collectors.[3]   Of the remaining 400 volumes Cosimo kept some

---

[1] Vespasiano, pp. 29, 264.   [2] *Ibid*. pp. 34, 265.
[3] See Vespasiano's *Life of Nicholas V.* p. 26.

for his own (the Medicean) library, and some he gave to
friends. At the same time he spared no pains in adding to
the Marcian collection. His agents received instructions to
buy codices, while Vespasiano and Fra Giuliano Lapaccini
were employed in copying rare MSS. As soon as Cosimo had
finished building the Abbey of Fiesole, he set about providing
this also with a library suited to the wants of learned ecclesiastics. Of the method he pursued, Vespasiano, who acted as
his agent, has transmitted the following account : [1]—'One
day, when I was in his room, he said to me, "What plan can
you recommend for the formation of this library ? " I answered
that to buy the books would be impossible, since they could
not be purchased. "What, then, do you propose ? " he
added. I told him that they must be copied. He then asked
if I would undertake the business. I replied that I was
willing. He bade me begin at my leisure, saying that he left
all to me ; and for the monies wanted day by day, he ordered
that Don Arcangelo, at that time prior of the monastery,
should draw cheques upon his bank, which should be
honoured. After beginning the collection, since it was his
will that it should be finished with all speed possible, and
money was not lacking, I soon engaged forty-five copyists, and
in twenty-two months provided two hundred volumes, following the admirable list furnished by Pope Nicholas V.'
The two libraries thus formed by Cosimo for the Convents of
S. Marco and Fiesole, together with his own private collections, constitute the oldest portion of the present Laurentian
Library. On the title-pages of many venerable MSS. may
still be read inscriptions, testifying to the munificence of the
Medici, and calling upon pious students to remember the
souls of their benefactors in their prayers [2]—*Orato itaque
lector ut gloria et divitiæ sint in domo ejus justitia ejus et
maneat in sæculum sæculi.*

[1] *Vita di Cosimo,* p. 254.   [2] See Von Reumont, vol. i. p. 578.

Cosimo's zeal for learning was not confined to the building of libraries or to book-collecting. His palace formed the
centre of a literary and philosophical society, which united
all the wits of Florence and the visitors who crowded to the
capital of culture. Vespasiano expressly states that ' he was
always the father and benefactor of those who showed any
excellence.' [1]   Distinguished by versatility of tastes and comprehensive intellect, he formed his own opinion of the men of
eminence with whom he came in contact, and conversed with
each upon his special subject. ' When giving audience to a
scholar, he discoursed concerning letters ; in the company of
theologians he showed his acquaintance with theology, a
branch of learning always studied by him with delight. So
also with regard to philosophy. Astrologers found him well
versed in their science, for he somewhat lent faith to astrology
and employed it on certain private occasions. Musicians in
like manner perceived his mastery of music, wherein he much
delighted. The same was true about sculpture and painting ;
both of these arts he understood completely, and showed
great favour to all worthy craftsmen. In architecture he
was a consummate judge, for without his opinion and advice
no building was begun or carried to completion.' [2]

The discernment of character, possessed by Cosimo in a
very high degree, not only enabled him to extend enlightened
patronage to arts and letters, but also to provide for the future
needs of erudition. Stimulated by the presence of the Greeks
who crowded Florence during the sitting of the Council in
1438, he formed a plan for encouraging Hellenic studies. It
was he who founded the Platonic Academy, and educated
Marsilio Ficino, the son of his physician, for the special
purpose of interpreting Greek philosophy. Ficino, in a letter
to Lorenzo de' Medici, observes that during twelve years he

[1] *Vita di Cosimo*, p. 266.
Condensed from Vespasiano, p. 258.

had conversed with Cosimo on matters of philosophy, and always found him as acute in reasoning as he was prudent and powerful in action. 'I owe to Plato much, to Cosimo no less. He realised for me the virtues of which Plato gave me the conception.' Thus the man whose political cynicism is enshrined in such apophthegms as these :—'A few ells of scarlet would fill Florence with citizens;' 'You cannot govern a State with paternosters;' 'Better the city ruined than the city lost to us'—must, by his relations to scholars and his enthusiasm for culture, still command our admiration and respect.

Among the friends of Cosimo, to whose personal influence at Florence the Revival of Learning owed a vigorous impulse, Niccolo de' Niccoli claims our earliest attention.[1] The part he took in promoting Greek studies has been already noticed, and we have seen that his private library formed the nucleus of the Marcian collection. Of the eight hundred volumes bequeathed to his executors, the majority had been transcribed by his own hand; for he was assiduous in this labour, and plumed himself upon his skill in cursive as well as printed character.[2] His whole fortune was expended long before his death in buying manuscripts or procuring copies from a distance. 'If he heard of any book in Greek or Latin not to be had in Florence, he spared no cost in getting it ; the number of the Latin books which Florence owes entirely to his generosity cannot be reckoned.'[3] Great, therefore, must have been the transports of delight with which he welcomed on one occasion a manuscript containing seven tragedies of

[1] What follows I have based on Vespasiano's Life of Niccolo. Poggio's Funeral Oration, and his letter to Carlo Aretino on the death of his friend Niccolo, are to the same effect. *Poggii Opera*, pp. 270, 342.

[2] Vespasiano, p. 471. 'Le scriveva di sua mano o di lettera corsiva o formata, che dell' una lettera e dell' altra era bellissimo scrittore.'

[3] *Ibid.* p. 473.

Sophocles, six of Æschylus, and the 'Argonautica' of Apollonius
Rhodius.[1] Nor was he only eager in collecting for his own
use. He lent his books so freely that, at the moment of his
death, two hundred volumes were out on loan ;[2] and, when it
seemed that Boccaccio's library would perish from neglect, at
his own cost he provided substantial wooden cases for it in the
Convent of S. Spirito. We must not, however, conclude that
Niccolo was a mere copyist and collector. On the contrary,
he made a point of collating the several MSS. of an author
on whose text he was engaged, removed obvious errors, and
suggested emendations, helping thus to lay the foundations of
modern criticism. His judgment in matters of style was so
highly valued that it was usual for scholars to submit their
essays to his eyes before they ventured upon publication.
Thus Lionardo Bruni sent him his 'Life of Cicero,' calling him
' the censor of the Latin tongue.'[3] Notwithstanding his fine
sense of language, Niccolo never appeared before the world
of letters as an author. His enemies made the most of this
reluctance, averring that he knew his own ineptitude, while
his friends referred his silence to an exquisite fastidiousness of
taste.[4] It may have been that he remembered the Tacitean
epigram on Galba—*omnium consensu capax imperii nisi
imperásset*—and applied it to himself. Certainly his reserve,
in an age noteworthy for arrogant display, has tended to confer on him distinction. The position he occupied at Florence
was that of a literary dictator. All who needed his assistance
and advice were received with urbanity. He threw his house
open to young men of parts, engaged in disputations with the
curious, and provided the ill-educated with teachers. Foreigners from all parts of Italy and Europe paid him visits :
' the strangers who came to Florence at that time, if they

[1] See a letter of Ambrogio Traversari, quoted by Voigt, p. 155.
[2] Vespasiano, p. 476. Poggio, p. 271.
[3] Vespasiano, pp. 473, 478.   [4] *Ibid.* p. 478. Poggio, p. 343.

missed the opportunity of seeing him at home, thought they had not been in Florence.'[1] The house where he lived was worthy of his refined taste and cultivated judgment; for he had formed a museum of antiquities—inscriptions, marbles, coins, vases, and engraved gems. There he not only received students and strangers, but conversed with sculptors and painters, discussing their inventions as freely as he criticised the essays of the scholars. It is probable that the classicism of Brunelleschi and Donatello, both of whom were among his intimate friends, may be due in part at least to his discourses on the manner of the ancients.[2] Pliny, we know, was one of his favourite authors; for, having heard that a complete codex of the 'Natural Histories' existed at Lübeck, he left no stone unturned till it had been transferred to Florence.[3]

Vespasiano's account of his personal habits presents so vivid a picture that I cannot refrain from translating it at length:—'First of all, he was of a most fair presence; lively, for a smile was ever on his lips; and very pleasant in his talk. He wore clothes of the fairest crimson cloth, down to the ground. He never married, in order that he might not be impeded in his studies. A housekeeper provided for his daily needs. He was above all men the most cleanly in eating, as also in all other things. When he sat at table, he ate from fair antique vases; and, in like manner, all his table was covered with porcelain and other vessels of great beauty. The cup from which he drank was of crystal or of some other precious stone. To see him at table—a perfect model of the men of old—was of a truth a charming sight. He always willed that the napkins set before him should be of the whitest, as well as all the linen. Some might wonder at the many vases he possessed, to whom I answer that things of that sort were neither so highly valued then, nor so much regarded, as they

---

[1] Vespasiano, p. 477.   [2] *Ibid.* p. 479.
[3] *Ibid.* p. 474.

have since become ; and Niccolo having friends everywhere, anyone who wished to do him a pleasure would send him marble statues, or antique vases, carvings, inscriptions, pictures from the hands of distinguished masters, and mosaic tablets. He had a most beautiful map, on which all the parts and cities of the world were marked ; others of Italy and Spain, all painted. Florence could not show a house more full of ornaments than his, or one that had in it a greater number of graceful objects ; so that all who went there found innumerable things of worth to please varieties of taste.' What distinguished Niccolo was the combination of refinement and humane breeding with open-handed generosity and devotion to the cause of culture. He knew how to bring forward men of promise, and to place them in positions of eminence. Yet, in return for benefits conferred, he exacted more compliance than could be expected from the haughty and unbending temper of distinguished scholars. Opposition and contradiction roused his jealousy and barbed his caustic speech with sarcasm. Chrysoloras and Guarino, Aurispa and Filelfo, after visiting Florence at his invitation, found the city unendurable through the opposition raised by Niccolo against them.

Among the men of ability who adorned Florence at this period, no one stands forth with a more distinguished personality than Lionardo Bruni. In his boyhood at Arezzo, where his parents occupied a humble position, he used, as he tells us in his 'Commentaries,' [1] to gaze on Petrarch's portrait, fervently desiring that he might win like laurels in the field of scholarship. At first, however, being poor and of no reputation, he was forced to apply his talents to the study of the law. From these uncongenial labours the patronage of Salutato and the

---

[1] Muratori, xix. p. 917. 'Erat in ipso cubiculo picta Francisci Petrarchæ imago, quam ego quotidie aspiciens, incredibili ardore studiorum ejus incendebar.'

influence of Chrysoloras [1] saved him. Having begun to write
for the public, his fame as a Latinist soon spread so wide that
he was appointed Apostolic Secretary to the Roman Curia.
After sharing the ill fortunes of John XXIII. at Constance,
and serving under Martin V. at Florence, he was appointed
to the Chancery of the Republic in 1427, a post which he
occupied until his death in 1443. His biography, therefore,
illustrates all that has been said concerning the employment
of humanists in high offices of Church and State. His diplomatic letters were regarded as models in that kind of composition, and his public speeches, carefully prepared before-
hand, were compared with those of Pericles. Florence was
crowded with the copyists who multiplied his MSS., dispersing
them all over Europe ; and when he walked abroad, a numerous
train of scholars and of foreigners attended him. [2] He moved
with gravity and majesty of person, wearing the red robes
of a Florentine burgher, using few words, but paying marked
courtesy to men of wealth. Among the compositions which
secured his reputation should first be mentioned the Latin
'History of Florence,' a work unique in its kind at that time
in Italy. [3] The grateful Republic rewarded their chancellor
by bestowing upon him the citizenship of Florence, and by
exempting the author and his children from taxation. The
high value at which Bruni rated his own Latin scholarship
is proved by his daring to restore the second Decade of Livy
in a compilation entitled 'De Primo Bello Punico.' His
mediæval erudition was exercised in the history of the Gothic
invasion of Italy, while his more elegant style found ample
scope in Latin Lives of Cicero and Aristotle, in a book of Commentaries on his own times, and in ten volumes of Collected
Letters. These original works were possibly of less importance than Bruni's translations from the Greek, which passed

[1] See above, pp. 77, 80.   [2] See Vespasiano, p. 436
[3] See Vol. I., *Age of Despots*, pp. 216–218.

in his own age for models of sound scholarship as well as pure
Latinity.　The erudition of the fifteenth century had to thank
his industry for critical renderings of Aristotle's 'Ethics,'
'Politics,' and 'Economics.'[1]　The 'Politics' were dedicated to
the Earl of Worcester, and the autograph was sent to England.
Some delay in the acknowledgment of so magnificent a tribute
of respect caused the haughty scholar to transfer the honour
of his dedication to Eugenius IV.　He cancelled his first preface, substituted a new one, and received the praise and thanks
he sought, in plenty from his Holiness.[2]　Of Plato Bruni translated the 'Phædo,' 'Crito,' and 'Apology,' the 'Phædrus' and
the 'Gorgias,' together with the 'Epistles.'　To these versions
must be added six Lives of Plutarch and two Orations of
Demosthenes.　Nor have we thus by any means exhausted the
list of Bruni's Latin compositions, which included controversial writings, invectives, moral essays, orations, and tracts
on literary or antiquarian topics.　If we consider that, in the
midst of these severe labours, and under the pressure of his
public engagements, he still found time to compose Italian
Lives of Dante and Petrarch, we shall understand the admiration universally expressed by his contemporaries for his comprehensive talents, and share their gratitude for services so
numerous in the cause of learning.　When Messer Lionardo
died in 1443, the priors decreed him a public funeral, 'after the
manner of the ancients.'　His corpse was clothed in dark silk,
and on his breast was laid a copy of the Florentine History.
Thus attired, he passed in state to S. Croce, where Giannozzo
Manetti, in the presence of the Signory, the foreign ambassadors,
and the Court of Pope Eugenius, pronounced a funeral oration,
and placed the laurel crown upon his head.[3]　The monument

[1] These last were then thought genuine.
[2] Vespasiano, p. 436.
[3] *Ibid. Vita di Manetti*, p. 452.　Manetti was himself a prior at this
time.

beneath which Messer Lionardo's bones repose is an excellent specimen of Florentine sepulchral statuary, executed by
Bernardo Rossellino.

Facing Bruni's tomb in S. Croce is that of Carlo Aretino,
wrought with subtler art and in a richer style by Desiderio da
Settignano.   Messer Carlo, who succeeded Bruni in the Chancery of the Republic, shared during his lifetime, as well as in
the public honours paid him at his death, very similar fortunes.
His family name was Marsuppini, and he was born of a good
family in Arezzo.   Having come to Florence while a youth to
study Greek, he fell under the notice of Niccolo de' Niccoli,
who introduced him to the Medicean family, and procured
him an engagement at a high salary from the Uffiziali dello
Studio.   At the time when he began to lecture, Eugenius was
holding his Court at Florence.   The cardinals and nephews
of the Pope, attended by foreign ambassadors, and followed
by the apostolic secretaries, mingled with burghers of
Florence and students from a distance round the desk of the
young scholar.   Carlo's reading was known to be extensive,
and his memory was celebrated as prodigious.   Yet on the
occasion of this first lecture he far surpassed all that was
expected of him.   'Before a crowd of learned men,' says
Vespasiano, 'he gave a great proof of his memory, for neither
Greeks nor Romans had an author from whom he did not
quote.'[1]   Filelfo, who was also lecturing in Florence at the
time, had the mortification of seeing the larger portion of
his audience transfer themselves to Marsuppini.   This wound
to his vanity he never forgave.   Through the influence of
Lorenzo de' Medici (Cosimo's younger brother), Carlo
Marsuppini was first made Apostolic Secretary, and then
promoted to the Chancery of Florence.   He was grave in
manner, taciturn in speech, and much given to melancholy.
His contemporaries regarded him as a man of no religion,

[1] *Vita di Carlo d' Arezzo*, p. 440.

and he was said to have died without confession or communion.[1] This did not prevent his being buried in S. Croce with ceremonies similar to those decreed for Messer Lionardo. Matteo Palmieri pronounced the funeral oration, and placed the laurel on his brows. Marsuppini's contributions to scholarship were chiefly in verse ; among these his translations of the ' Batrachomyomachia ' and the first book of the ' Iliad ' were highly valued.

Matteo Palmieri, who pronounced the funeral oration of Messer Carlo Aretino, sprang from an honourable Florentine stock, and by his own abilities rose to a station of considerable public influence. He is principally famous as the author of a mystical poem called ' Città di Vita,' which, though it was condemned for its heretical opinions, obtained from Ficinus for its author the title of *Poeta Theologicus*. To discuss the circumstances under which this allegory in the style of Dante was composed, the secresy in which it was involved until the poet's death, and the relation of Palmieri's views to heresies in vogue at Florence, belongs to a future section of my work.[2] He claims a passing notice here among the humanists who acquired high place and honour by the credit of his eloquence and style.

Giannozzo Manetti belonged to an illustrious house, and in his youth, like other well-born Florentines, was trained for mercantile affairs.[3] At the age of five-and-twenty he threw off the parental control, and gave himself entirely to letters. So obstinate was his industry in the acquisition of knowledge, that he allowed himself only five hours of sleep, and spent the

[1] See Tiraboschi, tom. vi. p. 1094.
[2] See Vespasiano, p. 500. Tiraboschi, vol. vi. p. 678. App. iii. to vol. v. of this work.
[3] The sources for Manetti's Life are Vespasiano and an anonymous Latin biography in Muratori. Besides the small Life of Vespasiano in his *Vite d' Uomini Illustri*, I have had recourse to his *Comentario della Vita di Gianozo Manetti*, Turin, 1862.

rest of his life in study. During nine whole years he never crossed the Arno, but remained within the walls of his house and garden, which communicated with the Convent of S. Spirito. Being passionately fond of disputation, he sought his chief amusement there in the debating society founded by Marsigli. Ambrogio Traversari was his master in Greek. Latin he had no difficulty in acquiring, and soon gained such facility in its exercise that even Lionardo Bruni is said to have envied his fluency. He was not, however, contented with these languages, and in order to perfect himself in Hebrew he kept a Jew in his own house.[1] When he had acquired sufficient familiarity with Hebrew, he turned the arms supplied him by his tutors against their heresies, basing his arguments upon such interpretations of texts as his superior philology suggested to him. The great work of his literary leisure was a polemical discourse 'Contra Judæos et Gentes,' for, unlike Marsuppini, he placed his erudition solely at the service of the Christian faith. Another fruit of his Hebrew studies was a new translation of the Psalms from the original.

Manetti was far from being a mere student. During the best years of his life he was continually employed as ambassador to the Republic at Venice, Naples, Rome, and other Courts of Italy. He administered the government of Pescia, Pistoja, and Scarparia in times of great difficulty, winning a singular reputation for probity and justice. On all occasions of state his eloquence made him indispensable to the Signory, while the lists of his writings include numerous speeches upon varied topics addressed to potentates and princes throughout Italy.[2] There is a curious story related in his Life, which illustrates the importance attached at this time to public

[1] 'Tenne in casa dua Greci et uno Ebreo che s'era fatto Cristiano, et non voleva che il Greco parlasse con lui se non in greco, et il simile il Ebreo in ebreo.'—*Comentario*, p. 11.

[2] 'Se ignuna cosa difficile o cura disperata, la davano a Messer Gianozo.'—*Ibid.* p. 22.

speaking.   After the coronation of the Emperor Frederick III.,
the Florentines sent fifteen ambassadors, including Manetti,
attended by the Chancellor Carlo Aretino, to congratulate
him.   Manetti was a Colleague of the Signory, and on him
would therefore have naturally fallen the fulfilment of the
task, had not this honour been conferred, by private machina-
tions of the Medicean family, on Carlo.   The Chancellor duly
delivered a prepared oration, which was answered by Æneas
Sylvius in the name of the Emperor.   Some topics raised in
this reply required rejoinder from the Florentines ; but Messer
Carlo declared himself unable to speak without previous study.
To be forced to hold their tongues before the Emperor and
all his suite was a bitter humiliation to the men of Florence.
How could they return home and confess that the rhetoric of
their Chancellor had been silenced by a witty secretary ?   In
their sore distress they besought Manetti to help them ; whereupon he rose and delivered an extempore oration.   ' When it was
finished,' says Vespasiano,[1] ' all competent judges who understood Latin, and could follow it, declared that Messer Gian-
nozzi's extempore speech was superior to that which Messer
Carlo had prepared.'

The Latin Life of Manetti contains innumerable instances
of the miracles wrought by his rhetoric.[2]   Yet we should err
if we imagined that the speeches pronounced upon solemn
occasions, by even such illustrious orators as Manetti or
Pius II., were marked by any of the nobler qualities of
eloquence.[3]   They consist of commonplaces freely interspersed
with historical examples and voluminous quotations.   Without charm, without originality, they survive as monuments of

[1] *Vita di Gianozo Manetti*, p. 462.   Compare Burckhardt, p. 182.
There is another story, told in the *Comentario*, of Manetti's speaking
before Alfonso at Naples.   The King remained so quiet that he did not
even brush the flies from his face.   P. 90.

[2] Muratori, vol. xx.

[3] For Pius II.'s reputation see Burckhardt, **p. 182.**

the enthusiasm of that age for classic erudition, and of the patience with which popes and princes lent their ears for two or three hours at a stretch to the self-complacent mouthings of a pompous pedant.

Giannozzo Manetti became at last so great a power in Florence that he excited the jealousy of the Medicean party. They ruined him by the imposition of extravagant taxes, and he was obliged to end his life an exile from his native land.[1] Florence never behaved worse to a more blameless citizen; for Manetti, by his cheerful acceptance of public burdens, by his prudence in the discharge of weighty offices, by the piety and sobriety of his private life, by his vast acquirements, and by the single-hearted zeal with which he burned for learning, had proved himself the model of such men as might have saved the State, if safety had been possible. He retired to the Court of Nicholas V., who had previously named him Apostolic Secretary; and on the death of that Pope he sought a final refuge with Alfonso at Naples.[2] There he devoted himself entirely to literature, translating the whole of the New Testament and the ethical treatises of Aristotle into Latin, and carrying his great controversial work against the Jews and Gentiles onwards to completion.

Few men deserve a higher place on the muster-roll of Italian worthies than Manetti. He was free from many vices of the Renaissance; his piety and morality remaining untainted by the contact with antiquity. Nor did he sink the citizen in the student. His learning was varied and profound. Instead of applying himself to Greek and Latin scholarship alone, he mastered Hebrew, and sought to acquire a comprehensive grasp of all the knowledge of the ancient world. At the same time he lived in constant sympathy with his age, sharing its

[1] Vespasiano, p. 465. Muratori, xx. 600.
[2] Alfonso gave him a pension of 900 scudi. He wrote a history of his life and deeds.

delight in rhetorical displays and wordy disputations, and
furthering the diffusion of knowledge by his toil as a translator.
It may well be wondered how it happens that a man in many
points akin to Pico should have fallen so far short of him in
fame. The explanation lies in this : Manetti was deficient
in all that elevates mere learning to the rank of art. His
Latin style was tedious ; his thoughts were commonplace.
When the influence of his voice and person passed away,
nothing remained to prove his eloquence but ill-digested facts
and ill-applied citations. Still the work which he effected in
his day was good, and the place he held was honourable.
Posterity may be grateful to him as one of the most active
pioneers of modern culture.

A man of different stamp and calling claims attention
next. Ambrogio Traversari was far from sharing the neopagan
impulse of the classical revival ; yet he owed political influence
and a high place among the leaders of his age to humanistic
enthusiasm. Born in Romagna, and admitted while yet a
child into the Convent degli Angeli at Florence, he gave early
signs of his capacity for literature. At a time when knowledge
of Greek was still a rare title to distinction,[1] Ambrogio
mastered the elements of the language and studied the Greek
Fathers in the original. His cell became the meeting-place
of learned men, where Cosimo and Lorenzo de' Medici, the
stately Bruni and the sombre Marsuppini, joined with caustic
Niccoli and lively Poggio in earnest conversation. His voluminous correspondence connected him with students in all
parts of Italy ; nor was there any important discovery of MSS.
or plan for library or university in which he did not take his
part among the first.

It seemed as though he were destined to pursue a peace-

---

[1] Niccolo de' Niccoli, it must be remembered, was not a Grecian.
Ambrogio used to insert the Greek words into his transcripts of Latin
codices.

ful student's life among his books; and for this career nature had marked out the little, meagre, lively, and laborious man. To be eminent in scholarship, however, and to avoid the burdens of celebrity, was impossible in that age. Eugenius IV., while resident in Florence, was so impressed with his literary eminence and strength of character that he made him General of the Camaldolese Order in 1431; and from this time forward Traversari's life was divided between public duties, for which he was scarcely fitted, and private studies that absorbed his deepest interests. He presented the curious spectacle of a monk distracted between the scruples of the cloister and the wider claims of humanism, who showed one mind to his Order and another to his literary friends. He made a point of never citing heathen poets in his writings, as though the verses of Homer or of Virgil were inconsistent with the sobriety of a Christian; yet his anxiety to round his style with Ciceronian phrases, and to bequeath models of pure Latinity in his epistles to posterity, proved how much he valued literary graces. Having vowed to consecrate his talents to the services of ecclesiastical learning, he undertook the translation of Diogenes Laertius, at Cosimo's request, with reluctance, and performed the task with bitter self-bemoaning. In his person we witness the conflict of the humanistic spirit with ecclesiastical tradition—a conflict in which the former was destined to achieve a complete and memorable victory.

These men—Niccoli, Bruni, Marsuppini, Manetti, and Traversari—formed the literary oligarchy who surrounded Cosimo de' Medici, and through their industry and influence restored the studies of antiquity at Florence. While they were carrying on the work of revival, each in his own sphere, with impassioned energy, a combination of external circumstances gave fresh impulse to their activity. Eugenius IV., having been expelled from Rome in 1434, had fixed his headquarters in Florence, whither in 1438 he transferred the

Council which had first been opened at Ferrara for negotiating the union of the Greek and Latin Churches. The Emperor of the East, John Palæologus, surrounded by his theologians and scribes, together with the Pope of Rome, on whom a train of cardinals and secretaries attended, now took up their quarters in the city of the Medici. A temporary building at Santa Maria Novella was erected for the sessions of the Council, and for several months Florence entertained as guests the chiefs of the two great sections of Christendom. Unimportant as were the results, both political and ecclesiastical, of this Council, the meeting of the Eastern and the Western powers in conclave vividly impressed the imagination of the Florentines, and communicated a more than transient impulse to their intellectual energies. Italy was on the eve of becoming not only the depositary of Greek learning, but also the sole interpreter of the Greek spirit to the modern world. Fifteen years after the closing of the Council, the thread which had connected Byzantium with Athens through an unbroken series of historical traditions, was snapped; already it was beginning to be felt in Europe that nothing but the ghost of Greek culture survived upon the shores of the Bosphorus, and that if the genius of antiquity was to illuminate the modern world, the light must dawn in Italy.[1]

The feelings with which the Florentines regarded their Greek guests were strangely mingled. While honouring them as the last scions of the noblest nation of the past, as the authentic teachers of Hellenic learning and the masters of the Attic tongue, they despised their empty vanity, their facile apostasy, their trivial pedantry, their personal absurdities. The long beards, trailing mantles, painted eyebrows, and fantastic headgear of the Byzantine sophists moved the

[1] See the emphatic words of Poliziano, quoted by Voigt, p. 189, on the revival of extinct Hellenism by the Florentines, and on their fluent command of the Attic idiom.

laughter of the common folk, accustomed to the grave and simple *lucco* of their own burghers. In vain did Vespasiano tell them that this costume descended from august antiquity through fifteen centuries of unchanged fashion.[1] The more educated citizens, again, soon discovered that the erudition of these strangers was but shallow, and that their magnificent pretensions reduced themselves to the power of speaking the emasculated Greek, which formed their mother tongue, with fluency. The truth is that, however necessary the Byzantines were at the very outset of the Revival of Learning, Greek studies owed less to their traditional lore than to the curiosity of Italian scholars. The beggarly elements of grammar, caligraphy, and bibliographical knowledge were supplied by the Greeks ; but it was not Chrysoloras even, nor yet Argyropoulos, so much as Ficino and Aldo, Palla degli Strozzi and Cosimo de' Medici, who opened the literature of Athens to the comprehension of the modern world.

Some exceptions must be made to these remarks; for it is not certain that, without guidance, the Florentines would have made that rapid progress in philosophical studies which contrasts so singularly with their comparative neglect of the Attic dramatists. Gemistos Plethon in particular stands forth as a man who combined real knowledge with natural eloquence, and who materially affected the whole course of the Renaissance by directing the intelligence of the Florentines to Plato. Inasmuch as Plethon's residence in Italy during the session of the Council formed a decisive epoch in the Revival of Learning, to pass him by without some detailed notice would be to omit one of the most interesting episodes in the history of the fifteenth century. At the same time, his biography so well illustrates the state of thought in the Greek Empire at the moment of its fall, as well as the speculations which inte-

---

[1] See the curious passage in the *Vita di Eugenio IV.*, *Papa*, p. 14.

rested philosophic intellects at that period in Italy, that I trust the following digression will be judged excusable.

Georgios Gemistos was born of noble parents at Byzantium about the year 1355.[1] During a long lifetime, chiefly spent in the Morea, he witnessed all the miseries that racked his country through its lingering agony of a hundred years, and died at last in 1450, just before the final downfall of the Greek Empire. Of his early life little is known beyond the fact that he left Constantinople as a young man in order to study philosophy at Brusa. Brusa and Adrianopolis, at that time the two Western seats of the Mahommedan power, outrivalled Byzantium in culture, while the mental vigour of the Mussulmans was far in advance of that of their effete neighbours. The young Greek, who seems already to have lost his faith in Christianity, was attracted to the Moslem Court by Elissaios, a sage of Jewish birth. From this teacher he learned what then passed for the doctrines of Zoroaster. After quitting Brusa, Gemistos settled at Mistra in the Peloponnese, upon the site of ancient Sparta, where with some interruptions he continued to reside until his death. The Greek Emperor was still nominally lord of the Morea, though the conquests of Frankish Crusaders and the incursions of the Turks had rendered his rule feeble. Gemistos, who enjoyed the confidence of the Imperial House, was made a judge at Mistra, and thus obtained clear insight into the causes of the decadence of the Hellenic race upon its ancient soil. The picture he draws of the anarchy and immorality of the peninsula is frightful. He also professed philosophy, and at the age of thirty-three became a teacher of repute. The views he formed concerning the corruption of the Greek Church and the degradation of the Greek people, combined with his

[1] I owe the greater part of the facts presented in this sketch of Gemistos to Fritz Schultze's *Geschichte der Philosophie der Renaissance*, vol. i.

philosophical opinions, inspired him with the visionary ambition of reforming the creed, the ethics, and the political conditions of Hellas on a Pagan basis. There is something ludicrous as well as sad in the spectacle of this sophist, nourishing the vain fancy that he might coin a complete religious system, which should supersede Christianity and restore vigour to the decayed body of the Greek Empire. In the dotage of Hellenism Gemistos discovered no new principle of vitality, but returned to the speculative mysticism of the Neoplatonists. Their attempt at a Pagan revival had failed long ago in Alexandria, while force still remained to the Greek race, and while the Christian Church was still comparatively ill-assured. To propose it as a panacea in the year 1400 for the evils of the Empire threatened by the Turks was mere childishness. Perhaps it is doing the sage injustice to treat his system seriously. Charity prompts us to regard it as a plaything invented for the amusement of his leisure hours. Yet nothing can be graver than his own language and that of his disciples.

The work in which he embodied his doctrine was called 'The Laws'—ἡ τῶν νόμων συγγραφή, or simply νόμοι. It comprised a metaphysical system, the outlines of a new religion, an elaborate psychology and theory of ethics, and a scheme of political administration. According to his notions, there is one Supreme God, Zeus, the absolute and eternal reality, existing as homogeneous and undiscriminated Being, Will, Activity, and Power. Zeus begets everlasting Ideas, or Gods of the second order ; and these gods, to whom Gemistos gave the name of Greek divinities, constitute a hierarchy corresponding to the abstract notions of his logic. With the object of harmonising the double series of immortal and mortal existences they are subdivided, by a singularly clumsy contrivance, into genuine and spurious children of Zeus. First among the genuine sons stands Poseidon, the idea of ideas, the logical *summum genus*, who includes within him-self the intellectual universe potentially. Next in rank is Hera, the female deity, created immediately by Zeus, but by a second act, and therefore inferior to Poseidon. These two are the primordial authors of the world as it exists. After them come three series, each of five deities, whereof the first set, including Apollo, Artemis, Hephæstus, Dionysus, and Athena, represent the most general categories. The second set, among whom we find Atlas and Pluto, are the ideas of im-mortal substance existing for ever in the world of living beings. The third, which reckons among others Hecate and Hestia, are the ideas of immortal substance existing for ever in the inanimate world. Next in the descending order come the spurious offspring of Zeus, or Titans, two of whom, Cronos and Aphrodite, are the ideas respectively of form and matter in things subject to decay and dissolution; while Koré, Pan, and Demeter are the specific ideas of men, beasts, and plants. Hitherto we have been recording the genealogy of divine beings subject to no laws of time or change, who are, in fact, pure thoughts or logical entities. We arrive in the last place at deities of the third degree, the genuine and the spurious children, no longer of Zeus, but of Poseidon, chieftain of the second order of the hierarchy. The planets and the fixed stars constitute the higher of these inferior powers, while the dæmons fill the lowest class of all. At the very bottom of the scale, below the gods of every quality, stand men, beasts, plants, and the inorganic world.

It will be perceived that this scheme is bastard Neo-platonism—a mystical fusion of Greek mythology and Greek logic, whereby the products of speculative analysis are hypo-stasised as divine persons. Of many difficulties patent in his doctrine Gemistos offered no solution. How, for example, can we ascribe to Zeus the procreation of spurious as well as genuine offspring? It is possible that the philosopher, if questioned on such topics, would have fallen back on the convenient theory of progressively diminished efficacy in the creative act; for though he guards against adopting the hypothesis of emanation, it is clear, from the simile of multiplied reflections in a series of mirrors, which he uses to explain the genealogy of gods, that some such conception modified his views. To point out the insults offered to the ancient myths, whereof he made such liberal and arbitrary use, or to insist upon the folly of the whole conceit, considered as the substance of a creed which should regenerate the world, would be superfluous; nothing can be more grotesque, for instance, than the personification of identity and self-determining motion under the titles of Apollo and Dionysus, nor any confusion more fatal than the attribution of sex to categories of the understanding. The sole merit of the system consists in the classification of notions, the conception of an intellectual hierarchy, descending by interdependent stages from the primordial cause through pure ideas to their copies and material manifestations in the world of things. Dreams of this kind have always haunted the metaphysical imagination, giving rise to hybrids between poetry and logic; and the system of Gemistos may fairly take rank among a hundred similar attempts between the days of Plato and of Hegel.

Such as it was, his metaphysic supplied Gemistos with the basis of a cult, a psychology, a theory of ethics, and a political programme. He founded a sect, and was called by his esoteric followers 'the mystagogue of sublime and celestial dogmas.'[1] They believed that the soul of Plato had been reincarnated in their master, and that the new creed, professed by him, would supersede the faiths existing in the world. Among the most distinguished of these neophytes was the famous Bessarion, who adopted so much at any rate of his teacher's doctrine as rendered him indifferent to the

points at issue between the Greek and Latin Churches, when
a cardinal's hat was offered as the price of his apostasy.
Bessarion, however, was too much a man of the world to
dream that Gemistos would triumph over Christ and
Mahomet.[1] While using the language of the mystic, and
recording his conviction that Plato's soul, released from the
body of Gemistos, had joined the choir of the Olympian
deities,[2] it is probable that he was only playing, after the
fashion of his age, with speculations that amused his fancy
though they took no serious hold upon his life. It was a
period, we must remember, when scholars affected the manners of the antique world, Latinised their names, and
adopted fantastic titles in their academics and learned clubs.
At no time of the world's history has this kind of masquerad-
ing attained to so much earnestness of rather more than half-
belief. The attitude assumed by Gemistos and his disciples
is, therefore, not without its value for illustrating the intellectual conditions of the earlier Renaissance. Practical religion
had but little energy among the educated classes. The
interests of the Church were more political than spiritual.
Science had not yet asserted her real rights in any sphere of
thought. Art and literature, invigorated by the passion for
antiquity, meanwhile absorbed the genius of the Italians; and
through a dim æsthetic haze the waning lights of Hellas
mingled with the dayspring of the modern world.

The most important event of Gemistos's life was the
journey which he took to Italy in the train of John Palæologus
in 1438. Secretly disliking Christianity in general, and the
Latin form of it in particular, he had endeavoured to dissuade
the emperor from attending the Council. Now he found
himself elected as one of the six champions of the cause of
the Greek Church. For the subtle Greek intellect in that
dotage of a doomed civilisation, no greater interest survived

[1] See Schultze, p. 77, note.   [2] Ibid. p. 107.

than could be found in dialectic ; and to dispute about the *filioque* of the Christian creed was fair sport, when no chance offered itself of forcing rationalistic Paganism down the throat of popes and cardinals. Therefore it is probable that Gemistos did not find his position at the Council peculiarly irksome, even though he had to listen to reasonings about purgatory and the procession of the Holy Ghost, and to suggest arguments in favour of the Eastern dogma, while in his inmost soul he equally despised the combatants on either side.

The effect he produced outside the Council was far more flattering than the part he had to play within the walls of Santa Maria Novella. Instead of power-loving ecclesiastics and pig-headed theologians, anxious only to extend their privileges and establish their supremacy, he found a multitude of sympathetic and enthusiastic listeners. The Florentines were just then in the first flush of their passion for Greek study. Plato, worshipped as an unknown god, whose rising would dispel the mists of scholastic theology, was upon the lips of every student. Men were thirsting for the philosophy that had the charm of poetry, that delighted the imagination while it fortified the understanding, and that lent its glamour to the dreams and yearnings of a youthful age. What they wanted, Gemistos possessed in abundance. From the treasures of a memory stored with Platonic, Pythagorean, and Alexandrian mysticism he poured forth copious streams of indiscriminate erudition. The ears of his audience were open ; their intellects were far from critical. They accepted the gold and dross of his discourse alike as purest metal. Hanging upon the lips of the eloquent, grave, beautiful old man, who knew so much that they desired to learn, they called him Socrates and Plato in their ecstasy. It was during this visit to Florence that he adopted the name of Plethon, which, while it played upon Gemistos, had in it the

ring of his great master's surname.[1]   The devotion of his
Greek disciples bore no comparison with the popularity he
acquired among Italians ; and he had the satisfaction of being
sure that the seed of Platonic philosophy sown by him would
spring up in the rich soil of those powerful and eager minds.
Cosimo de' Medici, convinced of the importance of Platonic
studies by his conversations with Gemistos, founded the
famous Florentine Academy, and designated the young
Marsilio Ficino for the special task of translating and explaining the Platonic writings.[2]   When we call to mind the
influence which the Platonic Academy of Florence, through
Ficino and Pico della Mirandola, exerted over the whole
thought of Italy, and, through Reuchlin and his pupil
Melanchthon, over that of Germany, we are able to estimate
the impulse given by Gemistos to the movement of the
fifteenth century.   It may be added that Platonic studies
in Italy never recovered from the impress of Neoplatonic
mysticism which proceeded from his mind.

While resident in Florence he published two treatises on
Fate and on the differences between Plato and Aristotle.   The
former was an anti-Christian work, in so far as it denied the
freedom of arbitrary activity to God as well as men.   The
latter raised a controversy in Italy and Greece, which long
survived its author, exercising the scholars of the Renaissance
to some purpose on the texts and doctrines of the chief great

---

[1] Γεμιστός and γεμίζω, Πλήθων and πλήθω. Both mean to be full.
Plato, however, is said to have been called Πλάτων, because of his broad
shoulders or his breadth of eloquence.

[2] See the translation of Plotinus by Ficino, quoted by Schultze, p. 76 :
‘ Magnus Cosmus, Senatûs consulto patriæ pater, quo tempore concilium
inter Græcos atque Latinos sub Eugenio pontifice Florentiæ tractabatur,
philosophum Græcum nomine Gemistum, cognomine Plethonem quasi
Platonem alterum, de mysteriis Platonicis disputantem frequenter
audivit.   E cujus ore ferventi sic afflatus est protinus, sic animatus, ut
inde Academiam quandam altâ mente conceperit, hanc opportuno
primum tempore pariturus.’

thinkers of antiquity. Gemistos attacked Aristotle in general for atheism and irreligious morality, while he proved that the Platonic system, as interpreted by him, was deeply theological. Without entering into the details of a dispute that continued to rage for many years, and aroused the bitterest feelings on both sides, it is enough to observe that Aristotle had for centuries been regarded as the pillar of orthodoxy in the Latin Church, while Plato supplied eclectic thinkers with a fair cloak for rationalistic speculations and theistic heresies. The opponents of Aristotle were undermining the foundations of the time-honoured scholastic fabric. The opponents of Plato accused his votaries of drowning the Christianity they pretended to maintain, in a vague ocean of heretical mysticism. It is indeed difficult to understand how Ficino, who worshipped Plato no less fervently than Christ, could avoid reducing Christianity to the level of Paganism, while he attempted to demonstrate that the Platonic system contained the essence of the Christian faith. This was, in fact, nothing less than abandoning the exclusive pretensions of revealed religion and the authority of the Church.

Before the year 1441 Gemistos had returned to Mistra, where he continued to exercise his magistracy. His old age was embittered by the fierce attacks directed by Gennadios,[1] afterwards Patriarch of Constantinople, against the esoteric doctrines of the Νόμοι. Gennadios accused him roundly of Paganism, continuing his polemic against the book long after the death of its author. That event happened in 1450. Gemistos was buried at Mistra; but five years later Sigismondo Pandolfo Malatesta, moved by ardent love of learning and by veneration for the philosopher, exhumed his bones, and transferred them to the Church of S. Francesco at Rimini, which Leo Alberti had but recently built for him.[2]

[1] Schultze, p. 92. His secular name was Georgios Scholarios.
[2] See Vol. I., *Age of the Despots*, pp. 134, 135, and *Sketches in Italy and Greece*, article ' Rimini.'

Of Bessarion I shall have to speak elsewhere; but, in order to complete the review of Greek studies in Florence at this epoch, mention must now be made of two Greeks who filled the chair of the University with distinguished success.

That John Argyropoulos, a native of Byzantium, visited Italy before the fall of the Greek Empire, appears from Vespasiano's account of his residence with Palla Strozzi at Padua during the first years of his exile.[1] In 1456 Cosimo called him to Florence, secured him good appointments from the *studio pubblico*, and installed him as public and private teacher of Greek language and philosophy. Argyropoulos laboured at Florence for a space of fifteen years, counting the most distinguished citizens among his pupils. From Florence he removed to Rome, where Reuchlin heard him lecture upon Thucydides in the pontificate of Sixtus IV. Reuchlin's scholarship, if we may trust Melanchthon, was rated at so high a value by this master that, on his departure from Rome, he exclaimed, 'Now hath Greece flown beyond the Alps!' A more commanding personage than Argyropoulos was Georgios Trapezuntios, who came to Italy as early as 1420, and professed Greek at Venice, Florence, Rome, and other cities. His temper was proud, choleric, and quarrelsome; but the history of his disputes belongs to the next chapter, which will treat of Rome. I may here mention that, during the residence of the Papal Court at Florence, he gave instruction both public and private,[2] without, however, entering into intimacy with the Medicean circle. After Manuel Chrysoloras, it can be said with certainty that the revival of Hellenism in the fifteenth century at Florence was due to the three men of whom I have been speaking—Georgios Gemistos, Joannes Argyropoulos, and Georgios Trapezuntios. Of the labours of the last in Rome, as well as of Theodoros Gaza,

---

[1] *Vita di Palla di Noferi Strozzi*, p. 284.
[2] See Vespasiano, p. 436.

Demetrius Chalcondylas, Andronicus Callistus and the Lascari, it is not yet time to speak in detail. Each deserves a separate commemoration, since to their joint activity in teaching, Europe owes Greek scholarship.[1]

Before passing from Florence to Rome, which at this time formed the second centre of Italian humanism, something should be said about the state of learning in the other republics. The causes that decided the pre-eminence of Florence have been already touched upon. It is enough to observe here that, while the Universities of Bologna, Siena, and Perugia engaged professors of eloquence at high salaries, the literary enthusiasm of those cities was in no way comparable to that of Florence. Their culture depended on the illustrious visitors who fixed their residence from time to time within their walls. Genoa remained almost dead to learning. At Venice the study of the classics engaged the attention of a few nobles, without permeating the upper classes or giving a decided tone to society at large. Though the illustrious Greek refugees made it their custom to halt for a season at Venice, while nearly all Italian teachers of note lectured there on short engagements, it is none the less true that the Venetians were backward to encourage literature. They opened no public libraries, made no efforts to retain the services of scholars for the State, and regarded the pretensions of the humanists with cold contempt. In letters, as in the fine arts, Venice waited till the rest of Italy had blossomed. Bembo succeeded to Poliziano, as Titian to Raphael. Much good, however, was done by men like the Giustiniani and Paolo Zane, who furnished young students with the means of visiting Constantinople, and who provided them with professorial chairs on their return. The *gentiluomini* could also count among their number Francesco Barbaro, no less distinguished

[1] See long lists in Tiraboschi, vol. vi. pp. 812, 822 837, of foreign and Italian Grecians.

by his knowledge of both learned languages than by the correspondence he maintained with all the scholars of his time. While yet a young man, he had imbibed the Florentine spirit in the house of Cosimo de' Medici. On his return to Venice he studied under the best masters, and soon attained such excellence of style that Poggio compared his treatise on marriage to the ' De Officiis ' of Cicero. The Republic of Venice, however, demanded more of patriotic service from her high-born citizens than the commonwealth of Florence; and Barbaro had to spend his life in the discharge of grave State duties, finding little leisure for the cultivation of his literary talents. It remained for him to win the fame of a Mæcenas, who, had he chosen, might have disputed laurels with the ablest of the scholars he protected.

CHAPTER V

SECOND PERIOD OF HUMANISM

Transition from Florence to Rome—Vicissitudes of Learning at the
Papal Court — Diplomatic Humanists — Protonotaries — Apostolic
Scribes—Ecclesiastical Sophists—Immorality and Artificiality of
Scholarship in Rome—Poggio and Bruni, Secretaries—Eugenius IV.
—His Patronage of Scholars—Flavio Biondo—Solid Erudition—
Nicholas V.—His Private History—Nature of his Talents—His
unexpected Elevation to the Roman See — Jubilation of the
Humanists—His Protection of Learned Men in Rome—A Workshop
of Erudition—A Factory of Translations—High Sums paid for
Literary Labour—Poggio Fiorentino—His Early Life—His Journeys
—His Eminence as a Man of Letters—His Attitude toward Ecclesias-
tics—His Invectives—Humanistic Gladiators—Poggio and Filelfo—
Poggio and Guarino—Poggio and Valla—Poggio and Perotti—Poggio
and Georgius Trapezuntios—Literary Scandals—Poggio's Collections
of Antiquities—Chancellor of Florence—Cardinal Bessarion—His
Library—Theological Studies—Apology for Plato—The Greeks in
Italy—Humanism at Naples—Want of Culture in Southern Italy—
Learning an Exotic—Alfonso the Magnificent—Scholars in the
Camp—Literary Dialogues at Naples—Antonio Beccadelli—'The
Hermaphroditus'—Lorenzo Valla—The Epicurean—The Critic—
The Opponent of the Church—Bartolommeo Fazio—Giannantonio
Porcello—Court of Milan—Filippo Maria Visconti—Decembrio's
Description of his Master—Francesco Filelfo—His Early Life—Visit
to Constantinople—Place at Court—Marriage—Return to Italy
—Venice—Bologna—His Pretensions as a Professor—Florence—
Feuds with the Florentines—Immersion in Politics—Siena—Settles
at Milan—His Fame—Private Life and Public Interests—Overtures
to Rome—Filelfo under the Sforza Tyranny—Literary Brigandage—
Death at Florence—Filelfo as the Representative of a Class—Vit-
torino da Feltre—Early Education—Scheme of Training Youths as
Scholars—Residence at Padua—Residence at Mantua—His School
of Princes—Liberality to Poor Students—Details of his Life and
System—Court of Ferrara—Guarino da Verona—House Tutor of

In passing from Florence to Rome, we are struck with the fact
that neither in letters nor in art had the Papal city any real
life of her own. Her intellectual enthusiasms were imported;
her activity varied with the personal interests of successive
Popes. Stimulated by the munificence of one Holy Father,
starved by the niggardliness of another; petted and caressed
by Nicholas V., watched with jealous mistrust by Paul II.;
thrust into the background by Alexander, and brought into
the light by Leo—learning was subjected to rude vicissitudes
at Rome. Very few of the scholars who shed lustre on the
reigns of liberal Pontiffs were Romans, nor did the nobles of
the Papal States affect the fame of patrons. We have, therefore, in dealing with humanism at Rome, to bear in mind that
it flourished fitfully, precariously, as an exotic, its growth
being alternately checked and encouraged at the pleasure of
the priest in office.

In spite of these variable conditions, one class of humanists
never failed at Rome. During the period of schisms and
councils, when Pope and Anti-pope were waging wordy warfare in the Courts of congregated Christendom, it was impossible to dispense with the services of practised writers and
accomplished orators. As composers of diplomatic despatches,
letters, bulls, and protocols; as disseminators of squibs and
invectives; as redactors of state papers; as pleaders, legates,
ambassadors, and private secretaries—scholars swarmed
around the person of the Pontiff. Their official titles varied,
some being called Secretaries to the Chancery, others Apostolic Scriptors, others again Protonotaries; while their duties
were divided between the regular business of the Curia and
the miscellaneous transactions that arose from special emer-
gencies of the Papal See. Their services were well rewarded.

In addition to about 700 florins of pay and perquisites, they, for the most part, entered into minor orders and held benefices. Men of acute intellect and finished style, who had absorbed the culture of their age, and could by rhetoric enforce what arguments they chose to wield, found, therefore, a good market for their talents at the Court of Rome. They soon became a separate and influential class, divided from the nobility by their birth and foreign connections, and from the churchmen by their secular status and avowed impiety, yet mingling in society with both and trusting to their talents to support their dignity. At the Council of Basle the protonotaries even claimed to take precedence of the bishops on occasions of high ceremony, arguing, from the nature of their office and the rarity of their acquirements, that they had a better right than priests to approach the person of the Sovereign Pontiff. Poggio and Bruni, Losco, Aurispa, and Biondo raised their voices in this quarrel, which proved how indispensable the mundane needs of the Papacy had rendered these free-lances of literature. Through them the spirit of humanism, antagonistic to the spirit of the Church, possessed itself of the Eternal City; and much of the flagrant immorality which marked Rome during the Renaissance may be ascribed to the influence of paganising scholars, freed from the restrictions of family and local opinion, indifferent to religion, and less absorbed in study for its own sake than in the profits to be gained by the exercise of a practised pen. There was a real discord between the principles which the Church professed, and the new culture that flourished on a heathen soil. While merely secular interests blinded the Popes to the perils which might spring from fostering this discord, humanistic enthusiasm had so thoroughly penetrated Italy that to exclude it from Rome was impossible. Neopagan scholarship added, therefore, lustre to the Papal Court, as one among the many splendours of that worldly period which raised the See of

Rome to eminence above the States of Italy. The light it shed, however, had no vital heat. Learning was always an article of artificial luxury at Rome, not, as at Florence, part of the nation's life; and when the gilded pomp of Leo dwindled down to Clement's abject misery and utter ruin, it was found that such encouragement as Popes had given to literature had been a source of weakness and decay. We may still be sincerely thankful that the Pontiffs took the line they did; for had they placed themselves in a position of antagonism to the humanistic movement, instead of utilising and approving of it, the free development of Italian scholarship might have sustained a dangerous check.

It was from Florence that Rome received her intellectual stimulus. The connection began in 1402, when Bonifaco IX. appointed Poggio to the post of Apostolic Secretary, which he held for fifty years. In 1405 Lionardo Bruni obtained the same office from Innocent VII. The powerful personality of these men, in whom the energies of the humanistic revival were concentrated, impressed the Roman Curia with a stamp it never lost. Good Latinity became a *sine qua non* in the Papal Chancery; and when Gregory XII. named Antonio Losco of Verona one of his secretaries, it was natural that this distinguished scholar, following the Florentine example of Coluccio Salutato, should compose a book of forms in Ciceronian style for the use of his office.[1] During the insignificant pontificate of Martin V., while the Curia resided in exile at Florence, the chain which was binding Rome to the city of Italian culture continued to gain strength. The result of all the discords which rent the Church in the first half of the fifteenth century was to Italianise the Papal See; nor did anything contribute to this end more powerfully than the Florentine traditions of three successive Popes—Martin V., Eugenius IV., and Nicholas V.

[1] See Facius, *De Viris Illustribus*, p. 9, quoted by Voigt, p. 278.

Eugenius was a Venetian of good family, who inherited considerable wealth from his father. Having realised his fortune, he bestowed 20,000 ducats on charitable institutions and took orders in the Church.[1] In 1431 he was raised to the Papacy; but the disturbed state of Rome obliged him to quit the Vatican in mean disguise, and to seek safety by flight from Ostia. He spent the greater portion of his life in Tuscany, occupied less with humanistic interests than with the reformation of monastic orders and the conduct of ecclesiastical affairs in the Councils of Basle and Florence. Though he did not share the passion of his age for learning, the patronage which he extended to scholars was substantial and important. Giovanni Aurispa received from him the title of Apostolic Secretary, and was appointed interpreter between the Greeks and Italians at the Council of the two Churches. Even the paganising Carlo Marsuppini was enrolled upon the list of Papal secretaries, while Filelfo and Piero Candido Decembrio, who added lustre at this epoch to the Court of Milan, were invited by Eugenius with highly flattering promises. The value of these meagre statements consists in this, that even a Pope, whose personal proclivities were monastic rather than humanistic, felt the necessity of borrowing all the strength he could obtain from men of letters in an age when learning itself was power. More closely attached to his Court than those who have been mentioned, were Maffeo Begio, the poet, and Flavio Biondo, one of the soundest and most conscientious students of the time.[2]

Though Biondo had but little Greek, and could boast of no beauty of style, his immense erudition raised him to high rank among Italian scholars. The work he undertook was to illustrate the antiquities of Italy in a series of historical, topo-

[1] See Vespasiano, p. 6.
[2] He was born at Forli in 1388, and died in 1463, the father of five sons.

graphical, and archæological studies. His 'Roma Instaurata,' 'Roma Triumphans,' and 'Italia Illustrata,' three bulky encyclopædias of information concerning ancient manners, laws, sites, monuments, and races, may justly be said to have formed the basis of all subsequent dictionaries of Roman antiquities. Another product of his industry was entitled 'Historiarum ab Inclinatione Romanorum.' Three decades and a portion of the fourth were written, when death put a stop to the completion of this gigantic task. In estimating the value of Biondo's contributions to history, we must remember that he had no previous compilations whereon to base his own researches. The vast stores of knowledge he collected and digested were derived from original sources. He grasped the whole of Latin literature, both classical and mediæval, arranged the results of his comprehensive reading into sections, and furnished the learned world with tabulated materials for the study of Roman institutions in the State, the camp, the law courts, private life, and religious ceremonial. Obstinate indeed must have been the industry of the scholar, who, in addition to these classical researches, undertook to narrate the dissolution of antique society and to present a faithful picture of Italy in the dark ages. Biondo's 'History of the Decline and Fall of the Roman Empire,' conceived in an age devoted to stylistic niceties and absorbed by the attractions of renascent Hellenism, inspires our strongest admiration. Yet its author failed in his lifetime to win the distinction he deserved. Though he held the office of Apostolic Secretary under four Popes, his marriage stopped the way to ecclesiastical preferment, while his incapacity to use the arts of the stylist, the sophist, the flatterer, and the translator, lost him the favour his more solid qualities had at first procured. Eugenius could appreciate a man of his stamp better than Nicholas V., whose special tastes inclined to elegant humanism rather than to ponderous erudition.

The lives of all the humanists illustrate the honours and the wealth secured by learning for her votaries in the Renaissance. No example, however, is so striking as that furnished by the biography of Nicholas V. Tommaso Parentucelli was born at Pisa in 1398. While he was still an infant his parents, in spite of their poverty and humble station, which might have been expected to shield them from political tyranny, were exiled to Sarzana; [1] and at the age of nine he lost his father at that place. Sarzana has consequently gained the credit of giving birth to the first great Pope of the Renaissance period. The young Tommaso found means, though extremely poor, to visit the University of Bologna, where he studied theology and made himself a master in the seven liberal arts. After six years' residence at Bologna, his total destitution, combined, perhaps, with a desire for more instruction in elegant scholarship than the university afforded, led him to seek work in Florence. He must have already acquired some reputation, since Rinaldo degli Albizzi received him as house-tutor to his children for one year, at the expiration of which time he entered the service of Palla degli Strozzi in a similar capacity. The money thus obtained enabled him to return to Bologna, and to take his degree as Doctor of Theology at the age of twenty-two. He was now fully launched in life. The education he had received at Bologna qualified him for office in the church, while his two years' residence at Florence had rendered him familiar with men of polite learning and of gentle breeding. Niccolo degli Albergati, Archbishop of Bologna, became his patron, and appointed him controller of his household. Albergati was one of the cardinals of Eugenius IV., a man of considerable capacity, and alive to the intellectual interests of his age. When he followed the Papal Court to Florence, Tommaso attended him, and here began the period which was destined

[1] So Vespasiano relates the cause of their removal from Pisa. P. 20.

to influence his subsequent career. Inspired with a passionate devotion to books for their own sake, and gifted with
ardent curiosity and all-embracing receptivity of intellect, the
young scholar found himself plunged into a society of which
literature formed the most absorbing occupation. He soon
became familiar with Cosimo de' Medici, and no meetings of
the learned were complete without him. A glimpse may be
obtained of the literary circle he frequented at this time from
a picturesque passage in Vespasiano.[1] 'It was the wont of
Messer Lionardo d' Arezzo, Messer Giannozzo Manetti, Messer
Poggio, Messer Carlo d' Arezzo, Messer Giovanni Aurispa,
Maestro Gasparo da Bologna, and many other men of learning
to congregate every morning and evening at the side of the
Palazzo, where they entered into discussions and disputes on
various subjects. As soon, then, as Maestro Tommaso had
attended the Cardinal to the Palazzo, he joined them, mounted
on a mule, with two servants on foot ; and generally he was
attired in blue, and his servants in long dresses of a darker
colour. At that time the pomp of the Court of Rome was not
by any means what it is nowadays. In the place I have
named he was always to be found, conversing and disputing,
since he was a most impassioned debater.'

Tommaso was not a man of genius ; his talents were
better suited for collecting and digesting what he read, than
for original research and composition. He had a vast memory,
and was an indefatigable student, not only perusing but
annotating all the books he purchased. Pius II. used to say
of him that what he did not know, must lie outside the sphere
of human knowledge. In speech he was fluent, and in
disputation eager ; but he never ranked among the ornate
orators and stylists of the age. His wide acquaintance with
all branches of literature, and his faculty for classification,
rendered him useful to Cosimo de' Medici, who employed him

[1] P. 23.

on the catalogue of the Marcian Library. From Cosimo in
return, Tommaso caught the spirit which sustained him in his
coming days of greatness. Already, at this early period,
while living almost on the bounty of the Medici, he never lost
an opportunity of accumulating books, and would even borrow
money to secure a precious MS.[1] He used to say that, if
ever he acquired wealth, he would expend it in book-buying
and building—a resolution to which he adhered when he rose
to the Pontificate.

Soon after the death of Albergati in 1443, Eugenius promoted Tommaso to the see of Bologna; a cardinal's hat
followed within a few months; and in 1447 he was elected
Pope of Rome. So sudden an elevation from obscurity and
poverty to the highest place in Christendom has rarely
happened; nor is it even now easy to understand what combinations of unsuccessful intrigues among the princes of the
Church enabled this little, ugly, bright-eyed, restless-minded
scholar to creep into S. Peter's seat. Perhaps the simplest
explanation is the best. The times were somewhat adverse
to the Papacy, nor was the tiara quite as much an object
of secular ambition as it afterwards became. Humanism
meanwhile exercised strong fascination over every class in
Italy, and it would seem that Tommaso Parentucelli had
nothing but his reputation for learning to thank for his
advancement. 'Who in Florence would have thought that a
poor bell-ringer of a priest would be made Pope, to the confusion of the proud?' This was his own complacent exclamation to Vespasiano, who had gone to kiss his old friend's
feet, and found him seated on a throne with twenty torches
blazing round him.[2]

The rejoicings with which the humanists hailed the elevation of one of their own number to the Papal throne may be
readily imagined; nor were their golden expectations, founded

---

[1] Vespasiano, p. 27.   [2] *Ibid.* p. 33.

on a previous knowledge of his liberality in all things that pertained to learning, destined to be disappointed. Nicholas V., to quote the words of Vespasiano, who knew him well, ' was a foe to ceremonies and vain flatteries, open and candid, without knowing how to feign ; avarice he never harboured, for he was always spending beyond his means.' [1] His revenues were devoted to maintaining a splendid Court, rebuilding the fortifications and palaces of Rome, and showering wealth on men of letters. In the protection extended by this Pope to literature we may notice that he did not attempt to restore the *studio pubblico* of Rome, and that he showed a decided preference for works of solid learning and translations. His tastes led him to delight in critical and grammatical treatises, and his curiosity impelled him to get Latin versions made of the Greek authors. It is possible that he did nothing for the Roman university because he considered Florence sufficient for the humanistic needs of Italy, and his own Alma Mater for the graver studies of the three professions. Still this neglect is noticeable in the case of a Pontiff whose one public aim was to restore Rome to the rank of a metropolis, and whose chief private interest was study.

The most permanent benefit conferred by him on Roman studies was the foundation of the Vatican Library, on which he spent about 40,000 scudi forming a collection of some 5,000 volumes.[2] He employed the best scribes, and obtained the rarest books ; nor was there anyone in Italy better qualified than himself to superintend the choice and arrangement of such a library. It had been his intention to place it in S. Peter's and to throw it open to the public ; but he died before this plan was matured. It remained for Sixtus IV. to carry out his project.

During the pontificate of Nicholas Rome became a vast workshop of erudition, a factory of translations from Greek

[1] Vespasiano, pp. 25, 27.　　　　[2] *Ibid.* p. 38.

into Latin. These were done for the most part by Greeks who had an imperfect knowledge of Latin, and by Italians who had not complete mastery of Greek. The work achieved was unequal and of no great permanent value; yet for the time being it served a purpose of utility, nor could the requirements of the age have been so fully satisfied by any other method. Nearly all the eminent scholars at that time in Italy were engaged in this labour. How liberally they were rewarded may be gathered from the following details. Lorenzo Valla obtained 500 scudi for his version of Thucydides; Guarino received the larger sum of 1,500 scudi for Strabo; Perotti 500 ducats for Polybius; while Manetti was pensioned at the rate of 600 scudi per annum to enable him to carry on his sacred studies. Nicholas delighted in Greek history. Accordingly, Appian was translated by Piero Candido Decembrio, Diodorus Siculus and the 'Cyropædia' of Xenophon by Poggio,[1] Herodotus by Valla. Valla and Decembrio were both engaged upon the 'Iliad' in Latin prose; but the dearest wish of Nicholas in his last years was to see the poems of Homer in the verse of Filelfo. Nor were the Greeks then resident in Italy neglected. To Georgios Trapezuntios the Pope entrusted the 'Physics,' 'Problems,' and 'Metaphysics' of Aristotle. The same scholar tried his hand at the 'Laws' of Plato, and, in concert with Decembrio, produced a version of the 'Republic.' Gregorios Tifernas undertook the 'Ethics' of Aristotle, and Theodorus Gaza the 'History of Animals.' To this list should be added the Greek Fathers, Theophrastus, Ptolemy, and minor works which it would be tedious to enumerate.[2]

The profuse liberality of Nicholas brought him thus into relation with the whole learned world of Italy. Among the humanists who resided at his Court in Rome, mention must

---

[1] The latter was intended for Alfonso of Naples.
[2] Tiraboschi is the authority for these details.

be made of Lorenzo Valla, who was appointed Apostolic Scriptor in 1447, and who opened a school of eloquence in 1450. Piero Candido Decembrio obtained the post of secretary and overseer of the Abbreviators.[1] Giovanni Tortello, of Arezzo, the author of a useful book on the orthography of Greek words, superintended the Pope's library. Piero da Noceto, whose tomb in the cathedral at Lucca is one of Matteo da Civitale's masterpieces, was private secretary and comptroller of the Pope's affairs. Of the circle gathered round Bessarion I shall have occasion to speak later on. Our present attention must be concentrated on a man who, more even than Nicholas himself, might claim the right to give his own name to this age of learning.

Gian Francesco Poggio Bracciolini is better known in the annals of literature as Poggio Fiorentino, though he was not made a burgher of Florence until late in life. Born in 1380 at Terranova, a village of the Florentine *contado*, he owed his education to Florence. In Latin he was the pupil of John of Ravenna, and in Greek of Manuel Chrysoloras. During his youth he supported himself by copying MSS. for the Florentine market. Coluccio Salutato and Niccolo de' Niccoli befriended the young student, who entered as early as the year 1402 or 1403 into the Papal Chancery.[2] Though Poggio's life for the following half-century was spent in the service of the Roman Curia, he refused to take orders in the Church, and remained at heart a humanist. With the

---

[1] The more complete notices which Valla and Decembrio deserve will be given in the history of scholarship at Naples and at Milan.

[2] Of his debt to Niccolo de' Niccoli Poggio speaks with great warmth of feeling in a letter on his death addressed to Carlo Aretino : ' Quem enim patrem habui cui plus debuerim quam Nicolao ? Hic mihi parens ab adolescentiâ, hic postmodum amicus, hic studiorum meorum adjutor atque hortator fuit, hic consilio, libris, opibus semper me ut filium et amicum fovit atque adjuvit.'—*Poggii Opera, Basileæ, ex ædibus Henrici Petri*, MDXXXVIII. p. 342. To this edition of Poggio's works my future references are made.

Florentine circle of scholars he maintained an unremitting correspondence, sending them notices of his discoveries in the convents of Switzerland and Germany, receiving from them literary gossip in return, joining in their disputes, and more than once engaging in fierce verbal duels to befriend his Medicean allies. His duties and his tastes alike made him a frequent traveller, and not the least of the benefits conferred by him upon posterity are his pictures of foreign manners. At the Council of Constance, for example, he saw and heard Jerome of Prague, in whom he admired the firmness and intrepid spirit of a Cato.[1] At Baden in Switzerland he noticed the custom, strange to Italian eyes, of men and women bathing together, eating, drinking, and playing at chess or cards upon floating tables in the water, while visitors looked down upon them from galleries above, as they now do at Leukerbad.[2] In England he observed that the gentry preferred residence in their country houses and secluded parks to the town life then, as now, fashionable in Italy, and commented upon the vast wealth and boorish habits of the great ecclesiastics.[3] Concerning his discoveries of MSS. I have had already occasion to write ; nor need I here repeat what I have said about his antiquarian researches among the ruins of ancient Rome. Poggio was a man of wide sympathies, active curiosity, and varied interests—no mere bookworm, but one whose eyes and mind were open to the world around him.

In literature he embraced the whole range of contemporary studies, making his mark as a public orator, a writer of

[1] 'Stabat impavidus, intrepidus, mortem non contemnens solum sed appetens ut alterum Catonem dixeris.'—*Opp. Omnia*, p. 301. This most interesting letter, addressed to Lionardo Bruni, is translated by Shepherd, *Life of Poggio Bracciolini*, pp. 78–88.

[2] *Opera Omnia*, p. 297. See Shepherd, pp. 67–76, for a translation of this letter to Niccolo de' Niccoli.

[3] Cardinal Beaufort had invited him to England.

rhetorical treatises and dialogues, a panegyrist of the dead, a violent impeacher and impugner of the living, a translator from the Greek, an elegant epistolographer, a grave historian, and a facetious compiler of anecdotes and epigrams. He possessed a style at once easy and pointed, correct in diction and varied in cadence, equally adapted for serious discourse and witty trifling, and not less formidable in abuse than delicate in flattery. This at least was the impression which his copious and facile Latin, always fluent and yet always full of sense, produced on his contemporaries. For us its finest flights of rhetoric have lost their charm, and its best turns of phrase their point. So impossible is it that the fashionable style of one age should retain its magic for posterity, unless it be truly classical in form, or weighted with sound thought, or animated with high inspiration. Just these qualities were missed by Poggio and his compeers. Setting no more serious aim before them than the imitation of Livy and Cicero, Seneca and Cæsar, they fell far short of their originals ; nor had they matter to make up for their defect of elegance. Poggio's treatises ' De Nobilitate,' 'De Varietate Fortunæ,' ' De Miseriâ Humanæ Conditionis,' ' De Infelicitate Principum,' ' An Seni sit Uxor ducenda,' ' Historia Disceptiva Convivialis,' and so forth, were as interesting to Italy in the fifteenth century as Voltaire's occasional essays to our more immediate ancestors. His controversial writings passed for models of destructive eloquence, his satires on the clergy for masterpieces of sarcastic humour, his Florentine history for a supreme achievement in the noblest Latin manner. Yet the whole of this miscellaneous literature seems coarse and ineffective to the modern taste. We read it, not without repugnance, in order to obtain an insight into the spirit of the author's age.

Two important points in Poggio's biography will serve to illustrate the social circumstances of the humanists. The first is the attitude adopted by him toward the churchmen, with whom he passed the best years of his life in close intimacy ; the second, his fierce warfare waged with rivals and opponents in the field of scholarship. Though Poggio served the Church for half a century, no one exposed the vices of the clergy with more ruthless sarcasm, or turned the follies of the monks to ridicule with more relentless scorn. After reading his 'Dialogue against the Hypocrites,' his 'Invective against Felix the Antipope,' and his 'Facetiæ,' it is difficult to understand how a satirist who knew the weak points of the Church so intimately, and exposed them so freely, could have held high station and been honoured in the Papal Curia. They confirm in the highest degree all that has been written in the previous volume about the division between religion and morality in Italy, the cynical self-satisfaction of the clergy, and the secular indifference of the Papacy, proving at the same time the proudly independent position which the talents of the humanists had won for them at Rome. At the end of the 'Facetiæ'—a collection of grossly indecent and not always very witty stories—Poggio refers to the meetings with which he and his comrades entertained themselves after the serious business of the day was over.[1] Their place of resort was in the precincts of the Lateran, where they had established a club which took the name of 'Bugiale,' or Lie Factory.[2] Apostolic secretaries, writers to the Chancery, protonotaries, and Papal scribes here met together after laying down the pens they had employed in drafting Bulls and dispensations, encyclical letters and diplomatic missives. To make puns, tell scandalous stories, and invent amusing plots for novelettes was the chief amusement of these Roman

[1] *Poggi Florentini Facetiarum Libellus Unicus*, Londini, 1798, vol. i. p. 282.

[2] 'Mendaciorum veluti officina' is Poggio's own explanation of the phrase.

wits. Their most stinging shafts of satire were reserved for
monks and priests; but they spared no class or profession,
and made free with the names of living persons.[1] Against
the higher clergy it might not have been safe to utter even
the truth, except in strictest privacy, seeing that preferment
had to be expected from the Sacred College and the Holy
Father. The mendicant orders and the country parsons,
therefore, bore the brunt of their attack, while the whole tone
of their discourse made it clear how little they respected the
religion and the institutions of the Church. Such fragments
of these conversations as Poggio thought fit to preserve,
together with anecdotes borrowed from the 'Cent Nouvelles
nouvelles' and other sources, he committed to Latin, and
printed in the later years of his life. The title given to
the book was 'Facetiarum Liber.' It ran speedily through
numerous editions, and was read all over Europe with the
same eagerness that the 'Epistolæ Obscurorum Virorum'
afterwards excited. Underneath its ribaldry and nonsense,
however, there lay no serious intention. The satires on the
clergy were contemptuous and flippant, arguing more liking
on the part of their author for scurrilous jests than any
earnest wish to prove the degradation of monasticism. Not a
word of censure from the Vatican can I find recorded against
this marvellous production of a Papal secretary's pen. Here,
by way of illustration, it may be mentioned that Filelfo, on
his way through Rome to Naples, placed his satires—the
most nauseous compositions that coarse spite and filthy fancy
ever spawned—in the hands of Nicholas V. The Pope retained them for nine days, read them, returned them with
thanks, and rewarded their author with a purse of 500
ducats.

The 'Dialogue against the Hypocrites' contains less of

---

[1] 'Ibi parcebatur nemini, in lacessendo ea quæ non probabantur a
nobis.'

mere scurrility and more that bears with real weight on the vices of the clergy. Begging friars, preachers, confessors, and aspirants to the fame of holiness are cited by name and scourged with pitiless impartiality, while the worldly ambition of the Roman churchmen is unmasked. The 'Fratres Observantiæ,' who flourished under Pope Eugenius, receive stern castigation at the hands of Carlo Aretino. Shepherd remarks, not without justice, on this dialogue that, had the author 'ventured to advance the sentiments which it contains in the days of Eugenius, he would in all probability have expiated his temerity by the forfeit of his life.[1] Nicholas V., who appreciated the pungency of its satiric style, instead of resenting its free speech, directed his friend Poggio's pen against his rival Felix. Raised to the Papacy by the Council of Basle in 1439, Amadeus, the ex-Duke of Savoy, still persisted in his Papal title after the election of Nicholas; and though the Sovereign of the Vatican could well afford to scorn the hermit of Ripaille, he thought it prudent to discharge the heavy guns of humanistic eloquence against the Antipope. A ponderous invective was the result, wherein Poggio described the unfortunate Felix as 'another Cerberus,' 'a rapacious wolf,' 'a golden calf,' 'a perverter of the faith and foe to true religion,' 'a high priest of malignity,' 'a roaring lion '— stigmatising the Council to whom he owed his election as 'that sink of iniquity the Synagogue of Basle,' 'a monstrous birth,' 'conventicle of reprobates,' 'tumultuary band of debauched men,' ' apostates, fornicators, ravishers, deserters, men convicted of most shameful crimes, blasphemers, rebels against God.'[2] To such amenities of controversial rhetoric did even Popes descend, substituting sound and fury for sense, and trusting to vituperation in the absence of more valid arguments.

Poggio, next to Filelfo, was the most formidable gladiator in that age of literary duellists. ' In his invectives he

[1] *Life of Poggio*, p. 423.   [2] *Opera Omnia*, pp. 155-164.

displayed such vehemence,' writes Vespasiano,[1] 'that the
whole world was afraid of him.'   Even Alfonso of Naples
found it prudent to avert his anger by a timely present of 600
ducats, when Poggio complained of his remissness in acknowledging the version of Xenophon's 'Cyropædia,'[2] and hinted
at the same time that a scholar's pen was powerful enough
to punish kings for their ingratitude.   The overtures, again,
made to Poggio by Filippo Maria Visconti, and the consideration he received from Cosimo de' Medici, testified to the desire
of princes for the goodwill of a spiteful and unscrupulous
pamphleteer.[3]   The most celebrated of Poggio's feuds with
men of letters began when Filelfo assailed the character of
Cosimo, and satirised the whole society of Florence in 1433.
The full history of Filelfo's animosity against the Florentines
belongs to the biography of that famous scholar.   It is enough
here to mention that he ridiculed Cosimo under the name
of Mundus, described Poggio as Bambalio, Carlo Aretino as
Codrus, and Niccolo de' Niccoli as Outis,[4] accusing them of
literary imbecility, and ascribing to them all the crimes and
vices that disgrace humanity.   Poggio girded up his loins for
the combat, and, in reply to Filelfo's ponderous hexameters,
discharged a bulky invective in prose against the common
adversary.   This was answered by more satires, Poggio re-
plying with new invectives.   The quarrel lasted over many
years ; when, having heaped upon each other all the insults it
is possible for the most corrupt imagination to conceive, they
joined hands and rested from the contest.[5]   To sully these

---

[1] P. 422.   [2] *Ibid.* p. 423.

[3] See the correspondence between Filippo Maria and Poggio, *Opp.*
pp. 333–358.   Letter to Cosimo, p. 339.

[4] 'The World, the Stammering Simpleton, the Execrable Poet, and
the Nobody.' See *Auree Francisci Philelphi Poete Oratorisque Cele-
berrimi Satyre.* Paris, 1508.   Passim.

[5] *Opp. Omn.* pp. 164–187.   The first invective is the most venomous, and deserves to be read in the original.   The last, entitled

pages with translations of Poggio's rank abuse would be
impossible.   I must content myself with referring readers,
who are anxious to gain a more detailed acquaintance with
the literary warfare of that age, to the excerpts preserved
by Shepherd and Rosmini.[1]   Suffice it to say that he poured
a torrent of the filthiest calumnies upon Filelfo's wife and
mother, that he accused Filelfo himself of the basest vice in
youth and the most flagrant debauchery in manhood, that he
represented him as a public thief, a professed cut-purse, a
blasphemous atheist, soiled with sordid immoralities of every
kind, and driven by his exposed felonies from town to town in
search of shelter for his hated head.   Filelfo replied in the
same strain.   All the resources of the Latin language were
exhausted by the combatants in their endeavours to befoul
each other's character, and the lowest depths of human
nature were explored to find fresh accusations.   The learned
world of Italy stood by applauding, while the valiant antagonists, like gladiators of the Roman arena, plied their
diverse weapons, the one discharging darts of verse, the other
wielding a heavy club of prose.[2]   Unhappily, there was enough
of scandalous material in both their lives to give some colour
to their accusations.   Yet the virulence with which they lied
against each other defeated its own object.   Raking that literary dunghill, it is now impossible to distinguish the true from
the false; all proportion is lost in the mass of overcharged
and indiscriminate scurrility.   That such encounters should
have been enjoyed and applauded by polite society is one of
the strangest signs of the times; and that the duellists them-

'Invectiva Excusatoria et Reconciliatoria,' is amusing from its tone of
sulky and sated exhaustion.

[1] *Life of Poggio*, pp. 263–272, 354.   *Vita di Filelfo.*

[2] The language of the arena was used by these literary combatants.
Thus Valla, in the exordium of his *Antidote*, describes his weapon of
attack in this sentence :—'Hæc est mea fusana, quandoquidem gladiator
a gladiatore fieri cogor, et ea duplex et utraque tridens,' p. 9.

selves should have imagined they were treading in the steps of Cicero and Demosthenes is even more astounding.

The dispute with Filelfo was rather personal than literary. Another duel into which Poggio entered with Guarino turned upon the respective merits of Scipio and Julius Cæsar. Poggio had occasion to explain, in correspondence with a certain Scipione Ferrarese, his reasons for preferring the character of Scipio Africanus. Guarino, with a view to pleasing his pupil Lionello d' Este, a professed admirer of Cæsar, tcok up the cudgels in defence of the dictator,[1] and treated Poggio, whom he called Cæsaromastix, with supreme contempt. Poggio replied in a letter to the noble Venetian scholar Francesco Barbaro.[2] Hard words were exchanged on both sides, and the antagonists were only reconciled on the occasion of Poggio's marriage in 1435. Rome, however, was the theatre of his most celebrated exploits as a disputant. It chanced one day that he discovered a copy of his own epistles annotated by a Spanish nobleman who was a pupil of Lorenzo Valla.[3] Poggio's Latinity was not spared in the marginal strictures penned by the young student; and the fiery scholar, flying to the conclusion that the master, not the pupil, had dictated them, discharged his usual missile, a furious invective, against Valla. Thus attacked, the author of the ' Elegantiæ ' responded in a similar composition, entitled ' Antidotum in Poggium,' and dedicated to Nicholas V.[4] Poggio followed with another invective ; nor did the quarrel end till he had added five of these disgusting compositions to his previous achievements in the

[1] See Rosmini, *Vita di Guarino da Verona*, vol. ii. p. 96.

[2] *Poggii Opera*, p. 365.

[3] ' Adolescens quidam auditor meus,' says Valla in the *Antidotum*, p. 2. The story is told at length, p. 151. I quote from the Cologne edition of 1527 : 'Laurentii Vallæ viri clarissimi in Pogium Florentinum antidoti libri quatuor : in eundem alii duo libelli in dialogo conscripti.'

[4] See Shepherd's *Poggio*, pp. 470, 471, for specimens of the scurrility on both sides.

same style, and had drawn a young Latinist of promise, Niccolo Perotti, into the disgraceful fray.[1] What makes the termination of the squabble truly comic is that Filelfo, himself the worst offender in this way, was moved at last to write a serious letter of admonishment to the contending parties, exhorting them to consult their own dignity and to lay down arms.[2] Concerning the invectives and antidotes by which this war was carried on Tiraboschi writes, 'Perhaps they are the most infamous libels that have ever seen the light; there is no sort of vituperation which the antagonists do not vomit forth against each other, no obscenity and roguery of which they are not mutually accused.'

The inconceivably slight occasions upon which these learned men rushed into the arena, and flung dirt upon one another, may be imagined when we find Lorenzo Valla at feud on the one side with Georgios Trapezuntios because the one preferred Cicero and the other Quintilian, and on the other with Benedetto Morando because that scholar doubted whether Lucius and Aruns were the grandsons of Tarquinius Priscus. Sometimes private incidents aroused their wrath, as in the curious rupture between Lionardo Bruni and Niccolo de' Niccoli at Florence. The story, since it is characteristic of the time, may be briefly told. Niccolo had stolen his brother's mistress Benvenuta, and made her his concubine.[3] His relatives,

[1] The invectives against Valla fill from p. 188 to p. 251 of Poggio's collected works. Part of them is devoted to a defence of his own Latinity, and to a critique of Valla's *Elegantiæ*. But by far the larger part consists of vehement incriminations. Heresy, theft, lying, forgery, cowardice, filthy living of the most odious description, drunkenness, and insane vanity—such are the accusations, supported with a terrible array of apparent evidence. As in the case of Filelfo, Poggio does not spare his antagonist's father and mother, but heaps the vilest abuse upon everyone connected with him. Valla's *Antidote* is written in a more tempered spirit and a purer Latin style.

[2] Shepherd, *Life of Poggio*, p. 474.

[3] Ambrogio Traversari, General of the Camaldolese Order, called her 'fidelissima fœmina.'

indignant at the domestic scandal, insulted Benvenuta in the street, and Niccolo bemoaned himself to all his friends. Lionardo, to whom he applied for sympathy, very properly observed that a student ought to be better occupied than with the misfortunes of a kitchen wench. This tart reply roused Niccolo's bile, and set his caustic tongue wagging against his old friend ; whereupon Lionardo Bruni launched a fierce invective *in nebulonem maledicum* against him, and the learned society of Florence indulged in a free fight on both sides.

Such quarrels were not always confined to words. There is no doubt that the dagger was employed against Filelfo by the Medicean party, while it now and then happened that the literary gladiators came to actual fisticuffs. A scene of this sort occurred at Rome in public. Georgios Trapezuntios complained that the credit of Poggio's translations from Diodorus and Xenophon really belonged to him, since he had done the work of them. Poggio shrieked out, ' You lie in your throat !' Georgios retorted with a box on Poggio's ears. Then Poggio came to close quarters, catching his adversary by the hair ; and the two professors pommelled each other till their respective pupils parted them.[1] Such anecdotes might be multiplied indefinitely. Nor would it be unprofitable to give some account of the vehement warfare waged in Italy between the Platonists and Aristotelians, were it not that enough has already been said to illustrate the acrimonious temper of the times.

The animosity displayed by scholars in these disputes may be taken as a proof of their enthusiasm for their studies. Men have always quarrelled about politics, because politics furnish matter of profound interest to everyone. Theology, for a similar reason, never fails to rouse the deepest rancours, hatreds, and hostilities of which the human breast is capable. Science, as we know from the annals of our days, sets the

[1] Thaboschi, vol. vi lib. ii. cap. 2, sect. 15.

upholders of antagonistic theories by the ears; and at times
when politics have been dull, theology dormant, and science
undemonstrative, even music has been found sufficient to
excite a nation. In the fifteenth century scholarship was all-
absorbing. It corresponded to science in our age, since it
engaged the talents of the strongest workers and supplied
the sources of progressive intellectual discovery. Moreover, it
included both philosophy and theology, and formed the most
attractive topic in all conversation. No wonder, therefore, that
the limpid fountains of classical erudition were troubled by
the piques and jealousies of students.

It is pleasant to turn from Poggio's wrangling to more
honourable passages in his biography. Since the year 1434
he had owned a farm not far from Florence. Here he built
a country residence, vying, if not in splendour, at least in
elegance, with the villas of the Florentine burghers. He
called it his Valdarniana, and adorned it with the fragments
of antique sculpture, inscriptions, and coins, collected by him
partly in person on the Roman Campagna and partly by
purchase from Greece. In the following year (1435) Poggio,
then a man of fifty-five, married a girl of eighteen, named
Vaggia, of the noble Buondelmonte blood. In forming this
connection he had to separate from a mistress who had borne
him fourteen children, four of them then living. His biographer, Shepherd, indulges in some sentimental reflections
upon the pain this leave-taking must have cost him. Yet the
impartial critic will hardly be brought to pity Poggio, seeing
that he cancelled the brief whereby he had previously legiti-
mised his natural children, and responded with raptures to
the congratulations of friends upon his new engagement. He
had already been admitted to the burghership of Florence,
and exempted from its taxes in consideration of his literary
services; so that, on the death of his friend Carlo Aretino, in
1453, no one was found more fitting for the post of Chancellor

to the Republic. As an increase of dignity, Poggio fulfilled the office of Prior, and sat among the Signory. The 'History of the Florentine Republic,' written in continuation of Lionardo Aretino's, occupied the closing years of his life. He left it still unfinished in the year 1459, when he died, and was buried in the Church of Santa Croce. I cannot find that his funeral was accompanied by the peculiar honours voted in the case of his two predecessors. The Florentines, however, erected his statue on the façade of Santa Maria del Fiore, and placed his picture by Antonio dal Pollajuolo in the hall of the Proconsolo. The fate of this statue, a work of Donatello's, was not a little curious. On the occasion of some alterations in 1560, it was removed from its first station, and set up as one among the Twelve Apostles in another part of the cathedral.

Any survey of the Court of Nicholas V. would be incomplete without some notice of the Cardinal Bessarion. Early in life he rose to high station in the Greek Church, and attended the Council of Florence as Archbishop of Nicea. Eugenius IV., by making him a cardinal in 1439, converted him to the Latin faith ; and, as it so happened, he missed the Papacy almost by an accident thirty-two years later.[1] His palace at Rome became the meeting-place of scholars of all nations,[2] where refugee Greeks in particular were sure of finding hearty welcome. In obedience to the reigning passion for book-collecting, he got together a considerable library of Greek and Latin authors, the number of which Vespasiano estimated at 600 volumes, while Platina reckoned their total cost at 30,000 scudi. In 1468 he offered this collection to the Church of S. Mark at Venice. The Republic accepted his gift, but showed no alacrity to build the library. It was not until

[1] Vespasiano, p. 146.
[2] See Platina's panegyric, quoted by Tiraboschi, vol. vi. lib. i. cap. 3, 22. Platina and Perotti were among his Italian protégés.

the next century that Bessarion's books were finally housed according to their dignity.[1] The Cardinal's own studies lay in the direction of theological philosophy. We have already seen that in his youth he was a pupil of Gemistos, and he now appears as the defender of Plato. Georgios Trapezuntios had published a treatise in the year 1458, in which, on the pretence of upholding Aristotle, he vilified Plato's moral character, accused him of having ruined Greece, and maintained that Mahomet was a far better legislator. Bessarion replied by the oration 'In Calumniatorem Platonis,' vindicating the morality of the philosopher and supporting him against Aristotle. This book was printed by Sweynheim and Pannartz in the infancy of the Roman press. Theodoros Gaza,[2] who, on his settlement in Rome in 1450, had been received into Bessarion's household, entered the lists with a critique of Gemistos; to which Bessarion replied: and so the warfare begun by Gennadios at Byzantium was continued by the Greek exiles at Rome. The titles of the works issued in this contest, among which we find 'De Naturâ et Arte,' 'Utrum Natura Consilio Agat,' 'Comparationes Philosophorum Aristotelis et Platonis,' sufficiently indicate the extent of ground traversed. The chief result was the rousing of Italian scholars to weightier points of issue in philosophy than had at first been raised by mystical Neoplatonists and pedantic Peripatetics.

Among the Greeks protected by Bessarion, passing notice may be made of Andronicus Callistus, whose lectures found less favour at Rome than they afterwards obtained at Florence, where he had the great Poliziano for his pupil. He was one

[1] A striking instance of the want of literary enthusiasm at Venice.
[2] He first came to Italy in 1430, professed Greek at Ferrara from 1441 to 1450, and died in Campania about 1478. He translated many works of Aristotle. His own book on Grammar was printed by Aldus in 1495.

of the first of the Greeks to seek fortune in France.[1] Nor must Demetrius Chalcondylas be omitted, who fled from Byzantium to Rome about the year 1447, and afterwards professed Greek in the University of Perugia. A letter written by one of his pupils, Gian Antonio Campano,[2] gives such an agreeable impression of the effect he produced in the city of the Baglioni, that I will translate a portion of it. 'A Greek has just arrived, who has begun to teach me with great pains, and I to listen to his precepts with incredible pleasure, because he is a Greek, because he is Athenian, and because he is Demetrius. It seems to me that in him is figured all the wisdom, the civility, and the elegance of those so famous and illustrious ancients. Merely seeing him, you fancy you are looking on Plato; far more when you hear him speak.' It was a young man of twenty-three who wrote this, the companion, probably, of such magnificent youths as Signorelli loved to paint and Matarazzo to describe.[3] It is interesting to compare this letter with the panegyric passed upon Ognibene da Lonigo five years after his death by Bartolommeo Pagello in an oration delivered at Vicenza. The young men of Vicenza, said the rhetorician, left their dice, their duels, their wine cups, and their loves to listen to this humanist; his learning wrought a reformation in the morals of the town.[4] Such were the fascinations of scholarship in the fifteenth century.

The Greeks hitherto mentioned quitted their country before the capture of Constantinople. It is, therefore, wrong to ascribe to that event the importation of Hellenic studies into Italy. Their Italian pupils carried on the work they had begun, with wider powers and nobler energy. All the great

[1] Raffaello Volaterrano, quoted by Tiraboschi, vol. vi. lib. iii. cap. 2, 16.

[2] See Tiraboschi, vol. vi. lib. iii. cap. 2, 17.

[3] See my *Sketches in Italy and Greece*, article ' Perugia.'

[4] Tiraboschi, vol. vi. lib. iii. cap. 5, 46.

Grecians of the third age of humanism are Italians. Florence received learning from Byzantium at the very moment when the Greek Empire was about to be extinguished, and spread it far and wide through Europe, herself achieving by far the largest and most arduous portion of the task.

In passing down to Naples, we find a marked change in the external conditions under which literature flourished. Men of learning at the Courts of Italy occupied a position different from that of their brethren in the Papal Chancery. They had to suit their habits to the customs of the Court and camp, to place their talents at the service of their patron's pleasure, to entertain him in his hours of idleness, to frame compliments and panegyrics, and to repay his bounty by the celebration of his deeds in histories and poems. Their footing was less official, more subject to the temper and caprices of the reigning sovereign, than at Rome; while the peculiar advantages, both political and social, which, even under the sway of the Medicean family, made Florence a real republic of letters, existed in no other town of Italy.

At Naples there was no such thing as native culture. The semi-feudal nobility of the South were addicted to field sports, feats of arms, and idleness. The people of the country were sunk in barbarism. In the cities there was no middle class analogous to that of the more northerly republics. Nevertheless, the kingdom of the Two Sicilies played an important part in the development of Italian literature. While the Mussulmans held sway at Palermo, Sicily was the most refined and enlightened state of Southern Europe. Under the Norman dynasty this Arabic civilisation began to influence North Italy, and during the reign of Frederick II. Naples bade fair to become the city of illumination for the modern world. The failure of Frederick's attempt to restore life to arts and letters in the thirteenth century belongs to the history of his warfare with the Church. What his courtiers effected for the

earliest poetry of the Italians is told by Dante in the treatise
De Vulgari Eloquio.' For our present purpose it is enough
to notice that the zeal for knowledge planted by the Arabs,
tolerated by the Normans, and fostered by the House of
Hohenstauffen in the south of Italy, was an exotic which took
no deep root in the people. No national poem was produced
in the golden age of Frederick's brief supremacy ; no stories
are told of Neapolitan carters and boatmen reciting the
sonnets of his courtiers. As culture began, so it continued to
exist at Naples—flourishing at intervals in close connection
with the sovereign's taste, and owing to local influences not
life and vigour, but colour and complexion, suavity and soft-
ness, caught from the surrounding beauties of the sea and
shore.

Each of the dynasties which held the throne of the Two
Sicilies could boast a patron of literature. Robert of Anjou
was proud to call himself the friend of Petrarch, and Boccaccio found the flame of inspiration at his Court.[1] In the
second age of humanism, with which we are now occupied,
Alfonso of Aragon deserved the praise bestowed on him by
Vespasiano of being, next to Nicholas V., the most munificent
promoter of learning.[2] His love of letters was genuine.
After making all deductions for the flattery of official historiographers, it is clear that Alfonso found his most enduring
satisfaction in the company of students, listening to their
debates on points of scholarship, attending their public
lectures, employing them in the perusal of ancient poets and
historians, insisting on their presence in his camp, and freely
supplying them with money for the purchase of books and
for their maintenance while engaged in works of erudition.
Vespasiano relates that Beccadelli's daily readings to his

[1] I may refer to Petrarch's Letters passim, and to the solemn peroration of the *Africa*.

[2] See Vol. I., *Age of the Despots*, pp. 445, 446.

master were not interrupted during the campaign of 1443, when Alfonso took the field against Francesco Sforza's armies in the March.[1] The Neapolitan captains might be seen gathered round their monarch, listening to the scholar's exposition of Livy, instead of wasting their leisure at games of hazard. Beccadelli himself professes to have cured an illness of Alfonso's in three days by reading aloud to him Curtius's Life of Alexander, while Lorenzo Valla describes the concourse of students to his table during the recitations of Virgil or of Terence.[2] Courtiers with no taste for scholarship were excluded from these literary meetings; but free access was given to poor youths who sought to profit by the learning of the lecturers. The king, meantime, sat at meat, now and then handing fruits or confectionery to refresh the reader when his voice seemed failing. His passion for the antique assumed the romantic character common in that age. When the Venetians sent him one of the recently discovered bones of Livy, he received it like the relic of a saint; nor could the fears of his physicians prevent him from opening and reading the MS. of Livy forwarded from Florence by Cosimo de' Medici, who was then suspected of wishing to poison him. On his military excursions he never neglected the famous sites of antiquity, saluting the *genius loci* with pious thanks at Ovid's birthplace, and expressly forbidding his engineers to trespass on the site of Cicero's villa at Gaeta.[3] Alfonso was no less assiduous than his contemporaries in the collection of books. The Palace library at Naples was his favourite place of recreation; here Giannozzo Manetti found him among his scholars on the famous occasion when the king sat through a long congratulatory oration like a brazen statue, without so

---

[1] *Vita di Alfonso*, p. 59. *Vita di Manetti*, p. 451.

[2] See Tiraboschi, vol. vi. lib. i. cap. 2, 17.

[3] Pontano, *De Principe*, and Panormita, *De Dictis et Factis Alphonsi Regis*, furnish these anecdotes.

much as brushing away the flies that settled on his face. His MSS. were dispersed when Charles VIII. occupied Naples, and what became of them is doubtful.[1]

Among the humanists who stood nearest to the person of this monarch, Antonio Beccadelli, called from his birth-place Il Panormita, deserves the first place. Born at Palermo in 1894, he received his education at Siena, where he was a fellow-student with Æneas Sylvius Piccolomini. The city of Siena, *molles Senæ*, as the poet himself called it, was noto-rious throughout Italy for luxury of living. Here, therefore, it may be presumed that Beccadelli in his youth enjoyed the experiences which he afterwards celebrated in ' Hermaphro-ditus. '[2] Nothing is more striking in that amazing collection of elegies than the frankness of their author, the free and liberal delight with which he dwells on shameless sensualities, and the pride with which he publishes his own name to the world. Dedicated to Cosimo de' Medici, welcomed with applause by the grey-headed Guarino da Verona,[3] extolled to the skies by Antonio Losco, eagerly sought after by Bartolommeo, Bishop of Milan—this book, which Strato and Martial might have blushed to own, passed from copyist to copyist, from hand to hand. Among the learned it found no serious adversaries. Poggio, indeed, gently reminded the poet that even the elegance of its Latinity and the heat of its author's youth were hardly sufficient excuses for its wantonness.[4] Yet the almost unanimous verdict of students was favourable. Its open animalism, as free from satire as from concealment, took

[1] The MS. of Livy referred to above is now in the library at Holk-ham ; see Roscoe's *Lorenzo*, p. 389.

[2] Published at Paris in 1791 among *Quinque illustrium Poetarum Lusus in Venerem*, and again at Coburg in 1824, with annotations by F. G. Forberg.

[3] A man of about sixty-three, and father of twelve legitimate children.

[4] *Poggii Opera*, pp. 349–354.

the world by storm; while the facile elegance of fluent verse
with which the sins of Sodom and Gomorrha were described
placed it, in the opinion of scholars, on a level with Catullus.[1]
When the Emperor Sigismund crowned Beccadelli poet at
Siena in 1433, he only added the weight of Imperial approval
to the verdict of the lettered public.

The Church could not, however, tolerate the scandal.
Ever since the days of Petrarch and Boccaccio, monks had
regarded the study of antique poetry with suspicion. Now
their worst fears were realised. Beccadelli had proved that the
vices of renascent Paganism were not only corrupting Italian
society in secret, but that a young scholar of genius could
openly proclaim his participation in the shame, abjure the
first principles of Christian morality, and appeal with confidence to princes and humanists for sympathy. The Minorite
Friars denounced the 'Hermaphroditus' from their pulpits,
and burned it, together with portraits of the poet, on the public
squares of Bologna, Milan, and Ferrara.[2]   Eugenius IV.
proscribed the reading of it under penalty of excommunication.
Dignitaries of the Church, who found it in the hands of their
secretaries, did not scruple to tear it to pieces, as a book forbidden by the Pope and contrary to sound morality.[3]   Yet all
this made but little difference to Beccadelli's reputation.[4]   He
lectured with honour at Bologna and Pavia, received a stipend

[1] Poggio, while professing to condemn the scandals of these poems,
writes thus :—'Delectatus sum mehercle varietate rerum et elegantiâ
versuum, simulque admiratus sum res adeo impudicas, adeo ineptas,
tam venuste, tam composite, a te dici, atque ita multa exprimi turpius-
cula ut non enarrari sed agi videantur, nec ficta a te jocandi causâ, ut
existimo, sed acta existimari possint.'—*Poggii Opera*, p. 349.

[2] Especially Bernardino da Siena, Roberto da Lecce, and Alberto da
Sarteano.   See the note to p. 353 of Vol. I., *Age of the Despots*.

[3] See Vespasiano, *Vita di Giuliano Cesarini*, p. 134.

[4] A curious letter from Guarino to Beccadelli (Rosmini's *Vita di
Guarino*, vol. ii. p. 44, and notes, p. 171) describes the enthusiastic reception given in public to an impostor who pretended to be the author
of *Hermaphroditus*.

of 800 scudi from the Visconti, and in 1435 was summoned to the Court of Naples. Alfonso raised him to the rank of noble, and continually employed him near his person, enjoying his wit, and taking special delight in his readings of classic authors. As official historiographer, Beccadelli committed to writing the memorable deeds and sayings of his royal master.[1] As ambassador and orator, he represented the King at foreign Courts. As tutor to the Crown Prince, Ferdinand, he prepared a sovereign for the State of Naples. This favour lasted till the year 1471, when he died, old, rich, and respected, in his lovely villa by the Bay of Naples. A more signal instance of the value attached in this age to pure scholarship, irrespective of moral considerations, and apart from profound learning— since Beccadelli was, after all, only an elegant Latinist— cannot be adduced. The 'Hermaphroditus,' therefore, deserves a prominent place in the history of Renaissance manners.

Those among us who have had the curiosity to study Beccadelli's 'Hermaphroditus' will find sufficient food for reflection upon his post of confidence and honour at the Court of Alfonso.[2] Yet the position of Lorenzo Valla at the same Court is even more remarkable. While Beccadelli urged the levity of youth in extenuation of his heathenism, and spoke with late regret of his past follies,[3] Valla showed the steady front of a deliberate critic, hostile at all points to the traditions and the morals of the Church. The parents of this remark-

---

[1] *De Dictis et Factis Alphonsi Regis Memorabilibus.* Æneas Sylvius wrote a commentary on this work, in the preface to which he says, 'Legere potui, quod feci, corrigere vero non potui ; nam quid est quod manu tuâ emissum correctione indigeat ? '—*Opp. Omnia*, p. 472. This proves Beccadelli's reputation as a stylist.

[2] What the biographers, especially Vespasiano, relate of Alfonso's ceremonious piety and love of theological reading makes the contrast between him and his Court poet truly astounding.

[3] ' Hic fæces varias Veneris moresque profanos,
    Quos natura fugit, me docuisse pudet.'

able man were natives of Piacenza, though, having probably been born at Rome, he assumed to himself the attribute of Roman.[1] Before he fixed his residence at Naples, he had already won distinction by a 'Dialogue on Pleasure,' in which he contrasted the principles of the Stoics and Epicureans, making it clear, in spite of cautious reservation, that he upheld the rights of the flesh in opposition to the teaching of philosophies and Churches. The virtue of virginity, so strongly prized by Christian saints, was treated by him as a violence to nature's laws, an intolerable torment inflicted upon man as God has made him.[2]

The attack opened by Valla upon the hypocrisies and false doctrines of monasticism was both powerful and novel. Humanistic freedom of thought, after assuming the form of witty persiflage in Poggio's anecdotes and appearing as pure Paganism in Beccadelli's poems, now put on the sterner mask of common sense and criticism in Lorenzo Valla. The arms which he assumed in his first encounter with Church doctrine, he never laid aside. To the end of his life Valla remained the steady champion of unbiassed criticism, the living incarnation of that 'verneinender Geist' to which the reason of the modern world has owed its motive force.

Before leaving Rome at the age of twenty-four, Valla tried to get the post of Apostolic Secretary, but without success. It is probable that his youth told less against him than his reputation for plain speech and fearlessness. In 1431 we hear of him at Pavia, where, according to the slanders of his enemies,[3] he forged a will and underwent public penance at

[1] 'Romam, in quâ natus sum . . . ego sum ortus Romæ oriundus a Placentiâ.'

[2] The naïve surprise with which Vespasiano records the fact of virginity (see especially the Lives of Ambrogio Traversari and the Cardinal Portogallo) shows how rare the virtue was, and what mysterious honour it conferred upon men who were reputed to be chaste.

[3] Poggio and Fazio are the authorities for this incident.

the order of the Bishop. This, however, is just one of those stories on which the general character of the invectives that contain it, throws uncertainty. Far more to our purpose is the fact that at this period he became the supreme authority on points of Latin style in Italy by the publication of his 'Elegantiæ.' True to his own genius, Valla displayed in this masterly treatise the qualities that gave him a place unique among the scholars of his day. The forms of correct Latinity which other men had picked out as they best could by close adherence to antique models, he subjected to critical analysis, establishing the art of style on scientific principles.

When Alfonso invited Valla to Naples in 1437, giving him the post of private secretary, together with the poet's crown, he must have known the nature of the man who was to play so prominent a part in the history of free thought. It is not improbable that the feud between the House of Aragon and the Papal See, which arose from Alfonso's imperfect title to the throne of Naples, and was embittered by the intrigues of the Church, disposed the King to look with favour on the uncompromising antagonist of Papacy. At all events, Valla's treatise on 'Constantine's Donation,' which appeared in 1440, assumed the character of a political pamphlet.[1] The exordium contained fierce personal abuse of Eugenius IV. and Cardinal Vitelleschi. The body of the tract destroyed the fabric of lies which had imposed upon the Christian world for centuries. The peroration ended with a menace. Worse chastisement was in store for a worldly and simoniacal priesthood, if the Popes refused to forego their usurped temporalities, and to confess the sham that criticism had unmasked. War to the death was thus declared between Valla and Rome. The storm his treatise excited, raged at first so wildly that Valla thought it prudent to take flight. He crossed the sea to Barcelona, and remained there a short

[1] *De falso Creditâ et Ementitâ Constantini Donatione.*

while, until, being assured of Alfonso's protection, he once more returned to Naples. From beneath the shield of his royal patron, he now continued to shoot arrow after arrow at his enemies, affirming that the letter of Christ to Abgarus, reported by Eusebius, was a palpable forgery, exposing the bad Latin style of the Vulgate, accusing S. Augustine of heresy on the subject of predestination, and denying the authenticity of the Apostles' Creed. That a simple humanist, trusting only to his learning, should have dared to attack the strong places of orthodoxy—its temporalities, its favourite code of ethics, its creed, and its patristic authorities—may well excite our admiration. With the stones of criticism and the sling of rhetoric, this David went up against the Goliath of the Church; and though he could not slay the Philistine, he planted in his forehead the first of those many missiles with which the battery of the reason has assailed tyrannical tradition in the modern world.

The friars, whom Valla attacked with frigid scorn, and whose empire over the minds of men he was engaged in undermining, could not be expected to leave him quiet. Sermons from all the pulpits of Italy were launched at the heretic and heathen; the people were taught to loathe him as a monster of iniquity; and finally a Court of Inquisition was opened, at the bar of which he was summoned to attend. To the interrogatories of the inquisitors Valla replied that 'he believed as Mother Church believed: it was quite true that she *knew* nothing: yet he believed as she believed.' That was all they could extract from the disdainful scholar, who, after openly defying them, walked away to the king and besought him to suspend the sitting of the Court. Alfonso told the monks that they must leave his secretary alone, and the process was dropped.

On the death of Eugenius, Nicholas V. summoned Valla to Rome, not to answer for his heresies and insults at the

Papal bar, but to receive the post of Apostolic Writer, with magnificent appointments. The entry of Valla into the Roman Curia, though marked by no external ceremony, was the triumph of humanism over orthodoxy and tradition. We need not suppose that Nicholas was seeking to bribe a dangerous antagonist to silence. He simply wanted to attach an illustrious scholar to his Court, and to engage him in the labour of translation from the Greek. To heresy and scepticism he showed the indifference of a tolerant and enlightened spirit; with the friars who hated Valla the Pope in Rome had nothing whatsoever in common. The attitude assumed by Nicholas on this occasion illustrates the benefit which learning in the Renaissance derived from the worldliness of the Papacy. It was not until the schism of the Teutonic Churches, and the intrusion of the Spaniards into Italy, that the Court of Rome consistently adopted a policy of persecution and repression.

A large portion of Valla's biography is absorbed by the history of his quarrels with Poggio, Georgios Trapezuntios, and other men of mark. Enough has already been said about these literary feuds; nor need I allude to them again, except for the purpose of bringing a third Court-scholar of Alfonso's into notice. Bartolommeo Fazio, a native of La Spezzia, occupied the position of historiographer at Naples. In addition to his annals of the life of Alfonso, he compiled a book on celebrated men, and won the reputation of being the neatest Latinist in prose of his age. Fazio ventured to criticise the style of Valla, in whose works he professed to have detected five hundred faults of language. Eight books of invectives and recriminations were exchanged between them; and when both died in 1457, this epigram was composed in celebration of their animosity :—

> Ne vel in Elysiis sine vindice Valla susurret,
> Facius haud multos post obit ipse dies.

The amusement afforded to Roman emperors by fights in

the arena, and to feudal nobles by the squabbles of their fools,
seems to have been extracted by Italian patrons from the
duels of well-matched humanists.   What personal jealousies,
what anxious competition for the princely favour, such warfare concealed may be readily imagined ; nor is it improbable
that Fazio's attack on Valli was prompted by the covert spite
of Beccadelli.   Scarcely less close to the person of Alfonso
than the students with whom we have been occupied, stood
Giannantonio Porcello, a native of Naples.   He was distinguished by his command of versification : the fluency with
which he poured fourth Latin elegiacs and hexameters approached that of an improvisatore of the Molo.   Alfonso sent
him to the camp of the Venetians during the war waged by
their general Piccinino in 1452-3 with Sforza.   Porcello, who
shared the tent of Piccinino on this occasion, wrote a Latin
history of the campaign in the style of Livy, with moral
reflections, speeches, and all the apparatus of Roman rhetoric.
Piccinino figured as Scipio Æmilianus ; Sforza as Hannibal.
The work was dedicated to Alfonso.[1]

With the exception of Lorenzo Valla,[2] the scholars of the
Court of Naples were stylists and poets rather than men of
erudition.   Freedom both of speculation and of morals marked
society in Southern Italy, where the protection of a powerful
monarch at war with the Church, and the license of a luxurious
capital, released the humanists from such slight restraints as
public opinion and conventional decorum placed on them in
Rome and Florence.

Owing to the marked diversity exhibited by the different
states of Italy, the forms assumed by art and literature are
never exactly the same in any two cities.   If the natives of

[1] It is printed in Muratori, vol. xx.
[2] The protection extended to Manetti and to Filelfo ought, however,
to be here mentioned.   Nearly all the contemporary scholars of Italy
dedicated works to Alfonso.

the Two Sicilies were not themselves addicted to severe
scholarship, the lighter kinds of writing flourished there
abundantly, and Naples gave her own peculiar character to
literature. This was not the case with Milan. Yet Milan,
during the reigns of the last Visconti and the first Sforza,
claims attention, owing to the accident of Filelfo's residence
at the Ducal Court. Filippo Maria Visconti was one of the
most repulsive tyrants who have ever disgraced a civilised
country. Shut up within his palace walls among astrologers,
minions, and monks, carefully protected from the public eye,
and watched by double sets of mutually suspicious body-
guards, it was impossible that he should extend the free encouragement to learned men which we admire at Naples.
Around despots of the stamp of the Visconti there must of
necessity reign the solitude and silence of a desert, where arts
and letters cannot flourish, though Pactolus be poured forth
to feed their roots. The history of humanism at Milan has,
therefore, less to do with the city or the Ducal circle than
with the private labours of students allured to Lombardy by
promise of high pay.

Piero Candido Decembrio began life as Filippo Maria's
secretary. To his vigorous pen the student of Italian history
owes the minutest and most vivid sketch now extant of the
habits and the vices of a tyrant. This remains the best title
of Decembrio to recollection, though his works, original and
translated, if we may trust his epitaph in S. Ambrogio,
amounted to 127 books when he died in 1447. Contemporary
with Decembrio, Gasparino da Barzizza, of whom mention
has already been made,[1] occupied the place of Court orator
and letter-writer. This office he transmitted to his son,
Guiniforte, who was also employed in the education of Francesco Sforza's children. None of these men, however, shed
much splendour upon Milan; they were simply the instru-

[1] Above, p. 78.

ments of ducal luxury, part of a prince's parade, at an epoch when éven warlike sovereigns sought to crowd their Courts with pedagogues and rhetoricians.

With Filelfo the case was different. His singular abilities rendered him independent of local patronage, and drew universal attention to any place where he might choose to fix his residence. Of all the humanists he was the most restless in his humour and erratic in his movements. Still Milan, during a long period of his life, formed his head-quarters; to Milan he returned when fortune frowned on him elsewhere; and with Milan his name will always be connected.

Francesco Filelfo was born in 1398 at Tolentino, in the March of Ancona. He studied grammar, rhetoric, and Latin literature at Padua, where he was appointed professor at the early age of eighteen. In 1417 he received an invitation to teach eloquence and moral philosophy at Venice. Here he remained two years, deriving much advantage from the society of Guarino da Verona and Vittorino da Feltre, and forming useful connections with the Venetian nobility. Young as he was, Filelfo had already made his mark, and won the consideration which attaches to men of decided character and extraordinary powers. The proof of this is that, after being admitted citizen of Venice by public decree, he was appointed Secretary to the Baily (*Bailo*, or Consul-General) of Constantinople through the interest of his friend Lionardo Giustiniani. Giustiniani having also provided him with money for his voyage, Filelfo set off in 1419 for the capital of Greek learning. Of the three Italian teachers—Guarino, Aurispa, and Filelfo—who made this journey for the express purpose of acquiring the Greek language and collecting Greek books, Filelfo was by far the most distinguished. The history, therefore, of his adventures may be taken as a specimen of what befell them all. The time spent at sea between Venice and Byzantium was five months; Filelfo did not arrive till the year 1420 was already well advanced. He put himself at once under the tuition of John Chrysoloras, the brother of Manuel, whose influence at the Imperial Court brought Filelfo into favour with John Palæologus. The young Italian student, having speedily acquired familiarity with the Greek tongue, received the titles of Secretary and Counsellor, and executed some important diplomatic missions for his Imperial master. We hear, for instance, of his being sent to Sigismund, the German Emperor, at Buda, and of his reciting an Epithalamial Oration at Cracow on the marriage of King Ladislaus. The Venetian Baily, again, despatched him to the Court of Amurath II., in order to negotiate terms of treaty between the Republic and the Turk.

The confidence extended alike by his Venetian and Greek patrons to Filelfo may well have inclined Chrysoloras to look with favour on the affection which now sprang up between the Italian stranger and his daughter Theodora. Theodora was but fourteen years of age; yet her youth probably suggested no impediment to marriage in the semi-Oriental society of the Greek capital. That she was connected by blood with the Imperial family made the alliance honourable to Filelfo; still there is no sufficient reason to conclude for certain that the match was so unequal as to justify the malignant suggestions thrown out at a later date by Poggio.[1]

[1] 'Itaque Chrysoloras, mœrore confectus, compulsus precibus, malo coactus, filiam tibi nuptui dedit a te corruptam, quæ si extitisset integra, ne pilum quidem tibi abrasum ab illius natibus ostendisset. An tu illam unquam duxisses uxorem si virginitatem per te servare potuisset? Tibi pater illam dedisset profugo, ignobili, impuro? Primariis suæ civitatis viris servabatur virgo, non tibi, insulsæ pecudi et asello bipedali, quem ille domi alebat tanquam canem aliquem solent senio et ætate confectum.'—*Poggii Opp.* p. 167. This is just one of the tales with which the invectives of that day abound, and with which it is almost impossible to deal. It may be true; for certainly Filelfo, by his immorality and grossness in after-life, justified the worst calumnies that his enemies could invent. Yet there is little but Poggio's word to prove it, while Rosmini has shown that Filelfo's position at Byzantium was

Of ancient blood there was enough and to spare at Constantinople; but wealth was wanting, while the talent which rendered Filelfo serviceable to great states and empires was itself sufficient guarantee for Theodora's maintenance in a becoming station.

Not long after their marriage Filelfo received an offer of the Chair of Eloquence at Venice, with a stipend of 500 sequins. In 1427, tempted by the prospect of good pay and growing fame, he landed with his wife, their infant son, four female slaves, and two men servants on the quay before S. Mark's.[1] The object of his journey to Constantinople had been amply attained. After an absence of seven and a half years, he returned to his native country with Greek learning, increased reputation, and a large supply of Greek books.[2] His proud

very different from what his foe suggests. Tiraboschi accepts the charge as 'not proven;' but he clearly leans in private against Filelfo, moved by the following passage from a letter of Ambrogio Traversari :— 'Nuper a Guarino accepi litteras, quibus vehementer in fortunam invehitur quod filiam Joannis Chrysoloræ clarissimi viri is acceperit, exterus, qui quantum libet homo bono ingenio, longe tamen illis nuptiis impar esset, queriturque substomachans uxorem Chrysoloræ venalem habuisse pudicitiam, mœchumque ante habuisse quam socerum.' Vol. vi. lib. iii. cap. v. 21. All that can be said now is that Filelfo's own morality and the corruption of Byzantine society render a story believed by Guarino and Traversari, and openly told by Poggio, not improbable.

[1] This retinue shows that Filelfo was at least able to support a large household.

[2] The catalogue of his library, communicated by him in a letter to Ambrogio Traversari, shows so clearly what the most indefatigable student and omnivorous reader of the age, to whom all the museums and bookshops of Byzantium must have been open, could then collect, that I will transcribe it :—'Qui mihi nostri in Italiam libri gesti sunt, horum nomina ad te scribo : alios autem nonnullos per primas ex Byzantio Venetorum naves opperior. Hi autem sunt Plotinus, Ælianus, Aristides, Dionysius Halicarnasseus, Strabo Geographus, Hermogenes, Aristotelis Rhetoricæ, Dionysius Halicarnasseus de Numeris et Characteribus, Herodotus, Dio Chrysostomus, Appollonius Pergæus, Thucydides, Plutarchi Moralia, Proclus in Platonem, Philo Judæus, Ethica Aristotelis, Ejus magna Moralia et Eudemia, et Œconomica

boast, frequently repeated in after-life, that no man living but
himself had mastered the whole literature of the ancients in
both languages, that no one else could wield the prose of
Cicero, the verse of Horace and of Virgil, and the Greek of
Homer and of Xenophon with equal versatility, was not
altogether an empty vaunt.[1] We may indeed smile at his
pretension to have surpassed Virgil because he was an orator,
and Cicero because he was a poet, and both of them together
because he could write Greek as well as Latin.[2] We know
that his Latin hexameters are such as not only Virgil but
Cicero would have scorned to own, that his Latin orations
would have been hissed before the Roman rostra, and that his

et Politica, quædam Theophrasti Opuscula, Homeri Ilias, Odyssea,
Philostrati de Vitâ Appollonii, Orationes Libanii, et aliqui Sermones
Luciani, Pindarus, Aratus, Euripidis Tragœdiæ Septem, Theocritus,
Hesiodus, Suidas, Phalaridis, Hippocratis, Platonis et multorum ex
veteribus Philosophis Epistolæ, Demosthenes, Æschinis Orationes et
Epistolæ, Pleraque Xenophontis Opera, Una Lysiæ Oratio, Orphei
Argonautica et Hymni, Callimachus, Aristoteles de Historiis Animalium,
Physica, et Metaphysica, et de Animâ, de Partibus Animalium, et alia
quædam, Polybius, Nonnulli Sermones Chrysostomi, Dionysiaca, et
alii Poetæ plurimi. Habes qui mihi sint, et his utere æque ac tuis.'

[1] ‘ Unum Philelphus audet affirmare, vel insaniente Candido, neminem esse hâc tempestate, nec fuisse unquam apud Latinos, quantum
constat ex omni hominum memoriâ, qui præter se unum idem unus
tenuerit exercuitque et Græcam pariter et Latinam orationem in omni
dicendi genere et prosâ et versu. Tu si quidem habeas alterum, me-
mora. Quid taces, homo miserrime ? ' Letter to Piero Candido Decembrio. Cf. what P. C. Decembrio wrote to Poggio in 1453 :—‘ Dixit (i.e.
Philelphus) enim neminem litteras scire præter ipsum, alios semilatinos
et semigræcos esse, se autem principatum inter stultos obtinere.'
Rosmini, vol. iii. p. 150.

[2] ‘ Quod si Virgilius superat me carminis ullis
        Laudibus, orator ille ego sum melior.
    Sin Tulli eloquio præstat facundia nostro,
        Versibus ille meis cedit ubique minor.
    Adde quod et linguâ possum hæc præstare Pelasgâ
        Et Latiâ.   Talem quem mihi des alium ? '

Lib. ix., De Jocis et Seriis. Elegy to Alessandro Sforza. Reported by
Rosmini, vol. iii. p. 149. One specimen of these boasts may stand for
thousands.

Greek style is at the same time tame and tumid. Neither he
nor his contemporaries were sufficiently critical to comprehend the force of these objections. They only saw that he
possessed the keys to all the learning of the ancient world,
and that, besides unlocking those treasures for modern
students, he was also competent to give to current thoughts a
form that aped the classic masterpieces each in its own kind.
Taken at their lowest valuation, the claims of Filelfo, well
founded in fact, mark him out as the most universal scholar
of his age. A genius he was not : for while his perceptions
were coarse, his intellect was receptive rather than originative.
Of deep thought, true taste, penetrative criticism, or delicate
fancy he knew nothing. The unimaginable bloom of style is
nowhere to be found upon his work. Yet a man of his stamp
was needed at that epoch to act as a focus for the streams of
light which flooded Italy from divers sources, to collect them
in himself, and to bequeath to students of a happier age
the ideal of comprehensive scholarship which Poliziano and
Erasmus realised.

Filelfo's reception at Venice by no means corresponded to
the promises by which he had been tempted, or to the value
which he set on his own services. The plague was in the
city ; the nobles had taken flight to their country houses ; and
there was no one to attend his lectures. He therefore very
readily accepted an offer sent him from Bologna, and early in
the year 1428 we find him settled in that city as professor
of eloquence and moral philosophy, with a stipend of 450
sequins. He was not destined to remain there long, however,
for the disturbed state of the town rendered teaching impossible ; and when flattering proposals arrived from the Florentines, he set off in haste and transferred his whole family
across the Apennines from Imola.[1] The delight which he

---

[1] The invitation came from Niccoli, Lionardo Bruni, Ambrogio
Traversari, and Palla Strozzi.

experienced in viewing the architectural monuments of Florence, and the enthusiasm he aroused by his stupendous learning
in an audience of unprecedented variety and multitude, are
expressed with almost childish emphasis in his correspondence.
' The whole State,' he writes,[1] ' is turned to look at me. All
men love and honour me, and praise me to the skies. My
name is on every lip. Not only the leaders of the city, but
women also of the noblest birth make way for me, paying
me so much respect that I am ashamed of their worship. My
audience numbers every day four hundred persons, mostly
men advanced in years and of the dignity of senators.' These
were the halcyon days of Filelfo's residence at Florence,[2] when
he was still enjoying the friendship of learned men, receiving
new engagements from the University with augmentations of
pay,[3] and when as yet he had not won the hatred of the
Medicean faction. His industry at this epoch was amazing.
He began the day by reading and explaining the ' Tusculans '
and rhetorical treatises of Cicero ; then he proceeded to Livy
or Homer ; after a brief rest at midday he resumed his labours
with Terence and a Greek author, Thucydides or Xenophon.
On holidays he read Dante to an audience assembled in the
Duomo, bestowing these lectures as a free gift on the people
of Florence. Amid these public labours, the weight of which
may be estimated by remembering what was required of professors in the fifteenth century,[4] Filelfo still found leisure for
private work. He translated two speeches of Lysias, the
' Rhetoric ' of Aristotle, two Lives of Plutarch, and Xenophon's
panegyrics of Agesilaus and the Spartan institutions.

At the same time he had abundant energy for the prosecution of the feuds in which he soon found himself engaged with

[1] Quoted by Cantù, p. 128.
[2] He stayed there from 1429 till the autumn of 1434.
[3] Engagement renewed October 17, 1431, for two years, with stipend
of 350 sequins ; again, in 1433, with stipend of 450 sequins.
[4] See above, pp. 90, 91.

the Florentine scholars. So great was the arrogance displayed by Filelfo, his meanness in private life, and his imprudence in public,[1] that even the men who had invited him became his bitter foes. Niccolo de' Niccoli, always jealous of superiority, and apt to take offence, was the first with whom he quarrelled ; then followed Carlo Marsuppini and Ambrogio Traversari, until at last the whole of the Medicean party were inflamed against him. Filelfo on his side spared neither satires nor slanders ; and when the political crisis, which for a time depressed the Medicean faction, was impending, he declared himself the public opponent of Cosimo. Already in the spring of 1433 he had been stabbed in the face while walking to the University one morning by Filippo, a cut-throat from Casale ; nor does there seem any reason to doubt that, as Filelfo himself firmly believed, the man was paid to kill him by the Medici. When the same bravo afterwards followed him to Siena,[2] Filelfo hired a Greek, by name Antonio Maria, to retaliate upon his foes in Florence. It is not probable that a merely literary quarrel would have run to these extremities. Even the foulness of Poggio's invectives and the fury of Filelfo's satires fail to account for the intervention of assassins. We know, however, that Filelfo had not confined himself to calumnies and criticisms of his literary rivals. During Cosimo's imprisonment he urged the Signory in open terms to take his life ; when he was living in exile at Venice, he pursued him with abominable slanders ; and now, on Cosimo's return, though himself expelled from the city as a rebel and a proscript, he kept stirring up the burghers of Florence and the Courts of Italy against the tyrant.[3]

[1] See Rosmini, vol. i. pp. 43, 48.
[2] *Ibid.* vol. i. p. 83, for the trial, torture, and confession of this bravo.
[3] The original source of information concerning Filelfo's quarrels with the Florentines is his Satires, divided into ten books or decades, each consisting of ten satires or hecatostichæ of one hundred verses each.

The occasion of Filelfo's removal to Siena was this:—
When his position at Florence had become untenable, he
received an invitation from Antonio Petrucci to lecture for
two years, with a stipend of 350 florins. Filelfo replied that
he preferred small pay and quiet to a larger income among the
swords and poisons of his envious rivals. Accordingly he
took up his abode at Siena for four years in the Piccolomini
Palace. Like many greater and more admirable men, he had
a restless disposition, always pleased with what is new, yet
always grumbling when the taste of bitter mounted to his lips.
The most honourable invitations now began to shower upon
him. The Council of Basle, the Venetian Senate, the Emperor of the East, Eugenius IV., the Universities of Perugia
and Bologna, and the Duke of Milan applied for his services.
It was not, however, until the year 1439 that his love of change,
combined with the allurements of higher pay, induced him to
close with the offers of the Senate of Bologna. Once more,
then, he crossed the Apennines, and once more, after a brief
sojourn of a few months, he again quitted Bologna, and
transferred himself to Milan. His reception by Filippo
Maria Visconti was most flattering. Placing a diamond ring

In the copy of this book, printed at Paris, 1508, by Robert and John
Gourmont, these virulent libels are called ' Divinum Francisci Philelphi
Poetæ Christiani Satyrarum Opus.' As their motto the publishers give
these sentences :—'Finis laus Deo, Spes mea Jesus.' For the abuse of
the Medicean circle see Dec. i. Hec. 5 ; Dec. i. Hec. 6 ; Dec. ii. Hec. 1,
3, 7 ; Dec. iii. Hec. 10 ; Dec. vi. 10 ; Dec. viii. 5. For Filelfo's attack
on Cosimo during his imprisonment, see Dec. iv. Hec. 1. For his invective against Cosimo on his return from exile, see Dec. iv. Hec. 9.
For an appeal to Filippo Maria Visconti against Cosimo, see Dec. v.
Hec. 1. For a similar appeal to Eugenius IV., see Dec. v. Hec. 2. For
the episode of the assassin Filippo, see Dec. v. Hec. 6. A political
attack on Cosimo addressed to Rinaldo Albizzi is contained in Dec. v.
Hec. 8. A furious denunciation of Cosimo's tyranny, in Dec. v. Hec. 9.
Palla degli Strozzi, as an opponent of Cosimo, is praised in Dec. iii. 1 ;
Dec. vi. 4. In Dec. vii. 8, Filelfo promises to moderate his fury. In
addition to these sources see the MS. invectives mentioned in Rosmini,
vol. i. p. 47.

upon his finger, the Duke welcomed him among the nobles of
his Court on New Year's Day in 1440. Thus began Filelfo's
connection with the Lombard capital, which, though often
interrupted, was never wholly broken till his death.

The munificence of the Visconti exceeded that of any of
Filelfo's patrons,[1] while the mode of life at Milan exactly
suited his vainglorious temperament. He loved to throw his
money about among lords, to appear at high Court festivals,
and to take the lead on ceremonial occasions in his rank of
orator. There was, moreover, no rival strong enough to
threaten the blasting of his popularity.[2] We find him,
during his residence at Milan, continually engaged in the
exercise of rhetoric. Public and private incidents of the most
various character employed his skill, nor is there any doubt
that his large professorial income was considerably increased
by presents received from patrons and employers.[3] In addition

---

[1] His professorial stipend was soon raised from 500 to 700 golden
florins.

[2] Vespasiano says that the concourse of people to Carlo Aretino's
lectures was the first cause of Filelfo's feuds at Florence.

[3] Here are the dates of some of these displays :—

1440. Funeral oration on Stefano Federigo Todeschini.
1441. Epithalamial on the Marriage of Giovanni Marliani.
1442. Discourse on Duties of a Magistrate.
1446. Panegyric of Filippo Maria Visconti, and oration on the Election
      of Jacopo Borromeo to the See of Pavia.
1450. Oration of Welcome to Francesco Sforza.
1455. Epithalamial on the Marriage of Tristano Sforza to Beatrice
      d' Este.
1458. Epithalamials for Antonio Crivelli and Teodoro Piatti.
1459. Oration to Pius II. on his Crusade.
1460. Oration on the Election of the Bishop of Como.
1464. Funeral oration for the Senator Filippo Borromeo.
1466. Ditto for Francesco Sforza.

It is probable that all of these were not recited ; but all were conceived in
the lumbering and pedantic style that passed for eloquence at that
period. With regard to rewards received on these occasions, note the
gift of a silver basin from Jacopo Antonio Marcello in return for a
consolatory epistle. Rosmini, vol. ii. p. 127. Cf. p. 197.

to the labours of his chair, he engaged in various literary works. His Satires and Odes were gradually growing into ponderous volumes.[1] Other fugitive pieces in prose he put together under the title of 'Convivia Mediolanensia.' Meanwhile he carried on an active correspondence, both familiar and hortatory, with the scholars and the princes of his day.[2] There was no branch of letters with which, sustained by sublime self-approval, he was not willing and eager to meddle. As he had professed Dante at Florence, so here at Milan, by ducal command, he undertook to comment upon Petrarch, and actually composed a poem on S. John the Baptist in *terza rima*. There is something ludicrous in the thought of this Visconti, would-be Herod as in truth he was, commissioning Filelfo, the outrageous Pagan, to versify the life of Christ's forerunner. If Filelfo despised anything more than sacred history, it was the Italian language; and if there was a task for which he was unfitted, it was the composition of poetry.

During the second year of his Milanese residence Filelfo lost his wife Theodora. He speedily married again, choosing for his bride a beautiful young lady of good family in Milan. Her name was Orsina Osnaga. Since I have touched upon this matter of Filelfo's private life, it may be well to add that

---

[1] The Satires, collected into ten decades, each satire consisting of 100 lines, were dedicated to Alfonso of Naples in 1451. Printed at Milan, 1446. The Odes, entitled *De Seriis et Jocis*, were finished in 1465, and dedicated partly to Malatesta Novello of Cesena, partly to Alessandro Sforza. There were ten books, each book containing 1,000 lines. Never printed. Rosmini, who inspected the MSS., reports that their obscenity exceeds description, and is only equalled by the vulgarity of the author's fancy and the coarseness of his style. In addition to these unpublished Latin poems, Filelfo collected three books of Greek elegies and epigrams, amounting to 2,400 verses. It is significant that he measured his poetry by lines, and trained his jog-trot muse to paces of 100 verses.

[2] The Epistle to Ladislaus of Hungary on his victories over the Turks, for instance.

when he lost his second wife, he took in wedlock for the third time Laura Magiolini. By each of his marriages he acquired no inconsiderable property, and all his brides belonged to highly distinguished families. The best thing that can be said about Filelfo as a man is, that he was undoubtedly attached to his wives and to the numerous children they bore him.[1] This feeling did not, however, protect him from numerous infidelities, or save his fortune from the burden of illegitimate children.[2] It is even doubtful whether credence should not be accorded to suggestions of worse debauchery, repeated with every appearance of belief by his enemies, and on his side but imperfectly refuted. Filelfo was, in truth, a man of great physical vigour, whose energies the mere labour of the student was insufficient to exhaust. Loves and hatreds, domestic sympathies and turbulent passions, absorbed a portion of his superfluous force; nor was he at any time restrained by scruples of religion or morality. What was good for Greeks and Romans was good for him. It is also to be noted that the innate sense of delicacy which sometimes forms the safeguard of excessive temperaments was altogether alien to his nature.

During the disasters that befell the State of Milan on the death of Filippo Maria, Filelfo at first espoused the cause of the burghers. A letter to the Florentines is extant, in which he exhorts them to aid their sister commonwealth at the extreme hour of her peril. It was not natural, however, that a humanist, who had no zeal for freedom, and whose personal interests led him to desire a settled government at any price, should continue staunch to a republic so unnerved as that of

---

[1] He had twelve sons and twelve daughters. They did not all live.

[2] A curious sign of current feeling is that Filelfo frequently boasted of being τριόρχης. See Rosmini, i. p. 15, and the verse quoted, *ib.* p. 113. He mentioned two natural children in his will and had many more. Rosmini, vol. iii. p. 78.

Milan. When Carlo Gonzaga played the Milanese false by
admitting the troops of Francesco Sforza, Filelfo was the first
to welcome the new monarch with a set oration. He professed
great admiration for the general who, by careful management
and double-dealing, had placed himself at the head of the third
state in the peninsula. Yet his correspondence at this period
proves that his mind was uneasy, and that he desired a change.
In an impudent letter addressed to Nicholas V., he solicited
ecclesiastical preferment, suggesting that the promise of a
bishop's mitre would secure his splendid talents for the service
of the Papacy.[1] However desirous the Pope might be to
engage Filelfo for his translation factory at Rome, the price
demanded was too great. He could not recognise a vocation
so clearly inspired by mercenary motives; and to receive into
the high places of the Church, at his own request, a man
accused of many vices, who had twice been married, would
have established a dangerous precedent. Filelfo, receiving
neither substantial encouragement nor a flat refusal, turned
his thoughts to matrimony for the third time, and addressed a
prayer on this occasion to Dame Venus, in which he besought
the mother of Priapus to befriend her votary. The intelligent
student of the Renaissance will not fail to notice the state of
mind implied by the juxtaposition of this letter to the Holy
Father and this ode to Venus.

Filelfo was now fain to content himself with the patronage
of Francesco Sforza, a prince who had no natural turn for
literature, but who was wise enough to know that a *parvenu*
could least of all afford to neglect the ruling fashions of his
age. The letters he wrote at this period abound in impudent
demands for money, querulous outcries over the poverty to
which the first scholar of the century was condemned, and
violent menaces of retaliation if his salary remained in

---

[1] Rosmini, vol. ii. p. 54. It may be remembered that Pietro Aretino
hinted he should like to be a cardinal.

arrears.[1] Not only Francesco Sforza, but all the patrons upon
whom Filelfo thought he had a claim, were assailed with
reptile lamentations and more reptile menaces. Alessandro
Sforza, Lodovico Gonzaga, and three Popes in succession may
be mentioned among the more distinguished princes who
suffered from this literary brigandage.[2] Not without strict justice did a contemporary describe him in the following severe
terms :—'He is calumnious, envious, vain, and so greedy of
gold that he metes out praise or blame according to the gifts
he gets, both despicable as proceeding from a tainted source.'[3]
Filelfo's rapacity is truly disgusting when we remember that
he received far more than any equally distinguished student of
his age. Not the illiberality of patrons, but his own luxurious

---

[1] As a specimen of Filelfo's Grub Street style of begging, I transcribe the following elegy (Rosmini, vol. ii. p. 285) : —

> 'Hæc autem altisone dum carmina celsius effert
>   Defecisse suo sentit ab ore tubam,
> Nam quia magnifici data non est copia nummi
>   Cogitur huic uti carmine raucidulo.
> Quod neque mireris ; vocem pretiosa canoram
>   Esca dat, et potus excitat ingenium.
> Ingenium spurco suevit languescere vino,
>   Humida mugitum reddere rapa solet.'

Francesco Sforza's anxiety to retain Filelfo in his service is expressed
in a letter to his treasurer (*ib.* p. 295) :—'Noi per niuno modo el vogliamo
perdere, la qual cosa seguirebbe quando gli paresse essere deluso, e non
potesse seguitare per manchamento delli dicti 250 fiorini la nobilissima
opera per lui in nostra gloria comenzata nè suplire agli altri suoi bisogni.'
The *tuba* and the *nobilissima opera* both refer to Filelfo's Sforziad.

[2] I may call particular attention to Filelfo's behaviour with regard
to Pius II.—the free pension of 200 florins granted (Rosmini, vol. ii.
p. 106), the menaces because it is not paid (*ib.* p. 115), the scurrilous
epigrams on the Pope's death (*ib.* p. 321), the abusive letter addressed
to Paul II. (*ib.* p. 136), the sentence of imprisonment for calumny issued
against him and his son Mario (*ib.* p. 140), the final palinode in which
he basely praises the Pope whom he had basely abused (*ib.* p. 146). The
whole series of transactions is disgraceful.

[3] Letter of Gregorio Lollio to the Cardinal of Pavia, reported by
Rosmini (vol. ii. p. 147).

habits, reduced him to beggary. All the while that he was screaming in bad Latin verse, he lived expensively, indulging ostentatious tastes, and finding money for unclean indulgences. In order to confirm his claim on the Duke of Milan's generosity, he began a gigantic Latin epic upon the life of Sforza. Without plan, a mere versified chronicle, encumbered with foolish mythological machinery, and loaded with fulsome flatteries, this leaden Sforziad crawled on until 12,800 lines had been written. Only the first eight books of it were published in MS., nor were these ever printed.[1]

By fair means and by foul, Filelfo had managed to secure a splendid reputation throughout Italy. His journey to Naples in 1453 resembled a triumphal progress. Nicholas V. entertained him with distinction, read his infamous satires, presented him with a purse of 500 ducats, and offered him a yearly stipend of 600 if he would dedicate his talents to translation. Alfonso dubbed him knight, and placed the poet's laurel on his brow with his own royal hands. As he passed through their capitals, the princes received him like an equal. At Ferrara he enjoyed the hospitalities of Duke Borso, at Mantua the friendship of the Marchese Lodovico Gonzaga; the terrible Gismondo Pandolfo Malatesta welcomed him in Rimini, and the General Jacopo Piccinino in his camp at Fossombrone. Nor was this fame confined to Italy. On the fall of Constantinople he addressed a letter to the Sultan, beseeching him to release his mother-in-law and her two daughters from captivity; the humanist's eloquence obtained this favour from the Turkish conqueror, who refused to accept a ransom for the relatives of so illustrious an orator.[2]

Until the death of Francesco Sforza Milan continued to be

[1] The whole poem ran to sixteen books. Therefore, according to Filelfo's art of poetry, the first eight contained 6,400 verses.

[2] See Rosmini, vol. ii. p. 90. The Greek epistle which he sent is printed, *ib.* p. 305.

the city of Filelfo's choice. After that event he turned his
thoughts to Rome. Pius II., Paul II., and Sixtus IV., in
succession, had testified their regard for him, either by
moderate presents, sufficient to excite his cupidity and check
his slanderous temper, or by negotiations which came to
nothing. At last, in 1474, he received from Rome the offer
of a professorial chair, with a stipend of 600 florins, and the
promise of the first vacant post in the Apostolic Chancery.

The old man of seventy-seven years once more journeyed
across the plains of Lombardy, ascended the Apennines,
passed through Florence,[1] and began his lectures with the
'Tusculans' of Cicero, on the twelfth day of January, 1475, in
Rome. The marks of favour with which Sixtus had received
him were highly honourable. Filelfo was permitted to sit in
the Pope's presence, and on Christmas Day he stood among
the ambassadors while Sixtus celebrated mass. The vigorous
old scholar at first felt that all his previous life had been
a tedious prologue to this blissful play. Soon, however, a
cloud arose on the horizon. The Pope's treasurer, Milliardo
Cicala, was remiss in payments. Filelfo retaliated by describing Cicala's vices in the most lurid colours to Sixtus.[2]
Though his style and eloquence were always vulgar, the concentrated fury and impassioned hatred of these invectives
cannot fail to impress the imagination. Such a picture of the
dissolute and grasping treasurer, painted by Filelfo and sent
to Sixtus, has a sinister humour which might recommend
itself to the audience of an infernal comedy. It is only
necessary to have some knowledge of the three men in order
to perceive its force. Nor did Sixtus himself long continue
in Filelfo's graces. Frequent journeys prove how unsettled
he became ; at last he left Rome in 1476, never to return.
When the Pazzi Conjuration failed at Florence, Filelfo wrote

[1] He had long since made peace with the Medici.
[2] See the original letters in Rosmini, vol. ii. pp. 411–419.

to congratulate Lorenzo de' Medici on his escape, and undertook the task of composing a history of the whole intrigue.
Two long and violent letters addressed to Sixtus, accusing
him of participation in the conspiracy, and heaping on
him charges of vice, were the result of this determination.
These epistles were dated from Milan, whither Filelfo had
retired in 1476, to find his third wife dead of the plague, and
buried on the eve of his arrival. His sorrow on this occasion
was genuine ; nor is it likely that he derived much comfort
from a curious epistle addressed to him by Paolo Morosini,
who, himself a husband and father, attempted to console the
septuagenarian professor by elaborate abuse of matrimony.[2]
To such ridiculous vagaries did the rhetorical spirit of humanism lead its votaries.

Filelfo's last journey was undertaken in 1481.   Ill at ease,
and sore of heart, the veteran of scholarship still longed for
further triumphs. All his wishes for some time past had
been set on ending his days at Florence, near the person of
Lorenzo de' Medici ; and when an invitation to the Chair of
Greek Literature arrived, it found him eager to set forth. He
was so poor, however, that the Duke's secretary, Jacopo
Antiquari, had to lend him money for the journey.[2] He just
managed to reach Florence, where he died of dysentery a fort-
night after his arrival, at the age of eighty-three. The Florentines buried him in the Church of the Annunziata.

[1] Rosmini, vol. ii. p. 261, note.   [2] *Ib.* p. 248.
[3] I cannot allow this mention of Antiquari's name to pass without
a note upon his life and services to letters. He was born and educated
at Perugia, entered the service of the Papal Legate Battista Savelli as
secretary at Bologna, and afterwards received the post of secretary and
diplomatic writer to the Sforza family at Milan. The Duke Galeazzo
Maria was his first master. At Milan he played the part of an amiable
and refined Mæcenas, while he carried on a correspondence in Latin—
still delightful to read—with Poliziano and all the greatest scholars of
his age. His biography, written at some length, with valuable miscellaneous appendices by Vermiglioli, was published at Perugia in 1819.

The sketch which I have given of Filelfo's life, abounds in details beyond the just proportions of the present chapter. This is due partly to the copiousness and the excellence of the authorities collected by Rosmini in his exhaustive biography, but more to the undoubted fact that Filelfo ranks as the typical humanist of his age. The universality of his acquirements and the impression they made upon contemporaries, his enormous physical vigour and incessant mental activity, the vehemence with which he prosecuted his literary warfares and the restlessness that drove him from capital to capital in Italy, are themselves enough to mark him out as the representative hero of the second period of humanism. Not less characteristic were the quality and the form of his literary work—ridiculously over-valued then, and now perhaps too readily depreciated. There is something pathetic in the certainty of everlasting fame that sustained the student through so many years of unremitting labour. It makes us wonder whether the achievements of the human intellect, in science and discovery, acceptable as these may be to their own time, are not, equally with Filelfo's triumph of scholarship, foredoomed to speedy obscuration. Nothing is imperishable but high thought, to which art has communicated the indestructible form of beauty.

The ' Age of the Despots '[1] contains a promise of further details concerning Vittorino da Feltre, to redeem which the time has now come. His father's name was Bruto de' Rambaldoni; but having been born at Feltre in the year 1378, he took from his birthplace the surname by which he is best known.

Like the majority of his contemporaries, Vittorino studied Latin under John of Ravenna and rhetoric under Gasparino da Barzizza. His poverty compelled him at the same time to support himself by taking pupils; this drudgery, however,

[1] Pp. 138, 139.

was so unremunerative that, when he wanted to attend the
mathematical lectures of Biagio Pelacane, he had to pay
that avaricious and eccentric teacher by personal service. As
Haydn got his much-desired instruction from Porpora by
playing the part of valet,[1] so Vittorino became the scullery boy
of Pelacane,[2] in order that he might acquire geometry. These
early studies were carried on at Padua, from which town he
appears to have moved about the year 1417 to Venice. Here
he entered into friendship with Guarino da Verona, and
having learned Greek, returned to his old university as
professor of rhetoric.[3] The bias of Vittorino's genius inclined
toward private teaching, and it is this by which he is distinguished among contemporary humanists. Accordingly we
find that, as soon as he was settled in Padua, he opened a
school for a fixed number of young men, selected without
regard to rank or wealth. From the richer pupils he required
fees proportioned to their means ; from the poor he exacted
nothing : thus the wealthy were made to support the needy,
while the teacher obtained for himself the noble satisfaction
of relieving aspirants after knowledge from the pressure of
want and privation. Other gain than this he never thought
of. Only genuine students were allowed to remain in
Vittorino's school ; the moral rule was strict, and high
thinking and plain living were expected from all his pupils.
This generous devotion to the cause of learning for its own
sake contrasts strongly with the self-seeking and vainglory of
other humanists. When Filelfo was urged on one occasion
to open a school for promising young men of noble birth,
he asked disdainfully whether his friends expected him to
take rank as a licensed victualler.[4] He was unable to

---

[1] Grove's *Dictionary of Music and Musicians*, vol. i. p. 704 b.

[2] 'Usque ad mundandam supellectilem quæ sumpto cibo lavare
consuerit.'—Rosmini, *Vita di Vittorino*, p. 38, note.

[3] In 1422 apparently.   [4] *Locandiere.* Rosmini, vol. i. p. 67.

comprehend the possibility of doing anything that would not reflect lustre on himself or place him in the light of popular applause.

Vittorino found it difficult to govern his school at Padua as strictly as he wished. The public Gymnasium was ill-ordered, and great license of life was permitted to its students. He therefore removed to Venice in 1423, where he continued his work as private tutor. By this time, however, he had acquired considerable reputation as an educator, to whose care the youth of both sexes might be entrusted with implicit confidence—no small testimony to his goodness in that age of ungoverned passions and indescribable vices. The Marchese Gian Francesco Gonzaga was looking out for a master for his children, and his choice fell on Vittorino. The admiration of antiquity was no mere matter of fashion with this prince. He loved history for its own sake, and professed a special reverence for the Roman Camillus. His practical good sense made him understand that, if he wished his sons and daughters to become thoroughly educated, not only in the humanities and mathematics, but also in the republican virtues of the ancients, which then formed the ideal of life in Italy, he must be willing to commit them wholly to the charge of their appointed governor. Vittorino, who would have undertaken the duty on no other condition, obtained full control of the young princes and their servants. An appointment of twenty sequins per month was assigned to him, together with a general order on the treasury of Mantua. A villa, called Casa Zojosa, which we may translate Joyous Gard, was allotted to the new household, and there Vittorino established himself as master in 1425. He had much to do before this dwelling could be converted from the pleasure house of a mediæval sovereign into the semi-monastic resort of earnest students. Through its open galleries and painted banquet chambers the young Gonzaghi lounged with favourite friends selected from the Mantuan nobility. The tables groaned under gold and silver plate, while perfumed lacqueys handed round rich wines and highly seasoned dishes, and the garden alleys echoed to the sound of lute and viol. Without making any brusque or sudden reformation, Vittorino managed, by degrees, and on various pretexts, to dismiss the more dangerous friends and servants of his pupils. A strict house-porter was engaged, with orders to exclude suspicious visitors. Plain clothes, simple habits, and frugal meals became the rule of the household, Vittorino contriving to render these changes no less agreeable than salutary to his pupils. When complaints arose from the former companions of the princes and their parents, he laid his plan of training clearly before the Marquis, who had the good sense to approve of all that he had done.

The eldest of Gian Francesco's children, Lodovico, was a youth of lazy habits, inclined to gluttony, and already too fat for his age. The next, Carlo, had outgrown his strength, and needed more substantial food. Vittorino devised systems of diet and physical training suited to their several temperaments, making it his one object to increase their vigour, and by multiplying sources of rational enjoyment to dispose them to the energetic exercise of their faculties. He by no means neglected what we call athletics. Indeed, it was a fundamental axiom of his method that a robust body could alone harbour a healthy mind. Boys who sat poring over books, or haunted solitary places, lost in dreaming, found no favour in his eyes. To exercises in the gymnasium or the riding-school he preferred games in the open air; hunting and fishing, wrestling and fencing, running and jumping, were practised by his pupils in the park outside their palace. To harden them against severities of heat and cold, to render

them temperate in food and drink, to train their voices, and
to improve their carriage was his first care. Since he could
not himself superintend their education in all its branches,
he engaged a subordinate staff of tutors; grammarians,
logicians, mathematicians, painters, and masters of riding,
dancing, singing, swimming, fencing, began to crowd the
halls of Joyous Gard. Each had his own allotted task to
perform, while Vittorino surveyed the whole scheme.
'Perhaps,' says Rosmini,[1] 'the only sciences that were not
taught in this academy were civil and canon law and
natural physics.'

It must not be imagined that so extensive an apparatus
existed solely for the young Gonzaghi. Noble youths from
all the Courts of Italy, and students from remote parts of
Europe, sought admittance to Vittorino's school. The more
promising of these pupils, who were fitted by their rank and
disposition to associate with his princely charges, the master
housed under his own roof; while for the rest he provided
suitable lodgings near at hand. Many were the poor
students who thus owed to his generosity participation in the
most refined and scientific culture their century afforded.[2]
While paying this tribute to Vittorino da Feltre, we must
remember the honour that is also due to Gian Francesco
Gonzaga. Had this prince not been endowed with true
liberality of soul and freedom from petty prejudice,
Vittorino could never have developed a system based upon
pure democratic principles, which even now may rank as an
unrivalled educational ideal. If the master, again, was able
to provide for sixty poor scholars at a time—teaching,
feeding, clothing, and furnishing them with costly books,

[1] P. 111.

[2] Sixty poor scholars were taught, fed, clothed, and provided with
implements of study at his cost. He also subsidised their families in
distress. Rosmini, *Vita di Vittorino*, pp. 165, 166.

his friend the Marquis must, we feel sure, have supplied his purse with extra funds for charitable purposes.[1]

The numerous biographers of Vittorino have transmitted many details in illustration of his method of teaching. He used to read the classic authors aloud, prefixing biographical notices by way of introduction, and explaining the matter, as well as the language of his text, as he proceeded. Sometimes he made his pupils read, correcting their pronunciation, and obliging them to mark the meaning by emphasis. He relied much on learning by heart and repetition, as the surest means of forming a good style. Gifted with a finer instinct for language than the majority of his contemporaries, he was careful that his pupils should distinguish between different types of literary excellence, not confounding Cicero with Seneca or Virgil with Lucan, but striving to appreciate the special qualities of each. With a view to the acquisition of pure principles of taste, he confined them at first to Virgil and Homer, Cicero and Demosthenes. These four authors he regarded as the supreme masters of expression. Ovid was too luxuriant, Juvenal too coarse, to serve as guides for tiros. Horace and Persius among the satirists, Terence among the comic poets, might be safely studied. In spite of Seneca's weight as a philosophic essayist, Vittorino censured the affectations of his rhetoric; and while he praised the beauty of the Latin elegists, he judged them ill-suited for the training of the young. Criticism of this kind, though it may sound to us obvious and superficial, was extremely rare in the fifteenth century, when scholars were too apt to neglect differences of style in ancient authors, and to ignore the ethics of their works. The refinement which distinguished Vittorino, made him prefer the graces of a chastened manner

---

[1] Rosmini, *Vita di Vittorino*, p. 165. Vespasiano, p. 492, tells a story which illustrates these relations between Vittorino and the Marquis. Cf., too, p. 494.

to the sounding phrases of emphatic declamation. His pupils were taught to see that they had something to say first, and then to say it with simplicity and elegance.

This purity of taste was no mere matter of æsthetic sensibility with Vittorino. Habits which brutalise the mind or debase the body, however sanctioned by the usage of the times, met with little toleration in his presence. Swearing, obscene language, vulgar joking, and angry altercation were severely punished. Personal morality and the observance of religious exercises he exacted from his pupils. Lying was a heinous offence. Those who proved intractable upon these points were excluded from his school. Of the rest Vespasiano writes with emphasis that ' his house was a sanctuary of manners, deeds, and words.' [1]

Concerning the noble Italian youths who were educated with the Gonzaga family at Mantua, enough has been said in another place.[2] Appended to Rosmini's copious biography will be found, by those who are curious to read such details, the notices of forty more or less distinguished pupils.[3] Beside the two sons of Gian Francesco Gonzaga already mentioned, Vittorino educated three other children of his master—Gian-lucido, Alessandro, and Cecilia.[4] Wholly dedicated to the cares of teaching, and more anxious to survive in the good fame of his scholars than to secure the immortality of literature, Vittorino bequeathed no writings to posterity. He lived to a hale and hearty old age; and when he died, in 1446, it was found that the illustrious scholar, after enjoying for so many years the liberality of his princely patron, had not accumulated enough money to pay for his own funeral.

---

[1] P. 492. [2] Vol. I., *Age of the Despots*, p. 138.

[3] Pp. 249–476.

[4] See Rosmini, p. 183, and Vespasiano, p. 493, for the record of her virtues, her learning, and her refusal to wed the infamous Oddo da Montefeltro.

Whatever he possessed, he spent in charity during his lifetime, trusting to the kindness of his friends to bury him when dead. Few lives of which there is any record in history, are so perfectly praiseworthy as Vittorino's; few men have more nobly realised the idea of living for the highest objects of their age; few have succeeded in keeping themselves so wholly unspotted by the vices of the world around them.

By the patronage extended to Vittorino da Feltre the Court of Mantua took rank among the high schools of humanism in Italy. Ferrara won a similar distinction through the liberality of the House of Este. What has already been said about Milan applies, however, in a less degree to Ferrara. The arts and letters, though they flourished with exceeding brilliance beneath the patrons of Boiardo, Ariosto, and Tasso, were but accessories to a splendid and voluptuous Court life. Literature was little better than an exotic, cultivated for its rarity and beauty by the princes of the Este family.

The golden age of culture at Ferrara began in 1402, when Niccolo III. reopened the university. Twenty-seven years later Guarino da Verona made it one of the five chief seats of Southern learning. The life of this eminent scholar in many points resembles that of Filelfo, though their characters were very different. Guarino was born of respectable parents at Verona in 1370. He studied Latin in the school of Giovanni da Ravenna, and while still a lad of eighteen travelled to Constantinople at the cost of a noble Venetian, Paolo Zane, in order to learn Greek. After a residence of five years in Greece he returned to Venice, and began to lecture to crowded audiences.[1] Like all the humanists, he seems to have preferred temporary to permanent engagements—passing from Venice to Verona, from Trent to Padua, from Bologna to Florence, and everywhere acquiring that substantial reputation

[1] See his Life by Rosmini, p. 11, for his brilliant reception at Venice.

as a teacher to which he owed the invitation of Niccolo d' Este in 1429. He was now a man of nearly sixty, master of the two languages, and well acquainted with the method of instruction. The Marquis of Ferrara engaged him as tutor to his illegitimate son Lionello, heir apparent to his throne. For seven years Guarino devoted himself wholly to the education of this youth, who passed for one of the best scholars of his age. Granting that the reputation for learning was lightly conferred on princes by their literary parasites, it seems certain that Lionello derived more than a mere smattering in culture from his tutor. Amid the pleasures of the chase, to which he was passionately devoted, and the distractions of the gayest Court in Italy, he found time to correspond on topics of scholarship with Poggio, Filelfo, Decembrio, and Francesco Barbaro. His conversation turned habitually upon the fashionable themes of antique ethics, and his favourite companions were men of polite education. It is no wonder that the humanists, who saw in him a future Augustus, deplored his early death with unfeigned sorrow, though we, who can only judge him by the general standard of his family, may be permitted to reserve our opinion. The profile portrait of Lionello, now preserved in the National Gallery, does not, at any rate, prepossess us very strongly in his favour.

Guarino, like his friend Vittorino, was celebrated for the method of his teaching and for the exact order of his discipline.[1] Students flocked from all the cities of Italy to his lecture-room; for, as soon as his tutorial engagements with the prince permitted, he received a public appointment as professor of eloquence from the Ferrarese Consiglio de' Savi. In this post he laboured for many years, maintaining his reputation as a student and filling the universities of Italy with his pupils. A sentence describing his manner of life in

---

[1] See the details collected by Rosmini, *Vita di Guarino*, pp. 79–87.

extreme old age might be used to illustrate the enthusiasm
which sustained the vital energy of scholars in that generation :—'His memory is marvellous, and his habit of reading
is so indefatigable, that he scarcely takes the time to eat, to
sleep, or to go abroad ; and yet his limbs and senses have the
vigour of youth.'[1]   Guarino was one of the few humanists
whose moral character won equal respect with his learning.
When he died at the age of ninety, the father of six boys and
seven girls by his wife Taddea Cendrata of Verona, it was
possible to say with truth that he had realised the ideal of a
temperate scholar's life.   Yet this incomparable teacher of
youth undertook the defence of Beccadelli's obscene verses :
this anchorite of humanism penned virulent invectives with
the worst of his contemporaries.[2]   Such contrasts were common enough in the fifteenth century.

The name of Giovanni Aurispa must not be omitted in
connection with Ferrara.   Born in 1369 at Noto in Sicily, he
lived to a great age, and died in 1459.   He too travelled in
early youth to Constantinople, and returned, laden with MSS.
and learning, to profess the humanities in Italy.   His life
forms, therefore, a close parallel with that of both Guarino
and Filelfo.   Aurispa, however, was gifted with a less un-
resting temper than Filelfo ; nor did he achieve the same
professorial success as Guarino.   In his school at Ferrara
he enjoyed the calmer pleasures of a student's life, 'devoted,'
as Filelfo phrased it, ' to the placid Muses.'[3]

To give an account of all the minor Courts, where humanism flourished under the patronage of petty princes, would be
tedious and unprofitable.   It is enough to notice that the

[1] Timoteo Maffei, quoted by Tiraboschi, vol. vi. lib. iii. cap. 5, 8.

[2] He carried on literary feuds with Niccolo de' Niccoli, Poggio, Filelfo,
and Georgios Trapezuntius.

[3] 'Placidis Aurispa Camœnis Deditus,' Sat., dec. i. hec. 5.   Valla,
Antid. in Pogium, p. 7, describes him as ' virum suavissimum et ab
omni contentione remotissimum.'

universities, in this age of indefatigable energy, kept forming scholars, eager to make their way as secretaries and tutors, while the nobles competed for the honour and the profit to be derived from the service of illustrious wits and ready pens. The seeds of classic culture were thus sown in every little city that could boast its castle. Carpi, for example, was preparing the ground where Aldus and Musurus flourished. At Forli the Ordelaffi, doomed to extinction at no distant period, gave protection to Codrus Urceus.[1] Mirandola was growing fit to be the birthplace of the mighty Pico. Alessandro and Costanzo Sforza were adorning their lordship of Pesaro with a library that rivalled those of Rome and Florence.[2] In the fortress of Rimini, Sigismondo Pandolfo Malatesta conversed with men of learning whenever his intrigues and his military duties gave him leisure. The desperate and godless tyrant, whose passions bordered upon madness, and whose name was a byeword for all the vices that disgrace humanity, curbed his temper before petty witlings like Porcellio, and carved a record of his burning love for learning on the temple raised to celebrate his fame in Rimini. To the same passion for scholarship in his brother, Malatesta Novello, the tiny burgh of Cesena owed the foundation of a library, not only well supplied with books, but endowed with a yearly income of 300 golden florins for its maintenance. The money spent on scholarship at these minor Courts was gained, for the most part, in military service—the wealth of Florentine and Venetian citizens, of Milanese despots, and ambitious Popes flowing through the hands of professional war-captains into the pockets of booksellers and students. It consequently happened that the impulse given at this time to learning in the lesser cities was but temporary. With the fall of the Malatesti and the

[1] Cf. Tiraboschi, vi. lib. iii. cap. 5, 58.
[2] Vespasiano, pp. 113–117, gives an interesting account of these lettered and warlike princes.

Sforza family, for instance, erudition died at Rimini and
Pesaro.

This might have been the case at Urbino also, if the
House of Montefeltro had not succeeded, by wise conduct
and prudent marriages, in resisting the encroachments of
the Church, and transmitting its duchy to the Della Rovere
family. As it was, Urbino retained for three generations
the stamp of culture and refinement impressed upon it by
the good Duke Frederick. Of his famous library, Vespasiano,
who was employed in its formation, has given us minute
and interesting details.[1] During more than fourteen years
the Duke kept thirty or forty copyists continually employed
in transcribing Greek and Latin MSS. Not only the classics
in both languages, but the ecclesiastical and mediæval authors,
the Italian poets, and the works of contemporary humanists
found a place in his collection. The cost of the whole was
estimated at considerably over 30,000 ducats. Each volume
was bound in crimson, with silver clasps ; the leaves were
of vellum, exquisitely adorned with miniatures ; nor could
you find a printed book in the whole library, for the Duke
would have been ashamed to own one. Vespasiano's admiration for these delicately finished MSS. and the contempt
he expresses for the new art of printing are highly characteristic.[2] Enough has been already said by me elsewhere
about Federigo da Montefeltro and his patronage of learning.[3]
The Queen's collection at Windsor contains a curious picture,
attributed to Melozza da Forli, of which I may be allowed
to speak in this place, since it possesses more than usual
interest for the student of humanism at the Italian Courts.
In a large rectangular hall, lighted from above by windows
in a dome, the Duke of Urbino is seated, wearing the robes
and badges of the Garter, and resting his left hand on a

[1] See pp. 94–99.   [2] P. 99.
[3] Vol. I., *Age of the Despots*, pp. 136–142.

folio. His son Guidobaldo, a boy of about eleven years of age, or little more, stands at the Duke's knee, dressed in yellow damask trimmed with pearls. Behind them, on a raised bench with a desk before it, sit three men, one attired in the red suit of a prelate, the second in black ecclesiastical attire, and the third in secular costume. At a door, opening on a passage, stand servants and lesser courtiers. The whole company are listening attentively to a grey-haired, black-robed humanist, seated in a sort of pulpit opposite to the Duke and his son. A large book, bound in crimson, with silver clasps is open on the desk before him; and by the movement of his mouth it is clear that he is reading aloud passages from some classical or ecclesiastical author, and explaining them for the benefit of his illustrious audience. To identify the scholar and the three men behind Federigo would not be impossible, if the exact date of this curious work could be ascertained; for they are clearly portraits. I like to fancy that in the layman we may perhaps recognise the excellent Vespasiano. Such conjectures are, however, hazardous; meanwhile the picture has intrinsic value as the unique representation, so far as I know, of a scene of frequent occurrence in the Courts of Italy, where listening to lectures formed a part of every day's occupation.

This is the proper place to speak of Vespasiano da Bisticci, on whose 'Lives of Illustrious Men' I have had occasion to draw so copiously. Peculiar interest attaches to him as the last of mediæval scribes, and at the same time the first of modern booksellers.[1] Besides being the agent of Cosimo de' Medici, Nicholas V., and Frederick of Urbino, Vespasiano supplied the foreign markets, sending MSS. by order to Hungary, Portugal, Germany, and England. The extent of his trade rendered him the largest employer of copyists in Europe at the moment when this industry was about to

[1] In the register of his death he is described as Vespasiano, Cartolaro

be superseded, and when scholars were already inquiring
for news about the art that saved expense and shortened the
labour of the student.[1] Vespasiano, who was born in 1421
at Florence, lived until 1498 ; so that after having helped
to form the three greatest collections of MSS. in Italy, he witnessed the triumph of printing, and might have even handled
the Musæus issued from the Aldine Press in 1493. Vespasiano was no mere tradesman. His knowledge of the books
he sold was accurate ; continual study enabled him to over-
look the copyists, and to vouch for the exactitude of their
transcripts.[2] At the same time his occupation brought him
into close intimacy with the chief scholars of the age, so
that the new culture reached him by conversation and
familiar correspondence. As a biographer Vespasiano possessed rare merit. Personally acquainted with the men of
whom he wrote, he drew their characters with praiseworthy
succinctness and simplicity. There is no panegyrical emphasis, no calumnious innuendo, in his sketches. It may
even be said that they suffer from reservation of opinion
and suppression of facts. Vespasiano's hatred of vice and
love of virtue were so genuine that, in his eagerness to
honour men of letters and their patrons, he softened down
harsh outlines and passed over all that is condemnable in
silence. He was less anxious to paint character in the style

[1] See Rosmini, *Vita di Filelfo*, vol. ii. p. 201. 'I have made up my
mind to buy some of those codices they are now making without any
trouble, and without the pen, but with certain so-called types, and whic
seem to be the work of a skilled and exact scribe. Tell me, then, at
what price are sold the *Natural History* of Pliny, the three Decades of
Livy, and Aulus Gellius.' Letter to Nicodemo Tranchedino, sent from
Siena to Rome, dated July 25, 1470.

[2] See this passage from a panegyric quoted by Angelo Mai :—'Tu
profecto in hoc nostro deteriori sæculo hebraicæ, græcæ atque latinæ
linguarum, omnium voluminum dignorum memoratu notitiam, eo-
rumque auctores memoriæ tradidisti.'—*Vite di Uomini Illustri*, preface,
p. xxiii

of Tacitus or Guicciardini, than to relate what he knew about the progress of learning in his age. The ethical intention in his work is obvious. The qualities he loves to celebrate are piety, chastity, generosity, devotion to the cause of liberal culture, and high-souled patriotism. Of the vices that added a lurid lustre to the age in which he lived, of the political rancours that divided the cities into hostile parties, and of the imperfections in the characters of eminent men, we hear nothing from Vespasiano. It is pleasant to conclude this chapter with an expression of gratitude to a man so blameless in his life, so charitable in his judgments, and so trustworthy in his record of contemporary history.

CHAPTER VI

THIRD PERIOD OF HUMANISM

Improvement in Taste and Criticism—Coteries and Academies—Revival
of Italian Literature—Printing—Florence, the Capital of Learning—
Lorenzo de' Medici and his Circle—Public Policy of Lorenzo—
Literary Patronage—Variety of his Gifts—Meetings of the Platonic
Society—Marsilio Ficino—His Education for Platonic Studies—
Translations of Plato and the Neoplatonists—Harmony between
Plato and Christianity—Giovanni Pico—His First Appearance in
Florence—His Theses proposed at Rome—Censure of the Church—
His Study of the Cabbala—Large Conception of Learning—Occult
Science—Cristoforo Landino—Professor of Fine Literature—Virgilian
Studies — Camaldolese Disputations — Leo Battista Alberti — His
Versatility—Bartolommeo Scala—Obscure Origin—Chancellor of
Florence—Angelo Poliziano—Early Life—Translation of Homer—
The 'Homericus Juvenis'—True Genius in Poliziano—Command of
Latin and Greek—Resuscitation of Antiquity in his own Person—
His Professorial Work—The 'Miscellanea'—Relation to Medici—
Roman Scholarship in this Period—Pius II.—Pomponius Lætus
—His Academy and Mode of Life—Persecution under Paul II.—
Humanism at Naples—Pontanus—His Academy—His Writings—
Academies established in all Towns of Italy—Introduction of Print-
ing — Sweynheim and Pannartz—The Early Venetian Press—
Florence—Cennini—Alopa's Homer—Change in Scholarship effected
by Printing—The Life of Aldo Manuzio—The Princely House of
Pio at Carpi—Greek Books before Aldo—The Aldine Press at Venice
—History of its Activity—Aldo and Erasmus—Aldo and the Greek
Refugees—Aldo's Death—His family and Successors—The Ne-
academia—The Salvation of Greek Literature.

IN the four preceding chapters I have sketched the rise and
progress of Italian humanism with more minuteness than
need be now employed upon the history of its further development. By the scholars of the first and second period the
whole domain of ancient literature was reconquered; the

classics were restored in their integrity to the modern world. Petrarch first inflamed the enthusiasm without which so great a work could not have been accomplished, his immediate successors mastered the Greek language, and explored every province of antiquity. Much still remained, however, to be achieved by a new generation of students : for as yet criticism was but in its cradle ; the graces of style were but little understood ; indiscriminate erudition passed for scholarship, and crude verbiage for eloquence. The humanists of the third age, still burning with the zeal that animated Petrarch, and profiting by the labours of their predecessors, ascended to a higher level of culture. It is their glory to have purified the coarse and tumid style of mediæval Latinists, to have introduced the methods of comparative and æsthetic criticism, and to have distinguished the characteristics of the authors and the periods they studied.

The salient features of this third age of humanism may be briefly stated. Having done their work by sowing the seeds of culture broadcast, the vagrant professors of the second period begin to disappear, and the republic of letters tends to crystallise round men of eminence in coteries and learned circles. This, therefore, is the age of the academies. Secondly, it is noticeable that Italian literature, almost totally abandoned in the first fervour of enthusiasm for antiquity, now receives nearly as much attention as the classics. Since the revival of Italian in the golden age of the Renaissance will form the subject of my final volume, the names of Lorenzo de' Medici and Poliziano at Florence, of Boiardo at Ferrara, and of Sannazzaro at Naples may here suffice to indicate the points of contact between scholarship and the national literature. A century had been employed in the acquisition of humanistic culture ; when acquired, it bore fruit, not only in more elegant scholarship, but also in new forms of poetry and prose for the people. A third marked feature of the period is the establish-

ment of the printing press. The energy wherewith in little
more than fifty years the texts of the classic authors were
rendered indestructible by accident or time, and placed within
the reach of students throughout Europe, demands particular
attention in this chapter.

Florence is still the capital of learning. The most brilliant humanists, gathered round the person of Lorenzo de'
Medici, give laws to the rest of Italy, determining by their
tastes and studies the tone of intellectual society. Lorenzo is
himself in so deep and true a sense the master spirit of this
circle, that to describe his position in the republic will hardly
be considered a digression.

Before his death in 1464 Cosimo de' Medici had succeeded
in rendering his family necessary to the State of Florence.
Though thwarted by ambitious rivals and hampered by the
intrigues of the party he had formed to rule the commonwealth, Cosimo contrived so to complicate the public finances
with his own banking business, and so to bind the leading
burghers to himself by various obligations, that, while he in
no way affected the style of a despot, Florence belonged to his
house more surely than Bologna to the Bentivogli. For the
continuation of this authority, based on intrigue and cemented
by corruption, it was absolutely needful that the spirit of
Cosimo should survive in his successors. A single false move,
by unmasking the tyranny so carefully veiled, by offending
the republican vanities of the Florentines, or by employing
force where everything had hitherto been gained by craft,
would at this epoch have destroyed the prospects of the
Medicean family. So true it is that the history of this age in
Italy is not the history of commonwealths so much as the
history of individualities, of men. The principles reduced to
rule by Machiavelli in his essay on the Prince may be studied
in the lives of fifteenth-century adventurers, who, like Cesare
Borgia, discerned the necessity of using violence for special

ends, or, like the Medici, perceived that sovereignty could be better grasped by a hand gloved with velvet than mailed in steel. The Medici of both branches displayed through eight successive generations, in their general line of policy, in the disasters that attended their divergence from it, and in the means they used to rehabilitate their influence, the action of what Balzac calls *l'homme politique*, with striking clearness to the philosophic student.

Both the son and grandson of Cosimo well understood the part they had to play, and played it so ably that even the errors of the younger Piero, the genius of Savonarola, and the failure of the elder Medicean line were insufficient to check the gradual subjugation of the commonwealth he had initiated. Lorenzo's father, Piero, called by the Florentines *Il Gottoso*, suffered much from ill-health, and was unable to take the lead in politics.[1] Yet the powers entrusted to his father were confirmed for him. The elections remained in the hands of the Medicean party, and the *balia* appointed in their favour continued to control the State. The dangerous conspiracy against Piero's life, engaged in by Luca Pitti and Diotisalvi Neroni, proved that his enemies regarded the chief of the Medici as the leader of the republic. It was due to the prudent action of the young Lorenzo that this conspiracy failed; and the Medici were even strengthened by the downfall of their foes. From the tone of the congratulations addressed on this

---

[1] It may be useful to add a skeleton pedigree of the Medici in this place:—

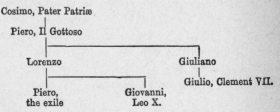

Cosimo, Pater Patriæ
Piero, Il Gottoso
Lorenzo — Giuliano
Giulio, Clement VII.
Piero, the exile — Giovanni, Leo X.

occasion by the ruling powers of Italy to Piero and Lorenzo, we may conclude that they were already reckoned as princes outside Florence, though they still maintained a burgherlike simplicity of life within the city walls.

In the marriage of his son Lorenzo to Clarice degli Orsini, of the princely Roman house, Piero gave signs of a departure from the cautious policy of Cosimo. Foreign alliances were regarded with suspicion by the Florentines, and Pandolfini's advice to his sons, that they should avoid familiarity with territorial magnates, exactly represented the spirit of the republic.[1] In like manner, the education of both Lorenzo and Giuliano, their intercourse with royal guests, and the prominent places assigned them on occasions of ceremony, indicated an advance toward despotism. It was concordant with the manners of the age that one family should play the part of host for the republic. The discharge of this duty by the Medici aroused no jealousy among the burghers; yet it enabled the ambitious house to place themselves in an unique position, and, while seeming to remain mere citizens, to take a step in the direction of sovereignty.

On the death of Piero, in 1469, the chief men of the Medicean party waited upon Lorenzo, and, after offering their condolences, besought him to succeed his father in the presidency of the State. The feeling prevailed among the leaders of the city that it was impossible, under the existing conditions of Italian politics, to carry on the commonwealth without a titular head. Lorenzo, then in his twenty-second year, entered thus upon the political career in the course of which he not only maintained a balance of power in Italy, but also remodelled the internal government of Florence in the interests of his family, and further strengthened their position by establishing connections with the Papal See. While bending all the faculties of his powefrul and subtle intellect to the one

See Vol. I., *Age of the Despots*, p. 190.

end of consolidating a tyranny, Lorenzo was far too wise to assume the bearing of a despot. He conversed familiarly with the citizens, encouraged artists and scholars to address him on terms of equality, and was careful to adopt no titles. His personal temperament made the task of being in effect a sovereign, while he acted like a citizen, comparatively easy, his chief difficulties arose from the necessity under which he laboured, like his grandfather Cosimo, of governing through a party composed of men distinguished by birth and ability, and powerful by wealth and connections. To keep this party in good temper, to flatter its members with the show of influence, and to gain their concurrence for the alterations he introduced into the State machinery of Florence, was the problem of his life. By creating a body of clients, bound to himself by diverse interests and obligations, he succeeded in bridling the Medicean party and excluding from offices of trust all dangerous and disaffected persons. The goodwill of the city at large was secured by the prosperity at home and peace abroad which marked the last fourteen years of his administration, while the splendour of his foreign alliances contributed in no small measure to his popularity. The Florentines were proud of a citizen who brought them into the first rank of Italian Powers, and who refrained from assuming the style of sovereign. Thus Lorenzo solved the most difficult of political problems—that of using a close oligarchy for the maintenance of despotism in a free and jealous commonwealth. None of his rivals retained power enough to withhold the sceptre from his sons when they should seek to grasp it.

The roots of the Medici clung to no one part of Florence in particular. They seemed superficial; yet they crept beneath the ground in all directions. Intertwined as they were with every interest both public and private in the city, to cut them out implied the excision of some vital member.

This was the secret of their power in the next generation, when, banished and reduced to bastards, the Medici returned from two exiles, survived the perils of the siege and Alessandro's murder, and finally assumed the Ducal crown in the person of the last scion of their younger branch. The policy, so persistently pursued for generations, so powerfully applied by Lorenzo, might be compared to the attack of an octopus, which fastens on its victim by a multitude of tiny tentacles, and waits till he is drained of strength before it shoots its beak into a vital spot.

In one point Lorenzo was inferior to his grandfather. He had no commercial talent. After suffering the banking business of the Medici to fall into disorder, he became virtually bankrupt, while his personal expenditure kept continually increasing. In order to retrieve his fortunes it was necessary for him to gain complete disposal of the public purse. This was the real object of the constitutional revolution of 1480, whereby his Privy Council assumed the active functions of the State. Had Lorenzo been as great in finance as in the management of men, the way might have been smoothed for his son Piero in the disastrous year of 1494.

If Lorenzo neglected the pursuit of wealth, whereby Cosimo had raised himself from insignificance to the dictatorship of Florence, he surpassed his grandfather in the use he made of literary patronage. It is not paradoxical to affirm that in his policy we can trace the subordination of a genuine love of arts and letters to statecraft. The new culture was one of the instruments that helped to build his despotism. Through his thorough and enthusiastic participation in the intellectual interests of his age, he put himself into close sympathy with the Florentines, who were glad to acknowledge for their leader by far the ablest of the men of parts in Italy. According as we choose our point of view, we may regard him either as a tyrant, involving his country in debt

and dangerous wars, corrupting the morals and enfeebling
the spirit of the people, and systematically enslaving the
Athens of the modern world for the sake of founding a petty
principality ; or else as the most liberal-minded noble of his
epoch, born to play the first part in the Florentine republic,
and careful to use his wealth and influence for the advancement of his fellow-citizens in culture, learning, arts, amenities
of life. Savonarola and the Florentine historians adopt the
former of these two opinions. Sismondi, in his passion for
liberty, arrays against Lorenzo the political assassinations
he permitted, the enervation of Florence, the national debt
incurred by the republic, the exhausting wars with Sixtus
carried on in his defence. His panegyrists, on the contrary,
love to paint him as the pacificator of Italy, the restorer
of Florentine poetry, the profound critic, and the generous
patron. The truth lies in the combination of these two
apparently contradictory judgments. Lorenzo was the representative man of his nation at a moment when political
institutions were everywhere inclining to despotism, and
when the spiritual life of the Italians found its noblest expression in art and literature. The principality of Florence
was thrust upon him by the policy of Cosimo, by the vote of
the chief citizens, and by the example of the sister republics,
all of whom, with the exception of Venice, submitted to the
sway of rulers. Had he wished, he might have found it
difficult to preserve the commonwealth in its integrity. Few
but doctrinaires believed in a *governo misto* ; only aristocrats
desired a *governo stretto* ; all but democrats dreaded a
governo largo. And yet a new constitution must have been
framed after one of these types, and the Florentines must
have been educated to use it with discretion, before Lorenzo
could have resigned his office of dictator with any prospect
of freedom for the city in his charge. Such unselfish
patriotism, in the face of such overwhelming difficulties, and

in antagonism to the whole tendency of the age, was not to be expected from an oligarch of the Renaissance, born in the purple, and used from infancy to intrigue.

Lorenzo was a man of marvellous variety and range of mental power. He possessed one of those rare natures, fitted to comprehend all knowledge and to sympathise with the most diverse forms of life. While he never for one moment relaxed his grasp on politics, among philosophers he passed for a sage, among men of letters for an original and graceful poet, among scholars for a Grecian sensitive to every nicety of Attic idiom, among artists for an amateur gifted with refined discernment and consummate taste. Pleasure-seekers knew in him the libertine, who jousted with the boldest, danced and masqueraded with the merriest, sought adventures in the streets at night, and joined the people in their May-day games and Carnival festivities. The pious extolled him as an author of devotional lauds and mystery plays, a profound theologian, a critic of sermons. He was no less famous for his jokes and repartees than for his pithy apophthegms and maxims, as good a judge of cattle as of statues, as much at home in the bosom of his family as in the riot of an orgy, as ready to discourse on Plato as to plan a campaign or to plot the death of a dangerous citizen. An apologist may always plead that Lorenzo was the epitome of his nation's most distinguished qualities, that the versatility of the Renaissance found in him its fullest incarnation. It was the duty of Italy in the fifteenth century not to establish religious or constitutional liberty, but to resuscitate culture. Before the disastrous wars of invasion had begun, it might well have seemed even to patriots as though Florence needed a Mæcenas more than a Camillus. Therefore the prince who in his own person combined all accomplishments, who knew by sympathy and counsel how to stimulate the genius of men superior to himself in special arts and sciences, who spent

his fortune lavishly on works of public usefulness, whose
palace formed the rallying-point of wit and learning, whose
council chamber was the school of statesmen, who expressed
his age in every word and every act, in his vices and his
virtues, his crimes and generous deeds, cannot be fairly
judged by an abstract standard of republican morality.   It
is nevertheless true that Lorenzo enfeebled and enslaved
Florence. At his death he left her socially more dissolute,
politically weaker, intellectually more like himself, than he
had found her. He had not the greatness to rise above the
spirit of his century, or to make himself the Pericles instead
of the Pisistratus of his republic. In other words, he was
adequate, not superior, to Renaissance Italy.

   This, then, was the man round whom the greatest
scholars of the third period assembled, at whose table sat
Angelo Poliziano, Cristoforo Landino, Marsilio Ficino, Giovanni Pico della Mirandola, Leo Battista Alberti, Michael
Angelo Buonarroti, Luigi Pulci. The mere enumeration of
these names suffices to awake a crowd of memories in the
mind of those to whom Italian art and poetry are dear.
Lorenzo's villas, where this brilliant circle met for grave discourse or social converse, heightening the sober pleasures of
Italian country life with all that wit and learning could
produce of delicate and rare, have been so often sung by
poets and celebrated by historians that Careggi, Caffagiolo,
and Poggio a Cajano are no less familiar to us than the
studious shades of Academe. 'In a villa overhanging the
towers of Florence,' writes the austere Hallam, moved to
more than usual eloquence by the spirit-stirring beauty of
his theme, ' on the steep slope of that lofty hill crowned by
the mother city, the ancient Fiesole, in gardens which Tully
might have envied, with Ficino, Landino, and Politian at
his side, he delighted his hours of leisure with the beautiful
visions of Platonic philosophy, for which the summer still-

ness of an Italian sky appears the most congenial accompani-
ment.' As we climb the steep slope of Fiesole, or linger
beneath the rose-trees that shed their petals from Careggi's
garden walls, once more in our imagination ' the world's
great age begins anew ; ' once more the blossoms of that
marvellous spring unclose. While the sun goes down
beneath the mountains of Carrara, and the Apennines grow
purple-golden, and Florence sleeps beside the silvery Arno,
and the large Italian stars come forth above, we remember
how those mighty master spirits watched the sphering of
new planets in the spiritual skies. Savonarola in his cell
below once more sits brooding over the servility of Florence,
the corruption of a godless Church. Michael Angelo, seated
between Ficino and Poliziano, with the voices of the prophets
vibrating in his memory, and with the music of Plato sounding in his ears, rests chin on hand and elbow upon knee, like
his own Jeremiah, lost in contemplation, whereof the after-
fruit shall be the Sistine Chapel and the Medicean tombs.
Then, when the strain of thought, ' unsphering Plato from
his skies,' begins to weary, Pulci breaks the silence with a
brand-new canto of Morgante, or a singing boy is bidden to
tune his mandoline to Messer Angelo's last-made *ballata*.

There is no difficulty in explaining Plato's power upon
the thinkers of the fifteenth century. Among philosophers
Plato shines like a morning star—οὔθ' ἕσπερος οὔτε ἐῷος οὕτω
θαυμαστός—an auroral luminary, charming and compelling
the attention of the world when man is on the verge of new
discoveries. That he should have enslaved the finest intellects at a time when the sense of beauty was so keenly stimulated, and when the stirrings of fresh life were so intense, is
nothing more than natural. To philosophise and humanise
the religious sentiments that had become the property of
monks and pardon-mongers ; to establish a concordat between
the Paganism that entranced the world, and the Catholic

faith whereof the world was not yet weary; to satisfy the
new-born sense of a divine and hitherto unapprehended
mystery in heaven and earth; to dignify with a semblance
of truth the dreams of magic and astrology that passed for
science—all this the men of the Renaissance passionately
craved. Who could render better help than Plato and the
Neoplatonists, whose charm of style and high-flown mysticism suited the ambitious immaturity of undeveloped
thought? For the interpretation of Platonic doctrine a
hierophant was needed. Marsilio Ficino had been set apart
from earliest youth for this purpose—selected in the wisdom
of Cosimo de' Medici, prepared by special processes of study,
and consecrated to the service of the one philosopher.[1]

When Marsilio was a youth of eighteen, he entered the
Medicean household, and began to learn Greek, in order that
he might qualify himself for translating Plato into Latin.
His health was delicate, his sensibilities acute; the temper
of his intellect, inclined to mysticism and theology, fitted
him for the arduous task of unifying religion with philosophy.
It would be unfair to class him with the paganising humanists,
who sought to justify their unbelief or want of morals by
the authority of the classics. Ficino remained throughout
his life an earnest Christian. At the age of forty, not without
serious reflection and mature resolve, he took orders, and
faithfully performed the duties of his cure. Antiquity he
judged by the standard of the Christian creed. If he asserted
that Socrates and Plato witnessed, together with the evan-
gelists, to the truth of revelation, or that the same spirit
inspired the laws of Moses and the Greek philosopher—this,
as he conceived it, was in effect little else than extending the
catena of authority backward from the Christian fathers to
the sages of the ancient world. The Church, by admitting

---

[1] Marsilio Ficino, the son of Cosimo's physician, was born at Figline
in 1433.

the sibyls into the company of the prophets, virtually sanctioned the canonisation of Plato; while the comprehensive survey of history as an uninterrupted whole, which since the days of Petrarch had distinguished the nobler type of humanism, rendered Ficino's philosophical religion not unacceptable even to the orthodox. The speculative mystics of the fifteenth century failed, however, to perceive that by recognising inspiration in the classic authors, they were silently denying the unique value of revelation; and that by seeking the religious tradition far and wide, they called in question the peculiar divinity of Christ. Savonarola saw this clearly; therefore he denounced the Platonists as heretics, who vainly babbled about things they did not understand. The permanent value of their speculations, crude and uncritical as they may now appear, consists in the large claim made for human reason as against bibliolatry and Church authority.

Ficino was forty-four years of age when he finished the translation of Plato's works into Latin. Five more years elapsed before the first edition was printed in 1482 at Filippo Valori's expense. It may here be mentioned incidentally that, by this help, the aristocracy of Florence materially contributed to the diffusion of culture. A genuine philosopher in his lack of ambition and his freedom from avarice, Ficino was too poor to publish his own works; and what is true of him, applies to many most distinguished authors of the age. Great literary undertakings involved in that century the substantial assistance of wealthy men, whose liberality was rewarded by a notice in the colophon or on the title-page.[1] When, for instance, the first edition of Homer was issued from the press by Lorenzo Alopa in 1488, two brothers of the

---

[1] Thus Ficino's edition of Plotinus, printed at Lorenzo de' Medici's expense, and published one month after his death, bears this notice:—'Magnifici sumptu Laurentii patriæ servatoris.'

Nerli family, Bernardo and Neri, defrayed the expense.[1] The
Plato was soon followed by a Life of the philosopher, and a
treatise on the 'Platonic Doctrine of Immortality.' The latter
work is interesting as a repertory of the theories discussed
by the Medicean circle at their festivals in honour of Plato's
birthday. It has, however, no intrinsic value for the critic
or philosopher, being in effect nothing better than a jumble
of citations culled from antique mystics and combined with
cruder modern guesses. In 1486 the translation of Plotinus
was accomplished, and in 1491 a voluminous commentary
had been added; both were published one month after
Lorenzo's death in 1492. A version of Dionysius the Areo-
pagite, whose treatise on the 'Hierarchies,' though rejected by
Lorenzo Valla, was accepted as genuine by Ficino, closed the
long list of his translations from the Greek. The importance
of Ficino's contributions to philosophy consists in the impulse he communicated to Platonic studies. That he did
not comprehend Plato, or distinguish his philosophy from
that of the Alexandrian mystics, is clear in every sentence
of his writings. The age was uncritical, nor had scholars
learned the necessity of understanding an author's relation
to the history of thought in general before they attempted
to explain him. Thus they were satisfied to read Plato by
the reflected light of Plotinus and Gemistos Plethon, and
to assimilate such portions only of his teaching as accorded
with their own theology. The doctrine of planetary influences, and the myths invented to express the nature of
the soul—in other words, the consciously poetic thoughts of
Plato—seemed of more value to Ficino than the theory of
ideas, wherein the deepest problems are presented in a logical
shape to the understanding. The Middle Ages had plied
dialectic to satiety; the Renaissance dwelt with passion

[1] See, however, Didot's *Alde Manuce*, p. 4, where Giovanni Acciaiuoli
is credited with this generosity.

upon vague and misty thoughts that gave a scope to its imagination. No dreams of poet or of mystic could surpass reality in the age of Lionardo da Vinci and Christopher Columbus.

If Plato has been studied more exactly of late years, he has never been loved better or more devotedly worshipped than by the Florentine Academy. Who builds a shrine and burns a lamp before his statue now? Who crowns his bust with laurels, or celebrates his birthday and his deathday with solemn festivals and pompous panegyrics? Who meet at stated intervals to read his words, and probe his hidden meaning, feeding his altar-flame with frankincense of their most precious thoughts? It was by outward signs like these, then full of fair significance, now puerile and void of import, that the pageant-loving men of the Renaissance testified their debt of gratitude to Plato. Of one of these birthday feasts Ficino has given a lively picture in his letter to Jacopo Bracciolini ('Prolegomena ad Platonis Symposium'). After partaking of a banquet, the text of the 'Symposium' was delivered over to discussion. Giovanni Cavalcanti interpreted the speeches of Phædrus and Pausanias, Landino that of Aristophanes; Carlo Marsuppini undertook the part of Agathon, while Tommaso Benci explained the esoteric meaning of Diotima. Was there anyone, we wonder, to act Alcibiades; or did Lorenzo, perhaps, sit drinking till day flooded the meadows of Valdarno, passing round a two-handled goblet, and raising subtle questions about comedy and tragedy?

Among the academicians who frequented Lorenzo's palace at Florence there appeared, in 1484, a young man of princely birth and fascinating beauty. 'Nature,' wrote Poliziano, 'seemed to have showered on this man, or hero, all her gifts. He was tall and finely moulded; from his face a something of divinity shone forth. Acute, and gifted with prodigious

memory, in his studies he was indefatigable, in his style
perspicuous and eloquent. You could not say whether his
talents or his moral qualities conferred on him the greater
lustre. Familiar with all branches of philosophy, and the
master of many languages, he stood on high above the reach
of praise.' This was Giovanni Pico della Mirandola, whose
portrait in the Uffizzi Gallery, with its long brown hair and
penetrating grey eyes, compels attention even from those who
know not whom it is supposed to figure. He was little more
than twenty when he came to Florence. His personal attractions, noble manners, splendid style of life, and varied
accomplishments made him the idol of Florentine society;
and for a time he gave himself, in part at least, to love and
the amusements of his age.[1] But Pico was not born for
pleasure. By no man was the sublime ideal of humanity,
superior to physical enjoyments and dignified by intellectual
energy, that triumph of the thought of the Renaissance, more
completely realised.[2] There is even reason to regret that,
together with the follies of youth, he put aside the collection
of his Latin poems, which Poliziano praised, and took no
pains to preserve those Italian verses, the loss whereof we
deplore no less than that of Lionardo's. While Pico continued to live as became a Count of Mirandola, he personally

[1] See Von Reumont, vol. ii. p. 108.

[2] Fine expression was given to this conception of life by Aldus in
the dedication to Alberto Pio of vols. ii., iii., iv. of Aristotle:—'Es nam
tu mihi optimus testis an potiores Herculis ærumnas credam, sævosque
labores, et Venere, et cœnis et plumis Sardanapali. Natus nam homo
est ad laborem et ad agendum semper aliquid viro dignum, non ad
voluptatem quæ belluarum est et pecudum.' The last sentence is a
translation of Ulysses' speech in the *Inferno*—

'Considerate la vostra semenza,
Fatti non foste a viver come bruti,
Ma per seguir virtute e conoscenza.'

Cf. Aldus's preface to Lascaris' Grammar; Renouard, vol. i. p. 7; and
again *Alde Manuce*, p. 143, for similar passages.

inclined each year to graver and more abstruse studies and to greater austerity, until at last the prince was merged in the philosopher, the man of letters in the mystic.

Pico's abilities displayed themselves in earliest boyhood. His mother, a niece of the great Boiardo, noticed his rare aptitude for study, and sent him at the age of fourteen to Bologna. There he mastered not only the humanities, but also what was taught of mathematics, logic, philosophy, and Oriental languages. He afterwards continued his education at Paris, the head-quarters of scholastic theology. Pico's powerful memory must have served him in good stead: it is recorded that a single reading fixed the language and the matter of the texts he studied, on his mind for ever. Nor was this faculty for retaining knowledge accompanied by any sluggishness of mental power. To what extent he relied upon his powers of debate as well as on his vast stores of erudition, was proved by the publication of the famous nine hundred theses at Rome in 1486. These questions seem to have been constructed in defence of the Platonic mysticism, which already had begun to absorb his attention. The philosophers and theologians who were challenged to contend with him in argument had the whole list offered to their choice. Pico was prepared to maintain each and all of his positions without further preparation. Ecclesiastical prudence, however, prevented the champions of orthodoxy from descending into the arena. They found it safer to prefer a charge of heresy against Pico, whose theses were condemned in a brief of Innocent VIII., dated August 5, 1486. It was not until June 18, 1493, that he was finally purged from the ban of heterodoxy by a brief of Alexander VI. During that long interval he suffered much uneasiness of mind, for even his robust intelligence quailed before the thought of dying under Papal interdiction. That a man so pure in his life and so earnest in his piety should have been stigmatised as a heretic,

and then pardoned, by two such Popes, is one of the curious
anomalies of that age.

To harmonise the Christian and classical tradition was
a problem which Manetti had crudely attempted. Pico approached it in a more philosophical spirit, and resolved to
devote his whole life to the task. The antagonism between
sacred and profane literature appeared more glaring to Renaissance scholars than to us, inasmuch as they attached
more serious value to the teaching of the latter as a rule of
life. Yet Pico was not intent so much on merely reconciling
hostile systems of thought, or on confuting the errors of the
Jews and Gentiles. He had conceived the great idea of the
unity of knowledge; and having acquired the *omne scibile* of
his century, he sought to seize the soul of truth that animates
all systems. Not the classics nor the Scriptures alone, but
the writings of the schoolmen, the glosses of Arabic philosophers, and the more obscure products of Hebrew erudition
had for him their solid value. Estimating authors at the
worth of their matter, and despising the trivial questions
raised by shallow wits among style-mongering students, he
freed himself from the worst fault of humanism, and conceived of learning in a liberal spirit. The best proof of this
wide acceptance of all literature conducive to sound thinking,
is given in a latter to Ermolao Barbaro.[1] After courteously
adverting to the Ciceronian elegance of his correspondent's
style he continues, 'And that I meantime should have lost
in the studies of Thomas Aquinas, John Scotus, Albertus
Magnus, and Averrhoes the best years of my life—those long,
laborious vigils wherein I might perchance have made myself
of some avail in polite scholarship ! The thought occurred
to me, by way of consolation, if some of them could come to

---

[1] Dated Florence, 1485 ; in the Aldine edition of Poliziano's Letters,
book ix.

life again, whether men so powerful in argument might not
find sound pleas for their own cause; whether one among
them, more eloquent than Paul, might not defend, in terms
as free as possible from barbarism, their barbarous style,
speaking perchance after this fashion : We have lived illustrious, friend Ermolao, and to posterity shall live, not in the
schools of the grammarians and teaching-places of young
minds, but in the company of the philosophers, conclaves of
sages, where the questions for debate are not concerning the
mother of Andromache or the sons of Niobe and such light
trifles, but of things human and divine ; in the contemplation,
investigation, and analysis whereof we have been so subtle,
searching, and eager that we may sometimes have seemed to
be too scrupulous and captious, if indeed it be possible to be
too curious or fastidious in seeking after truth.   Let him who
accuses us of dulness, prove by experience whether we barbarians have not the god of eloquence in our hearts rather
than on our lips ; whether, if the faculty of ornamented
speech be lacking, we have wanted wisdom : and to trick out
wisdom with ornaments may be more a crime than to show it
in uncultured rudeness.'

During the period of his Platonic studies at Florence
chance brought Pico into contact with a Jew who had a copy
of the Cabbala for sale. Into this jungle of abstruse learning
Pico plunged with all the ardour of his powerful intellect.
Asiatic fancies, Alexandrian myths, Christian doctrines,
Hebrew traditions, are so wonderfully blended in that laby-
rinthine commentary that Pico believed he had discovered the
key to his great problem, the quintessence of all truth.   It
seemed to him that the science of the Greek and the faith of
the Christian could only be understood in the light of the
Cabbala. He purchased the MS., devoted his whole attention to its study, and projected a mighty work to prove the
harmony of philosophies in Christianity, and to explain the

Christian doctrine by the esoteric teaching of the Jews.[1]
Pico's view of the connection between philosophy, theology,
and religion is plainly stated in the following sentence from
a letter to Aldus Manutius (February 11, 1491) :—' Philo-
sophia veritatem quærit, theologia invenit, religio possidet '
(' Philosophy seeks truth, theology discovers it, religion hath
it '). Death overtook him before the book intended to demonstrate these positions, and by so doing to establish the concord
of all earnest and truth-seeking systems, could be written.
He died at the age of thirty-one, on the very day when
Charles VIII. made his entry into Florence.

While accepting the Cabbala it was impossible for Pico to
reject magic. He showed his good sense, however, by an
energetic attack upon the so-called science of judicial astrology. Strictly speaking, the spirit of humanism was opposed
to this folly. Petrarch had long ago condemned it, together
with the charlatans who used its jargon to impose upon the
world ; yet, in spite of humanism, the folly not only persisted,
but seemed to increase with the spread of rational knowledge.
The universities founded Chairs of Astrology, Popes consulted
the stars on occasions of importance, nor did the Despots dare
to act without the advice of their soothsayers. These men
not unfrequently accompanied the greatest generals on their
campaigns. Their services were bought by the republics ;
citizens employed them for the casting of horoscopes, the
building of houses, the position of shops, the fit moment for
journeys, the reception of guests into their families, and the
date of weddings. To take a serious step in life without the
approval of an astrologer had come to be regarded as perilous.
Even Ficino believed in horoscopes and planetary influences ;
so did Cardan at a later date. It may be remembered that
Catherine de' Medici allowed the Florentine Ruggieri to share

[1] In the introduction to Pico's *Apologia* may be read the account
he gives of the codex of the pseudo-Esdras purchased by him.

her secret counsels during the reigns of three kings, and that Paul III. always obtained the sanction of his star-gazer before he held a consistory. In proportion as religion grew less real, and the complex dangers of a corrupt society increased, astrology gained in importance. It was not, therefore, a waste of eloquence, as Poliziano complained, when Pico directed his attack against this delusion, accusing it of debasing the intellect and opening the way for immorality of all kinds.[1]

Since Pico's keen intellect discerned the shallowness of astrological pretensions, it is the more to be deplored that he fell a victim to the hybrid mysticism and magical nonsense of the Cabbala. We have here another proof that criticism was as yet in its infancy. It was easier for men of genius in the Renaissance to win lofty vantage-ground for contemplation, to divine the unity of human achievements, and to comprehend the greatness of the destiny of man, than to accept the learning of the past at a simple historical valuation. What fascinated their imagination passed with them too easily for true and proved. Yet all they needed was time for the digestion and assimilation of the stores of knowledge they had gained. If the Counter-Reformation had not checked the further growth of Italian science, the spirit that lived in Pico would certainly have produced a school of philosophy second to none that Europe has brought forth. Of this Pico's own short treatise on the 'Dignity of Man,' as I have said already, is sufficient warrant.

[1] Poliziano's Greek epigram addressed to Pico on this matter may be quoted from the *Carmina Quinque Poetarum*, p. 412 :—

καὶ τοῦτ' ἀστρολόγοις ἐπιμέμφομαι ἱερολέσχαις,
ὅττι σοφοὺς Πίκου μοι φθονέουσ' ὀάρους.
καὶ γὰρ ὃ ἐνδυκέως τούτων τὸν λῆρον ἐλέγχων
μουνάξει ἐν ἀγρῷ δηρὸν ἑκὰς πόλεως.
Πῖκε τί σοι καὶ τούτοις ; οὔ σ' ἐπέοικεν ἀγύρταις
ἀντᾶραι τὴν σὴν εὐτυχέα γραφίδα.

As Pico was the youngest so was Cristoforo Landino the oldest member of the Medicean circle. He was born at Florence in 1424, nine years before Ficino, with whom he shared the duties of instructing Lorenzo in his boyhood. Landino obtained the Chair of Rhetoric and Poetry in 1457, and continued till his death in 1504 to profess Latin literature at Florence. While Ficino and Pico represented the study of philosophy, he devoted himself exclusively to scholarship, annotating Horace and Virgil, and translating Pliny's 'Natural Histories.' A marked feature in Landino's professorial labours was the attention he paid to the Italian poets. In 1460 he began to lecture on Petrarch, and in 1481 he published an edition of Dante with voluminous commentaries. The copy of this work, printed upon parchment, splendidly bound, and fastened with niello clasps, which Landino presented with a set oration to the Signory of Florence, may still be seen in the Magliabecchian library. The author was rewarded with a house in Borgo alla Collina, the ancient residence of his family.

Though the name of Cristoforo Landino is now best known in connection with his Dantesque studies, one of his Latin works, the 'Camaldolese Discussions,'[1] will always retain peculiar interest for the student of Florentine humanism. This treatise is composed in imitation of the Ciceronian rather than the Platonic dialogues; the 'Tusculans' may be said to have furnished Landino with his model. He begins by telling how he left his villa in the Casentino, accompanied by his brother, to pay a visit to the hill-set sanctuary of S. Romualdo.[2] There he met with Lorenzo and Giuliano de' Medici, attended by noble youths of Florence—Piero and Donato

---

[1] *Disputationum Camaldulensium* lib. iv., dedicated to Frederick of Urbino.
[2] The legend of the foundation of this Order is well known through Sacchi's picture in the Vatican.

Acciaiuoli, Alamanno Rinuccini, Marco Parenti, and Antonio
Canigiani—all of whom had quitted Florence to enjoy the
rest of summer coolness among the firs and chestnuts of
the Apennines. The party thus formed was completed by the
arrival of Leo Battista Alberti and Marsilio Ficino. The
conversation maintained from day to day by these close friends
and ardent scholars forms the substance of the dialogue.
Seated on the turf beside a fountain, near the spot where
Romualdo was bidden in his trance to exchange the black
robes of the Benedictine Order for the snow-white livery of
angels, they not unnaturally began to compare the active life
that they had left at Florence with the contemplative life of
philosophers and saints. Alberti led the conversation by a
panegyric of the βίος θεωρητικός, maintaining the Platonic
thesis with a wealth of illustration and a charm of eloquence
peculiar to himself. Lorenzo took up the argument in favour
of the βίος πρακτικός. If Alberti proved that solitude and
meditation are the nurses of great spirits, that man by com-
muning with nature enters into full possession of his mental
kingdom, Lorenzo pointed out that this completion of self-
culture only finds its use and value in the commerce of the
world. The philosopher must descend from his altitude and
mix with men, in order to exercise the faculties matured by
contemplation. Thus far the artist and the statesman are
supposed to hold debate on Goethe's celebrated distich—

> Es bildet ein Talent sich in der Stille,
> Sich ein Charakter in dem Strom der Welt.

The audience decided, in the spirit of the German poet, that
a fully-formed man, the possessor of both character and talent,
must submit himself to each method of training. Thus ended
the first day's discussion. During the three following days
Alberti led the conversation to Virgil's poetry, demonstrat-
ing its allegorical significance, and connecting its hidden

philosophy with that of Plato. It is clear that in this part of his work Landino was presenting the substance of his own Virgilian studies. The whole book, like Castiglione's 'Courtier,' supplies a fair sample of the topics on which social conversation turned among refined and cultivated men. The tincture of Platonism is specially characteristic of the Medicean circle.

The distinguished place allotted in this dialogue to Leo Battista Alberti proves the singular regard in which this most remarkable man was held at Florence, where, however, he but seldom resided. His name will always be coupled with that of Lionardo da Vinci ; for though Lionardo, arriving at a happier moment, has eclipsed Alberti's fame, yet both of them were cast in the same mould. Alberti, indeed, might serve as the very type of those many-sided, precocious, and comprehensive men of genius who only existed in the age of the Renaissance. Physical strength and dexterity were given to him at birth in measure equal to his mental faculties. It is recorded that he could jump standing over an upright man, pierce the strongest armour with his arrows, and so deftly fling a coin that it touched the highest point of a church or palace roof. The wildest horses are said to have trembled under him, as though brutes felt, like men, the magnetism of his personality. His insight into every branch of knowledge seemed intuitive, and his command of the arts was innate. At the age of twenty he composed the comedy of ' Philodoxius,' which passed for an antique, and was published by the Aldi as the work of Lepidus Comicus in 1588. Of music, though he had not made it a special study, he was a thorough master, composing melodies that gave delight to scientific judges. He painted pictures, and wrote three books on painting ; practised architecture and compiled ten books on building. Of his books, chiefly portraits, nothing remains ; but the Church of S. Andrea at Mantua, the Palazzo Rucellai at Florence, and the remodelled Church of S. Francesco at Rimini attest his greatness as an architect. The façade of the latter building is more thoroughly classical than any other monument of the earlier Renaissance. As a transcript from Roman antiquity it ranks with the Palazzo della Ragione of Palladio at Vicenza. While still a young man, Alberti, overtaxed, in all probability, by the prodigious activity of his mental and bodily forces, suffered from an illness that resulted in a partial loss of memory. The humanistic and legal studies on which he was engaged had to be abandoned ; yet, nothing daunted, he now turned his plastic genius to philosophy and mathematics, rightly judging that they make less demand upon the passive than the active vigour of the mind. It is believed that he anticipated some modern discoveries in optics, and he certainly advanced the science of perspective. Like his compeer Lionardo, he devoted attention to mechanics, and devised machinery for raising sunken ships. Like Lionardo, again, he was never tired of interrogating nature, conducting curious experiments, and watching her more secret operations. As a physiognomist and diviner, he acquired a reputation bordering on wizardry. It was as though his exquisite sensibilities and keenness of attention had gifted him with second sight. The depth of his sympathy with the outer world is proved by an assertion of his anonymous biographer that, when he saw the cornfields and vineyards of autumn, tears gathered to his eyes. All living creatures that had beauty won his love, and even in old persons he discovered a charm appropriate to old age. Foreigners, travellers, and workmen skilled in various crafts formed his favourite company, for in the acquisition of varied knowledge he was indefatigable. In general society his wisdom and his wit, the eloquence of his discourse and the brilliance of his improvisation, rendered him most fascinating. Collections of maxims culled from his table talk were made, whereof the anonymous biography contains a fair selection. At the same time we are told that, in the midst of sparkling sallies or close arguments, he would suddenly subside into reverie, and sit at table lost in silent contemplation. Alberti was one of the earliest writers of pure Italian prose at the period of its revival; but this part of his intellectual activity belongs to the history of Italian literature, and need not be touched on here. It is enough to have glanced thus briefly at one of the most attractive, sympathy-compelling figures of the fifteenth century.

In order to complete the picture of the Florentine circle, we have in the last place to notice two men raised by the Medici from the ranks of the people. ' I came to the republic, bare of all things, a mere beggar, of the lowest birth, without money, rank, connections, or kindred. Cosimo, the father of his country, raised me up, by receiving me into his family.' So wrote Bartolommeo Scala,[1] the miller's son, who lived to be the Chancellor of Florence. The splendour of that office had been considerably diminished since the days when Bruni, Marsuppini, and Poggio held it; nor could Scala, as a student, bear comparison with those men. His Latin history of the first crusade was rather a large than a great work, of which no notice would be taken if Tasso had not used it in the composition of his epic. Honours and riches, however, were accumulated on the Chancellor in such profusion that he grew arrogant, and taunted the great Poliziano with inferiority. The feud between these men was not confined to literature. Scala's daughter, a far better scholar than himself, attracted Poliziano's notice, and Greek epigrams were exchanged between them. The dictator of Italian letters now sought the hand of the fair Alessandra, who was rich not only in learning but in world's gear also. When she gave herself to Michael Marullus Tarcagnota, a Greek, his anger knew no bounds; instead of penning amatory he now composed satiric epigrams,

[1] Born at Colle in 1430.

abusing Marullus in Latin no less than he had praised Alessandra in Greek.[1]

Angelo Poliziano was born in 1454. His name, so famous in Italian literature, is a Latinised version of his birthplace, Montepulciano. His father, Benedetto Ambrogini, was a man of some consequence, but of small means, who fell a victim to the enmity of private foes among his fellow-citizens, leaving his widow and five young children almost wholly unprovided for.[2] This accounts for the obscurity that long enveloped the history of Poliziano's childhood, and also for the doubts expressed about the surname of his family. At the age of ten he came to study in the University of Florence, where he profited by the teaching of Landino, Argyropoulos, Andronicos Kallistos, and Ficino. The precocity of his genius displayed itself in Latin poems and Greek epigrams composed while he was yet a boy. At thirteen years of age he published Latin letters ; at seventeen he distributed Greek poems among the learned men of Florence ; at eighteen he edited Catullus, with the boast that he had shown more zeal than any other student in the correction and illustration of the ancients.

---

[1] The following verses on Alessandra are so curious a specimen of Poliziano's Greek style that I transcribe them here (*Carmina Quinque Illustrium Poetarum*, p. 304) :—

εὕρηχ' εὕρηχ' ἣν θέλον, ἣν ἐζήτεον αἰεί,
    ἣν ἤτουν τὸν ἔρωθ', ἣν καὶ ὀνειροπόλουν ·
παρθενικὴν ἧς κάλλος ἀκήρατον, ἧς ὅγε κόσμος
    οὐκ εἴη τέχνης ἀλλ' ἀφελοῦς φύσεως ·
παρθενικὴν γλώττῃσιν ἐπ' ἀμφοτέρῃσι κομῶσαν,
    ἔξοχον ἔντε χοροῖς ἔξοχον ἔντε λύρᾳ ·
ἧς περὶ σωφροσύνῃ τ' εἴη χαρίτεσσι θ' ἁμίλλα,
    τῇ καὶ τῇ ταύτην ἀντιμεθελκομέναις.
εὕρηκ' οὐδ' ὄφελος, καὶ γὰρ μόλις εἰς ἐνιαυτὸν
    οἰστροῦντι φλογερῶς ἐστιν ἅπαξ ἰδέειν.

The satires on Mabilius (so he called Marullus) are too filthy to be quoted. They may be read in the collection cited above, pp. 275-280.

[2] See Carducci, preface to *Le Stanze*, Florence, 1863, and Isidoro del Lungo in *Arch. Stor.* series iii. vol. ii.

As early as the year 1470 he had not only conceived the ambitious determination to translate Homer into Latin verse,
but had already begun upon the second Iliad. The first book
was known to scholars in Marsuppini's Latin version. Poliziano carried his own translation as far as the end of the
fifth book, gaining for himself the proud title of *Homericus
juvenis* ; further than this, for reasons unexplained, he never
advanced, so that the last wish of Nicholas V., the chief desire
of fifteenth-century scholarship—a Latin Iliad in hexameters
—remained still unaccomplished.

The fame of this great undertaking attracted universal
attention to Poliziano. It is probable that Ficino first introduced him to Lorenzo de' Medici, who received the young
student into his own household, and made himself responsible
for his future fortunes. ' The liberality of Lorenzo de' Medici,
that great and wise man,' wrote Poliziano in after years,
' raised me from the obscure and humble station where my
birth had placed me, to that degree of dignity and distinction
I now enjoy, with no other recommendation than my literary
abilities.' Before he had reached the age of thirty, Poliziano
professed the Greek and Latin literatures in the University
of Florence, and received the care of Lorenzo's children. If
Lorenzo represents the statecraft of his age, Poliziano is no
less emphatically the representative of its highest achievements in scholarship. He was the first Italian to combine
perfect mastery over Latin and a correct sense of Greek with
a splendid genius for his native literature. Filelfo boasted
that he could write both classic languages with equal ease,
and exercised his prosy muse in *terza rima*. But Filelfo had
no fire of poetry, no sense of style. Poliziano, on the contrary,
was a born poet, a *sacer vates* in the truest sense of the word.
I shall have to speak elsewhere of his Italian verses : those
who have studied them know that the ' Orfeo,' the ' Stanze,'
and the ' Rime ' justify Poliziano's claim to the middle place

of honour between Petrarch and Ariosto. Italian poetry took
a new direction from his genius, and everything he penned
was fruitful of results for the succeeding generation. Of his
Latin poetry, in like manner, I propose to treat at greater
length in the following chapter.

The spirit of Roman literature lived again in Poliziano.
If he cannot be compared with the Augustan authors, he will
pass muster at least with the poets of the silver age. Neither
Statius nor Ausonius produced more musical hexameters, or
expressed their feeling for natural beauty in phrases marked
with more spontaneous grace. Of his Greek elegiacs only a
few specimens survive. These, in spite of certain licenses
not justified by pure Greek prosody, might claim a place in
the 'Anthology,' among the epigrams of Agathias and Paulus
Silentiarius.[1] The Doric couplets on two beautiful boys, and
the love sonnet to the youth Chrysocomus, read like extracts
from the Μοῦσα παιδική.[2] What is remarkable about the
Greek and Latin poetry of Poliziano is that the flavour
of the author's Italian style transpires in them. They are
no mere imitations of the classics. The 'roseate fluency' of
the 'Rime' reappears in these *prolusiones*, making it manifest that the three languages were used with equal facility,
and that on each of them the poet set the seal of his own
genius.

What has been said about his verse, applies with no less

[1] Julius Cæsar Scaliger wrote thus about them in the *Hypercri-
ticus* :—' Græcis vero, quæ puerum se conscripsisse dicit, ætatem
minus prudenter apposuit suam ; tam enim bona sunt ut ne virum
quidem Latina æque bene scripsisse putem.'

[2] *Quinque Illustrium Poetarum Carmina*, pp. 299, 301. These epigrams, as well as two on pp. 303, 307, are significant in their illustration of the poet's morality. Giovio's account of Poliziano's death
was certainly accepted by contemporaries :—' *Ferunt eum ingenui
adolescentis insano amore percitum facile in letalem morbum incidisse.*'
The whole *Elogium*, however, is a covert libel, like many of Giovio's
sketches.

force to his prose composition. Poliziano wrote Latin, as
though it were a living language, not culling phrases from
Cicero or reproducing the periods of Livy, but trusting to
his instinct and his ear, with the facility of conscious power.
The humanism of the first and second periods attained to the
freedom of fine art in Poliziano. Through him, as through a
lens, the rays of previous culture were transmitted in a column
of pure light. He realised what the Italians had been striving
after—the new birth of antiquity in a living man of the
modern world. By way of modifying this high panegyric, it
may be conceded that Poliziano had the defects of his qualities.
Using Latin with the freedom of a master, he was not careful
to purge his style of obsolete words and far-fetched phrases,
or to maintain the diction of one period in each composition.
His fluency betrayed him into verbiage, and his descriptions
are often more diffuse than vigorous. Nor will he bear comparison with some more modern scholars on the point of
accuracy. The merit, however, remains to him of having
been the most copious and least slavish interpreter of the
ancient to the modern world. His very imperfections, when
judged by the standard of Bembo, place him above the purists,
inasmuch as he possessed the power and courage to express
himself in his own idiom, instead of treading cautiously in
none but Ciceronian or Virgilian footprints.

As a professor, none of the humanists achieved more
brilliant successes than Poliziano. Among his pupils could
be numbered the chief students of Europe. Not to mention
Italians, it will suffice to record the names of Reuchlin,
Grocin, Linacre, and the Portuguese Tessiras, who carried
each to his own country the culture they had gained in
Florence. The first appearance of Poliziano in the lecture-
room was not calculated to win admiration. Ill-formed, with
eyes that had something of a squint in them, and a nose
of disproportionate size, he seemed more fit to be a solitary

scholar than the Orpheus of the classic literature.[1] Yet no sooner had he opened his lips and begun to speak, with the exquisite and varied intonations of a singularly beautiful voice, than his listeners were chained to their seats. The ungainliness of the teacher was forgotten; charmed through their ears and their intellect, they eagerly drank in his eloquence, applauding the improvisations wherewith he illustrated the spirit and intention of his authors, and silently absorbing the vast and well-ordered stores of knowledge he so prodigally scattered. It would not be profitable to narrate here at any length what is known about the topics of these lectures. Poliziano not only covered the whole ground of classic literature during the years of his professorship, but also published the notes of courses upon Ovid, Suetonius, Statius, the younger Pliny, the writers of Augustan histories, and Quintilian. Some of his best Latin poems were written by way of preface to the authors he explained in public. Virgil was celebrated in the 'Manto,' and Homer in the 'Ambra;' the 'Rusticus' served as prelude to the 'Georgics,' while the 'Nutricia' formed an introduction to the study of ancient and modern poetry. Nor did he confine his attention to fine literature. The curious prælection in prose called 'Lamia' was intended as a prelude to the prior 'Analytics' of Aristotle. Among his translations must be mentioned Epictetus, Herodian, Hippocrates, Galen, Plutarch's 'Eroticus,' and the 'Charmides' of Plato. His greatest achievement, however, was the edition of the 'Pandects' of Justinian from the famous MS. of which Florence had robbed Pisa, as the Pisans had previously taken it from Amalfi. It must not be forgotten that all these

---

[1] 'Erat distortis sæpe moribus, uti facie nequaquam ingenuâ et liberali ab enormi præsertim naso, subluscoque oculo perabsurdâ.' Giovio, *Elogia.* Cf. Poliziano's own verses to Mabilius, beginning :—

Quod nasum mihi, quod reflexa colla
Demens objicis.

Carmina Quinque Poetarum, p. 277.

undertakings involved severe labours of correction and criticism. MSS. had to be compared and texts settled, when as yet the apparatus for this higher form of scholarship was miserably scanty. Though students before Poliziano had understood the necessity of collating codices, determining their relative ages, and tracing them, if possible, to their authoritative sources, he was the first to do this systematically and with judgment. To emendation he only had recourse when the text seemed hopeless. His work upon the 'Pandects' alone implies the expenditure of enormous toil.

The results of Poliziano's more fugitive studies, and some notes of conversations on literary topics with Lorenzo, were published in 1489 under the title of ' Miscellanea.' [1] The form was borrowed from the 'Noctes Atticæ' of Aulus Gellius ; in matter this collection anticipated the genial criticisms of Erasmus. The excitement caused by its appearance is vividly depicted in the following letter of Jacopus Antiquarius, secretary to the Duke of Milan : [2]—' Going lately, according to my custom, into one of the public offices, I found a number of the young clerks neglecting their prince's business, and lost in the study of a book which had been distributed in sheets among them. When I asked what new book had appeared, they answered, Politian's "Miscellanies." I mounted their desk, sat down among them, and began to read with equal eagerness. But, as I could not spend much time there, I sent at once to the bookseller's stall for a copy of the work.' By this time Poliziano's fame had eclipsed that of all his contemporaries. He corresponded familiarly with native and foreign princes, and held a kind of court at Florence among men of learning who came from all parts of Italy to converse with him. This

[1] The first words of the dedication run as follows :—' Cum tibi superioribus diebus Laurenti Medices, nostra hæc Miscellanea *inter equitandum* recitaremus.'

[2] *Angeli Politiani Epistolæ*, lib. iii. ed. Ald. 1498. The letter is dated Nov. 1488.

popularity grew even burdensome, or at any rate he affected to find it so. ' Does a man want a motto for his sword's hilt or a posy for a ring,' he writes,[1] 'an inscription for his bedroom or a device for his plate, or even for his pots and pans, he runs like all the world to Politian. There is hardly a wall I have not besmeared, like a snail, with the effusions of my brain. One teazes me for catches and drinking-songs, another for a grave discourse, a third for a serenade, a fourth for a Carnival ballad.' In executing these commissions he is said to have shown great courtesy; nor did they probably cost him much trouble, for in all his work he was no less rapid than elegant. He boasted that he had dictated the translation of Herodian while walking up and down his room, within the space of a day or two; and the chief fault of his verses is their fluency.

It still remains to speak of Poliziano's personal relations to the Medicean family. When he first entered the household of Lorenzo, he undertook the tuition of his patron's sons, and continued to superintend their education until their mother Clarice saw reason to mistrust his personal influence. There were, no doubt, many points in the great scholar's character that justified her thinking him unfit to be the constant companion of young men. Whatever may be the truth about the cause of his last illness, enough remains of his Greek and Italian verses to prove that his morality was lax, and his conception of life rather Pagan than Christian.[2] Clarice contrived that he should not remain under the same roof with her children; and though his friendly intercourse with the Medicean family continued uninterrupted, it would seem that after 1480 he only gave lessons in the classics to his former pupils.

[1] In a letter to Hieronymus Donatus, dated Florence, May 1480, *Angeli Politiani Epistolæ*, lib. ii.

[2] The well-known scandal about Poliziano's death is traceable to the *Elogia* of Paulus Jovius—very suspicious authority. See above, p. 252, note 2.

Poliziano, proud as he was of his attainments, lacked the nobler quality of self-respect. He condescended to flatter Lorenzo, and to beg for presents, in phrases that remind us of Filelfo's prosiest epigrams.[1] That a scholar should vaunt his own achievements[2] and extol his patron to the skies, that he should ask for money and set off his panegyrics against payment, seemed not derogatory to a man of genius in the fifteenth century. Yet these habits of literary mendicancy and toad-eating proved a most pernicious influence. Italian literature never lost the superlatives and exaggerations imported by the humanists, and Pietro Aretino may be called the lineal descendant of Filelfo and Poliziano.

It must be allowed that to overpraise Lorenzo from a scholar's point of view would have been difficult, while the affection that bound the student to his patron was genuine. Poliziano, who watched Lorenzo in his last moments, described the scene of his death in a letter marked by touching sorrow which he addressed to Antiquari, and proved by the Latin monody which he composed and left unfinished, that grief for his dead master could inspire his muse with loftier strains than any expectation of future favours while he lived had done.

Two years after Lorenzo's death Poliziano died himself, dishonoured and suspected by the Piagnoni. Savonarola had swept the Carnival chariots and masks and gimcracks of Lorenzo's holiday reign into the dust-heap. Instead of *rispetti* and *ballate*, the refrain of Misereres filled the city, and the Dominican's prophecy of blood and ruin drowned with its thundrous reverberations the scholarlike disquisitions

---

[1] The most curious of these elegiac poems are given in *Carmina Quinque Illustrium Poetarum*, p. 234. It is possible that their language ought not to be taken literally, and that they concealed a joke now lost.

[2] Poliziano's letter to Matthias Corvinus is a good example of his self-laudation.

of Greek professors. Poliziano's lament for Lorenzo was therefore, as it were, a prophecy of his own fate :

> Quis dabit capiti meo
> Aquam ? quis oculis meis
> Fontem lachrymarum dabit ?
> Ut nocte fleam,
> Ut luce fleam.
> Sic turtur viduus solet,
> Sic cygnus moriens solet,
> Sic luscinia conqueri.

'Oh that my head were waters and mine eyes a fountain of tears, that I might weep day and night ! So mourns the widowed turtle dove ; so mourns the dying swan ; so mourns the nightingale.' Into these passionate words of wailing, unique in the literature of humanism by their form alike and feeling, breaks the threnody of the abandoned scholar. 'Ah, woe ! Ah, woe is me ! O grief ! O grief ! Lightning hath struck our laurel tree, our laurel dear to all the Muses and the dances of the Nymphs, beneath whose spreading boughs the God of Song himself more sweetly harped and sang. Now all around is dumb ; now all is mute, and there is none to hear. Oh that my head were waters, and mine eyes a fountain of tears ! '

This at least of grace the gods allowed Poliziano, that he should die in the same year as his friend Pico della Mirandola, a few weeks before the deluge prophesied by Savonarola burst over Italy. Upon his tomb in S. Marco a burlesque epitaph was inscribed—

> Politianus
> in hoc tumulo jacet
> Angelus unum
> qui caput et linguas
> res nova tres habuit.
> Obiit an. MCCCCLXXXXIV
> Sep. XXIV. Ætatis
> XL.[1]

---

[1] 'Poliziano lies in this grave, the angel who had one head and, what is new, three tongues. He died September 24, 1494, aged 40.'

Bembo, who succeeded him in the dictatorship of Italian letters, composed a not unworthy elegy upon the man whom he justly apostrophised as 'Poliziano, master of the Ausonian lyre.'

The fortunes of Roman scholarship kept varying with the personal tastes of each successive Pope. Calixtus III. differed wholly from his predecessor, Nicholas V. Learned in theology and mediæval science, he was dead to the interests of humanistic literature. Vespasiano assures us that, when he entered the Vatican library and saw its Greek and Latin authors in their red and silver bindings, instead of praising the munificence of Nicholas, he exclaimed, ' Vedi in che egli ha consumato la robba della Chiesa di Dio ! ' [1] Æneas Sylvius Piccolomini ranked high among the humanists. As an orator, courtier, state secretary, and man of letters, he shared the general qualities of the class to which he belonged. While a fellow-student of Beccadelli at Siena, he freely enjoyed the pleasures of youth, and thought it no harm to compose novels in the style of Longus and Achilles Tatius. These stories, together with his familiar letters, histories, cosmographical treatises, rhetorical disquisitions, apophthegms, and commentaries, written in a fluent and picturesque Latin style, distinguished him for wit and talent from the merely laborious students of his age.[2] A change, however, came over him when he assumed the title of Pius II. with the tiara.[3] Learning in Italy owed but little to his patronage, and though he

---

[1] 'Behold whereon he spent the substance of the Church of God ! ' Vespasiano adds that he gave away several hundred volumes to one of the cardinals, whose servants sold them for an old song. Vesp. p. 216. Assemani, the historian of the Vatican Library, on the contrary, asserts that Calixtus spent 40,000 ducats on books. It is not likely, however, that Vespasiano was wholly in error about a matter he understood so well, and had so much at heart.

[2] See the Basle edition of his collected works, 1571.

[3] See Vol. I., *Age of the Despots*, p. 299.

strengthened the position of the humanists at Rome by founding the College of Abbreviators, he was more eager to defend Christendom against the Turk than to make his See the capital of culture. For this it would be narrow-minded to blame Pius. The experience of European politics had extended his view beyond the narrower circle of Italian interests ; and there is something noble as well as piteous in his attempt to lead the forlorn hope of a cosmopolitan cause. Paul II. was chiefly famous for his persecution of the Roman Platonists ; [1] and Sixtus IV., though he deserves to be remembered as the Pontiff who opened the Vatican library to the public, plays no prominent part in the history of scholarship. Tiraboschi may be consulted for his refusal to pay the professors of the Roman Sapienza. Of Innocent VIII. nothing need be said ; nor will any student of history expect to find it recorded that Alexander VI. wasted money on the patronage of learning. To the Borgia, indeed, the world owes that curse of Catholicism, that continued crime of high treason against truth and liberal culture, the subjection of the press to ecclesiastical control.

Under these Popes humanism had to flourish, as it best could, in the society of private individuals. Accordingly, we find the Roman scholars forming among themselves academies and learned circles. Of these the most eminent took its name from its founder, Julius Pomponius Lætus. He was a bastard of the princely House of the Sanseverini, to whom, when he became famous and they were anxious for his friendship, he penned the celebrated epistle : '*Pomponius Lætus cognatis et propinquis suis salutem. Quod petitis fieri non potest. Valete.*' [2] Pomponius derived his scholarship from Valla, and devoted all his energies to Latin literature, refus-

---

[1] Vol. I., *Age of the Despots*, pp. 302–303.

[2] 'P. L. to his kinsmen and relatives, greeting. What you ask cannot be. Farewell.'

ing, it is even said, to learn Greek, lest it should distract him
from his favourite studies. He made it the object of his most
serious endeavours not only to restore a knowledge of the
ancients, but also to assimilate his life and manners to their
standard. Men praised in him a second Cato for sobriety of
conduct, frugal diet, and rural industry. He tilled his own
ground after the methods of Varro and Columella, went
a-fishing and a-fowling on holidays, and ate his sparing meal
like a Roman Stoic beneath the spreading branches of an oak
on the Campagna. The grand mansions of the prelates had
no attractions for him. He preferred his own modest house
upon the Esquiline, his garden on the Quirinal. It was here
that his favourite scholars conversed with him at leisure;
and to these retreats of the philosopher came strangers of
importance, eager to behold a Roman living in all points like
an antique sage. The high school of Rome owed much to his
indefatigable industry. Through a long series of years he
lectured upon the chief Latin authors, examining their text
with critical accuracy, and preparing new editions of their
works. Before daybreak he would light his lantern, take his
staff, and wend his way from the Esquiline to the lecture-
room, where, however early the hour and however inclement
the season, he was sure to find an overflowing audience. Yet
it was not as a professor that Pomponius Lætus acquired his
great celebrity, and left a lasting impress on the society of
Rome. This he did by forming an academy for the avowed
purpose of prosecuting the study of Latin antiquities and
promoting the adoption of antique customs into modern life.
The members assumed classical names, exchanging their
Italian patronymics for fancy titles like Callimachus Ex-
periens, Asclepiades, Glaucus, Volscus, and Petrejus. They
yearly kept the birthday feast of Rome, celebrating the Palilia
with Pagan solemnities, playing comedies of Plautus, and
striving to revive the humours of the old Atellan farces. Of

this circle Pontanus and Sannazzaro, Platina, Sabellicus and
Molza, Janus Parrhasius, and the future Paul III. were proud
to call themselves the members. It is only from the language
in which such men refer to Lætus that we gain a due notion
of his influence; for he left but little behind him as an author,
and used himself to boast that, like Socrates and Christ, he
hoped to be remembered through his pupils. In the year
1468 this Roman academy acquired fresh celebrity by the
persecution of Paul II., who partly suspected a political object
in its meetings, and partly resented the open heathenism of
its leaders. I need not here repeat the tale of his crusade
against the scholars. It is enough to mention that Lætus
was imprisoned for a short while, and that in prison he wrote
an apology for his life, defending himself against a charge of
misplaced passion for a young Venetian pupil, and professing
the sincerity of his belief in Christianity. After his release
from the Castle of S. Angelo he was obliged to discontinue
the meetings of his academy, which were not resumed until
the reign of Sixtus. Pomponius Lætus lived on into the
Papacy of Alexander, and died in 1498 at the age of seventy.
His corpse was crowned with a laurel wreath in the Church of
Araceli. Forty bishops, together with the foreign ambassadors
in Rome and the representatives of the Borgia, who were
specially deputed for that purpose, witnessed the ceremony
and listened to the funeral oration. Lætus had desired that
his body should be placed in a sarcophagus upon the Appian
Way. This wish was not complied with. He was conveyed
from Araceli to S. Salvatore in Lauro, and there buried like a
Christian.

While the academy of Pomponius Lætus flourished at
Rome, that of Naples was no less active under the presidency
of Jovianus Pontanus. It appears to have originated in social
gatherings assembled by Beccadelli, and to have held its
meetings in a building called after its founder the *Porticus*

Antonianus. When death had broken up the brilliant circle surrounding Alfonso the Magnanimous, Pontanus assumed the leadership of learned men in Naples, and gave the formality of a club to what had previously been a mere reunion of cultivated scholars. The members Latinised their names; many of them became better known by their assumed titles than by their Italian cognomens. Sannazzaro, for instance, acquired a wide celebrity as Accius Syncerus. Pontanus was himself a native of Cereto in the Spoletano. Born in 1426, he settled in his early manhood at Naples, where Beccadelli introduced him to his royal patrons. During the reigns of Ferdinand I., Alfonso II., and Ferdinand II. Pontanus held the post of secretary, tutor, and ambassador, accompanying his masters on their military expeditions and negotiating their affairs at the Papal Court. When Charles VIII. entered Naples as a conqueror, Pontanus greeted him with a pane-gyrical oration, proving himself more courtly and self-seeking than loyal to the princes he had served so long. Guicciardini observes that this act of ingratitude stained the fair fame of Pontanus. Yet it may be pleaded in his defence that no moralist of the period had more boldly denounced the crimes and vices of Italian princes; and it is possible that Pontanus really hoped Charles might inaugurate a better age for Naples.

He was distinguished among the scholars of his time for the purity of his Latin style; to him belongs the merit of having written verse that might compete with good models of antiquity. His hexameters on stars and meteors, called ' Urania,' won the enthusiastic praise of his own generation, and subsequently served as model to Fracastoro for his own didactic poem. His amatory elegiacs have an exuberance of colouring and sensuous force of phrase that seem peculiarly appropriate to the Bay of Naples, where they were inspired. As a prose-writer it is particularly by his moral treatises that

Pontanus deserves to be remembered. Unlike the mass of contemporary dialogues on ethical subjects, they abound in illustrations drawn from recent history, so that even now they may be advantageously consulted by students anxious to gather characteristic details and to form a just opinion of Renaissance morality. Throughout his writings Pontanus shows himself to have been an original and vigorous thinker, a complete master of Latin scholarship, unwilling to abide contented with bare imitation, and bent upon expressing the facts of modern life, the actualities of personal emotion, in a style of accurate Latinity. When he died in 1503, he left at Naples one of the most flourishing schools of neopagan poets to be found in Italy; Lilius Gyraldus employs the old metaphor of the Trojan horse to describe the number and the vigour of the scholars who issued from it.

In the Church of Monte Oliveto at Naples there may be seen a group in terra cotta painted to imitate life. Alfonso II., Pontanus, and Sannazzaro are kneeling in adoration before the body of the dead Christ. Pontanus, who represents Nicodemus, is a stern, hard-featured, long-faced man, of powerful bone and fibrous sinews, built for serious labour in the study or the field. Sannazzaro, who stands for Joseph of Arimathea, is bald, fat-faced, with bushy eyebrows and a heavy cast of countenance. The physical characteristics of these men and their act of faith are in curious contradiction with the conception we form of them after reading the ‘Elegies’ and the ‘Arcadia.’

The Roman Academy of Pomponius Lætus and the Neapolitan Academy of Pontanus continued to exist after the death of their founders, while similar institutions sprang up in every town of Italy. To speak of these in detail would be quite impossible. With the commencement of the sixteenth century they lost their classical character, and assumed fantastic Italian titles. Thus the Roman coterie of wits and scholars called itself *I Vignaiuoli*. The members, among whom were Berni, La Casa, Firenzuola, Mauro, Molza, assumed titles like *L'Agreste*, *Il Mosto*, *Il Cotogno*, and so forth. The Cardinal Ippolito de' Medici founded a club in Rome for the study of Vitruvius. It met twice in the week, and was known as *Le Virtù*. At Bologna the *Viridario* devoted its energies to the correction of printed texts; the *Sitibondi* studied law, the *Desti* cultivated extinct chivalry. Besides these, the one town of Bologna produced *Sonnacchiosi*, *Oziosi*, *Desiosi*, *Storditi*, *Confusi*, *Politici*, *Instabili*, *Gelati*, *Umorosi*. As the century advanced, academies multiplied in Italy, and their titles became more absurd. Ravenna had its *Informi*, Faenza its *Smarriti*, Macerata its *Catenati*, Fabriano its *Disuniti*, Perugia its *Insensati*, Urbino its *Assorditi*, Naples its *Sereni*, *Ardenti*, and *Incogniti*—and so on *ad infinitum*. At Florence the Platonic Academy continued to flourish under the auspices of the Rucellai family, in whose gardens assembled the company described by Filippo de' Nerli,[1] until the year 1522, when it was suppressed on the occasion of the conspiracy against Giulio de' Medici. Duke Cosimo revived it under the name of the Florentine Academy in 1540, when its labours were wholly devoted to Petrarch and the Italian language. In 1572 appeared the famous academy called *Della Crusca*, the only one among these later societies which acquired an European reputation.

Those who are curious to follow the history of the academies, may be referred to the comprehensive notices of Tiraboschi. From the date of their Italianisation they cease to belong to the history of humanism; what justifies the mention of them here is the fact that they owed their first existence to the scholars of the third period. The worst faults of Italian erudition—pedantry and stylistic affectations—were perpetuated by coteries worshipping Petrarch and

---

[1] See Vol. I., *Age of the Despots*, p. 220, note.

peddling with the idlest of all literary problems, where so great a writer as Annibale Caro thought it in good taste to write a dissertation on the nose of a president, and where the industry of sensible men was absorbed in the concoction of sonnets by the myriad and childish puns on their own titles. During the following age of political stagnation and ecclesiastical oppression the academies were the playthings of a nation fast degenerating into intellectual hebetude. Not without amazement do we read the eulogies pronounced by Milton on the 'learned and affable meeting of frequent academies, and the procurement of wise and artful recitations, sweetened with eloquent and graceful incitements to the love and practice of justice, temperance, and fortitude.' What he had observed with admiration in Italy, he would fain have seen imitated in England, undeterred apparently by the impotence and sterility of academic dissertations.[1]

It remains to speak of the establishment of printing in Italy, an event no less important for the preservation and diffusion of classical learning than the previous discovery of MSS. had been indispensable for its revival. What has to be said about the erudite society of Venice may appropriately be introduced in this connection ; while the final honours of the third period will be seen to belong of right to one of Italy's most noble-minded scholars, Aldus Manutius.

In 1462 Adolph of Nassau pillaged Maintz and dispersed its printers over Europe. Three years later two Germans, by name Sweynheim and Pannartz, who had worked under Fust, set up a press in Subbiaco, a little village of the Sabine mountains. Here, in October 1465, the first edition of Lactantius saw the light. The German printers soon afterwards removed from Subbiaco, and settled, under the protection of the Massimi, in Rome, where they continued to issue

[1] See the *Reason of Church Government urged against Prelaty*, and the *Ready and Easy Way to Establish a Free Commonwealth*.

Latin authors from their press.[1] In 1646 John of Spires
established himself at Venice. He was soon afterwards joined
by his brother Vindelino (so the Italians write the name) and
by Nicholas Jenson, the Frenchman. Florence had no press
till 1471, when Bernardo Cennini printed the commentary of
Servius on Virgil's 'Bucolics.' The 'Georgics' and 'Æneid'
appeared in the following year. To Cennini, however, belongs
the honour of having been the first Italian to cast his own
type. Like many other illustrious artificers, he was by trade
a goldsmith; in his address to the reader he styles himself
aurifex omnium judicio præstantissimus, adding, with refe-
rence to the typography, *expressis ante calide caracteribus ac
deinde fusis literis volumen hoc primum impresserunt*. The
last sentence of the address should also be quoted : *Floren-
tinis ingeniis nil ardui est*. Other printers opened workshops
in Florence within the course of a few years—John of Maintz
in 1472, Nicholas of Breslau in 1477, Antonio Miscomini in
1481, and Lorenzo Alopa of Venice, who gave Homer with
Greek type to the world in 1488. Still, Florence had been
anticipated by many other cities ; for when once the new art
took root in Italy, it spread like wild fire. Omitting smaller
places from the calculation, it has been reckoned that, before
the year 1500, 4,987 books were printed in Italy, of which 298
are claimed by Bologna, 300 by Florence, 629 by Milan, 929 by
Rome, and 2,835 by Venice. The disproportion between the
activity of Florence and of Venice in the book trade deserves
to be noticed, though how it should be explained I hardly
know. Fifty towns and numbers of insignificant burghs—
Pinerolo, Savona, Pieve di Sacco, Cividale, Soncino, Chivasso,

[1] From a memorial presented by these printers to Sixtus IV. in
1472 we ascertain some facts about their industry. They had at that
date printed in all 12,495 volumes. It was their custom to issue 265
copies in each edition ; the double of that number for Virgil, Cicero's
separate works, and theological books in request. Cantù, *Lett. It.*
p. 112. See Cantù, p. 110, for details of the earliest Latin books.

Scandiano, for example—could boast of local presses. Ambulant printers established their machinery for half a year or so in a remote village, printed what came to hand there, and moved on.

While scholars rejoiced in the art that, to quote the words of one of them, 'had saved the labour of their aching joints,' the copyists complained that their occupation would be taken from them. The whistle of the locomotive at the beginning of this century was not more afflicting to stage-coachmen than the creaking of the wooden printing press to those poor scribes. Yet, however quickly a labour-saving invention may spread, there is generally time for the superseded industry to die an easy death, and for artisans to find employment in the new trade. Vespasiano, who during twenty-six years survived the first book printed in Florence, could even afford to despise the press.[1] The great nobles, on whose patronage he depended, did not suddenly transfer their custom from the scribe to the compositor ; nor was it to be expected that so essentially a democratic art as printing should find immediate favour with the aristocracy. A prince with a library of MSS. worth 40,000 ducats hated the machine that put an equal number of more readable volumes within the reach of moderate competency. Moreover, a certain suspicion of subversiveness and license clung about the press. This was to some extent justified by fact, since the press was destined to be the most formidable engine of the modern reason. Ecclesiastics, again, questioned whether the promiscuous multiplication of books were pious ; and Alexander VI. stretched his hand out to coerce the printer's devil. To check the spread of printing would, however, have overtaxed the powers of any human tyranny. All that the Church could do was to place its productions under episcopal control.

Though the copyists of MSS. were thrown out of work

_____
[1] See above, p. 220.

by the printing press, it gave important stimulus to other industries in Italy. The paper mills of Fabriano and of Colle in the Val d' Elsa became valuable properties ;[1] compositors and readers began to form a separate class of artisans, while needy scholars found a market for their talents in the houses of the publishers. When we consider the amount of literary work that had to be performed before Greek, Latin, and Hebrew texts could be prepared for the press, the difficulty of procuring correct copies of authoritative codices, and the scrupulous attention expended upon proof sheets, we are able to understand that men who lived by learning found the new art profitable.

Instead of having previous editions to work upon, the publishers were obliged, in the first instance, to collect MSS. For this purpose they either travelled themselves from city to city, or employed competent amanuenses. Next, it was necessary to study the philosophers, poets, historians, mathematicians, and mystics, whose works they intended to print, in order that no mistake in the sense of the words should be made. Orthography and punctuation had to be fixed ; and between many readings only one could be adopted. Giving a first edition to the world involved far more anxiety on these points than the reproduction of a book already often printed. No one man could accomplish such tasks alone. Therefore we find that scores of learned men were associated together for the purpose, living under the same roof, revising the copy for the compositor, overlooking the men at work, reading the text aloud, and correcting the proofs with a vigilance that is but little needed nowadays. All this labour, moreover, was

---

[1] It is supposed that the earliest paper factory established in Italy was at Fabriano. Colle, a little town near Volterra, made paper from a remote period ; by a deed, dated March 6, 1377, now preserved in the Florentine Archivio Diplomatico, one Colo da Colle rented a fall of water there *et gualcheriam ad faciendas cartas* for twenty years. Both places are still celebrated for their paper mills.

accomplished without the aid of grammars, lexicons, and other aids. Truly we may say without exaggeration that the Aldi of Venice and the Stephani of Paris are more worthy of commemoration for services rendered through scholarship to humanity than those modern castigators of ancient texts, the Porsons and the Lachmanns, whose names are on every lip. The enthusiasm of discovery, and the rich field for original industry offered to those early editors, may be reckoned as compensation for their otherwise overwhelming toil.

Teobaldo Mannucci, better known as Aldo Manuzio, was born in 1450 at Sermoneta, near Velletri. After residing as a client in the princely house of Carpi, he added the name Pio to his patronymic, and signed his publications with the full description, *Aldus Pius Manutius Romanus et Philhellen*, Ἄλδος ὁ Μανούτιος Ῥωμαῖος καὶ Φιλέλλην. He studied Latin at Rome under Gasparino da Verona, and Greek at Ferrara under Guarino da Verona, to whom he dedicated his Theocritus in 1495. Having qualified himself for undertaking the work of tutor or professor, according to the custom of the century, and having made friends with many of the principal Italian scholars, he went in 1482 to reside at Mirandola with his old friend and fellow student, Giovanni Pico. There he stayed two years, enjoying the society of the Phœnix of his age, and continuing his Greek studies in concert with Emmanuel Adramyttenos, a learned Cretan. Before Pico removed to Florence he procured for Aldo the post of tutor to his nephews Alberto and Lionello Pio. Carpi had owned the family of Pio for its masters since the thirteenth century, when they rose to power, like many of the Lombard nobles, by adroit use of Imperial privileges.[1] This little city, placed midway between Correggio, Mirandola, and Modena, is so

---

[1] Sansovino, in his *Famiglie Illustri*, after giving a fabulous pedigree of the Pio family, dates their signorial importance from the reign of Frederick II.

insignificant that its name has been omitted from the index
to Murray's handbook; nor is there indeed much but the
memory of Aldo and Alberto Pio, and a church built by
Baldassare Peruzzi, to recommend it to the notice of a traveller. Under the tuition of Aldo the two young princes
became excellent scholars. Alberto in particular proved, by
his aptitude for philosophical studies, that he had inherited
from his mother, the sister of Giovanni Pico, something of
the spirit of Mirandola. When Aldus published his great
edition of Aristotle, he inscribed it to his former pupil with
a Greek dedication, in which he styled him τῷ τῶν ὄντων
ἐραστῇ. There can be no doubt that Alberto's knowledge of
Greek language and philosophy was far more thorough than
that of many more belauded princes of the age. Yet he had
but little opportunity for the quiet prosecution of classical
studies, or for the patronage of learned men at Carpi. Driven
from his patrimony by the Imperialists, he died at Paris in
1530, after a life spent in foreign service and diplomatic
offices of trust. The bronze monument for his tomb may
still be seen [1] in the Gallery of the Louvre. The princely
scholar, clad in rich Renaissance armour, is reclining with
his head supported by his right hand; the left holds an open
book. The attitude of melancholy meditation, the ornamental
but useless cuirass, and the volume open while the scabbard
of the sword is shut, add to the portrait of this prince in exile
the value of an allegory. Such symbols suited the genius of
Italy during the age of foreign invaders.

To Alberto Pio the world owes a debt of gratitude, inasmuch as he supplied Aldo with the funds necessary for
starting his printing press, and gave him lands at Carpi, where
his family were educated. When Aldo conceived the ambitious
project of printing the whole literature of Greece, four Italian
towns could already claim the honours of Greek publications.

[1] Executed for the Church of the Cordeliers by Paulus Pontius.

Milan takes the lead.   In 1476 the Grammar of Lascaris was
printed   there   by   Dionysius   Paravisini, with   the   aid   of
Demetrius of Crete.[1]   In 1480 Esop and Theocritus appeared,
with no publisher's name.   In 1486 two Cretans, Alexander
and Laonicenus, edited a Greek psalter.   In 1493 Isocrates,
prepared by Demetrius Chalcondylas, was issued by Henry the
German and Sebastian of Pontremolo.   Next comes Venice,
where, as early as 1484, the 'Erotemata' of Chrysoloras had
been produced by a certain Peregrinus Bononiensis.   Vicenza
followed in 1488 with a reprint of Lascaris's Grammar due to
Leonard Achates of Basle, and in 1490 with a reprint of the
'Erotemata.'   Florence, as we have already seen, gave Homer
to the world in 1488.   Demetrius Chalcondylas revised the
text;   Demetrius the Cretan supplied the models for the
types;   Alopa of Venice was the publisher.   It will be remarked
that, with the exception of Homer and Theocritus, no true
classic of the first magnitude had appeared before the foundation of the Aldine Press.   I may also add that the Milanese
Isocrates   was   really   contemporaneous   with   the   Musæus,
Galeomyomachia, and Psalter issued by Aldo as precursors
of his Greek library—Πρόδρομοι τῆς Ἑλληνικῆς βιβλιοθήκης.
This fact makes his thirty-three first editions of all the
greatest and most voluminous Greek authors between 1494
and 1515 all the more remarkable.

It was at Carpi in 1490 that Aldo finally matured his

---

[1] Poliziano's epigram addressed to these earliest Greek printers
may be quoted here:

> Qui colis Aonidas, Grajos quoque volve libellos;
>   Namque illas genuit Græcia, non Latium.
> En Paravisinus quantâ hos Dionysius arte
>   Imprimit, en quanto cernitis ingenio !
> Te quoque, Demetri, ponto circumsona Crete
>   Tanti operis nobis edidit artificem.
> Turce, quid insultas ? tu Græca volumina perdis;
>   Hi pariunt : hydræ nunc age colla seca !

project of establishing a Greek press. His patrons desired
him to found it in their castle of Novi; but Aldo judged
rightly that at Venice he would be more secure from the disturbances of warfare, as well as more conveniently situated
for engaging the assistance of Greek scholars and compositors.
Accordingly, he took a house, and settled near S. Agostino.
This house speedily became a Greek colony. It may be
inferred from Aldo's directions to the printers that his trade
was carried on almost entirely by Greeks, and that Greek
was the language of his household. The instructions to the
binders as to the order of the sheets and mode of stitching
were given in Greek; and many curious Greek phrases
appear to have sprung up to meet the exigencies of the new
industry. Thus we find ἵνα ἑλληνιστὶ συνδεθήσεται for ‘Greek
stitching,’ and καττιτερίνῃ χειρὶ for ‘the type;’ while Aldo
himself is described as ἐφευρέτῃ τούτων γραμμάτων χαρακτῆρος
ὡς εἴρηται. The prefaces, almost always composed in Greek,
prove that this language was read currently in Italy, since
Aldo relied on numerous purchasers of his large and costly
issues. The Greek type, for the casting of which he provided
machinery in his own house, was formed upon the model
supplied by Marcus Musurus, a Cretan, who had taken Latin
orders and settled at Carpi, and from whom Aldo received
important assistance in the preparation of editions for the
press. The compositors, in like manner, were mostly Cretans.
We hear of one of them, by name Aristoboulos Apostolios,
while John Gregoropoulos, another Cretan, the brother-in-law
of Musurus, performed the part of reader. The ink used by
Aldo was made in his own house, where he had, besides, a
subordinate establishment for binding. The paper, excelled
by none that has been since produced, came from the mills of
Fabriano. It may easily be imagined that this beehive of
Greek industry often numbered over thirty persons, not including the craftsmen employed in lesser offices by the day.

The superintendence of this large establishment, added to the anxieties attending the production of so many books as yet not edited, sorely taxed the health and powers of Aldo. For years together he seems to have had no minute he could call his own. Continual demands were made by visitors and strangers upon his hours of leisure ; and in order to secure time for the conduct of his business, he was forced to placard his door with a prohibitory notice.[1] Besides the more ordinary interruptions, to which every man of eminence is subjected, he had to struggle with peculiar difficulties due to the novelty of his undertaking. The prefaces to many of his publications contain allusions to strikes among his workmen,[2] to the piracies of rival booksellers,[3] to the difficulty of procuring authentic MSS.,[4] and to the interruptions caused by war. Twice was the work of printing suspended, first in 1506, and then again in 1510. For two whole years at the latter period the industries of Venice were paralysed by the allied forces of the League of Cambray. The dedication of the first edition of Plato, 1513, to Leo X. concludes with a prayer, splendid in the earnestness and simplicity of its eloquence, wherein Aldo compares the miseries of warfare and the woes of Italy with

[1] See Didot's *Alde Manuce*, p. 417, the passage beginning ' Vix credas.' In the Latin preface to the *Thesaurus Cornucopiæ et Horti Adonidis*, 1495, Aldo complains that he has not been able to rest for one hour during seven years.

[2] ' Tot illico oborta sunt impedimenta malorumque invidiâ et domesticorum καὶ ταῖς τῶν καταράτων καὶ δραπετευόντων δούλων ἐπιβούλαις.' Preface to the *Poetæ Christiani Veteres*, 1501. Again in the ' monitum ' of the same, ' quater jam in ædibus nostris ab operariis et stipendiariis in me conspiratum et duce malorum omnium matre avaritiâ quos Deo adjuvante sic fregi ut valde omnes pœniteat suæ perfidiæ.'

[3] The French publishers of Lyons, the Giunti of Rome, and Soncino of Fano, were particularly troublesome. Didot has extracted some curious information about their tricks as well as Aldo's exposure of them. Pp. 167, 482-486.

[4] See especially the preface to Aristotle, vol. i. 1495 ; vol. v. 1498.

the sublime and peaceful objects of the student. All the terrible experiences of that wasteful campaign, from the effects of which the Republic of Venice never wholly recovered, seem to find expression in the passionate but reverent, address of the great printer to the scholar Pope. For two years previously the press of Aldo had been idle, while the French were deluging Brescia with blood, and the plains of Ravenna were heaped with dead Italians, Spaniards, Gauls, and Germans, met in passionate but fruitless conflict by the Ronco. Now, from the midst of her desolated palaces and silenced lagoons, Venice stretched forth to Europe the peace-gift of Plato. The student who had toiled to make it perfect, appealed before Christ and His vicar, from the arms that brutalise to the arts that humanise the nations.

In the midst of these occupations, disappointments, and distractions, Aldo, sustained by the enthusiasm of his great undertaking, never flagged. Some of his prefaces, after setting forth the impediments he had to combat, burst into a cry of triumph. What joy, he exclaims, it is to see these volumes of the ancients rescued from book-buriers ($\beta\iota\beta\lambda\iota o\tau\acute{a}\phi o\iota$) and given freely to the world ! [1] No man could have been more generously anxious than he was to serve the cause of scholarship by the widest possible diffusion of books at a moderate price. No artist was ever more scrupulously bent on giving the best possible form, the utmost accuracy, to every detail of his work. When we consider the beauty of the Aldine volumes, and the critical excellence of their texts, we may fairly be astonished at their prices. The Musæus was sold for something under one shilling of our money, the Theocritus for something under two shillings. The five

[1] See Preface to *Thesaurus Cornucopiæ*, quoted by Didot, p. 80; and cf. pp. 210, 221, 521, for further hints about selfish bibliomaniacs, who tried to hoard their treasures from the public and refused them to the press. Aldo, as a genuine lover of free learning, and also as a publisher, detests this class of men.

volumes which contained the whole of Aristotle, might be
purchased for a sum not certainly exceeding 8*l.* Each volume
of the pocket series, headed in 1501 by the 8vo. Virgil, and
comprising Greek, Latin, and Italian authors, fetched about
two shillings. For this library the celebrated Italic type,
known as Aldine, was adapted from the handwriting of
Petrarch, and cut by Francesco da Bologna.[1] It appears that,
as his trade increased, Aldo formed a company, who shared
the risks and profits of the business.[2] Yet the expenses of
publishing were so heavy, the insecurity of the book market
so great, and the privileges of copyright granted by the Pope
or the Venetian Senate so imperfect,[3] that Aldo, after giving
his life to this work, and bequeathing to the world Greek
literature, died comparatively poor. Erasmus, always somewhat snarling, accused him of avarice ; yet it was his liberality
to his collaborators, his openhandedness in buying the ex-
pensive apparatus for critical editions, that forced him to be
economical.

The first editions of Greek books published by Aldo
deserve to be separately noticed. In 1493, or earlier, appeared the 'Hero and Leander' of Musæus, a poem that
passed, in that uncritical age, for the work of Homer's
mythical predecessor.[4] In 1495 the first volume of Aristotle
saw the light, accompanied by numerous Greek epigrams and

[1] See Pannizzi's tract on 'Francesco da Bologna,' published by
Pickering, 1873. He was probably Francia the painter.

[2] In a letter to Marcello Virgilio Adriani, the teacher of Machiavelli, he mentions some books 'Cum aliis quibusdam communes,' as
distinguished from others which were his private property. Didot,
p. 233.

[3] On the subject of patents, privileges, and monopolies see Didot,
pp. 79, 166, 189, 371, 479–481.

[4] Μουσαῖον τὸν παλαιότατον ποιητὴν ἠθέλησα προοιμιάζειν τῷ τε
Ἀριστοτέλει καὶ τῶν σοφῶν τοῖς ἑτέροις αὐτίκα δι' ἐμοῦ ἐντυπησομένοις.
This πρόδρομος, or precursor, appeared without a date ; but it must
have come out earlier than 1494.

a Greek letter of Scipione Fortiguerra, who deplores in it the deaths of Pico, Poliziano, and Ermolao Barbaro. The remaining four volumes followed in 1497 and 1498. In the latter of these years Aldo, aided by his friend Musurus, produced nine comedies of Aristophanes ; the MSS. of the 'Lysistrata' and 'Thesmophoriazusæ' were afterwards discovered at Urbino, and published by Giunta in 1515. In 1502, Thucydides, Sophocles, and Herodotus appeared, followed in 1503 by Xenophon's 'Hellenics' and Euripides,[1] and in 1504 by Demosthenes. After this occurs a lull, occasioned in part by the disturbances ensuing on the League of Blois. In 1508 the list is recontinued with the Greek orators ; while 1509 has to show the minor works of Plutarch. Then follows another stoppage due to war. In 1513 Plato was published, and in 1514 Pindar, Hesychius, and Athenæus.

From the preceding account I have omitted the notice of minor editions as well as reprints. In order to complete the history of the Aldine issue of Greek books, it should be mentioned that Aldo's successors continued his work by giving Pausanias, Strabo, Æschylus, Galen, Hippocrates, and Longinus to the world ; so that when the Estiennes of Paris came to glean in the field of the Italian publishers, they only found Anacreon, Maximus Tyrius, and Diodorus Siculus as yet unedited.

We must not forget that, while the Greek authors were being printed thus assiduously by Aldo, he continued to send forth Latin and Italian publications from his press. Thus we find that the 'Etna' and the 'Asolani' of Bembo, the collected writings of Poliziano, the 'Hypnerotomachia Poliphili,' the 'Divine Comedy,' the 'Cose Volgari' of Petrarch, the 'Poetæ

---

[1] John Lascaris had edited four plays of Euripides for Alopa in 1496. This Aldine edition contained eighteen, one of which, the *Hercules Furens*, turned up while vol. ii. was in the press. The *Electra*, not discovered till later on, was printed at Rome, 1545.

Christiani Veteres,' including Prudentius, the poems of
Pontanus, the letters of the younger Pliny, the 'Arcadia' of
Sannazzaro, Quintilian, Valerius Maximus, and the 'Adagia'
of Erasmus were printed, either in first editions or with a
beauty of type and paper never reached before, between the
years 1495 and 1514.

The great Dutch scholar who made an epoch in the history
of learning, and transferred the sovereignty of letters to the
north of Europe, paid a visit in 1508 to the house of Aldo,
where he personally superintended the re-impression of his
'Proverbs.'[1] We have a lively picture of the printing of this
celebrated book in Aldo's workshop. 'Together we attacked
the work,' says Erasmus, 'I writing, while Aldo gave my copy
to the press.' In one corner of the room sat the scholar at his
desk, with the thin keen face so well portrayed by Holbein,
improvising new paragraphs, and making additions to his
previous collections in the brilliant Latin style that no one
else could write. Aldo took the MS. from his hand, and
passed it on to the compositors, revising the proofs as they
came fresh from the press, or conferring with his reader Sera-
phinus.[2] Erasmus had already gained the reputation of a
dangerous freethinker and opponent to the Church. As years
advanced, and the Reformation spread in Northern Europe, he
became more and more odious to ecclesiastical authority. The
spirit of revolt was incarnate in this Voltaire of the sixteenth
century, nor could the clergy raise other arms than those of
persecution against so radiant a champion of pure reason. All
reprints of the 'Adagia' were therefore forbidden by the bishops.
Paulus Manutius had to quote it on his catalogues as the work

[1] The *Adagia* were first printed in 1500 at Paris by John Philippi.
After the Aldine edition eleven were issued between 1509 and 1520 by
Matthew Schürer, ten by Froben between 1513 and 1539, while seven
or eight others appeared in various parts of Germany.

[2] See the passage quoted by Didot, pp. 297–299.

of *Batavus quidam homo*. To such an extent were liberal studies now gagged and downtrodden by the tyrants of the Counter-Reformation in that Italy which for two previous centuries had been the champion of free culture for Europe.

Before concluding the biography of Aldo Manuzio it may be well to give some account of the more illustrious assistants and collaborators whom he gathered around him in his academy at Venice.[1] The New Academy, or Aldine Academy of Hellenists, was founded in 1500 for the special purpose of promoting Greek studies and furthering the publication of Greek authors. Its rules were written in Greek ; the members were obliged to speak Greek ; their official titles were Greek ; and their names were Grecised. Thus Scipione Fortiguerra of Pistoja, who prepared the text of Demosthenes for Aldo, styled himself Carteromachos : and Alessandro Bondini, the Venetian physician who worked upon the edition of Aristotle, bore the name of Agathemeros.[2] The most distinguished Greeks at that time resident in Italy could be counted among the Neacademicians. John Lascaris, of Imperial blood, the teacher of Hellenism in France under three kings, was an honorary member. To this great scholar Aldo dedicated his first edition of Sophocles. Marcus Musurus occupied a post of more practical importance.[3] We have seen that his handwriting formed the model of Aldo's Greek type. To his scholarship the editions of Aristophanes, Plato, Pindar, Hesychius, Athenæus, and Pausanias owed their critical accuracy ; while, in concert with Nicolaos Blastos and

---

[1] Didot, pp. 147–151, 436–470, gives ample details concerning the foundation, constitution, and members of the Aldine Academy.

[2] We may compare the name of Melanchthon.

[3] A native of Rotino, in Crete (b. 1470, d. at Rome 1517). He acquired Latin so thoroughly that Erasmus wrote of him : 'Latinæ linguæ usque ad miraculum doctus, quod vix ulli Græco contigit præter Theodorum Gazam et Joannem Lascarem.' John Lascaris was his master.

Zacharias Calliergi, two Cretan printers settled in Venice, he published the first Latin and Greek lexicon.[1] It will be observed that the Cretans play a prominent part in this Venetian revival of Greek learning. Aristoboulos Apostolios, Joannes Gregoropoulos, Joannes Rhosos, and Demetrius Doucas, all of them natives of Crete, were members of the Neacademy. The first as a compositor, the second as a reader, the third as a scribe, the fourth as editor of the Greek Orators, rendered Aldo effective assistance. Among Italians, Pietro Bembo, Aleander, and Alberto Pio occupied positions of honorary distinction rather than of active industry. Those who worked in earnest for the Aldine press were chiefly Venetians. Girolamo Avanzi, professor of philosophy at Padua, revised the texts of Catullus, Seneca, and Ausonius. Andrea Navagero, the noble Venetian poet, corrected Lucretius, Ovid, Terence, Quintilian, Horace, and Virgil. Giambattista Egnazio performed the same service for Valerius Maximus, the Letters of Pliny, Lactantius, Tertullian, Aulus Gellius, and other Latin authors. To mention all the eminent Venetians who played their part in this Academy would be tedious; yet the two names of Marino Sanudo, the famous diarist, and of Marco Antonio Coccio, called Sabellicus, the historian of the Republic, cannot be omitted. Of northern foreigners the most illustrious was Erasmus; to Englishmen the most interesting is Thomas Linacre. Born in 1460 at Canterbury, he travelled into Italy, and studied at Florence under Poliziano and Chalcondylas. On his return to England he founded the Greek Chair at Oxford, and died in London in the year 1524. His translation into Latin of the ' Sphere ' of Proclus was published by Aldus in 1499. To him and to

---

[1] *Etymologicon Magnum*, 1499. Didot, pp. 544–578, may be consulted for information about this Greek press. Musurus boasts in his encomiastic verses that the work was accomplished entirely by Cretans. ἀναλώμασι Βλαστοῦ πόνῳ καὶ δεξιότητι Καλλιέργου in the colophon.

Grocin belongs the credit of having sought to plant the
culture of Italy in the universities of England.

During a severe illness in the year 1498 Aldo vowed to
take holy orders if he should recover. From this obligation
he subsequently obtained release by a brief of Alexander VI.,
and in the following year he married Maria, daughter of
Andrea Torresano, of Asola. Andrea, some years earlier, had
bought the press established by Nicholas Jenson in Venice, so
that Aldo's marriage to his daughter combined the interests
of two important firms. Henceforth the names of Aldus and
of Asolanus were associated on the title-pages of the Aldine
publications. When Aldo died in 1514 (1515 new style), he
left three sons—Manutio, in orders at Asola ; Antonio, a
bookseller at Bologna ; [1] and Paolo Manuzio. The last of
these sons, born at Venice in 1512, was educated by his grandfather Andrea till the year of the old man's death (1529).
He carried on the press at Venice and at Rome, separating
in the year 1540 from his uncles the Asolani, and bequeathing
his business to his son named Aldo. This grandson of Aldo
Manuzio, called by Scaliger a 'wretched and slow wit, the
mimic of his father,' began his career by printing, at the age
of eleven, a treatise on the 'Eleganze della Lingua Toscana
e Latina.' He married Francesca Lucrezia Giunta, of the
famous house of printers, and died, without surviving issue,
at Rome in 1597. Thus the industry of Aldo was continued
through two generations till the close of the sixteenth century.
The device of the dolphin and the anchor, intended to
symbolise quickness of execution combined with firmness of
deliberation, and the motto *Festina lente*, which Sir Thomas
Browne has rendered by 'Celerity contempered with cuncta-
tion,' though changed to suit varieties of taste from time to

---

[1] There is some discrepancy about this Antonio between Renouard
and Didot.

time, were never altogether abandoned by the Aldines.[1] As
years went on, however, their publications became of less
importance, and the beauty of their books degenerated.

In tracing the history of Aldo's enterprise, I have been
carried beyond the limits of the period included in this chapter.
Yet I knew not how to describe the activity of the press
in Italy better than by concentrating attention upon the
greatest publisher who ever lived. Aldo Manuzio was no
mere bookseller or printer. His learning won the hearty
praises of ripe scholars, nor did any student of the age express
more nobly and with fuller conviction his deep sense of the
dignity conferred by learning on the soul of man.[2] That he
was amiable in private life is proved by the intimate relations
he maintained with humanists, than whom even poets are not
a more irritable race of men.[3] To his fellow-workers he was
uniformly generous in pecuniary matters, free from jealousy,
and prodigal of praise. Seeking even less than his due share
of credit, he desired that the great work of his life should
pass for the common achievement of himself and his learned
associates. Therefore he called his Greek library the fruits of
the Neacademia, though no man could have known better
than he did that his own genius was the life and spirit of
the undertaking. His stores of MSS. were as open to the

---

[1] 'Sum ipse mihi optimus testis me semper habere comites, ut
oportere aiunt, delphinum et anchoram ; nam et dedimus multa cunc-
tando, et damus assidue.' Preface to the *Astronomici*, dedicated to
Duke Guidobaldo of Urbino, 1499. The observations of Erasmus on
the motto deserve to be read with attention. See Didot, p. 299.

[2] See the passages from his letters and prefaces quoted and referred
to on p. 239, above, note 2.

[3] The prospect of his visit to Milan in 1509 called forth these pretty
April verses from Antiquari :—

> Aldus venit en, Aldus ecce venit !
> Nunc, O nunc, juvenes, ubique in urbe
> Flores spargite. Vere namque primo
> Aldus venit en, Aldus ecce venit.

instruction of scholars as his printed books were given liberally
to the public.[1] 'Aldo,' writes Erasmus, 'had nothing in his
treasury but what he readily communicated.' Those who
read the estimate of his services to learning made by eminent
contemporaries, will find the language of Nicholas Leonicenus,
Erasmus, and Anton Francesco Doni not exaggerated.[2] But,
in order to comprehend their true value, we must bear in mind
that until the year 1516, when Froben printed the Greek
Testament at Basle, none but insignificant Greek reprints had
appeared in Northern Europe.[3] Finally, what makes the
place of Aldus in the history of Italian humanism all-im-
portant is the fact that, after about 1520, Greek studies began
to decline in Italy all together. As though exhausted by
the enormous energy wherewith Florence had acquired and
Venice had disseminated Greek culture, the Italians relapsed
into apathy. Posterity may be thankful that their pupils,
Grocin and Linacre, Reuchlin and Erasmus, the Stephani and
Budæus, had by this time transplanted erudition beyond the
Alps, while Aldo had secured the literature of ancient Greece
against the possibility of destruction.

[1] See above, p. 275, for his hatred of the βιβλιοτάφοι. He was the
very opposite of Henri Estienne the younger, who closed his library
against his son-in-law Casaubon.

[2] Didot, pp. 89, 299, 423.

[3] *Priscian*, at Erfurt, 1501; *Alphabet, Batrachomyomachia*, Musæus,
Theocritus, Grammar of Chrysoloras, Hesiod's *Works and Days*, Paris,
1507; Aristotle on *Divination by Dreams*, Cracow, 1529; Lucian, περὶ
διψάδων, Oxford, 1521, are among the earliest Greek books printed out of
Italy. The grammars of the Greek humanists were frequently reprinted
in the first quarter of the sixteenth century in Germany.

CHAPTER VII

FOURTH PERIOD OF HUMANISM

Fall of the Humanists—Scholarship permeates Society—A New Ideal
of Life and Manners—Latinisation of Names—Classical Periphrases
—Latin Epics on Christian Themes—Paganism—The Court of
Leo X.—Honours of the Church given to Scholars—Ecclesiastical
Men of the World—Mæcenases at Rome—Papal and Imperial Rome
—Moral Corruption—Social Refinement—The Roman Academy—
Pietro Bembo—His Life at Ferrara—At Urbino—Comes to Rome
—Employed by Leo—Retirement to Padua—His Dictatorship of
Letters—Jacopo Sadoleto—A Graver Genius than Bembo—Paulus
Jovius—Latin Stylist—His Histories—Baldassare Castiglione—Life
at Urbino and Rome—The Courtly Scholar—His Diplomatic Missions
—Alberto Pio—Gian Francesco Pico della Mirandola—The Vicissi-
tudes of his Life—Jerome Aleander—Oriental Studies—The Library
of the Vatican—His Mission to Germany—Inghirami, Beroaldo,
and Acciaiuoli—The Roman University—John Lascaris—Study of
Antiquities—Origin of the ' Corpus Inscriptionum '—Topographical
Studies—Formation of the Vatican Sculpture Gallery—Discovery of
the Laocoon—Feeling for Statues in Renaissance Italy—Venetian
Envoys in the Belvedere—Raphael's Plan for excavating Ancient
Rome—His Letter to Leo—Effect of Antiquarian Researches on the
Arts—Intellectual Supremacy of Rome in this Period—The Fall—
Adrian VI.—The Sack of Rome—Valeriano's Description of the
Sufferings of Scholars.

WHAT is known as the Revival of Learning was accomplished before the close of the fifteenth century, and about
this time humanism began to lose credit. The professional
scholars who had domineered in Italy during the last hundred
years, were now regarded with suspicion as pretentious sophists,
or as empty-pated pedants. Their place was taken by men of
the world, refined courtiers, and polite stylists who piqued

themselves on general culture. This revolution in public opinion was the result of various causes which I shall attempt to set forth in another chapter. It is enough for my present purpose to observe that the learning possessed at first by a few teachers, acquired with effort, and communicated with condescension, had now become the common property of cultivated men. In proportion as a knowledge of the classic authors diffused itself over a wider area, the mere reputation of sound scholarship ceased to form a valid title to celebrity. It was necessary that the man of letters, educated by antiquity, should give proof of his genius by some originality of mind. The age of acquisition had ended ; the age of application had begun. To this result the revived interest in Italian literature powerfully contributed. Writers were no longer, like Bruni and Poggio, ashamed of their *cose volgari*. On the contrary, the most splendid productions of the first half of the sixteenth century, the Histories of Guicciardini and Machiavelli, the Epic of Ariosto, the ' Cortegiano ' of Castiglione, and the burlesque poems of Berni were penned in powerful and delicate Italian. To what extent the influence of Lorenzo de' Medici, who was always more partial to vernacular literature than to scholarship, determined the change in question, is a matter for opinion. That Florence led the way by her great writers of Italian poetry and prose admits of no doubt.

At the same time the erudition of the fifteenth century had steeped the whole Italian nation. Humanism penetrated every sphere of intellectual activity, and gave a colour to all social customs. The arts of painting and of sculpture felt its influence. A new style of architecture, formed upon the model of Roman monuments, sprang up. Science took a special bias from the classics, and philosophy was so strongly permeated by antique doctrines that the Revival of Learning may be justly said to have checked the spontaneity of the Italian intellect. There was not enough time for students to absorb antiquity and pass beyond it, before the mortmain of the Church and the Spaniard was laid upon the fairest provinces of thought. To trace the course of Italian philosophy, is, however, no part of my scheme in this volume. The Aristotelian and Platonic controversies on the nature of the soul, the materialism of Pietro Pomponazzo, the gradual emergence of powerful thinkers like Bruno and Campanella, the theological rationalism of Aonio Paleario, and the final suppression of free thought by the Church, belong to the history of the Counter-Reformation. To the same sad chapter of Italian history must be relegated the labours of the earliest mathematicians, astronomers, and cosmographers, who, poring over the texts of Ptolemy and Euclid, anticipated Copernicus, impelled Columbus to his enterprise, and led the way for Galileo. The infamy of having rendered science and philosophy abortive in Italy, when its early show of blossom was so promising, falls upon the Popes and princes of the last half of the sixteenth century. The narrative of their emergence from the studies of the humanists must form the prelude to a future work treating of Farnesi and Caraffas, Inquisitors and Jesuits. Only by showing the growth which might have been, can we demonstrate the atrophy that was.

It remains in this chapter to describe the fourth period of humanism, when Italy, still permeated with the spirit of the classical revival, laid down laws of social breeding for the nations of the North. Few things are more difficult than to set forth without exaggeration, and yet with sufficient force, the so-called Paganism of Renaissance Italy. At first sight, and from certain points of view, it seems as though the exclusive study of the classics had wrought a thorough metamorphosis of morality and manners. When, on reflection, this appearance is seen to be illusory, we incline, perhaps, to the contrary conclusion that scholarship only set a kind of fashion without taking deep hold even on the imagination of the people. A more complete acquaintance with the period makes it clear that the imitation of the ancients in thought, sentiment, and language was no mere affectation, and that, however partial its influences may have been, they were not superficial. In the first volume of this work I tried to show to what extent the patriotism of tyrannicides and the profligacy of courtiers were alike related to the prevailing study of the ancient world. It was no small matter that the vices and the virtues, the worldliness and the enthusiasm, of that many-featured age, together with its supreme achievements in art, its ripest productions in literature, should have gradually assumed a classic form. The standards of moral and æsthetic taste were paganised, though the nation at large remained unchanged in Catholicity. It was precisely this discord between the professed religion of the people and the heathenism of its ideal that inspired Savonarola with his prophecy.

Classical style being the requirement of the age, it followed that everything was sacrificed to this. In christening their children the great families abandoned the saints of the calendar and chose names from mythology. Ettorre, Achille, Atalanta, Pentesilea, Lucrezia, Porzia, Alessandro, Annibale, Laomedonte, Fedro, Ippolito, and many other antique titles became fashionable. Those who were able to do so turned their baptismal names into Latin or Greek equivalents. Janus or Jovianus passed for Giovanni, Pierius for Pietro, Aonius for Antonio, Lucius Grassus for Luca Grasso; the German prelate John Goritz was known as Corycius,[1] and the Roman professor Gianpaolo Parisio as Janus Parrhasius. Writers who undertook to treat of modern or religious themes, were driven by their zeal for purism to the strangest expedients of

---

[1] Namque sub Œbaliæ memini me turribus altis
Qua niger humectat flaventia culta Galesus
Corycium vidisse *senem.*—Virg. *Georg.* lib. iv. 125.

language. God, in the Latin of the sixteenth century, is *Jupiter Optimus Maximus* ; Providence becomes *Fatum ;* the saints are *Divi,* and their statues *simulacra sancta Deorum.* Our Lady of Loreto is changed into *Dea Lauretana,* Peter and Paul into *Dii tutelares Romæ,* the souls of the just into *Manes pii,* and the Pope's excommunication into *Diræ.* The Holy Father himself takes the style of *Pontifex Maximus* ; his tiara, by a wild confusion of ideas, is described as *infula Romulea.* Nuns are Vestals, and cardinals Augurs. For the festivals of the Church periphrases were found, whereof the following may be cited as a fair specimen : [1]
'*Verum accidit ut eo ipso die, quo domum ejus accesseram, ipse piæ rei caussá septem sacrosancta Divûm pulvinaria supplicaturus inviserit ; erant enim lustrici dies, quos unoquoque anno quadragenos purificatione consecravit nostra pietas.*'

It need hardly be added that, when the obligations of Latinity had reached this point, to read Cicero was of far more importance than to study the Fathers of the Church. Bembo, it is well known, advised Sadoleto to 'avoid the Epistles of S. Paul, lest his barbarous style should spoil your taste : *Omitte has nugas, non enim decent gravem virum tales ineptiæ.*' The extent, however, to which formal purism in Latinity was carried, may be best observed in the 'Christiad' of Vida, and the poem 'De Partu Virginis' of Sannazzaro.[2] Sannazzaro not only invokes the muses of Helicon to sing the birth of Christ, but he also makes Proteus prophesy his advent to the river-god of Jordan. The archangel discovers Mary—described by the poet as *spes fida Deorum*—intent on

[1] From the exordium to Valeriano's treatise *De Infelicitate Literatorum.*

[2] Lilius Gyraldus, in his dialogue 'De Poetis Nostri Temporis,' *Opp.* vol. ii. p. 384, mentions a critic who was so stupid as to *desiderare in Pontano et si deis placet in Sanazario Christianam elocutionem, hoc est barbaram !*

reading nothing less humanistic than the Sibyls ; and after she has received his message, the spirits of the patriarchs are said to shout because they will escape from Tartarus and Acheron and the hideous baying of the triple-throated hound.

It might be reasonably urged against Milton that in the ' Paradise Regained ' he somewhat impairs the religious grandeur of his subject by investing it with the forms of the classical epic. If he has erred in this direction, it is as nothing compared with the pseudo-Pagan travesty of Vida. God the Father in the ' Christiad ' is spoken of as *Superum Pater nimbipotens* and *Regnator Olympi*—titles which had their real significance in Latin mythology, being transferred with frigid formalism to a Deity whose essence is spiritual, and whose cult has no admixture of nature worship. Jesus is invariably described as *Heros* ; this absurdity reaches its climax in the following phrase about the bad thief on the cross :—

> Ipse etiam verbis morientem heroa superbis
> Stringebat.

The machinery whereby the Jews are brought to will the death of Christ is no less ridiculous. Instead of attempting to set religious or ethical motives into play, Vida introduces a gang of Gorgons, Harpies, Centaurs, Hydras, and the like. The bread of the Last Supper appears under the disguise of *sinceram Cererem*. The wine mingled with gall, offered to our Lord upon the cross, is *corrupti pocula Bacchi*. The only excuse for these grotesque compromises between the Biblical subject-matter and its mythological expression is, that in any other way it would have been impossible to give the form of pure Latinity to the verse. The poet failed to comprehend that he was producing a masterpiece of *barocco* mannerism, spoiling at once the style he sought to use and the theme he undertook to illustrate. It was enough for him to fit the Roman toga to his saints and Pharisees, and to

tickle the taste of a learned audience by allusions that reminded them of Virgil. The same bathos was reached
by Bembo when he invented the paraphrase of 'heavenly
zephyr' for the Holy Ghost, and described the Venetian
Council bidding a Pope *uti fidat diis immortalibus, quorum
vices in terrâ gerit*. It is not the profanity of these phrases
so much as their æsthetic emptiness, the discord between the
meaning intended to be conveyed and the literary form, that
strikes a modern critic.

When the same poets break out into honest Paganism, in
the frank verses written by Bembo for Priapus, in Beccadelli's
epigrams, or in the elegies of Acon and Iolas, we feel that
they are more artistically justified. The following lines, for
instance, from Vida's 'Poetics,' have a true ring and beauty
of their own. He is addressing Virgil as a saint :—

> Te colimus, tibi serta damus, tibi thura, tibi aras,
> Et tibi rite sacrum semper dicemus honorem.

Or again--

> Nos aspice præsens,
> Pectoribusque tuos castis infunde calores
> Adveniens pater, atque animis te te insere nostris.

There is no confusion here between the feeling and the
language chosen to express it. The sentiment, if somewhat
artificial and unreal, is at least adequate to the form.

I have entered at some length into the illustration of
puristic Latinisms, because they seem to represent the cul-
minating point of classic studies, in so far as these affected
taste in general, and also because they are specially characteristic of the period of which I have now to treat. It was
at Rome, among the great ecclesiastics, that these Pagan
fashions principally flourished. Eminence of all kinds found
a home with Leo X., assuming the purple of the prelate and
the scarlet of the cardinal at his indulgent hands. The
genius of the Renaissance seemed to have followed this first

Medicean Pope from Florence. Though Leo was a man of merely pleasure-loving and receptive temperament, who left no lasting impress on his age, he knew at least how to appreciate ability, and found the height of his enjoyment in the arts and letters he enthusiastically patronised. This sybarite of intellectual and sensual luxury gave his name to what is called the golden age of Italian literature, chiefly because he attracted the best wits to Rome and received the flatteries of men whose work survived them.

History presents few spectacles more striking than that of Rome in the pontificate of Leo. While the Papacy has become a secular sovereignty, learning and arts have assumed the sacerdotal habit, and the boldest immoralities of a society comparable to that of the ancient Empire flourish in the petty Courts of ecclesiastical princes. The capital of Christendom is full of priests; but the priests are men of pleasure and the world—elegant Latinists and florid rhetoricians, raised to posts of eminence by reason of their brilliant gifts. We have seen already how the humanists made their way into the Roman Curia as writers and abbreviators, and how liberally Nicholas V. rewarded learning. Yet, however indispensable the scholars of the fifteenth century became, they rarely rose above the rank of Apostolic secretaries; while few of the professional humanists cared to take orders in the Church. They were satisfied with official emoluments and semi-secular benefices. All this was now altered. The most distinguished men of letters made the Church their profession. Sadoleto, Bembo, and Aleander, who began their career under Leo, received the hats of cardinals from Paul III. Paulus Jovius was consecrated Bishop of Nocera by Clement VII., and retired to Como in disgust because he failed to get the scarlet in 1549. Marcus Musurus, created Bishop of Malvasia, is said to have died of disappointment when he saw the same dignity beyond his reach. Vida, the

Latin poet, obtained the see of Alba in Piedmont, and Giberti, the accomplished stylist, that of Verona, from Clement VII. All these men had made their mark at Leo's Court, who set the example, followed by his Medicean successor, of rewarding mundane talents and accomplishments with ecclesiastical distinctions. The question, seriously entertained, of admitting Raphael to the Sacred College proves to what extent the highest honours of the Church had come to be esteemed as prizes, and justifies to some extent Pietro Aretino's arrogant offer to sell his services to the Papacy in exchange for a cardinal's hat.

The biographies of these favourites of fortune offer strong points of similarity. Whether born of noble families, like Bembo, or raised from comparative obscurity, like Bibbiena, they early in life attached themselves to some distinguished prince,[1] or entered the service of a great ecclesiastic. Their literary talents, social accomplishments, successes with women, and diplomatic service at the centres of Italian politics brought them still further into notice. Thus Sadoleto's Latin poem on the Laocoon, Bibbiena's ' Calandra,' Inghirami's acting of the part of Phædra in Seneca's ' Hippolytus,' and Bembo's friendship with Lucrezia Borgia might be cited as turning-points in the early history of these illustrious prelates. Having thus acquired position by their personal gifts, they travelled to Rome in the suite of their respective patrons, and obtained office at the hands of Leo. Sadoleto and Bembo became his secretaries. Inghirami superintended the Vatican Library.[2] Bibbiena's versatile abilities were divided between the duties of State minister and master of the revels. As they had built their fortunes by the help of eminent protectors, they now in their turn took the rank of patrons. In addition to the Vatican, Rome

---

[1] See Vol. I., *Age of the Despots*, p. 145.
[2] He held this post under Julius II.

displayed a multitude of petty Courts and minor circles.
Each cardinal and each ambassador held a jurisdiction independent of the Pope, and not unfrequently in opposition
to the ruling power. To found academies, to gather clever
men around them, and to play the part of Mæcenas was
the ambition of these subordinate princes. During the
pontificate of Leo the Cardinals Riario, Giulio de' Medici,
Bibbiena, Petrucci, Farnese, Alidosi, and Gonzaga, not to
mention others, entertained their own following of flatterers
and poets, who danced attendance at their levees, accompanied them in public, and earned a meagre pittance by
compliments and dedications. Some of these priestly patrons
affected the arts, others the sciences; others again, and these
the majority, bestowed their favours upon literature. Ippolito de' Medici is said to have maintained a retinue of three
hundred poets, among whom are mentioned the elegant Molza
and the learned Valeriano. The fashion thus set by Leo
and the Sacred College was followed by all the eminent men
in Rome. The banker Agostino Chigi made himself a name
not only by his patronage of painters, but also by the private
Greek press founded in his house.[1] Baldassare Turini
devoted himself to the arts of building and of decoration.
Baldassare Castiglione, as ambassador from Mantua and
Ferrara, and Alberto Pio, as prince of Carpi and ambassador
from France, dispensed the hospitality of their palaces to
scholars, among whom they held no inconsiderable rank on
their own merits.

Libraries, collections of statues and of pictures, frescoes
painted from mythological subjects, garden-houses planned
upon the antique model, Latin inscriptions, busts of the

[1] The first Greek book printed in Rome, an edition of Pindar by
Cornelius Benignius, 1515, issued from Chigi's press under the superintendence of Zacharias Kalliergos of Crete. Concerning this printer
see Didot, *Alde Manuce*, pp. 544-578.

emperors, baths and banquet chambers decorated in the manner of the Roman ruins—on such objects the wealth of the Church was being prodigally spent. Posterity has reason to deplore the non-appearance of a satirist in this Papal society, so curiously similar to that of Imperial Rome. Horace would, indeed, have found ample materials for humorous delineation, whether he had chosen to deride the needy clients leaving their lodgings before daybreak to crowd a prelate's antechamber, or the parasites on whom coarse practical jokes were played in the Pope's presence, or the flatterers who praised their master's mock virtues in hour-long declamations. Fouler vices than vanity, hypocrisy, and servility supplied fit subjects for invectives no less fiery than the second and the sixth of Juvenal. At Rome virtuous women had no place ; but Phryne lived again in the person of Imperia, and dignitaries of the Church thought it no shame to parade their preference for Giton.[1] In the absence of a Horace or a Juvenal, we have to content ourselves with Bandello and other novelists, and with one precious epistle of Ariosto describing the difficulty of conducting business at the Papal Court except by way of backstairs influence and antechamber intrigue.

To over-estimate the moral corruption of Rome at the beginning of the sixteenth century is almost impossible. To over-rate the real value of a literature that culminated in the subtleties of rhetoric and style is easy. Nor is it difficult to mistake, as many critics have done, the sunset of the fine arts for their meridian splendour. Yet, while we recognise the enervation of society in worse than heathen

---

[1] The epitaph of Bella Imperia proves that the title of Hetæra was thought honourable: 'Imperia, Cortisana Romana, quæ digna tanto nomine, raræ inter homines formæ specimen dedit. Vixit a. xxvi. d. xii. Obiit MDXI., die xv. Aug.' Berni's *Capitolo sopra un Garzone* may be referred to for the second half of the sentence.

vices, and justly regard Rome as the hostelry of alien arts
and letters rather than the mother city of great men, we
cannot blind our eyes to the varied lights and colours of
that Court, unique in modern history. The culture toward
which Italian society had long been tending, was here completed. The stamp of universality had been given to the
fine arts and to literature by the only potentate who at that
moment claimed allegiance from united Christendom. As
the eloquent historian of the town of Rome observes, ' the
richest intellectual life here blossomed in a swamp of vices.'
It was not the life of great poetry : that had perished long
ago with Dante. It was not the life of genuine science :
that was destined to be born with Galileo. It was not the
life of comprehensive scholarship : that slept in the grave
of Poliziano. It was not even the life of progressive art ;
for Raphael died in this age, and though Michael Angelo
survived it, his genius had no successors. But it was the
life of culture, rendering the rudest and most vicious sensitive to softening influences, and preparing for more powerful nations the possibilities of great achievements.

Amid political debility and moral corruption an ideal
of refinement, adopted from antiquity, and assimilated to
modern modes of living, had been formed. This was the
most perfect bloom of the Renaissance, destined to survive
the decay of humanism, and to be for subsequent civilisation
what chivalry was for the Middle Ages. Through the continued effort of patricians and of scholars to acquire the tone
of classic culture, something like antique urbanity had
reappeared at Florence and in Rome ; while several generations devoted to polite studies had produced a race distinguished above all things for its intellectual delicacy. The
effect of this æsthetic atmosphere upon visitors from the
North was singularly varied. Luther, who came to see the
City of the Saints, found in Rome the sink of all abominations,

the very lair of Antichrist. The *comitas* and the *facetiæ* of the prelates were to him the object of unmitigated loathing. Erasmus, on the contrary, wrote from London that nothing but Lethe could efface his memory of that radiant city its freedom of discourse, its light, its libraries, its honeyed converse of most learned scholars, its large style of life, and all those works of art that made of Rome the theatre of nations. The Italians themselves, lessoned by the tragedy of 1527, looked back with no less mingled feelings upon Leo's Rome. La Casa mentions the *nimia humanitatis suavitas*—the excess of sweetness in all that makes society humane—as a characteristic of the past age. That excessive sweetness of civility, the final product of the arts and scholarship of Italy, when diffused through Europe and tempered to the taste of sterner nationalities, became the politeness of France under Louis XIV., the *bel air* of Queen Anne's courtiers.

The Roman Academy still continued to be active, meeting at the palaces of more than one great prelate. The gardens of Angelo Colocci, Leo's secretary, a friend of John Lascaris, and himself no inconsiderable stylist, formed its headquarters. Sometimes the poet Blosius Palladius received the associates in his villa by the Tiber; sometimes they enjoyed the hospitality of Egidius Canisius, General of the Augustine Order; at one time they sought the house of Sadoleto on the Quirinal; at another they feasted in the vineyard of John Goritz, the Corycius Senex. The festivals of this learned society, to judge by the descriptions of its members, were distinguished by antique simplicity and good taste, contrasting powerfully with the banquets of mere mundane prelates.[1] When Agostino Chigi entertained the Academicians in the Villa Farnesina, he chastened his magnificence to suit the spirit of their founder, Lætus, and

[1] See Tiraboschi, vii. 1, lib. i. c. 2.

omitted those displays of vulgar pomp that marked his wedding banquet.[1]

The muster-roll of the Academy brings the most eminent wits of Rome before us. First and foremost stands Pietro Bembo, the man of letters, who, like Petrarch, Poggio, and Poliziano, may be chosen as the fullest representative of his own age of culture. His father, Bernardo Bembo, was a Venetian of noble birth and education. To his generous enthusiasm for Italian literature Ravenna owes the tomb of Dante. Pietro was born at Florence in 1470, and received his early education in that city. Therefore the Tuscans claim his much-praised purity of diction for their gift. He afterwards studied Greek at Messina under Constantine Lascaris, and learned philosophy from Pomponazzo at Padua. When his master's treatise on the 'Immortality of the Soul' was condemned by the Lateran Council, Bembo used his influence successfully in his behalf. Though he denied the demonstrability of the doctrine, and maintained that Aristotle gave it no support, Pomponazzo was only censured, instead of being burned like Bruno. This good fortune was due, however, less to his pupil's advocacy than to the nonchalance of Leo. Having completed his academical studies in 1498, Bembo joined his father at the brilliant Court of the Estensi. When Lucrezia Borgia entered Ferrara in 1502 she was still in the zenith of her beauty. Her father, Alexander, grew daily more powerful in Rome ; while her brother held the central States of Italy within his grasp. The greatness of the Borgias reflected honour on the bride of Alfonso d' Este ; and though the princes of Ferrara at first received her with reluctance, they were soon won over by her grace. Between the princess and the courtly scholar a friendship speedily sprang up, which strengthened with years and was maintained by correspondence at a distance. To Lucrezia Bembo

[1] See Vol. I., *Age of the Despots*, p. 342.

dedicated ' Gli Asolani,' a dialogue in the Italian tongue upon
Platonic love,[1] by far the freest and most genial of his
writings. The collection of his Latin poems contains an
epigram upon a golden serpent clasped above her wrist, and
an elegy in which he praises her singing, dancing, playing,
and recitation :—

> Quicquid agis, quicquid loqueris, delectat : et omnes
> Præcedunt Charites, subsequiturque decor.

This liaison, famous in the annals of Italian literature, gave
Bembo a distinguished place in the great world. A touching
memento of it—Lucrezia's letters and a tress of her long
yellow hair—is still preserved at Milan in the Ambrosian
Library.

From Ferrara Bembo passed to Urbino in 1506, where
Guidobaldo da Montefeltre had gathered round him the
brilliant group described in the ' Cortegiano.' The climax
of that treatise, our most precious source of information on
Court life in Italy, makes it clear that Bembo played the first
part in a circle distinguished above all others at that time
for refinement and wit. Many cities might boast of a larger
and more splendid concourse of noble visitors ; but none
competed with Urbino for the polish of its manners and the
breeding of its courtiers. In his dialogue in praise of Guidobaldo, Bembo paid a magnificent tribute to the prince from
whose society he learned so much, and in whose service he
remained till the Duke's death.[2] Giuliano de' Medici, with
whom he lived on terms of intimacy at Urbino, took him to
Rome in 1512. The reign of Leo was about to shed new
lustre on the Medicean exiles. His victorious exclamation
to his brother, ' Godiamoci il Papato poichè Dio ce l' ha dato,'
had a ring of promise in it for their numerous friends and

---

[1] Written 1504. First printed by Aldo, 1505.

[2] ' De Guido Ubaldo Feretrio deque Elisabetha Gonzaga Urbini
Ducibus.'

clients. Even without the recommendation of Giuliano, it
is not likely that Leo would have overlooked a man so
wholly after his own heart as Bembo. The qualities he most
admired—smooth manners, a handsome person, wit in conversation, and thorough mastery of Latin style, without
pretension to deep learning or much earnestness of purpose—
were incarnate in the courtly Venetian. Bembo was precisely
the man to make Leo's life agreeable by flattering his superficial tastes and subordinating the faculties of a highly cultivated mind to frivolous, if intellectual, amusements. The
churchman who warned Sadoleto against spoiling his style
by study of the Bible, the prosaist who passed his compositions through sixteen portfolios, revising them at each
remove, the versifier who penned a hymn to S. Stephen and
a monologue for Priapus with equal elegance, was cast in the
same mould as the pleasure-loving Pontiff. For eight years
he lived at Rome, honoured by the Medici and loved by all
who knew him. His duties as secretary to Leo, shared by
his old friend and fellow-student Sadoleto, were not onerous ;
while the society of the capital afforded opportunity for the
display of his most brilliant gifts. In 1520, wearied by nearly
thirty years of continual Court life, and broken down in health
by severe sickness, Bembo retired to Padua. The collection
of a library and museum, horticulture, correspondence, and
the cultivation of his studied Ciceronian style now occupied
his leisure through nineteen most disastrous years for Italy.
The learned courtiers of that age liked thus to play the
Roman in their villas, quoting Horace and Virgil on the
charms of rustic life, and fancying they caught the spirit of
Cincinnatus while they strolled about the farm. Bembo's
Paduan retreat became the rendezvous of all the ablest
men in Italy, the centre of a fluctuating society of highest
culture. Paul III. recalled him to Rome, and made him
cardinal in 1539. When he died in 1547 he was buried not

far from Leo in the Church of the Minerva. A fair slab of marble marks his grave.

Bembo succeeded Poliziano in the dictatorship of Italian letters. Like Poliziano, he was both a scholar and a writer of Italian ; but he was far from possessing the comprehensive understanding or the genius of his predecessor. Of all the 'apes of Cicero' scoffed at by Erasmus, he stood first and foremost. His exclusive devotion to one favourite author made his Latin stiff and mannered. Tuscan critics again have complained that his Italian style lacks nerve and idiom. He wrote like an alien, not one to the manner born. In his dread of not writing correctly, he ended by expressing tame thoughts with frigid formality. Even a foreigner can see that he used Italian, as he used Latin, without yielding to natural impulse, and with the constant effort to attain a fixed ideal. The mark of the file may be observed on every period. Raciness and spontaneity are words that have no meaning when applied to him. The decadence of Italian prose composition into laboured mannerism and meticulous propriety should be traced in a great measure to his influence. Yet Bembo deserves credit for having braved the opinion of the learned by his cultivation of the vulgar tongue; and on this point some verses from a Latin poem to Ercole Strozzi deserve quotation in a note.[1]

> [1] Nam pol quâ proavusque avusque linguâ
> Sunt olim meus et tuus loquuti,
> Nostræ quâque loquuntur et sorores
> Et matertera nunc et ipsa mater,
> Nos nescire loqui magis pudendum est,
> Qui Graiæ damus et damus Latinæ
> Studi tempora duplicemque curam,
> Quam Graiâ simul et simul Latinâ.
> Hac uti ut valeas tibi videndum est,
> Ne dum marmoreas remotâ in orâ
> Sumtu construis et labore villas,
> Domi te calamo tegas palustri.
>   *Carmina Quinque Illustrium Poetarum*, p. 25.

Jacopo Sadoleto's career was not dissimilar to that of his friend Bembo, though the two men offer many points of difference in character and turn of mind. Born at Modena in 1477, he studied Latin at Ferrara, and Greek at Rome, where he settled in the reign of Alexander VI. His copy of hexameters on the newly-discovered statue of Laocoon made him famous. Frigid and laboured as these verses may appear to us, who read them like a prize exercise, they had the merit of originality when first produced. Leo made the poet his secretary and Bishop of Carpentras. Sadoleto passed a good portion of his life in the duties of his see, composing moral treatises, annotating the Psalms, and publishing a 'Commentary on the Epistle to the Romans.'[1] Though strongly tinctured with Ciceronian purism, his taste was more austere than Bembo's. Nature had given him an intellect adapted to grave studies, sincerity of purpose, and true piety. Living in the dawn of the Reformation, Sadoleto was deeply conscious of the perils of the Church; nor did he escape the suspicion of sharing the new heresy.[2] His celebrated letter to Clement VII., after the sack of Rome in 1527, shows that he viewed this disaster as a punishment inflicted on the godless capital of Christendom. In 1536 Paul III. recalled him to Rome, and made him cardinal. He died in 1547, and was buried in S. Pietro in Vincoli. Sadoleto's correspondence may be reckoned among the most valuable materials for the literary annals of this period.

Next to Sadoleto a place must be found for the grave and studious Egidio Canisio. He was born at Viterbo in 1470, and was therefore an exact contemporary of Bembo. His powers of Latin oratory gained him the fame of a great speaker, and the address with which he opened the Lateran

---

[1] His most famous essays bore these titles: *De Liberis Instituendis* and *De Laudibus Philosophiæ*.

[2] His *Commentary on the Romans* was placed upon the Index.

Council in 1512 was committed to the press in that year. Egidius was already General of the Augustine Order. Five years later he received the red hat of a cardinal, and in 1518 he represented the Holy See as Legate at the Court of Spain. He died in 1532, leaving a vast mass of miscellaneous works on theology, philosophy, Biblical criticism, and universal history. Few of these have been printed. It is said that, besides Greek and Latin, he was a master of Hebrew and Chaldee, Turkish, Persian, and Arabic.

A more brilliant figure is presented by the witty but un-scrupulous historian Paulus Jovius. He was born at Como in 1483, and came at the age of thirty-three to Rome, with the beginning of his comprehensive History already written.[1] Leo, who delighted in listening to recitations of new literary works, declared that nothing had been penned more perfect since the days of Livy. This high praise induced Jovius to fix his residence at Rome, where Clement VII. made him Bishop of Nocera in 1528. After spending twenty-one years in the expectation, continually frustrated, of being received in the Sacred College, he retired to Como, and died at Florence in 1552. Jovius was the cleverest of all the Latinists produced by the Italians. His style is fluent, sparkling with anecdote, highly picturesque in its descriptive passages, and adorned by characteristic details. In addition to the histories, he produced a series of biographies of great and varied value, some of which are libels, others panegyrics, while all are marked by acute observation and mastery of the matter in hand. He was wont to say that he could use a golden or a silver pen at will: the golden was exercised upon the Life of Leo; the silver, dipped in ironic gall, upon the Life of

[1] Like the History of Guicciardini, it opens with the year 1494. It is carried down to 1547. A portion of the first decade was lost in the sack of Rome, and never rewritten by the author. Printed at Florence, 1550.

Hadrian. The sketches of eminent men, known by the name of 'Elogia,' were composed in illustration of a picture gallery of portraits collected in his villa. They include not only Italians, but Greeks, Germans, French and English worthies, dead and living notabilities of every kind.[1] If Brantôme had chosen Latin instead of French, he would have made a book not altogether unlike this of Jovius. The versatility of the author was further illustrated by a Latin treatise on Roman fishes, and by an Italian essay on mottoes and devices.[2]

Among the celebrities of the Roman Academy a place apart must be reserved for Baldassare Castiglione ; for though his biography belongs to the political even more than to the literary annals of the period, few men represent the age of Leo in its culture with more dignity and grace combined. He was born in 1478 at Casatico, in the Duchy of Mantua ; his father's family held the county of Castiglione, and his mother was a Gonzaga. In his youth he received an education framed upon the system set in vogue by Vittorino and Guarino, and became the living illustration of those varied accomplishments which he described in the 'Cortegiano.' His scholarship was sound and elegant ; as a writer of Latin verse he distinguished himself among the best men of his generation. Sensitive to the beauty of the arts, he proved an excellent critic of modern painting and of antique sculpture, and assisted Raphael in the composition of his famous letter to Leo on the exploration of old Rome. At the same time he did not neglect the athletic exercises which formed an indispensable branch of an Italian nobleman's training. Cultivated at all points, he early devoted his abilities to the service of

---

[1] *Elogia Virorum literis illustrium, quotquot vel nostrâ, vel avorum memoriâ vixere,* and *Elogia Virorum bellicâ virtute illustrium,* Basel, 1557.

[2] *De Piscibus Romanis,* Rome, 1524. *Ragionamento sopra i Motti e Disegni d' Arme e d' Amore.*

princes; for at this period in Italy there was no sphere for such a character outside the Courts. After spending some time at Milan and Naples, Castiglione removed to Rome, where Julius II. discerned the use that might be made of him in furthering the interests of his nephew Francesco Maria della Rovere. Federigo da Montefeltre, Duke of Urbino, had died in 1482, leaving his son Guidobaldo in possession of his fiefs and titles; but it was known that this prince could have no heirs. In him the male line of the Montefeltri ended. His sister Giovanna had been married to Giovanni della Rovere, a brother of the Pope, and Julius hoped that their son Francesco Maria might be declared successor to the Duchy of Urbino. Castiglione therefore attached himself to the person of Guidobaldo, with the special purpose of making himself necessary to the princes of Urbino and furthering the claims of Francesco, then a boy of about fifteen. Of his residence at Urbino, and of the polished splendour of Guidobaldo's Court, he has left an ever-memorable record in his ' Cortegiano,' that mirror of gentle breeding for the sixteenth century in Europe. Guidobaldo received the Count of Castiglione with marked favour, made him captain of fifty men at arms, and employed him in several offices of trust. Not the least important of these was the mission to England, undertaken in 1506 by Castiglione as Guidobaldo's proxy for receiving from Henry VII. the investiture of the Garter. After the death of Guidobaldo, Francesco Maria della Rovere was proclaimed Duke of Urbino, and Castiglione continued to enjoy his confidence until the year 1517, when Leo succeeded in placing his nephew Lorenzo de' Medici upon the Ducal throne.

Castiglione was now deprived of what had become the necessity of his life, a post of honour in the Court of a reigning sovereign. He therefore transferred his allegiance to his natural lord, the Marquis of Mantua, who appointed him ambassador at Rome. The first and most brilliant period of the courtier's life was passed at Urbino ; the second, less fruitful in literary achievements, embraced his residence among the wits of Leo's circle. At Rome Castiglione adapted himself to the customs of the papal society, penning Latin elegiacs, consorting with artists, and exercising the pleasant patronage of a refined Mæcenas. His friendship with Raphael is not the least interesting episode in this chapter of his biography. Substantial records of it still remain in the epitaph composed by the courtly scholar on the painter, and in Castiglione's portrait now preserved in the Louvre collection. That picture represents the very model of an Italian nobleman as culture and Court life had made him—tranquil, with grave open eyes, and a mouth as well suited for urbane discourse as gentle merriment. The owner of this face was not born to lead armies or to control unruly multitudes, but to pass his time in the *loggie* of princes—self-contained and qualified to win favour without the sacrifice of personal dignity. It forms a strong contrast to earlier and later portraits—to that of Sigismondo Pandolfo Malatesta, for example, and to the Spanish grandees of the next century. Castiglione was still in Rome during the pontificate of Clement VII., who, recognizing his great ability as a diplomatist, sent him to Charles V. At Madrid the Pope's nuncio was unable to avert the disaster of 1527, and Castiglione had the bitter mortification of hearing at a distance how the Rome he knew and loved so well, had been ravaged by the brigands of Germany and Spain. It is clear, however, from the diplomatic correspondence of that memorable moment, and from the letter addressed by Clement to Castiglione's mother in 1529, that he never lost the confidence of his master ; in spite of his failure to negotiate between them, he was respected alike by the Pope and the Emperor. He died at Toledo two years after the sack of Rome, worn out, it is said, by disappointment and regret.

Not only in his book of the 'Courtier,' but also in his life, Castiglione illustrated the best qualities of an Italian gentleman, moulded by the political and social conditions of the sixteenth century into a refined scholar and a courtly diplomatist.

Of Alberto Pio, whose life in some respects may be compared with Castiglione's, I have had occasion to speak in the last chapter. His first cousin, Gian Francesco Pico della Mirandola, demands more than passing notice. By no prince of that troubled period were the cruel vicissitudes of Italian politics more painfully experienced. Few of the scholars could boast of wider learning and a nobler spirit. He was born in 1470, and succeeded his father, Galeotto, in the lordship of Mirandola. In 1502 his brother Lodovico expelled him from his capital. Julius II. restored him. After being dispossessed a second time by Trivulzi, general of the French forces, he was once more reinstated, but only for a brief period. His nephew, Galeazzo, murdered him in 1533 before the crucifix, together with his heir, Alberto. In the intervals of his unquiet and unhappy life, Gian Francesco Pico devoted himself to studies not unlike those of his more famous uncle.[1] Early in his youth he had conceived the strongest admiration for Savonarola ; and the work by which he is best known to posterity is a Life of his great master. Savonarola's principles continued to rule his thought and conduct through life. During the pontificate of Leo he composed a long address to the Lateran Council upon the reformation of the Church,[2] and dared to entertain the friendship of Reuchlin and Willibad Pirkheimer. His residence in Rome, and the dedication of

[1] The titles of his philosophical works—*De Studio divinæ et humanæ philosophiæ, De amore Divino, Examen vanitatis doctrinæ gentium et veritatis Christianæ disciplinæ, De rerum prænotione*--show how closely he followed in the footsteps of Giovanni Pico.

[2] *Joannis Francisci Pici Mirandolæ et Concordiæ Comitis Oratio ad Leon X. et Concilium Lateranense de reformandis Ecclesiæ moribus.*

his treatise on 'Divine Love' to Leo, justify our ranking him with the Roman scholars.

If Gian Francesco Pico and Sadoleto bring us close upon the threshold of the German Reformation, we cross it in the company of Aleander. Jerome Aleander was born at Motta, in the Marches of Treviso, in the year 1480. His studies, more comprehensive than those of the stylists, included theology, philosophy, and science, together with the Oriental languages, in addition to the indispensable Greek and Latin culture. Before he reached the age of thirty he travelled to Paris, and professed Hebrew and the humanities at the University. French scholarship may be said to date from the impulse given to these subjects by Aleander, who rose to such fame that he was made Rector of the University. After leaving Paris, he spent some time in Germany, and came first to Rome in 1516 in the train of Erard van der Mark, Bishop of Lüttich. Here Leo appointed him librarian of the Vatican. The rest of Aleander's life was spent in the service of the Church. Despatched as *nuntius* to Germany by Leo in 1520, he vainly attempted, as all students of the Reformation know, to quench the fire of Luther's kindling. When he returned to Italy, Clement VII. gave him the archbishopric of Brindisi, and Paul III. raised him to the scarlet in 1538. He died in 1542, leaving in France the memory of his unrivalled learning, in Germany the fame of an intolerant persecutor, in Italy the reputation of a stanch though unsuccessful champion of the Church.

Aleander's three predecessors in the Vatican Library—Tommaso Inghirami of Siena, Filippo Beroaldo of Bologna, and Zanobio Acciaiuoli of Florence—made their mark in Roman society by erudition rather than by authorship.[1]

---

[1] Inghirami, made librarian 1510, died 1516. Beroaldo held the office two years, and died 1518. Acciaiuoli held it only for a few months. Aleander succeeded him in 1519.

Inghirami's eloquence won the admiration of contemporaries, who called him the second Cicero ; as a writer he had no celebrity.[1] A fortunate find of MSS. at Bobbio earned for him the post of Vatican librarian. Leo, like all the members of the Medicean family, was bent upon the rediscovery of buried classics. But the world had been already ransacked, and, though he employed agents for this purpose in the East as well as Europe, only one great treasure came to light. Gian Angelo Arcimboldi disinterred the first five books of Tacitus's 'Annals' at Corvey, and sold them to the Pope for 500 golden florins. Filippo Beroaldo, who was entrusted with the task of editing this precious codex, received the librarianship as his reward. Leo's privilege granted to the printers of Beroaldo's edition expresses in truly noble language the highest ideal of humanism, and reflects real credit on his patronage of letters.[2] Of Acciaiuoli there is not much to say. His knowledge of Hebrew and the classic languages gained for him a reputation for singular learning. In his capacity as librarian he began to catalogue the documents of the 'Secreta Bibliotheca,' founded by Sixtus IV. It is worthy of notice that Acciaiuoli is the only Florentine whom we have had occasion to mention among the learned courtiers of Leo. Florence, always foremost in the van of culture, had shaken off at this period the traditions of strict humanism. Her greatest writers, Guicciardini, Machiavelli, Varchi, Segni, and Giannotti, exchanged the Latin language for their mother speech, and sought for honour in fields removed from verbal scholarship or Ciceronian niceties of phrase.

The Roman Sapienza never held the same rank as the Universities of Padua or Bologna ; nor could it compete as

---

[1] ' Lingua verius quam calamo celebrem . . . dictus sui seculi Cicero,' says Erasmus. ' Affluentissimum eloquentiæ flumen ' is Valeriano's phrase.

[2] See Burckhardt, p. 174. Roscoe's Life of Leo X. vol. i. p. 357.

an academy of culture with the High Schools of Florence
and Ferrara. The Popes of the Renaissance, occupied with
nepotism and political aggrandisement, had but small care for
the interests of education. Nor did Rome, always overcrowded
by foreigners, require the students who brought custom and
prestige to minor cities.[1] Leo X. resolved, as far as he was
able, to raise the studies of his capital from the decadence
into which they had fallen. In 1513 he reformed the statutes
of the University, increased the appointments of the professors,
and founded several new chairs. Yet, though scholars no
less respectable than Janus Parrhasius of Cosenza, Tommaso
Inghirami, and Filippo Beroaldo were numbered among the
teachers, the Sapienza failed to take firm root in Rome :— the
most flourishing school of humanism at this period was
Ferrara, governed by Leoniceno, Celio Calcagnini, and Lilius
Gyraldus. To Hellenistic studies, just now upon the point
of decadence in Italy, Leo gave encouragement by the establishment of a Greek press, and by the foundation of the
Gymnasium Caballini Montis, where Joannes Lascaris and
Marcus Musurus lectured. Musurus we have already learned
to know as the inmate of Alberto Pio's palace at Carpi, and
as Aldo's most efficient helper. Soon after his elevation to
the Papacy, Leo invited the venerable Lascaris to Rome ; but
he did not long retain the services of so illustrious a Hellenist.
Lascaris, who had taught Greek in Paris during the reign of
Charles VIII., and who had long served Louis XII. as ambassador at Venice, was induced by Francis I. to superintend
the library at Fontainebleau in 1518. He once more visited
Rome during the pontificate of Clement, and died there at
the age of ninety—the last of the Greek exiles who transplanted Hellas into Latium. Between the visit of Manuel
Chrysoloras in 1398 and the death of John Lascaris in 1535
more than a century had elapsed, in the course of which

[1] See above, p. 86.

Italy,[1] after acquiring Greek literature and committing its
chief treasures to the press, had seen her learning pass
beyond the Alps and flourish with new vigour on a northern
soil. The epitaph composed by Lascaris for his own tomb in
Santa Agata touchingly expresses the grief of an exile for his
country's servitude, together with the gratitude of one who
found a new home in an alien land :—

> Λάσκαρις ἀλλοδαπῇ γαίῃ ἐνικάτθετο, γαίην
> οὔτι λίην ξείνην ὦ ξένε μεμφόμενος.
> εὕρετο μειλιχίην, ἀλλ' ἄχθεται εἴπερ Ἀχαιοῖς
> οὐδ' ἔτι χοῦν χεύει πάτρις ἐλευθέριον.

Any account of erudite society in Rome would be incomplete without some notice of its antiquaries. While the
Pope and his cardinals were bent on collecting statues, coins,
vases, and inscriptions, it was natural that the scholars should
devote themselves to their illustration. Much of this industry
was carried on by the academicians, who discussed difficult
readings and exchanged opinions at their meetings. Treatises
on Roman antiquities, topographical essays, and commentaries
on Vitruvius and Frontinus abounded. Amid a multitude of
minor works it will be enough to mention the cyclopædias of
Andrea Fulvio and Bartolommeo Marliano, the comprehensive
collection of inscriptions by Mazochi, and Valeriano's dissertation on the hieroglyphics of the Roman obelisks.[2] The
greater number of these compositions were published by
Jacopo Mazochi, bookseller to the Roman Academy, and himself no mean scholar. Together with his coadjutor, Francesco Albertini, he undertook what he describes as 'the Her-
culean labour' of saving inscribed tablets from the lime-kiln

---

[1] Cf. Giovio, close of the *Elogia*.

[2] *Andreas Fulvius Sabinus Antiquarius, Antiquitates Urbis Romæ*,
1527. *Bartholomæus Marlianus, Eques D. Petri, Urbis Romæ Topo-
graphia*, 1534. *Jacobus Mazochius, Epigrammata antiquæ urbis Romæ*,
1521. *Johannis Pierii Valeriani Hieroglyphica seu de Sacris Ægyptio-
rum*, &c., in his collected works, Ven. 1604.

and the mason's hammer. Built into the walls of houses, embedded in church pavements, mingled with the rubbish of the Forum, unearthed by the mattock or the plough in vine-yard and cornfield, these records of old history encumbered Rome. To decipher them as best he could, arrange them by the regions where they had been found, and incorporate his own readings with the previous collections of Ciriaco and Fra Giocondo,[1] was the object of Mazochi. His work formed the nucleus of the ponderous collection known as the *Corpus Inscriptionum*.

This is the proper occasion for resuming what has to be said about the Roman ruins, and the feeling for them shown in the Renaissance period. We have already listened to Poggio's lamentations over their gradual decay through wanton injury and lapse of time.[2] Pius II., who had a strong taste for topographical studies, endeavoured to protect the Roman monuments from depredation by a Bull in 1462. But his successors were less scrupulous. Even the scholarly Nicholas V. had shown more zeal for building modern Rome afresh than true regard for the imperial city. He levelled large portions of the wall of Servius Tullius, and quarried the Temple of Peace for his own edifices. In his days Blondus wrote that his life was embittered by the wholesale waste of ancient reliques. That Paul II. should have used the stone wall of the Coliseum for the Palace of S. Marco; that Sixtus IV. should have pulled down the circular Temple of Hercules, and destroyed the oldest bridge across the Tiber to make cannon balls; that Innocent VIII. should have em-powered his architects to take what antique masonry they pleased—excites in us no wonder; these Popes were acting according to the spirit that was in them. Nor can it be

---

[1] The architect of Verona who first edited Vitruvius, and was em-ployed by Lorenzo de' Medici in collecting inscriptions for him at Rome.
[2] See above, p. 111.

denied that for some of their acts of Vandalism the excuse of utility or even of necessity might have been pleaded. It is, however, singular that no steps were taken to preserve in Rome the basreliefs and sculptures of the monuments thus overthrown. Everyone who chose laid hands upon them. Poggio scraped together what he could; Pomponius Lætus formed a museum; Lorenzo de' Medici and the Rucellai employed agents to select and ship to Florence choicer fragments. At last the impulse to collect possessed the Popes themselves. The Capitol Museum dates from 1471. The pretty statue of the boy pulling a thorn from his foot, the group of the lion clinging to a horse, the urn of Agrippina, and the bronze Hercules from the Forum Boarium formed the nucleus of this collection. Soon afterwards the equestrian statue of Marcus Aurelius was unearthed and placed where it now stands. The Vatican Museum was founded in 1523, when Julius II. erected the Apollo on a marble basis near the entrance to the gardens of the Belvedere. It had been discovered some years earlier at Porto d'Anzo, and was bought by Giuliano della Rovere before he was made Pope. The Laocoon came to light in 1506 among the ruins of the Baths of Titus in the vineyard of Felix de Fredis. How Giuliano di San Gallo and Michael Angelo heard of it, and walked abroad to see it disinterred, may still be read in the letter of Francesco, nephew of the former. Julius bought this group for six hundred golden crowns, and placed it in the Vatican. He also purchased the statue of the sleeping Ariadne, which then passed for Cleopatra,[1] together with the torso of Hercules, found near the Palazzo Pio, and the statue of Commodus dug up in the Campo Fiore. Leo X. further enriched the collection by the reclining statues of the Nile and Tiber, found among the ruins of the Iseum near S. Stefano in Caco, and the so-called Antinous discovered in the Baths of Trajan.

[1] See Castiglione's verses.

The feeling of professed scholars for these masterpieces of classic art appears in Sadoleto's and Castiglione's poems, while a passage of Ghiberti's Commentary expresses the enthusiasm of technical sculptors. After describing an Hermaphrodite he saw in Rome, the Florentine sculptor adds : ' To express the perfection of learning, mastery, and art displayed in it is beyond the power of language. Its more exquisite beauties could not be discovered by the sight, but only by the touch of the hand passed over it.' Of another classic marble at Padua he says: ' This statue, when the Christian faith triumphed, was hidden in that place by some gentle soul, who, seeing it so perfect, fashioned with art so wonderful, and with such power of genius, and being moved to reverent pity, caused a sepulchre of bricks to be built, and there within buried the statue, and covered it with a broad slab of stone, that it might not in any way be injured. It has very many sweet beauties, which the eyes alone can comprehend not, either by strong or tempered light; only the hand by touching finds them out.' [1] Meanwhile a genuine sentiment for the truth and beauty of antique art passed downwards from the educated classes to the people. Like all powerful emotions that affect the popular imagination at epochs of imperfect knowledge and high sensibility, it took the form of fable. The beautiful myth of Julia's Corpse is our most precious witness to this moment in the history of the Revival.[2] At the same time the real intention of classic statuary was better understood. Donatello had not worked in vain for a public, finely tempered to receive æsthetic influences, and cultivated by two centuries of native art. The horsemen of Monte Cavallo ceased to be philosophers. Menander and Poseidippus were no longer reckoned among

[1] *Terzo Commentario del Ghiberti, Frammenti Inediti*, in Le Monnier's Vasari, vol. i. pp. xi.-xiii. I have paraphrased rather than translated the original, which is touching by reason of its naïveté.

[2] See Vol. I., *Age of the Despots*, p. 17.

the saints. In the age of Leo, Carlo Malatesta could not
have thrown Virgil's statue into the Mincio ;[1] nor would the
republic of Siena have buried their antique Venus by stealth
in the Florentine territory, hoping thereby to transfer to their
foes the curse of heathenism.[2] The effect produced on less
impressionable natures by the Belvedere statues transpires
in a curious document penned by a Venetian ambassador to
Rome in 1523.[3] It is so valuable for illustrating the average
culture of the Italians at that epoch, that I may allow myself
the pleasure of rendering a full account of it.

Adrian VI., soon after his accession, had walled up eleven
of the twelve doors, leading to the Belvedere. The Venetian
envoys, however, received permission to visit this portion of
the Vatican palace, and the single entrance was unlocked
for them. After describing the beauty of the gardens, their
cypresses and orangeries, the greenness of their lawns and
the stately order of their paved avenues, the writer of the
report arrives at the statues. 'In the midst of the garden
are two very large men of marble, facing one another, twice
the size of life, who lie in the attitude of sleep. One of
these is the Tiber, the other the Nile, figures of vast antiquity ; and from beneath them issue two fair fountains. On
the first entrance into the garden, on the left hand, there is a
kind of little chapel let into the wall, where, on a pedestal of
marble, stands the Apollo, famous throughout the world, a
statue of incomparable beauty and dignity, of life size and
of finest marble. Somewhat farther on, in a similar alcove
and raised on a like pedestal to the height of an altar from
the ground, opposite a well of most perfect fashion, is the
Laocoon, celebrated throughout the world, a statue of the
highest excellence, of size like a natural man, with hairy

[1] See Rosmini's *Vittorino da Feltre*, p. 63, note.

[2] See Ghiberti's *Commentario*, in Le Monnier's Vasari, vol. i. p. xiv.

[3] Alberi, *Relazioni Venete*, serie ii. vol. iii. p. 114, &c.

beard, all naked. The sinews, veins, and proper muscles in each part are seen as well as in a living body; breath alone is wanting. He is in a posture between sitting and standing, with his two sons, one on either hand, both, together with himself, twined by the serpents, as Virgil says. And herein is seen so great merit of the artist, that better could not be; the languishing and dying are manifest to sight, and one of the boys on the right side is most tightly clipped by the snake twice girdled round him; one of the coils crossing his breasts and squeezing his heart, so that he is on the point of dying. The other boy on the left side is also girdled round by another serpent. While he seeks to drag the raging worm from his leg with his little arm, and cannot help himself at all, he raises his face, all tearful, crying to his father, and holding him with his other hand by the left arm. And seeing his unhappy father more deadly struck than he is, the double grief of this child is clear to view, the one for his own coming death, the other for his father's helplessness; and he so faints withal, that nothing remains for him but to breathe his last. It is impossible that human art can arrive at producing so great and so natural a masterpiece. Every part is perfect, except that Laocoon's right arm is wanting. He seems about forty years of age, and resembles Messer Girolamo Marcello of S. Tommaso; the two boys look eight and nine respectively. Not far distant, and similarly placed, is a very beautiful Venus of natural size, naked, with a little drapery on her shoulder, that covers a portion of the waist; as very fair a figure as can be imagined by the mind; but the excellence of the Laocoon makes one forget this and the Apollo, who before was so famous.'

A systematic plan for exploring the monuments of old Rome, excavating its ruins, and bringing its buried treasures of statuary to light was furnished by Raphael in 1518. Leo had made him master of the works at S. Peter's and general

superintendent of antiquities.[1] For some time previously he
had been studying Vitruvius in the Italian translation prepared for his use by Fabio Calvi of Ravenna. How enthusiastically he followed in the traces of the ancients, the
arabesques of the Loggie, imitated from the frescoes of the
Baths of Titus, amply prove. He now, not long before his
death, laid down a ground-plan of the city, divided into
fourteen regions, and set forth his project in a memorable
letter to the Pope. This epistle, written in choice old Italian,
has more than once been printed : it will be found in Passa-
vant's Life of the painter. Raphael begins by describing the
abandonment and desolation of the city, and by characterising
its several styles of architecture—classical, Lombard, Gothic,
and modern.[2] Some phrases that occur in this exordium
deserve to be cited for the light they cast upon the passion
which inspired those early excavators. ' Considerando la
divinitate di quelli animi antichi . . . . vedendo quasi il
cadavere di quest' alma nobile cittate, che è stata regia del
mondo, così miseramente lacerato . . . . quanti pontefici
hanno permesso le ruine et disfacimenti delli templi antichi,
delle statue, delli archi et altri edificii, gloria delli lor fonda-
tori ! Quanti hanno comportato che solamente per pigliare
terra pozzolana si siano scavati i fondamenti ! Onde in poco
tempo li edificii sono venuti a terra. Quanta calcina si è fatta
di statue e d'altri ornamenti antichi ! che ardirei dire che
tutta questa nova Roma, che hor si vede, quanto grande
ch'ella vi sia, quanto bella, quanto ornata di pallazzi, di chiese
et di altri edificii, sia fabricata di calcina fatta di marmi antichi.'[3] He then observes that during his twelve years' resi-

[1] By a brief dated Aug. 27, 1515.
[2] It may be observed that he calls the round-arched buildings of the
Middle Ages Gothic ; the pointed style German.
[3] 'When we reflect upon the divinity of those intellects of the old
world . . . when we see the corpse of this noble city, mother and
queen of the world, so piteously mangled . . . how many Pontiffs have

dence in Rome the Meta in the Via Alexandrina, the arches
at the entrance to the Baths of Diocletian and the Temple of
Ceres in the Via Sacra, part of the Foro Transitorio, and the
larger portion of the Basilica del Foro have been destroyed.
Therefore he prays Leo to arrest this work of the new Van-
dals, and, by pursuing a well-considered scheme of operations,
to lay bare and to protect what still remains of antique
monuments in the Eternal City.

Raphael's own death followed close upon the execution
of the first part of a Roman map designed by him. Great
interest had been excited in the world of letters by his undertaking; and its failure through his untimely end aroused the
keenest disappointment. The epigrams quoted below in a
footnote express these feelings with more depth of emotion
than scholarly elegance.[1] How Raphael's design would have

---

allowed the ruin and defacement of ancient temples, statues, arches,
and other buildings, the glory of their founders! How many have
suffered their foundations to be undermined for the mere sake of
quarrying *pozzolana*, whereby in a short time the buildings themselves
have fallen to earth! How much lime has been made of statues and
other antique decorations! I should not hesitate to say that the whole
of this new Rome which now meets the eye, great as it is, and fair,
and beautified with palaces and churches and other buildings, has been
cemented with lime made from antique marbles.'

[1] Tot proceres Romam, tam longa struxerat ætas,
     Totque hostes et tot sæcula diruerant;
Nunc Romam in Româ quærit reperitque Raphael;
     Quærere magni hominis, sed reperire Dei est.
                              Celio Calcagnini.
Quod lacerum corpus medicâ sanaverit arte,
     Hippolytum Stygiis et revocarit aquis,
Ad Stygias ipse est raptus Epidaurius undas;
     Sic pretium vitæ mors fuit artifici.
Tu quoque dum toto laniatam corpore Romam
     Componis miro, Raphael, ingenio,
Atque urbis lacerum ferro, igne, armisque cadaver
     Ad vitam antiquum jam revocasque decus,
Movisti Superum invidiam; indignataque mors est
     Te dudum extinctis reddere posse animam,

been carried out it is impossible to guess. Archæological
zeal is impotent to stay the march of time, except by sacrifice
of much that neglect alone makes venerable; and it may
fairly be questioned whether it is wise to lay the hand of the
restorer on these relics of the past. We at least, who during
the last few years have seen the Coliseum and the Baths of
Caracalla stripped of their romantic vegetation, the Palatine
ruins fortified with modern masonry, and the dubious guesses
of antiquaries placarded upon sign-posts for the instruction
of Sunday visitors, may feel, perhaps, that a worse fate than
slow decay or ruthless mutilation was still in store for the
majestic corpse of ancient Rome. Nothing, in truth, is less
sublime or more pitiful than a dismantled brick wall, robbed
of its marbles and mosaics, naked of the covering of herbs
that nature gave it, patched with plaster, propped with stone-
work, bound by girders, and smeared over with the trail of
worse than snails or blindworms—pedants bent on restoration.

The immediate and most important consequence of these
antiquarian pursuits was the adoption of classic forms by
architects and artists. Fresco-painters imitated the newly-
discovered *grotteschi* in their arabesques.[1] Sculptors abandoned Christian subjects for antique mythology, or gave the
attributes of heroes to the saints of the Catholic Church.
The principles of Vitruvius were applied as strictly as possible to modern buildings, and the free decoration of the
earlier Renaissance yielded to what passed for purely classic
ornaments. It would be incorrect to maintain that this
reproduction of antiquity in art only dated from the age of

Et quod longa dies paullatim aboleverat, hoc te
　Mortali spretâ lege parare iterum.
Sic miser heu primâ cadis intercepte juventâ:
　Debere et morti nostraque nosque mones.
　　　　　　　　　　　　　Baldassare Castiglione.
[1] See Benvenuto Cellini, i. 31.

Leo. Alberti and Brunelleschi, Bramante and Michellozzo, had, each in his own way, striven to assimilate to modern use the style of Roman architecture. Donatello and Michael Angelo at Florence had carved statues in the classic manner; nor are the arabesques of Signorelli at Orvieto, of Perugino at Perugia, less fanciful than those of Raphael in the Loggie. What really happened was that the imitation of the ancients grew more puristic and precise through the formation of a common taste that imposed itself with the weight of authority on artists. Giulio Romano's Palazzo del Te at Mantua may be cited as the most perfect production of this epoch, combining, as it does, all forms of antique decoration and construction with the vivid individuality of genius. Giulio Romano comprehended the antique, and followed it with the enthusiasm of a neophyte. But his very defects prevented him from falling into the frigid formalism of Palladio.

The causes of Roman pre-eminence in this last age of humanism are not far to seek. By the policy of Alexander and Julius the Papal See had become the chief power in Italy. Venice never publicly encouraged literature, nor was the ambition of her nobles fixed on anything so much as the aggrandisement of the Republic. In the beginning of the sixteenth century their energy was needed no longer for the extension of Venetian rule, but for its preservation under the attack of Europe leagued against the city of the sea. Florence, divided between the parties of the Piagnoni and the Ottimati, reserved her failing vigour for the great struggle of 1529. The Medici, after absorbing what remained of mental force into their own circle, had transferred the Florentine traditions of culture with Giovanni and Giulio to Rome. At Naples the Aragonese dynasty had been already shaken to its foundation by the conspiracy of the Barons and by the conquest of Charles VIII. Ferdinand the Catholic and Louis XII. were now intent upon dividing the

southern provinces of Italy between them. Little opportunity was left, if inclination had remained, for patronising
men of letters at a Court suspicious of its aristocracy and
terrified by foreign interference. Milan, first among the
towns of Lombardy, was doomed to bear the brunt of French,
and Swiss, and German armies. To maintain the semblance
of their dukedom taxed the weakness of the Sforzas to the
utmost, while the people groaned beneath the fiendish cruelty
of Spanish governors. The smaller principalities had been
destroyed by Cesare Borgia and Julius. Ferrara, Mantua,
and Urbino, at the beginning of the century, alone continued
the traditions of the previous age. Rome, meanwhile, however insecure the Papal rule might be, still ranked among the
Powers of Europe, pursuing a policy on equal terms with
France and Spain. In Rome money abounded; nor had the
sacred city of Christendom felt as yet the scourge of war,
that broke the spirit of the Northern capitals. It was but
natural, therefore, that the political and intellectual energies
of the Italians should find their centre here.

Sad times, however, were in store for Rome. When Leo's
successor read the Latin letters of the Apostolic secretaries,
he cried, ' *Sunt litteræ unius poetæ*; ' and after walking
through the Belvedere Gallery, he gave vent to his feelings
in the famous exclamation, ' *Sunt idola antiquorum*.' The
humanists had nothing to expect from such a master. The
election of Giulio de' Medici restored the hope that Rome
might once more be as it had been beneath the sway of Leo.
Yet for Clement VII. was reserved the final bitterness of
utter ruin. In the fourth year of his papacy happened the
catastrophe that closed one period of Italian history, and
opened a new era for Rome and for the nation. The tale of
the sack has been already told.[1] A fitting conclusion for this
chapter may be found in Valeriano's discourse upon its con-

---

[1] Vol. I., *Age of Despots*, App. V.

sequences to the literary society assembled by the Medici at
the Papal Court.

Valeriano's dialogue ' De Literatorum Infelicitate ' opens
with a description of Rome in the pontificate of Leo.[1]   Never
since the downfall of the Empire, he says, had letters
flourished so freely or had men of learning found more
generous patronage.   Of that brilliant company Valeriano
was himself an ornament.   The friend of Egidius and the
favourite of Leo, he spent his time in the composition of
Latin poems, panegyrical and satiric, and in the exploration
of antiquities.   Afterwards he became the protonotary of
Clement, and supervised the education of the Medicean
bastards Alessandro and Ippolito.   His good fortune carried
him to Piacenza in the fatal year of 1527.   On his return to
Rome after the siege, he looked in vain for his old comrades
and associates.   ' Good God ! ' he exclaims in the dialogue
before us, ' when first I began to inquire for the philosophers,
orators, poets, and professors of Greek and Latin literature,
whose names were written on my tablets, how great, how
horrible a tragedy was offered to me !   Of all those
lettered men whom I had hoped to see, how many had
perished miserably, carried off by the most cruel of all fates,
overwhelmed by undeserved calamities : some dead of plague,
some brought to a slow end by penury in exile, others
slaughtered by a foeman's sword, others worn out by daily
tortures ; some, again, and these of all the most unhappy,
driven by anguish to self-murder.'   John Goritz, captured by
his countrymen, had ransomed himself with the sacrifice of
all his wealth, and now was dying of despair at Verona.
Colocci had seen his house, with its museums and MSS.,
burned before his eyes.   Angelo Cesi, maltreated by the
Spanish soldiers on a sick bed, died of his injuries before
the year was out.   Marone, the brilliant improvisatore,

Printed at Venice, 1620.

stripped of everything and deprived of his poems, the accumulated compositions of years spent in Leo's service, breathed his last in a miserable tavern. Marco Fabio Calvi, Raphael's friend and teacher, succumbed to sickness in a hospital. Julianus Camers, maddened by the sight of the torments inflicted on his servants, had thrown himself from a window in his house, and was killed. Baldus, the professor, after watching his commentary upon Pliny used to light the camp fires of the soldiery, had died himself of hunger. Casanova, the poet, fell a victim to the plague. Paolo Bombasi, another poet, was murdered in the streets of Rome. Cristoforo Marcello had been tortured by the Spaniards. Exposed naked on a tree, his nails were daily drawn from his fingers by these human fiends; he only escaped their clutches to die of his injuries at Gaeta. Laomedon Tardolus and John Bonifacius Victor suffered similar indignities and torments. Francesco Fortunio and John Valdes slew themselves. To enumerate all the scholars who succumbed to fear, plague, famine, torture, and imprisonment in this fatal year; to relate how numbers left Rome, robbed of everything, to wander over Italy, and die of hunger by the wayside, or of fever in low hovels; to describe the losses of their MSS., their madness, beggary, mysterious disappearances, and deaths by hands of servants or of brigands on the high roads, would occupy more space than I have left at my command. The ghastly muster roll is told with terrible concision by Valeriano, who adds divers examples, unconnected with the sack, of early deaths by over-study, lingering illnesses, murders by poison or the knife, and accidents of every kind, attributable more or less directly to the shifting career of students at that time in Italy.

Though the wars in Lombardy proved scarcely less fatal to men of letters than the siege of Rome, those disasters fell singly and at intervals. The ever-memorable stage of the

Eternal City was reserved for the crowning tragedy of arts
and letters.   Whatever vicious seeds had been sown in Italy
by the humanists had blossomed and borne fruit in Rome ;
and there the Nemesis of pride and insolence, and godlessness of evil living, fell upon them like a bolt from heaven.
In essays, epistles, and funeral orations they amply recognised
the justice of their punishment.   A phrase of Hieronymus
Niger's in a letter to Sadoleto—' Rome, that is the sink of
all things shameful and abominable '—might serve as the
epitome of their conscience-stricken Jeremiads.[1]   All Italy
re-echoed with these lamentations ; and though Clement VII.
and Paul III. did their best to repiece the ruins of Leo's
golden house of fame, the note of despair and anguish uttered
by the scholars in 1527 was never destined to be drowned by
chorus hymeneal or triumphal chant again.   What remained
of humanism among the Italians assumed a different form,
adapted to the new rule of the Spaniards and the new attitude of the Church.   To the age of the Humanists succeeded
the age of the Inquisitors and Jesuits.

[1] ' Quod Romæ, hoc est in sentinâ omnium rerum atrocium et puden-
darum deprehensi fuerimus.'   Quoted by Gregorovius, *Stadt Rom*, vol.
viii. p. 598, note 3.

CHAPTER VIII

LATIN POETRY

THE history of this last period of the Revival would be incomplete without a survey of its Latin poetry. I shall have
failed to convey a right notion of the tendencies of humanism,
if I have not shown that the Italians were seeking not merely
to acquire a knowledge of ancient literature, but also to effect
a resuscitation of antiquity in their own writings. Regarding
themselves as the heirs of Rome, separated from the brilliant
period of Latin civilisation by ten centuries of ignorance,
they strove with all their might to seize the thread of culture
at the very point where the poets of the Silver Age had
dropped it. In the opinion of Northern races it might seem
unnatural or unpatriotic to woo the Muses in a dead language; but for Italians the Camoenæ had not died; on the
hills of Latium, where they fell asleep, they might awake

again. Every familiar sight and sound recalled 'the rich Virgilian rustic measure' of the 'Georgics' and 'Bucolics.' Nature had not changed, nor did the poets feel the influence of Christianity so deeply as to find no meaning in the mythic phraseology of Fauns and Nymphs.

Latin, again, was far less a language of the past for the Italians than for other European nations. What risk the Tuscan dialect ran, when Dante wrote the first lines of the 'Divine Comedy' in Latin, and when Petrarch assumed the laurel crown by right of his 'Africa,' is known to every student. The serious efforts of the greatest writers were for centuries devoted to Latin composition, because they believed that the nation, in the modern as in the ancient world, might freely use the speech of Cicero and Virgil. Their *volgari cose* they despised as trifles, not having calculated the impotence of scholars or of kings to turn the streams of language from their natural courses. Nor was this blindness so inexplicable as it seems to us at first sight. Italy possessed no common dialect; Dante's 'Italiano Illustre,' or 'Cortegiano,' was even less native to the race at large, less universal in its use, than Latin.[1] Fashioned from the Tuscan for literary purposes, selected from the vocabulary of cultivated persons, stripped of vernacular idioms, and studied in the works of a few standard authors, it was itself, upon the soil that gave it birth, a product of high art and conscious culture. The necessity felt soon after Dante's death for translating the 'Divine Comedy' into Latin, sufficiently proves that a Latin poem gained a larger audience than the masterpiece of Italian literature. While the singer of a dialect, however noble, appealed to his own fellow-citizens, the Latin poet gave his verses *urbi et orbi.* If another proof

[1] Cf. Filelfo, quoted in a note to the next chapter, who says, 'Tuscan is hardly known to all Italians, while Latin is spread far and wide throughout the whole world.'

of the artificiality of Italian were needed, we should find it
in the fact that the phrases of Petrarch are not less obsolete
now than in the fourteenth century. The English require a
glossary for Chaucer, and even Elizabethan usages are out of
date; in other words, the language of the people has outgrown the style of its first poets. But Italian has undergone
no process of transformation and regeneration according
to the laws of organic growth, since it first started. The
different districts still use different dialects, while writers in
all parts of the peninsula have conformed their style as far
as possible to early Tuscan models. It may be questioned
whether united Italy, having for the first time gained the
necessary conditions of national concentration, is not now
at last about to enter on a new phase of growth in literature,
which, after many years, will make the style of the first
authors more archaic than it seems at present.

The foregoing observations were requisite in order to explain why the cultivation of Latin poetry was no mere play-
work to Italian scholars. The peculiar direction given by
Petrarch to classical studies at the outset must also be taken
into account. We have seen that he regarded rhetoric and
poetry as the two chief aims of humanism. To be either a
poet or an orator was the object of all students who had
slaked their thirst at the Castalian springs of ancient learning.
Philology and poetry, accordingly, went hand in hand through
the periods of the Revival; and to this first impulse we are
perhaps justified in tracing back the prominence assigned to
Latin verse in our own school studies.

Poetry being thus regarded as a necessary branch of
scholarship, it followed that few men distinguished for their
learning abstained from versification. Pedants who could
do no more than make prosaic elegiacs scan, and scholars
respectable for their acquirements, but destitute of inspiration,
were reckoned among the *sacri vates*. It would be a weari-

ful—nay, hopeless—task to pass all the Latin versifiers of the Renaissance in review. Their name is legion ; even to count them would be the same as to number the stars—*ad una ad una annoverar le stelle.* It may be considered fortunate that perhaps the larger masses of their productions still remain in manuscript, partly because they preceded the age of printing, and partly, no doubt, because the good sense of the age rejected them. What has been printed, however, exceeds in bulk the 'Corpus Poetarum Latinorum,' and presents so many varieties that to deal with more than a selection is impossible.[1]

The poetasters of the first two periods need not be taken into account. Struggling with a language imperfectly assimilated, and with the rules of a prosody as yet but little understood, it was as much as they could do to express themselves at all in metre. Elegance of composition was out of the question when a writer could neither set forth modern thoughts with ease nor imitate the classic style with accuracy. What he lost in force by the use of a dead language, he did not gain in polish ; nor was the taste of the age schooled to appreciate the niceties of antique diction. Beccadelli alone, by a certain limpid fluency, attained to a degree of moderate excellence ; and how much he owed to his choice of subject may be questioned. The obscenity of his themes, and the impudence required for their expression, may have acted as a stimulus to his not otherwise distinguished genius. There is, moreover, no stern conflict to be fought with phrases when the author's topic is mere animalism. The rest of his contemporaries, Filelfo included, did no more than smooth the way for their successors by practising the technicalities of

---

[1] I purpose in this chapter to use the *Deliciæ Poetarum Italorum,* two parts divided into 4 vols., 1608 ; *Carmina Quinque Illustrium Poetarum,* Bergomi, 1753 ; *Poemata Selecta Italorum,* Oxonii, 1808 ; and *Selecta Poemata Italorum,* accurante A. Pope, Londini, 1740.

verse and exciting emulation.   To surpass their rude achievements was not difficult, while the fame they enjoyed aroused
the ambition of younger rivals.   Exception to this sweeping
verdict may be made in favour of Alberti, whose Latin play,
called ' Philodoxus,' was a brilliant piece of literary workmanship.[1]   Not only did it impose on contemporaries as a genuine
classic, but, even when judged by modern standards, it shows
real familiarity with the language of Latin comedy and rare
skill in its employment.

Poliziano is the first Latin poet who compels attention in
the fifteenth century; nor was he surpassed, in fertility of
conception and mastery of metre, by any of his numerous
successors.   With all his faults of style and crudities of diction, Poliziano, in my opinion, deserves the chief place among
original poets of revived Latin literature.   Bembo wrote more
elegantly, Navagero more classically, Amalteo with a grace
more winning.   Yet these versifiers owe their celebrity to
excellence of imitation.   Poliziano possessed a manner of
his own, and made a dead language utter thoughts familiar
to the age in which he lived.   He did not merely traverse the
old ground of the elegy, the epigram, the satire, and the
idyll.   Striking out a new path for himself, and aiming at
instruction, he poured forth torrents of hexameters, rough
perhaps and over-fluent, yet marked by intellectual energy
and copious fancy, in illustration of a modern student's
learning.   This freedom of handling is shown to best advantage in his ' Sylvæ.' [2]

The ' Nutricia ' forms an introduction to the history of
poetry in general, and carries on its vigorous stream the
weight of universal erudition.   From it we learn how the

---

[1] Bonucci's edition of Alberti's works, vol. i.   Alberti's own preface,
in the form of a dedicatory letter to Lionello d' Este, describes how he
came to write this comedy, and how it was passed off upon contemporaries as an original play by Lepidus Comicus.   *Ib.* pp. cxxi.–cxxiii.

[2] See above, p. 254, for the purpose fulfilled by the *Sylvæ*.

most accomplished scholar of his century judged and distinguished the whole body of fine literature possessed by his
contemporaries. On the emergence of humanity from barbarism, writes Poliziano, poetry was given to men as a consolation for the miseries of life and as an instrument of
culture ; their first nurse in the cradle of civilisation was the
Muse :—

> Musa quies hominum, divomque æterna voluptas.[1]

After characterising the Pagan oracles, the mythical bards
of Hellas, and the poet-prophets of the Jewish race, with
brief but telling touches, Poliziano addresses himself in the
following lines to the delineation of the two chief epic-
singers :—

> . . . . etenim ut stellas fugere undique cælo,
> Aurea cum radios Hyperionis exeruit fax,
> Cernimus, et tenuem velut evanescere lunam;
> Sic veterum illustres flagranti obscurat honores
> Lampade Mæonides : unum quem dia canentem
> Facta virum, et sævas æquantem pectine pugnas,
> Obstupuit, prorsusque parem confessus Apollo est.
> Proximus huic autem, vel ni veneranda senectus
> Obstiterit, fortasse prior, canit arma virumque
> Vergilius, cui rure sacro, cui gramine pastor
> Ascræus, Siculusque simul cessere volentes.[2]

Then follows the enumeration of lesser Greek and Roman
epopœists. After them the lyrists and elegiac poets, among

---

[1] 'Of men the solace, and of gods the everlasting joy.'

[2] 'As from the heavens we see the stars on all sides fleeing, when the
golden torch of the sun-god rises, and the diminished moon appears to
fade ; so with his burning lamp Mæonides obscures the honours of the
earlier bards. Him alone, while he sang the divine deeds of heroes,
and with his lyre arrayed fierce wars, Apollo, wonder-struck, confessed
his equal. Close at his side, or higher even, but for the veneration due
to age, Vergil entones the song of arms and the hero—Vergil, to whom
from holy tilth and pasture land both Ascra's and Sicilia's shepherds
yield their sway with willing homage.'—*Quinque Illustrium Poetarum
Carmina*, p. 167.

whom Pindar is celebrated in the following magniloquent
paragraph :—

> Aërios procul in tractus, et nubila supra
> Pindarus it Dircæus olor, cui nectare blandæ
> Os tenerum libâstis apes, dum fessa levaret
> Membra quiete puer mollem spirantia somnum ;
> Sed Tanagræa suo mox jure poetria risit,
> Irrita qui toto sereret figmenta canistro ;
> Tum certare auso palmam intercepit opimam
> Æoliis prælata modis atque illice formâ.
> Ille Agathocleâ subnisus voce coronas
> Dixit Olympiacas, et quâ victoribus Isthmos
> Fronde comam, Delphique tegant, Nemeæaque tesqua
> Lunigenam mentita feram; tum numina divum
> Virtutesque, virosque undanti pectore torrens
> Provexit, sparsitque pios ad funera questus.
> Frugibus hunc libisque virum Cirrhæus ab arâ
> Phœbus, et accubitu mensæ dignatus honoro est :
> Panaque pastores solis videre sub antris
> Pindarico tacitas mulcentem carmine silvas.
> Inde senem pueri gremio cervice repostâ
> Infusum, et dulci laxantem corda sopore,
> Protinus ad manes, et odoro gramine pictum
> Elysium tacitâ rapuit Proserpina dextrâ.
> Quin etiam hostiles longo post tempore flammæ,
> Quæ septemgeminas populabant undique Thebas,
> Expavere domum tanti tamen urere vatis,
> Et sua posteritas medios quoque tuta per enses
> Sensit inexhaustâ cinerem juvenescere famâ.[1]

Sappho is described in the following lines :—

>   lyricis jam nona poetis
> Æolis accedit Sappho, quæ flumina propter
> Pierias legit ungue rosas, unde implicet audax
> Serta Cupido sibi, niveam quæ pectine blando
> Cyrinnem, Megaramque simul, cumque Atthide pulchram

---

[1] 'Far off into the tracts of air and high above the clouds soars
Pindar, the Dircæan swan, whose tender mouth ye gentle bees with
nectar fed, while the boy gave rest to weary limbs that breathed soft
slumber. But him the maid of Tanagra derided, what time she told

Cantat Anactorien, et crinigeram Telesippen ;
Et te conspicuum recidivo flore juventæ
Miratur revocatque, Phaon, seu munera vectæ
Puppe tuâ Veneris, seu sic facit herba potentem :
Sed tandem Ambracias temeraria saltat in undas.[1]

Having disposed of the lyrists, Poliziano proceeds to the
dramatic poets. His brief notice of the three Attic tragedians is
worthy of quotation, if only because it proves what we should
suspect from other indications, that the best scholars of the
earlier Renaissance paid them little attention. The facts
mentioned in the following lines seem to be derived from the
gossip of Athenæus :—

him that he sowed his myths from the whole sack to waste ; and when
he dared contend with her in song, she bore away the victor's palm,
triumphant by Æolian moods, and by her seductive beauty too. He
with his mighty voice, trained in the school of Agathocles, sang the
crowns of Olympia and the garlands wherewith the Isthmus and Delphi,
and the Nemean wastes that falsely claimed the moon-born monster,
shade the athlete's brows. Then, like a torrent, with swelling soul, he
passed to celebrate the powers and virtues of the gods and heroes, and
poured forth pious lamentations for the dead. Him Phœbus, lord of
Cirrha, honoured with food and drink from his altar, and made him
guest-fellow at his own board : shepherds too saw Pan in lonely caverns
charming the woods with a Pindaric song. At last, when he was old,
and lay with his neck reclined upon the bosom of the boy he loved,
soothing his soul in sleep, Proserpina with still right hand approached
and took him straight to join the shades and pace Elysium's fragrant
meads. Nay, more : long afterwards, the foeman's flames, which laid
seven-gated Thebes in ruins far and wide, these flames dared not to
burn so great a poet's house ; and his descendants, safe 'mid a thousand
swords, learned that his ashes still were young through fame that lives
for aye.'—*Carmina*, &c. p. 173.

[1] 'Ninth among lyric bards, Æolian Sappho joins the crew ; she
who by flowing water plucks Pieria's rose for venturous Love to twine
in wreaths for his own brow ; who with her dulcet lyre sings fair
Cyrinna's charms, and Megara, and Atthis and sweet Anactoria, and
Telesippa of the flowing hair. And thee, too, Phaon, beautiful in youth's
rathe flower, on thee she gazes, thee she calls again ; such power to
thee gave Venus for her freightage in thy skiff, or else the herb of love.
Yet at the last, not wisely bold, she leaps into the Ambracian waves.'
Ib. &c. p. 175.

Æschylus aëriæ casu testudinis ictus,
Quemque senem meritæ rapuerunt gaudia palmæ,
Quemque tegit rabidis lacerum pia Pella molossis.[1]

Nor are his observations on the comic dramatists less meagre.[2] The Roman poets having been passed in the same rapid review, Poliziano salutes the founders of Italian literature in the following fine passage :—

Nec tamen aligerum fraudarim hoc munere Dantem,
Per Styga, per stellas, mediique per ardua montis
Pulchra Beatricis sub virginis ora volantem :
Quique Cupidineum repetit Petrarcha triumphum :
Et qui bis quinis centum argumenta diebus
Pingit, et obscuri qui semina monstrat amoris :
Unde tibi immensæ veniunt præconia laudis,
Ingeniis opibusque potens Florentia mater.[3]

The transition to Lorenzo at this point is natural. A solemn peroration in praise of the Medicean prince, himself a poet, whose studies formed the recreation of severer labours, ends the composition. This is written in Poliziano's best style, and, though it is too long to quote, six lines may be selected as indicating the theme of the argument :—

Quodque alii studiumque vocant durumque laborem,
Hic tibi ludus erit ; fessus civilibus actis
Huc is emeritas acuens ad carmina vires :

---

[1] 'Æschylus, smitten by a tortoise falling from the air above his head, and he whose triumph, justly won in old age, killed him with excess of joy, and he whose body, torn by raging hounds, the reverent earth of Pella hides.'—*Carmina*, &c. p. 176.

[2] *Ib.* p. 177.

[3] 'Nor yet of this meed of honour would I cheat wing-bearing Dante, who flew through hell, through the starry heavens, and o'er the intermediate hill of purgatory beneath the beauteous brows of Beatrice ; and Petrarch too, who tells again the tale of Cupid's triumph ; or him who in ten days portrays a hundred stories, and lays bare the seeds of hidden love : from whom unmeasured fame and name are thine, by wit and wealth twice potent, Florence, mother of great sons ! '—*Ib.* p. 178.

Felix ingenio, felix cui pectore tantas
Instaurare vices, cui fas tam magna capaci
Alternare animo, et varias ita nectere curas.[1]

We possess the whole of Poliziano in the 'Nutricia.' It
displays the energy of intellect that carried him on bounding
verse through the intricacies of a subject difficult by reason
of its scope and magnitude. All his haste is here, his in-
ability to polish or select, his lava-stream of language hurrying the dross of prose and scoriæ of erudition along a burning
tide of song. His memory held, as it were, in solution all
the matter of antique literature ; and when he wrote, he
poured details forth in torrents, combining them with critical
remarks, for the double purpose of instruction and panegyric.
Taken at the lowest valuation by students to whom his
copious stores of knowledge are familiar, the vivid and
continuous melody of his leaping hexameters places the
' Nutricia' above the lucubrations of more fastidious Latinists.
We must also remember that, when it was recited from the
professorial Chair of Rhetoric at Florence, the magnetism
of Poliziano's voice and manner supplied just that touch of
charm the poem lacks for modern readers ; nor was the
matter so hackneyed at the end of the fifteenth century as it
is now. Lilius Gyraldus, subjecting the 'Sylvæ' to criticism
at a time when Latin poetry had been artistically polished
by the best wits of the age of Leo, passed upon them a judgment which may even now be quoted as final.[2] 'Poliziano's
learning was marvellous, his genius fervent and well-trained,
his reading extensive and uninterrupted ; yet he appears to

[1] 'What other men call study and hard toil, that for thee shall be
pastime ; wearied with deeds of state, to this thou hast recourse, and
dost address the vigour of thy well-worn powers to song : blest in thy
mental gifts, blest to be able thus to play so many parts, to vary thus
the great cares of thy all-embracing mind, and weave so many divers
duties into one.'—*Carmina*, &c. p. 179.

[2] 'Dialogus de Poetis nostri Temporis.' *Opp.* vol. ii. p. 388. Edition
of Basle, 1580.

have composed his verses with more heat than art, using too
little judgment both in the selection of his materials and in
the correction of his style. When, however, you read his
'Sylvæ,' the impression left upon your mind will be such that
for the moment you will lack nothing.'

The second poem of the 'Sylvæ,' entitled 'Rusticus,'
forms an induction to the study of bucolic poets, principally
Hesiod and Virgil. It is distinguished by more originality
and play of fancy than the 'Nutricia;' some of its delinea-
tions of landscape and sketches of country life compete not
unfavourably with similar passages in the author's 'Stanze.'
To dwell upon these beauties in detail, and to compare
Poliziano, the Latin poet, with Poliziano, the Italian, would
be a pleasant task. Yet I must confine myself to quoting
the last, and in some respects the least imaginative, lines, for
the sake of their historical interest. Careggi and Florence,
Lorenzo and his circle of literary friends, rise before us in
these verses :—

> Talia Fesuleo lentus meditabar in antro,
> Rure suburbano Medicum, quâ mons sacer urbem
> Mæoniam, longique volumina despicit Arni :
> Quâ bonus hospitium felix placidamque quietem
> Indulget Laurens, Laurens haud ultima Phœbi
> Gloria, jactatis Laurens fida anchora Musis ;
> Qui si certa magis permiserit otia nobis,
> Afflabor majore Deo, nec jam ardua tantum
> Silva meas voces, montanaque saxa loquentur,
> Sed tu, si qua fides, tu nostrum forsitan olim,
> O mea blanda altrix, non aspernabere carmen,
> Quamvis magnorum genitrix Florentia vatum,
> Doctaque me triplici recinet facundia linguâ.[1]

The third canto of the 'Sylvæ' is called 'Manto.' It
relates the birth of Virgil, to whom the Muses gave their

---

[1] 'On themes like these I spent my hours of leisure in the grottoes
of Fiesole, at the Medicean villa, where the holy hill looks down upon
the Mæonian city, and surveys the windings of the distant Arno.

several gifts, while the Sibyl of Mantua foretold his future course of life and all the glories he should gain by song. The poem concludes with a rhetorical eulogy of Rome's chief bard, so characteristic of Renaissance enthusiasm for Virgil that to omit a portion of it from these pages would be to sacrifice one of the most striking examples of Italian taste in scholarship :—

> At manet æternum, et seros excurrit in annos
> Vatis opus, dumque in tacito vaga sidera mundo
> Fulgebunt, dum sol nigris orietur ab Indis,
> Prævia luciferis aderit dum curribus Eos,
> Dum ver tristis hiems, autumnum proferet æstas,
> Dumque fluet spirans refluetque reciproca Tethys,
> Dum mixta alternas capient elementa figuras,
> Semper erit magni decus immortale Maronis,
> Semper inexhaustis ibunt hæc flumina venis,
> Semper ab his docti ducentur fontibus haustus,
> Semper odoratos fundent hæc gramina flores,
> Unde piæ libetis apes, unde inclyta nectat
> Serta comis triplici juvenalis Gratia dextrâ.[1]

Not less ingenious than the poem itself is the elegiac introduction. Poliziano feigns that when the Minyæ came to

There good Lorenzo gives his friends a happy home and rest from cares ; Lorenzo, not the last of Phœbus' glorious band; Lorenzo, the firm anchor of the Muses tempest-tost. If only he but grant me greater ease, the inspiration of a mightier god will raise my soul; nor shall the lofty woods alone and mountain rocks resound my words ; but thou—such faith have I—thou too shalt sometime hear, kind nurse of mine, nor haply scorn my song, thou, Florence, mother of imperial bards, and learned eloquence in three great tongues shall give me fame.' *Carmina*, &c. p. 196.

[1] 'Nay, but for everlasting lives our poet's work, abides, and goes forth toward the ages late in time. So long as in the silent firmament the stars shall shine ; so long as day shall rise from sun-burned Ind ; so long as Phosphor runs before the wheels of light ; so long as gloomy winter leads to spring, and summer to autumn ; while breathing ocean ebbs and flows by turns, and the mixed elements put on their changing shapes—so long, for ever, shall endure great Maro's fame, for ever shall flow these rivers from his unexhausted fount, for ever shall draughts of learning be drawn from these rills, for ever shall these meadows yield

Cheiron's cave on Pelion, and supped with him, Orpheus sang a divine melody, and then the young Achilles took the lyre, and with rude fingers praised the poet's song. The Minyæ smiled, but Orpheus was touched by the boy-hero's praises. Even so will Maro haply take delight in mine :—

> Finis erat dapibus; citharam pius excitat Orpheus,
>> Et movet ad doctas verba canora manus.
> Conticuere viri, tenuere silentia venti,
>> Vosque retro cursum mox tenuistis aquæ.
> Jam volucres fessis pendere sub æthera pennis,
>> Jamque truces videas ora tenere feras.
> Decurrunt scopulis auritæ ad carmina quercus,
>> Nudaque Peliacus culmina motat apex.
> Et jam materno permulserat omnia cantu,
>> Cum tacuit, querulam deposuitque fidem.
> Occupat hanc audax, digitosque affringit Achilles,
>> Indoctumque rudi personat ore puer.
> Materiam quæris? laudabat carmina blandi
>> Hospitis, et tantæ murmura magna lyræ.
> Riserunt Minyæ: sed enim tibi dicitur, Orpheu,
>> Hæc pueri pietas grata fuisse nimis.
> Me quoque nunc magni nomen celebrare Maronis,
>> Si qua fides vero est, gaudet et ipse Maro.[1]

The fourth poem, bearing the name of 'Ambra,' forms a similar induction to the study of Homer. The youth of

their perfumed flowers, to pasture holy bees, and give the youthful Graces garlands for their hair.'—*Carmina*, &c. p. 207.

[1] 'Supper was over; Orpheus awakes the lyre, and sings a melody to suit the tune he plays. The men were silent; the winds hushed; the rivers held their waters back to hear; the birds hung motionless in air; and the wild beasts grew calm. From the cliffs the oaks run down with listening ears, and the top of Pelion nods his barren head. And now the bard had soothed the whole world with his mother's song; when he ceased from singing and put down the thrilling lyre. This bold Achilles seizes; he runs his fingers o'er the strings, and chaunts an untaught lay, the simple boy. What was his theme? you ask. He praised the singing of the gentle guest, the mighty murmurs of that lyre divine. The Minyæ laughed; but yet, so runs the tale, even all too sweet, Orpheus, to thee was the boy's homage. Just so my praise of mighty Maro's name, if faith be not a dream, gives joy to Maro's self.'—*Carmina*, &c. p. 197.

Homer is narrated, and how Achilles appeared to him, blinding him with the vision of his heroic beauty, and giving him the wand of Teiresias. Then follow descriptions of both 'Iliad' and 'Odyssey,' and a passage of high-flown panegyric; the whole ending with these lines on Lorenzo's villa of Cajano:—

> Et nos ergo illi gratâ pietate dicamus
> Hanc de Pierio contextam flore coronam,
> Quam mihi Cajanas inter pulcherrima nymphas
> Ambra dedit patriæ lectam de gramine ripæ;
> Ambra mei Laurentis amor, quem corniger Umbro,
> Umbro senex genuit domino gratissimus Arno,
> Umbro suo tandem non erepturus ab alveo.[1]

Taking into consideration the purpose fulfilled by Poliziano's 'Sylvæ' in his professorial career, it is impossible to deny their merit. The erudition is borne with ease; it does not clog or overload the poet's impulse. The flattery of Lorenzo is neither fulsome nor unmerited. The verse flows strongly and majestically, though more variety of cadence in the hexameter may be desired. The language, in spite of repetitions and ill-chosen archaisms, is rich and varied; it has at least the charm of being the poet's own, not culled with scrupulous anxiety from one or two illustrious sources. Some of the pictures are delicately sketched, while the whole style produces the effect of eloquent and fervid improvisation. For fulness and rapidity of utterance, copious fancy, and wealth of illustration, these four poems will bear comparison with Roman work of the Silver Age. The Florentines who crowded Poliziano's lecture-room must have felt as in the

[1] 'We also, therefore, with glad homage dedicate to him this garland twined of Pieria's flowers, which Ambra, loveliest of Cajano's nymphs, gave to me, culled from meadows on her father's shores; Ambra, the love of my Lorenzo, whom Umbrone, the horned stream, begat— Umbrone, dearest to his master Arno, Umbrone, who now henceforth will never break his banks again.'—*Carmina*, &c. p. 224.

days of the Empire, when Statius declaimed his periods to a
Roman audience, and the patrician critics clapped applause.[1]

Among Poliziano's minor poems it is enough to mention
the elegiac couplets on some violets sent him by his mistress,
the verses descriptive of a beautiful girl, and the lamentation
for the wife of Sismondo della Stufa.[2] They illustrate the
delicacy of his style and the freedom of his fancy in the
treatment of occasional themes, and are far superior to his
epigrams and epitaphs.[3] The numerous encomiastic elegies
addressed to Lorenzo de' Medici and other patrons are wholly
without value. Poliziano was a genuine poet. He needed
the inspiration of true feeling or of lively fancy ; on a tame
occasion he degenerated into frigid baldness. Yet the satires
on Mabilius, where spite and jealousy have stirred his genius,
are striking for their volubility and pungency. A Roman
imitator of Catullus in his brutal mood could not have produced abuse more flexible and nauseous. Taken altogether,
Poliziano's Latin compositions display the qualities of fluency
and abundance that characterise his Italian verses, though
they have not the exquisite polish of the 'Giostra.' Their final
merit consists in their spontaneity. No stylist of the age of
Leo knew how to use the language of classic Rome with so
much ease.

Jovianus Pontanus deserves a high place among the writers
of Latin verse, whether we regard his didactic poems on
astronomy and the cultivation of the orange, his epigrams, or
the amorous elegies that, for their grace, may be compared
almost with Ovid.[4] Even during his lifetime Pontanus
became a classic, and after his death he was imitated by the

---

[1] Cf. Juvenal, *Satire*, i. 9-14 ; vii. 81-87. Persius, *Satire*, i. 79-82. And
cf. Petronius Arbiter for a detailed picture of these Roman recitations.

[2] *Carmina Quinque*, &c. pp. 250, 272, 276.

[3] The epitaphs on Giotto, Lippo Lippi, the fair Simonetta, and others,
are only valuable for their historic interest, such as that is.

[4] I shall quote from his *Collected Poems*, Aldus, 1513.

most ambitious versifiers of the late Renaissance.[1] The beauty of South Italian landscape—Sorrento's orange gardens and Baiæ's waters—passed into the fancy of the Neapolitan poets, and gave colour to their language. Nor was Pontanus, in spite of his severe studies and gravely-tempered mind, dead to the seductions of this siren. What we admire in Sannazzaro's ' Arcadia ' assumes the form of pure Latinity in his love poems.[2] Their style is penetrated with the feeling for physical beauty, Pagan and untempered by an afterthought of Christianity. Their vigorous and glowing sensuality finds no just analogue except in some Venetian paintings. It was not, however, by his lighter verses so much as by the five books called ' De Stellis' or ' Urania ' that Pontanus won the admiration of Italian scholars. In this long series of hexameters he contrived to set forth the whole astronomical science of his age, touching upon the mythology of the celestial signs, describing the zodiac, discussing the motion of the heavens, raising the question of planetary influences, and characterising the different regions of the globe by their relation to the sun's path across the sky. He seems to have taken the ' Metamorphoses ' of Ovid for his model of versification ; and though we miss the variety of Ovid's treatment, great ingenuity is displayed in adorning so difficult a subject with poetical episodes.[3] Personal interest is added to the conclusion of ' Urania ' by the lamentation poured forth for his daughter Lucia by the poet :—

> Ornabam tibi serta domi ; Syriumque liquorem
> Ad thalamos geminæ, geminæ, tua cura, sorores

---

[1] See the Elegy of Sannazzaro on the writings of Pontanus, *Poemata Selecta*, pp. 1–4, and Fracastoro's *Syphilis*, *ib.* p. 72.

[2] *Delitiæ Poetarum Italorum*, pt. ii. pp. 668–712. Specimens may also be read in the *Poemata Selecta Italorum*, pp. 1–24.

[3] See, for instance, the tale of Hylas, lib. v. p. 103 ; the tale of Cola Pesce, lib. iv. p. 79 ; the council of the gods, lib. i. p. 18 ; the planet Venus, lib. i. p. 5.

> Fundebant.   Quid pro sertis Syrioque liquore
> Liquisti ?   Sine sole dies, sine sidere noctes,
> Insomnes noctes.[1]

Lucia died before her marriage-day, and her grey-headed
father went mourning for her, fooled by memory, vainly
seeking the joy that could not come again.   Had she become,
he asks, a star in heaven, and did the blessed gods and
heroines enjoy her splendour ?   No voice replied when he
called into the darkness, nor did new constellations beam on
him with brightness from his daughter's eyes.   All through
the wakeful night he mourned, but when dawn went forth he
marked a novel lustre on the sea and in the sky.   Lucia had
been added to the nymphs of morning.   She smiled upon her
father as she fled before the wheels of day ; and now the sun
himself arose, and in his light her light was swallowed :
Hyperion scaled the heights of heaven with more than his
own glory.   With this apotheosis of his daughter, so curiously
Pagan in feeling, and yet so far from classical in taste, the
poem might have ended, had not Pontano reserved its final
honours for himself.   To Lucia, now made a goddess, he
addresses his prayers that she should keep his name and
fame alive on earth when he is dead :—

> Fama ipsa assistens tumulo cum vestibus aureis,
> Ore ingens, ac voce ingens, ingentibus alis,
> Per populos late ingenti mea nomina plausu
> Vulgabit, titulosque feret per sæcula nostros ;
> Plaudentesque meis resonabunt laudibus auræ,
> Vivet et extento celeber Jovianus in ævo.[2]

---

[1] Lib. v. pp. 105-108.   'For thee I hung the house with wreaths ;
and thy twin sisters poured forth Syrian perfumes at the marriage
chamber.   What for our garlands and our perfumes hast thou left ?
Days without light, nights without a star, long sleepless nights.'

[2] 'Fame herself, seated by my tomb with golden raiment, mighty-
mouthed, mighty-voiced, with mighty wings, shall spread abroad among
the people my names with mighty sound of praise, and carry through
the centuries my titles, and with my glory shall resound applauding
airs of heaven ; renowned through everlasting ages Jovian shall live.'

Sannazzaro's own elegies on the joys of love and country life, the descriptions of his boyhood at Salerno, the praises of his Villa Mergillina, and his meditations among the ruins of Cumæ, are marked by the same characteristics. Nothing quite so full of sensual enjoyment, so soft, and so voluptuous can be found in the poems of the Florentine and Roman scholars. They deserve study, if only as illustrating the luxurious tone of literature at Naples. It was not by these lighter effusions, however, that Sannazzaro won his fame. The epic on the birth of Christ cost him twenty years of labour; and when it was finished, the learned world of Italy welcomed it as a model of correct and polished writing. At the same time the critics seem to have felt, what cannot fail to strike a modern reader, that the difficulties of treating such a theme in the Virgilian manner, and the patience of the stylist, had rendered it a masterpiece of ingenuity rather than a work of genius.[1] Sannazzaro's epigrams, composed in the spirit of bitterest hostility towards the Borgia family, were not less famous than his epic. Alfonso of Aragon took the poet with him during his campaign against the Papal force in the Abruzzi; and these satires, hastily written in the tent and by the camp-fire, formed the amusement of his officers. From the soldiers of Alfonso they speedily passed, on the lips of courtiers and scholars, through all the cities of Italy; nor is it easy to say how much of Lucrezia Borgia's legend may not be traceable to their brief but envenomed couplets. What had been the scandal of the camp acquired consistency in lines too pungent to be forgotten and too witty to remain

---

[1] 'Lilius Gyraldus,' loc. cit. p. 384, writes about this epic, 'in quibus, ut sic dicam, statarius poeta videri potest. Non enim verborum volubilitate fertur, sed limatius quoddam scribendi genus consectatur, et limâ indies atterit, ut de illo non ineleganter dictum illud Apellis de Protogene Pontanus usurpare solitus esset, eum manum de tabulâ tollere nescire.'

unquoted.[1]   As a specimen of Sannazzaro's style, the epigram
on Venice may here be cited :—

> Viderat Hadriacis Venetam Neptunus in undis
>   Stare urbem, et toto ponere jura mari :
> Nunc mihi Tarpeias quantumvis, Jupiter, arces
>   Objice, et illa tui mœnia Martis. ait :
> Si Pelago Tybrim præfers, urbem aspice utramque ;
>   Illam homines dices, hanc posuisse deos.[2]

I have already touched upon the Virgilianism of Sannazzaro's ' Partus Virginis.'[3]   What the cold churches of
Palladio are to Christian architecture, this frigid epic is to
Christian poetry.   Leo X. delighted to recognise the Gospel
narrative beneath a fancy dress of mythological inventions,
and to witness the triumph of classical scholarship in the
holy places of the mediæval faith.   To fuse the traditions of
Biblical and secular antiquity was, as I have often said, the
dream of the Renaissance.   What Pico and Ficino attempted
in philosophical treatises, the poets sought to effect by form.
Religion, attiring herself in classic drapery, threw off the
cobwebs of the Catacombs, and acquired the right of *petites
entrées* at the Vatican. It did not signify that she had sacrificed
her majesty to fashion, or that her tunic *à la mode antique*
was badly made.   Her rouge and spangles enchanted the
scholarly Pontiff, who forthwith ordered Vida to compose the
' Christiad,' and gave him a benefice at Frascati in order that
he might enjoy a poet's ease.   Vida's epic, like Sannazzaro's,

---

[1] See *Delitiæ Poetarum Italorum*, second part, pp. 713–761. The
following couplet on the death of Cesare Borgia is celebrated :—

> Aut nihil aut Cæsar vult dici Borgia ; quidni ?
> Cum simul et Cæsar possit et esse nihil.

[2] ' When Neptune beheld Venice stationed in the Adriatic waters,
and giving laws to all the ocean, "Now taunt me, Jupiter, with the
Tarpeian rock and those walls of thy son Mars ! " he cried. " If thou
preferrest Tiber to the sea, look on both cities ; thou wilt say the one
was built by men, the other by gods." '

[3] See above, p. 288.

was not finished during the lifetime of Leo. Both the
'Christiad' and the 'Partus Virginis' reflected lustre on the
age of Clement.

Vida won his first laurels in the field of didactic poetry.
Virgilian exercises on the breeding of silkworms and the game
of chess displayed his faculty for investing familiar subjects
with the graces of a polished style.[1] Such poems, whether
written in Latin, or, like the 'Api' of Rucellai, in Italian,
gratified the taste of the Renaissance, always appreciative of
form independent of the matter it invested. For a modern
student Vida's metrical treatise in three books on the 'Art of
Poetry' has greater interest, since it illustrates the final
outcome of classic studies in the age of Leo. The 'Poetica'
is addressed to Francis, Dauphin of France, in his Spanish
prison : [2]—

> Primus ades, Francisce ; sacras ne despice Musas,
> Regia progenies, cui regum debita sceptra
> Gallorum, cum firma annis accesserit ætas.
> Hæc tibi parva ferunt jam nunc solatia dulces ;
> Dum procul a patriâ raptum, amplexuque tuorum,
> Ah dolor ! Hispanis sors impia detinet oris,
> Henrico cum fratre ; patris sic fata tulerunt
> Magnanimi, dum fortunâ luctatur iniquâ.
> Parce tamen, puer, o lacrymis ; fata aspera forsan
> Mitescent, aderitque dies lætissima tandem
> Post triste exilium patriis cum redditus oris
> Lætitiam ingentem populorum, omnesque per urbes
> Accipies plausus, et lætas undique voces ;
> Votaque pro reditu persolvent debita matres.
> Interea te Pierides comitentur ; in altos
> Jam te Parnassi mecum aude attollere lucos.[3]

Bombycum ; Libri duo. Scacchia, Ludus ; Liber unus. Pope's
Poemata Italorum, vol. i. pp. 103–130 ; pp. 190–210. The former poem
is addressed to Isabella Gonzaga, née D'Este.

[2] *Poemata Selecta*, pp. 207–266. It will be remembered that
Francis I., after Pavia, gave his two sons as hostages to Charles V.

[3] 'Thou, Francis, art the first to answer to my call. Scorn not the
sacred Muses, scion of a royal line, to whom the sceptre of the kings
of Gallia in due season of maturity will pass. Their sweetness even

After this dedication Vida describes the solace to be found
in poetry, and adds some precepts on the preparation of the
student's mind.[1] A rapid review of the history of poetry—
the decline of Greek inspiration after Homer, and of Latin
after Virgil ; the qualities of the Silver Age, and the Revival
of letters under the Medici at Florence—serves to show how
narrow the standard of Italian culture had become between
the period of Poliziano, who embraced so much in his sketch
of literature, and that of Vida, who confined himself to so
little. The criticism is not unjust ; but it proves that the
refinement of taste by scholarship had resulted in restricting
students to one or two models, whom they followed with
servility.[2] Having thus established his general view of the

now shall yield thee some slight solace, exiled from home and father-
land by fate impiteous on the Spanish shore, thee and thy brother
Henry. So the fortunes of thy mighty-hearted father willed, condemned
to strive against unequal doom. Yet spare thy tears : perchance hard
fate will soften, and a day of supreme joy will come at last, when, after
thy sad exile, once more given to thy nation, thou shalt behold thy
country's gladness, and hear the shouts of all her cities and the ringing
songs of happiness, and mothers shall perform their vows for thy return.
Meanwhile let the maidens of Pieria attend thee ; and, with me for
guide, ascend into the groves of high Parnassus.'

[1]   tibi digna supellex
        Verborum rerumque paranda est, proque videnda
        Instant multa prius, quorum vatum indiget usus.
                                Poemata Selecta, p. 209.

[2] After mentioning the glories of Virgil, Vida adds :—
                Sperare nefas sit vatibus ultra.
        Nulla mora, ex illo in pejus ruere omnia visa,
        Degenerare animi, atque retro res lapsa referri.
        Hic namque ingenio confisus posthabet artem ;
        Ille furit strepitu, tenditque æquare tubarum
        Voce sonos, versusque tonat sine more per omnes ;
        Dant alii cantus vacuos, et inania verba
        Incassum, solâ capti dulcedine vocis.
Poemata Selecta, p. 213. Cf. the advice (p. 214) to follow none but
Virgil :—
        Ergo ipsum ante alios animo venerare Maronem,
        Atque unum sequere, utque potes, vestigia serva.

poetic art, Vida proceeds to sketch a plan of education. The qualities and duties of a tutor are described; and here we may notice how far Vittorino's and Guarino's methods had created an ideal of training for Italy. The preceptor must above all things avoid violence, and aim at winning the affections of his pupil; it would be well for him to associate several youths in the same course of study, so as to arouse their emulation. He must not neglect their games, and must always be careful to suit his method to the different talents of his charges. When the special studies to be followed are discussed, Vida points out that Cicero is the best school of Latin style. He recommends the early practice of bucolic verse, and inculcates the necessity of treating youthful essays with indulgence. These topics are touched with more or less felicity of phrase and illustration; and though the subject-matter is sufficiently trite, the good sense and kindly feeling of the writer win respect. The first book concludes with a peroration on the dignity and sanctity of poets, a theme the humanists were never weary of embroidering.[1] The second describes the qualities of a good poem, as these were conceived by the refined but formal taste of the sixteenth century. It should begin quietly, and manage to excite without satisfying the curiosity of the reader. Vain displays of learning are to be avoided. Episodes and similes must occur at proper intervals; and a frugal seasoning of humour will be found agreeable. All repetitions should be shunned, and great care should be taken to vary the narrative with picturesque descriptions. Rhetoric, again, is not unworthy of attention, when the poet seeks to place convenient and specious arguments in the mouths of his personages.

[1] Dona deûm Musæ : vulgus procul este profanum.
Poemata Selecta, p. 224 ; and again, *ib.* p. 226 :—

      Tu Jovis ambrosiis das nos accumbere mensis ;
      Tu nos diis æquas superis, &c.

It is difficult in a summary to do justice to this portion of Vida's poem. His description of the ideal epic is indeed nothing more or less than a refined analysis of the ' Æneid ; ' and students desirous of learning what the Italians of the sixteenth century admired in Virgil will do well to study its acute and sober criticism. A panegyric of Leo closes the second book. From this peroration some lines upon the woes of Italy may be read with profit, as proving that the nation, conscious of its own decline, was contented to accept the primacy of culture in exchange for independence :—

> Dii Romæ indigetes, Trojæ tuque auctor, Apollo
> Unde genus nostrum cœli se tollit ad astra,
> Hanc saltem auferri laudem prohibete Latinis :
> Artibus emineat semper, studiisque Minervæ,
> Italia, et gentes doceat pulcherrima Roma ;
> Quandoquidem armorum penitus fortuna recessit,
> Tanta Italos inter crevit discordia reges ;
> Ipsi nos inter sacros distringimus enses,
> Nec patriam pudet externis aperire tyrannis.[1]

The third book treats of style and diction. To be clear and varied, to command metaphor and allusion, to choose phrases coloured by mythology and fancy, to suit the language to the subject, to vary the metrical cadence with the thought and feeling, and to be assiduous in the use of the file are mentioned as indispensable to excellence. A peroration on Virgil, sonorous and impassioned, closes the whole poem, which, rightly understood, is a monument erected to the fame of the Roman bard by the piety of his Italian pupil. The final lines are justly famous :—

[1] 'Ye native gods of Rome ! and thou, Apollo, Troy's founder ! by whom our race is raised to heaven ! let not at least this glory be withdrawn from Latium's children : may Italy for ever hold the heights of art and learning, and most beauteous Rome instruct the nations ; albeit all success in arms be lost, so great hath grown the discord of Italia's princes. Yea, one against the other, we draw bloody swords, nor feel we any shame in calling foreign tyrants into our own land.'—*Poemata Selecta*, p. 245.

O decus Italiæ ! lux o clarissima vatum !
Te colimus, tibi serta damus, tibi thura, tibi aras ;
Et tibi rite sacrum semper dicemus honorem
Carminibus memores.   Salve, sanctissime vates !
Laudibus augeri tua gloria nil potis ultra,
Et nostræ nil vocis eget ; nos aspice præsens,
Pectoribusque tuos castis infunde calores
Adveniens, pater, atque animis te te insere nostris.[1]

Vida's own intellect was clear, and his style perspicuous ;
but his genius was mediocre.   His power lay in the disposition of materials and in illustration.   A precise taste,
formed on Cicero and Virgil, and exercised with judgment in
a narrow sphere, satisfied his critical requirements.   Virgil
with him was first and last, and midst and without end.   In
a word, he shows what a scholar of sound parts and rhetorical
aptitude could achieve by the study and imitation of a single
author.

Since I have begun to speak of didactic poems, I may
take this opportunity of noticing Fracastoro, who seems to
have chosen Pontanus for his model, and, while emulating
both Lucretius and Virgil, to have fallen short of Vida's
elegance.   His work is less remarkable for purity of diction
than for massiveness of intellect, gravity of matter, and
constructive ability.   Jeronimo Fracastoro was born in 1483
at Verona, where he spent the greater portion of his life,
enjoying high reputation as a physician, philosopher,
astronomer, and poet.   During his youth he studied under
Pomponazzo at Padua.   The strong tincture of materialistic
science he there received, continued through life to colour his

[1] 'Hail, light of Italy, thou brightest of the bards !   Thee we
worship, thee we adore with wreaths, with frankincense, with altars ;
to thee, as duty bids, for everlasting will we chaunt our holy hymns.
Hail, consecrated bard !   No increase to thy glory flows from praise,
nor needs it voice of ours.   Be near, and look upon thy votaries ; come,
father, and infuse thy fervour into our chaste hearts, and plant thyself
within our souls.'—*Poemata Selecta*, p. 266.

thought. Among modern Pagans none is more completely
bare of Christianity than Fracastoro. As is well known, he
chose the new and terrible disease of the Renaissance for his
theme, and gave a name to it that still is current. To speak
of Fracastoro's 'Syphilis,' dedicated to Bembo, hailed with
acclamation by all Italy, preferred by Sannazzaro to his own
epic, and praised by Julius Cæsar Scaliger as a ' divine poem,'
is not easy now. The plague it celebrates appeared at Naples
in 1495, and spread like wildfire over Europe, assuming at
first the form of an epidemic sparing neither Pope nor king,
and stirring less disgust than dread among its victims.[1]
Whether the laws of its propagation were rightly understood
in the sixteenth century is a question for physicians to decide.
No one appears to have suspected that it differed in specific
character from other pestilent disorders ; and it is clear, both
from contemporary chronicles and from Fracastoro's poem,
that the *mal franzese*, as it was popularly called, suggested
to the people of that age associations different from those
that have since gathered round it. At the same time more
formidable and less loathsome, it was a not more unworthy
subject for verse than the plague at Athens described by
Lucretius. Treating the disease, therefore, as a curse common
to his generation, the scientific poet dared to set forth its
symptoms, to prescribe remedies, to discuss the question of
its origin, and to use it as an illustration of antagonistic
forces, pernicious and beneficent, in the economy of nature.
To philosophise his repulsive subject-matter was the author's
ambition. His contemporaries admired the poetic graces with
which he had contrived to adorn it.

The exordium of the first book states the problem.
Whence came this new scourge of humanity ? Not, surely,
from America, though it is there indigenous. Its diffusion
after the disasters of 1494 was too rapid to admit of this

[1] See Vol. I., *Age of the Despots*, p. 433, note.

hypothesis.[1] To the corruption of the atmosphere must be
referred the general invasion of the plague.[2] The theory of
infected and putrescent air is stated in a long Lucretian
passage, followed by a scientific account of the symptoms of
syphilis. At this point the poet diversifies his argument by
an episode, narrating the sad death of a young man born on
the banks of the Oglio, and leading by gradual transitions to
a peroration on the wars and woes of Italy.[3] Over all the
poets of this age the miseries of their country hung like a
cloud, and, touch the lyre as they may at the beginning of
their song, it is certain ere the ending to give forth a dolorous
groan. In the second book Fracastoro enters on the subject
of remedies. He lays stress on choice of air, abundant
exercise, avoidance of wine and heating diet, blood-letting,
abstinence from sensual pleasures, fomentations, herbs, and
divers minute rules of health. By attention to these matters
the disease may be, if not shunned, at least mitigated. The
sovereign remedy of quicksilver demanded fuller illustration ;
therefore the poet introduces the legendary episode of the
shepherd Ilceus, conducted by the nymph Liparë to the
sulphur founts and lakes of mercury beneath Mount Etna.
Ilceus bathed, and was renewed in health. The rigorously
didactic intention of Fracastoro is proved by the recipe for a
mercurial ointment and the description of salivation that
wind up this book.[4] The third opens with an allusion to the

[1]   quoniam in primis ostendere multos
Possumus, attactu qui nullius hanc tamen ipsam
Sponte suâ sensere luem, primique tulere.
                              Poemata Selecta, p. 67.

[2] Qunmque animadvertas, tam vastæ semina labis
Esse nec in terræ gremio, nec in æquore posse,
Haud dubie tecum statuas reputesque necesse est,
Principium sedemque mali consistere in ipso
Aëre, qui terras circum diffunditur omnes.
                              Ibid. p. 69.

[3] *Ibid.* pp. 79, 80.   [4] *Ibid.* pp. 95, 96.

discovery of America, and a celebration of the tree Hyacus (Guaiacum). It is noticeable that, with such an opportunity for singing the praises of Columbus, Fracastoro passed him by, nor cared to claim for Italy a share in the greatest achievement of the century. Mingling myth with history, he next proceeds to tell how the Spaniards arrived in the West Indies, and shot birds sacred to the Sun,[1] one of which spoke with human voice, predicting the evils that would fall upon the crew for their impiety. Not the least of these was to be a strange and terrible disease. The natives of the islands flocked to meet the strangers, and some of them were tettered with a ghastly eruption. This leads to the episodical legend of the shepherd Syphilus, who dared to deride the Sun god, and of the king Alcithous, who accepted divine honours in his stead. The Sun, to requite the insolence of Syphilus, afflicted him with a dreadful sickness. It yielded to no cure until the nymph Ammericë initiated him in the proper lustral rites, and led him to the tree Hyacus. The poem ends with a panegyric of Guaiacum.

I have sketched the subject of the 'Syphilis' in outline because of its importance not only for the neo-Latin literature of the Renaissance, but also for the history of medical opinion. As a didactic poem, it is constructed with considerable art; the style, though prosaic, is forcible, and the meaning is always precise. Falling short of classic elegance, Fracastoro may still be said to have fulfilled the requirements of Vida, and to have added something male and vigorous peculiar to himself. His adulatory verses to Alessandro Farnese, Paul III., and Julius III. might be quoted as curious examples of ful-some flattery conveyed in a *barocco* style. They combine

---

[1] These phrases he finds for a fowling-piece :—

Cava terrificis horrentia bombis
Aera, et flammiferum tormenta imitantia fulmen.
Poemata Selecta, p. 101.

Papal cant with Pagan mannerism, Virgilian and Biblical phraseology, masculine gravity of diction and far-fetched conceits, in a strange amalgam, as awkward as it is ridiculous.[1]

Another group of Latin versifiers, with Bembo at their head, cultivated the elegy, the idyll, and the ode. The authors of their predilection were Catullus, Propertius, and Tibullus. Abandoning the attempt to mould Christian or modern material into classic form, they frankly selected Pagan motives, and adhered in spirit as well as style to their models. Two elegiac poems of Bembo's, the 'Priapus' and the 'Faunus ad Nympeum Flumen,' may be cited as flagrant specimens of sixteenth-century licentiousness.[2] Polished language and almost faultless versification are wasted upon themes of rank obscenity. The 'Priapus,' translated and amplified in Italian *ottava rima*, gained a popular celebrity beyond the learned circles for whom it was originally written. We may trace its influence in many infamous Capitoli of the burlesque poets. Bembo excelled in elegiac verse. In a poem entitled 'De Amicâ a Viro Servatâ,' he treated a characteristically Italian subject with something of Ovid's graceful humour.[3] A lover complains of living near his mistress, closely watched by her jealous husband. Here, as elsewhere, the morality is less to be admired than the versification ; and that the latter, in spite of Bembo's scrupulous attention to metre, is not perfect, may be gathered from this line :—

Tunc quos nunc habeo et quos sum olim habiturus amicos.

After reading hexameters so constructed we are tempted to shut the book with a groan, wondering how it was that a

---

[1] Cf. the passage about Alessandro Farnese's journeys—

Matre deâ comitante et iter monstrante nepoti—

and the reformation in Germany. *Poemata Selecta*, p. 125. The whole idyll addressed to Julius III., *ib.* pp. 130-135, is inconceivably uncouth.

[2] *Carmina Quinque Illustrium Poetarum*, pp. 4 and 9-11.

[3] *Ib.* pp. 18-23.

Pope's secretary and a prince of the Church should have
thought it worth his while to compose a poem so injurious to
his reputation as a moralist, or to preserve in it a verse so
little favourable to his fame as a Latinist.   More beautiful,
because more true to classic inspiration, is the elegy of
' Galatea.' [1]   The idyllic incidents suggest a series of pretty
pictures for basreliefs or decorative frescoes in the manner of
Albano.   Bembo's masterpiece, however, in the elegiac metre,
is a poem with 'De Galeso et Maximo' for its title.[2]   It was
composed, as the epigraph informs us, at the command of a
great man at Rome; but whether that great man was also
the greatest in Rome, and whether Maximus was another
name for Leo, is matter of conjecture.   The boy Galesus had
wronged Maximus, his master.   When reproved, he offered no
excuses, called no witnesses, uttered no prayers to Heaven,
indulged in no asseverations of innocence, shed no tears :—

> Nil horum aggreditur; sed tantum ingrata loquentis
>   Implicitus collo dulce pependit onus.
> Nec mora, cunctanti roseis tot pressa labellis
>   Oscula cœlitibus invidiosa dedit,
> Arida quot levibus florescit messis aristis,
>   Excita quot vernis floribus halat humus.
> Maxime, quid dubitas?   Si te piget, ipse tuo me
>   Pone loco : hæc dubitem non ego ferre mala.[3]

Bembo's talent lay in compositions of this kind.   His
verses, to quote the phrase of Gyraldus, were uniformly
' sweet, soft, and delicate.'   When he attempted work involv-

---

[1] *Carmina Quinque Illustrium Poetarum*, p. 7.   [2] *Ib.* p. 23.
[3]   None of these things he tried; but only ran,
           And clasped with his sweet arms the angry man;
           Hung on his neck, rained kisses forth that Heaven
           Envied from those red lips to mortals given;
           In number like ripe ears of ruddy corn,
           Or flowers beneath the breath of April born.
           Still doubting, Maximus?   Change place with me:
           Gladly I'd bear such infidelity.

ing more sustained effort of the intellect and greater variety
of treatment, he was not so successful.   His hexameter poem
'Benacus,' a description of the Lago di Garda, dedicated to
Gian Matteo Giberti, reads like an imitation of Catullus
without the Roman poet's grace of style or wealth of fancy.[1]
Among Bembo's most perfect compositions may be reckoned
his epitaphs on celebrated contemporaries.   The following
written for Poliziano, deserves quotation.[2] Not only is the
death of the scholar, following close upon that of his patron,
happily touched, but the last line pays a proper tribute to
Poliziano as an Italian poet :—

> Duceret extincto cum mors Laurente triumphum,
> Lætaque pullatis inveheretur equis,
> Respicit insano ferientem pollice chordas,
> Viscera singultu concutiente, virum.
> Mirata est, tenuitque jugum ; furit ipse, pioque
> Laurentem cunctos flagitat ore Deos :
> Miscebat precibus lacrymas, lacrymisque dolorem ;
> Verba ministrabat liberiora dolor.
> Risit, et antiquæ non immemor illa querelæ,
> Orphei Tartareæ cum patuere viæ,
> Hic etiam infernas tentat rescindere leges,
> Fertque suas, dixit, in mea jura manus.
> Protinus et flentem percussit dura poetam,
> Rupit et in medio pectora docta sono.
> Heu sic tu raptus, sic te mala fata tulerunt,
> Arbiter Ausoniæ, Politiane, lyræ.[3]

---

[1] *Carmina Quinque Illustrium Poetarum*, pp. 26–34.   [2] *Ib.* p. 38.
[3] 'When Lorenzo was dead, and Death went by in triumph, drawn
by her black horses, her eyes fell on one who madly struck the chords,
while sighs convulsed his breast. She turned, and stayed the car; he
storms and calls on all the gods for Lorenzo, mixing tears with prayers,
and sorrow with his tears, while sorrow suggests words of wilder freedom.   Death laughed; remembering her old grudge, when Orpheus
made his way to hell, she cried, "Lo, he too seeks to abrogate our laws,
and lays his hand upon my rights !" Nor more delay; she struck the
poet while he wept, and broke his heart-strings in the middle of his
sighs. Alas ! thus wast thou taken from us, ravished by harsh fate,
Politian, master of the Italian lyre !'

More richly endowed for poetry than Bembo was his fellow-countryman Andrea Navagero. Few Latin versifiers of the Renaissance combined so much true feeling and fancy with a style more pure and natural. Some of his little compositions, half elegy, half idyll, have the grace and freedom of the Greek Anthology.[1] There is a simple beauty in their motives, while the workmanship reminds us of chiselling in smooth waxy marble; unlike the Roman epigrammatists, Navagero avoided pointed terminations.[2] The picture of Narcissus dead and transformed to a flower, in the elegy of 'Acon,' might be quoted as a fair specimen of his manner :—

> Magna Parens, quæ cuncta leves producis in auras,
>   Totaque diverso germine picta nites ;
> Quæ passim arboribus, passim surgentibus herbis,
>   Sufficis omnifero larga alimenta sinu ;
> Excipe languentem puerum, moribundaque membra,
>   Æternumque tuâ fac, Dea, vivat ope.
> Vivet, et ille vetus Zephyro redeunte quotannis
>   In niveo candor flore perennis erit.[3]

The warnings addressed to his mistress in her country rambles, to beware of rustic gods, and the whole eclogue of 'Iolas,' are written in a rich and facile style, that makes us wonder whether some poet of the Græco-Roman period did not live again in Navagero.[4] Only here and there, as in the

[1] Notice especially 'Thyrsidis vota Veneri,' 'Invitatio ad amœnum fontem,' 'Leucippem amicam spe præmiorum invitat,' 'Vota Veneri ut amantibus faveat,' and 'In Almonem.'—*Carmina*, &c. pp. 52, 53, 54, 55.

[2] Paolo Giovio noticed this; in his *Elogia* he writes, '*Epigrammata non falsis aculeatisque finibus, sed tenerâ illâ et prædulci priscâ suavitate claudebat.*'

[3] 'Mighty mother, thou who bringest all things forth to breathe the liquid air, who shinest in thy painted robe of diverse budding lives, thou who from thy teeming bosom givest nourishment to trees and sprouting herbs in every region of the earth, take to thyself the fainting boy, cherish his dying limbs, and make him live for ever by thy aid. Yes, he shall live ; and that white loveliness of his, each year as spring returns, shall blossom in a snowy flower.'—*Carmina*, &c. p. 57.

[4] 'Ad Gelliam rusticantem,' *Carmina*, &c. pp. 64-66. 'Iolas,' *ib.* pp. 66-68.

case of all this neo-Latin writing, an awkward word or a
defective cadence breaks the spell, and reminds us that it
was an artificial thing. A few lines forming the exordium to
an unfinished poem on Italy may be inserted here for their
intrinsic interest :—

> Salve, cura Deûm, mundi felicior ora,
> Formosæ Veneris dulces salvete recessus :
> Ut vos post tantos animi mentisque labores
> Aspicio, lustroque libens ! ut munere vestro
> Sollicitas toto depello e pectore curas ! [1]

Navagero, we are told, composed these verses on his return
from a legation to Spain. Born in 1483, he spent his youth
and early manhood in assiduous study. Excessive application
undermined his health, and Giovio relates that he began to
suffer from *atra bilis*, or the melancholy of scholars. The
Venetian Senate had engaged him to compose the history of
the Republic in Latin ; this work was already begun when
illness forced him to abandon it. He was afterwards employed
in an unsuccessful mission to Charles V. and in diplomatic
business at the Court of France. He died at Blois of fever,
contracted in one of his hurried journeys. He was only forty-
six when he perished, bequeathing to immediate posterity the
fame of a poet at least equal to the ancients. In that age of
affectation and effort the natural flow of Navagero's verse,
sensuous without coarseness and highly coloured without
abuse of epithets, raised a chorus of applause that may strike
the modern student as excessive. The memorial poems written
on his death praise the purity of sentiment and taste which
made him burn a copy of Martial yearly to the chaste Muses.[2]

---

[1] 'Hail, darling of the gods, thou happiest spot of earth ! hail
chosen haunt of beauty's queen ! What joy I feel to see you thus again,
and tread your shores after so many toils endured in mind and soul !
How from my heart by your free gift I cast all anxious cares !'—*Carmina*, &c. p. 84.

[2] See the Hendecasyllabics of Johannes Matthæus, *Carmina*, &c.
p. 86.

One friend calls upon the Nereids to build his tomb by the silent waters of the lagoons, and bids the Faun of Italy lament with broken reeds.[1] Another prophesies that his golden poems will last as many years as there are flowers in spring, or grapes in autumn, or storms upon the sea, or stars in heaven, or kisses in Catullus, or atoms in the universe of Lucretius.[2]

A place very close to Navagero might be claimed for Francesco Maria Molsa, a nobleman of Modena, who enjoyed great fame at Rome for his Latin and Italian poetry. After a wild life of pleasure he died at the age of forty-one, worn out with love and smitten by the plague of the Renaissance. The sweetest of his elegies celebrate the charms of Faustina Mancini, his favourite mistress. In spite of what Italians would call their *morbidezza*, it is impossible not to feel some contempt for the polished fluency, the sensual relaxation, of these soulless verses. A poem addressed to his friends upon his sick bed, within sight of certain death, combines the author's melody of cadence with a certain sobriety of thought and tender dignity of feeling.[3] It is, perhaps, of all his compositions the worthiest to live. The following couplets describe the place which he would choose for his sepulchre :—

> Non operosa peto titulos mihi marmora ponant,
>   Nostra sed accipiat fictilis ossa cadus ;
> Exceptet gremio quæ mox placidissima tellus,
>   Immites possint ne nocuisse feræ.
> Rivulus hæc circum dissectus obambulet, unda
>   Clivoso qualis tramite ducta sonat ;
> Exiguis stet cæsa notis super ossa sepulta,
>   Nomen et his servet parva tabella meum :
> Hic jacet ante annos crudeli tabe peremptus
>   Molsa ; ter injecto pulvere, pastor, abi.

---

[1] Basilius Zanchius, *Carmina*, &c. p. 85.
[2] M. Antonius Flaminius, *ib.* p. 85.
[3] *Poemata Selecta*, pp. 203–206. An elegy written by Janus Etruscus, Pope's *Poemata Italorum*, vol. ii. p. 25, on a similar theme, though very inferior to Molsa's, may be compared with it.

Forsitan in putrem longo post tempore glebam
  Vertar, et hæc flores induet urna novos;
Populus aut potius abruptis artubus alba
  Formosâ exsurgam conspicienda comâ.
Scilicet huc diti pecoris comitata magistro
  Conveniet festo pulchra puella die;
Quæ molles ductet choreas, et veste recinctâ
  Ad certos nôrit membra movere modos.[1]

The Paganism of the Renaissance, exchanging Christian
rites for old mythologies, and classic in the very tomb, has
rarely found sweeter expression than in this death song.
We trace in it besides a note of modern feeling, the romantic
sense of community with nature in the immortality of trees
and flowers.[2]

Castiglione cannot claim comparison with Navagero for
sensuous charm and easy flow of verse. Nor has he those
touches of genuine poetry which raise Molsa above the level
of a fluent versifier. His Latin exercises, however, offer
much that is interesting to a student of Renaissance literature; while the depth of feeling and the earnestness of
thought in his clear and powerful hexameters surpass the
best efforts of Bembo's artificial muse. When we read the

[1] 'I ask for no monument of wrought marble to proclaim my titles:
let a vase of baked clay receive these bones. Let earth, quietest of
resting-places, take them to herself, and save them from the injury of
ravening wolves. And let a running stream divide its waters round my
grave, drawn with the sound of music from a mountain-flank. A little
tablet carved with simple letters will be enough to mark the spot, and
to preserve my name: "Here lies Molsa, slain before his day by wasting sickness: cast dust upon him thrice, and go thy way, gentle shepherd." It may be that after many years I shall turn to yielding clay,
and my tomb shall deck herself with flowers; or, better, from my limbs
shall spring a white poplar, and in its beauteous foliage I shall rise
into the light of heaven. To this place will come, I hope, some lovely
maid attended by the master of the flock; and she shall dance above
my bones and move her feet to rhythmic music.'

[2] For the picture of the girl dancing on the lover's grave, cf. Omar
Khayyam. Cf. too Walt Whitman's metaphor for grass—'the beautiful
uncut hair of graves.'

idyll entitled ' Alcon,' a lamentation for the friend whom
he had loved in youth—

> Alcon deliciæ Musarum et Apollinis, Alcon
> Pars animæ, cordis pars Alcon maxima nostri—[1]

we are impelled to question how far Milton owed the form
of ' Lycidas ' to these Italian imitations of the Græco-Roman
style.   What seemed false in tone to Johnson, what still
renders that elegy the stumbling-block of taste to immature
and unsympathetic students, is the highly artificial form
given to natural feeling.   Grief clothes herself in metaphors,
and, abstaining from the direct expression of poignant
emotion, dwells on thoughts and images that have a beauty
of their own for solace.   Nor is it in this quality of art alone
that ' Lycidas ' reminds us of Renaissance Latin verse.   The
curious blending of allusions to Church and State with
pastoral images is no less characteristic of the Italian manner.
As in ' Lycidas,' so also in these lines from Castiglione's
' Alcon,' the truth of sorrow transpires through a thin veil of
bucolic romance :—

> Heu miserande puer, fatis surrepte malignis !
> Non ego te posthac, pastorum adstante coronâ,
> Victorem aspiciam volueri certare sagittâ ;
> Aut jaculo, aut durâ socios superare palæstrâ.
> Non tecum posthac molli resupinus in umbrâ
> Effugiam longos æstivo tempore soles :
> Non tua vicinos mulcebit fistula montes,
> Docta nec umbrosæ resonabunt carmina valles:
> Non tua corticibus toties inscripta Lycoris,
> Atque ignis Galatea meus nos jam simul ambos
> Audierint ambæ nostros cantare furores.
> Nos etenim a teneris simul usque huc viximus annis,
> Frigora pertulimusque æstus noctesque diesque,
> Communique simul sunt parta armenta labore.

---

[1] ' Alcon, the darling of Phœbus and the Muses ; Alcon, a part of
my own soul; Alcon, the greatest part of my own heart.'—*Carmina
Quinque Poetarum*, p. 89.

Rura mea hæc tecum communia; viximus una:
Te moriente igitur curnam mihi vita relicta est?
Heu male me ira Deûm patriis abduxit ab oris,
Ne manibus premerem morientia lumina amicis.[1]

Castiglione's most polished exercises are written on ficti·
tious subjects in elegiac metre. Thus he feigns a letter from
his wife, in the style of the 'Heroidum Epistolæ,' praying
him to beware of Rome's temptations, and to keep his heart
for her.[2] Again he warns his mistress to avoid the perils of
the sea-beach, where the Tritons roam :—

Os informe illis, rictus, oculique minaces,
Asperaque anguineo cortice membra rigent:
Barba impexa, ingens, algâ limoque virenti
Oblita, oletque gravi lurida odore coma.[3]

In these couplets we seem to read a transcript from some
fresco of Mantegna or Julio Romano. Two long elegies are
devoted to the theme of marine monsters, and the tale of
Hippolytus is introduced to clinch the poet's argument.
Among Castiglione's poems of compliment, forming a pleasant

[1] 'Alas! poor youth, withdrawn from us by fate malign. Never
again shall I behold thee, while the shepherds stand around, win
prizes with thy flying shafts or spear, or wrestle for the crown; never
again with thee reclining in the shade shall I all through a summer's
day avoid the sun. No more shall thy pipe soothe the neighbouring
hills, the vales repeat thy artful songs. No more shall thy Lycoris,
whose name inscribed by thee the woods remember, and my Galatea
hear us both together chaunt our loves. For we like brothers lived
our lives till now from infancy: heat and cold, days and nights, we
bore; our herds were reared with toil and care together. These fields
of mine were also thine: we lived one common life. Why, then, when
thou must die, am I still left to live? Alas! in evil hour the wrath
of Heaven withdrew me from my native land, nor suffered me to close
thy lids with a friend's hands!'—*Carmina*, &c. p. 91.

[2] *Ib.* p. 100.

[3] 'Hideous is their face, their grinning mouth, their threatening
eyes, and their rough limbs are stiff with snaky scales; their beard
hangs long and wide, uncombed, tangled with sea-weed and green ooze,
and their dusky hair smells rank of brine.'—*Ib.* p. 103.

illustration to his book of the ' Courtier,' may be mentioned
the lines on ' Elisabetta Gonzaga singing.' [1] Nor can I omit
the most original of his elegies, written, or at least conceived,
in the camp of Julius before Mirandola.[2] Walking by night
in the trenches under the beleaguered walls, Castiglione
meets the ghost of Lodovico Pico, who utters a lamentation
over the wrongs inflicted on his city and his race. The
roar of cannon cuts short this monologue, and the spectre
vanishes into darkness with a groan. During his long
threnody the prince of Mirandola apostrophises the warlike
Pope in these couplets :—

> O Pater, O Pastor populorum, O maxime mundi
>   Arbiter, humanum qui genus omne regis ;
> Justitiæ pacisque dator placidæque quietis,
>   Credita cui soli est vita salusque hominum ;
> Quem Deus ipse Erebi fecit Cœlique potentem,
>   Ut nutu pateant utraque regna tuo ! [3]

When the spiritual authority of the Popes came thus
to be expressed in Latin verse, it was impossible not to treat
them as deities. The temptation to apply to them the language of Roman religion was too great ; the double opportunity of flattering their vanity as Pontiffs, and their ears
as scholars, was too attractive to be missed. In another
place Castiglione used the following phrases about Leo :—

> Nec culpanda tua est mora, nam præcepta Deorum
>   Non fas, nec tutum est spernere velle homini :
> Esse tamen fertur clementia tanta Leonis
>   Ut facili humanas audiat ore preces.[4]

---

[1] 'De Elisabetta Gonzaga canente,' *Carmina*, &c. p. 97. Cf. Bembo's
'Ad Lucretiam Borgiam,' *ib.* p. 14, on a similar theme.

[2] *Ib.* p. 95.

[3] 'O father, O shepherd of the nations, O great master of the world
who rulest all the human race, giver of justice, peace, and tranquil ease ;
thou to whom alone is committed the life and salvation of men, whom
God Himself made lord of hell and heaven, that either realm might
open at thy nod.'

[4] 'I do not blame thee for delaying thy return, since neither is it

Navagero called Julius II. *novus ex alto demissus Olympo Deus* (a new God sent down from heaven to earth), and declared that the people of Italy, in thanksgiving for his liberation of their country from the barbarians, would pay him yearly honours with prayer and praise :—

> Ergo omnes, veluti et Phœbo Panique, quotannis
> Pastores certis statuent tibi sacra diebus,
> Magne Pater ; nostrisque diu cantabere silvis.
> Te rupes, te saxa, cavæ te, Maxime Juli,
> Convalles, nemorumque frequens iterabit imago.
> At vero nostris quæcumque in saltibus usquam
> Quercus erit, ut quæque suos dant tempora flores,
> Semper erit variis ramos innexa coronis ;
> Inscriptumque geret felici nomine truncum.
> Tum quoties pastum expellet, pastasve reducet
> Nostrum aliquis pecudes ; toties id mente revolvens
> Ut liceat, factum esse tuo, Pater optime, ductu ;
> Nullus erit, qui non libet tibi lacte recenti,
> Nullus erit qui non teneros tibi nutriat agnos.
> Quin audire preces nisi dedignabere agrestes,
> Tu nostra ante Deos in vota vocaberis omnes.
> Ipse ego bina tibi solenni altaria ritu,
> Et geminos sacrâ e quercu lauroque virenti
> Vicino lucos Nanceli in litore ponam.[1]

It will be remembered that the oak was the ensign of the Della Rovere family, so that when the poets exalted

safe nor right for man to set at naught a God's command ; and yet so great is Leo's kindness said to be that he inclines a ready ear to human prayers.'—*Ib.* p. 102.

[1] 'Therefore shall all our shepherds pay thee divine honours, as to Pan or Phœbus, on fixed days, great Father ; and long shalt thou be celebrated in our forests. Thy praise, Julius the Great, the cliffs, the rocks, the hollow valleys, and the woodland echoes shall repeat. Wherever in our groves an oak tree stands, as spring and summer bring the flowers, its branches shall be hung with wreaths, its trunk shall be inscribed with thy auspicious name. As often as our shepherds drive the flocks afield, or bring them pastured home, each one, remembering that he does this under thy protection, shall pour libations of new milk forth to thee, and rear thee tender lambs for sacrifice. Nay, if thou spurn not rustic prayers, before all gods shall we invoke

Julius to Olympus, they were not in want of a tree sacred to the new deity. To trace this Pagan flattery of the Popes through all its forms would be a tedious business. It will be enough to quote Poliziano's ' Sapphics ' to Innocent VIII. :—

> Roma cui paret dominusque Tibris,
> Qui vicem summi geris hic Tonantis,
> Qui potes magnum reserare et idem
> Claudere cœlum.[1]

A more quaint confusion of Latin mythology and mediæval superstition, more glibly and trippingly conveyed in flimsy verse, can hardly be imagined ; and yet even this, I think, is beaten by the ponderous conceits of Fracastoro, who, through the mouth of the goat-footed Pan, saluted Julius III. as the mountain of salvation, playing on his name Del Monte :—

> Hoc in Monte Dei pecudes pascentur et agni,
> Graminis æterni pingues et velleris aurei ;
> Exsilient et aquæ vivæ, quibus ubera capræ
> Grandia distendant, distendant ubera vaccæ.[2]

The mountain soon becomes a shepherd, and the shepherd not only rules the people, and feeds the sheep of God, but chains the monsters of the Reformation to a rock in Caucasus, and gives peace and plenty to Italy :—

> Æternis illum numeris ad sidera tollent,
> Heroemque, deumque, salutiferumque vocabunt.[3]

---

thee in our supplications. I myself will build and dedicate to thee two altars, and will plant twin groves of sacred oak and laurel evergreen for thee.'—*Carmina*, &c. pp. 58, 59.

[1] ' Thou whom Rome obeys, and royal Tiber, who wieldest upon earth the Thunderer's power, whose it is to lock and open the gates of heaven.'—*Ib.* p. 260.

[2] ' In this mountain of the Lord shall flocks and herds feed, fat with eternal pastures and golden-fleeced. Living waters too shall leap forth, wherewith the goats shall swell their udders, and the kine like-wise.'—*Poemata Selecta*, p. 132.

[3] ' Him with immortal verse the poets shall exalt to heaven, and call him hero, god, and saviour.'—*Ib.* p. 133.

Returning to Castiglione : I have already spoken of his epitaph on Raphael and his description of the newly-discovered 'Ariadne.'[1] The latter exercise in rhetoric competes with Sadoleto's laboured hexameters on the Laocoon. These verses, frigid as a prize poem in our estimation, moved Bembo to enthusiasm. When they appeared he wrote to Sadoleto, 'I have read your poem on Laocoon a hundred times. O wonder-working bard! Not only have you made for us, as it were, a second statue to match that masterpiece ; but you have engraved upon my mind the very statue itself.' This panegyric stirs a smile when we compare it with Sadoleto's own prolusion, the fruit of a grave intellect and cultivated taste rather than of genius and inspiration.[2]

Time would fail to tell of all the later Latin poets—of La Casa's polished lyrics in the style of Horace, of Amalteo's waxen eclogues, of Aonio Paleario's fantastic hexameters upon the 'Immortality of the Soul,'[3] of Strozzi's elegies, of Ariosto's epigrams, and Calcagnini's learned muse. When I repeat that every educated man wrote Latin verses in that century, and that all who could committed their productions to the press, enough has been said to prove the impossibility of dealing more than superficially with so vast a mass of meritorious mediocrity.

One name remains to be rescued from the decent obscurity

[1] See above, pp. 312, 317.
[2] See *Carmina Quinque Poetarum*, pp. 318-336.
[3] A didactic poem in three books ; Pope's *Poemata Italorum*, vol. i. pp. 211-270. The description of the Resurrection, the Last Judgment, and the entrance of the blessed into Paradise, forming the conclusion of the last book, is an excellent specimen of *barocco* style and bathos. Virgil had written, ' *Ite domum pasti, si quis pudor, ite juvenci !* ' Paleario makes the Judge address the damned souls thus : ' *Ite domum in tristem, si quis pudor, ite ruentes,*' &c. How close Milton's path lay to the worst faults in poetry, and how wonderfully he escaped, may well be calculated by the study of such verse as this.

of the 'Delitiæ Poetarum Italorum.' Marcantonio Flaminio was born at Seravalle in 1498. He came, while yet a young man, to the Court of Leo armed with Latin poetry for his credentials. No better claim on patronage from Pope or cardinal could be preferred in that age of twanging lyres. At Rome Flaminio lived in the service of Alessandro Farnese, whose hospitality he afterwards repaid with verses honourable alike to poet and patron by their freedom from vulgar flattery. The atmosphere of a Court, however, was uncongenial to Flaminio. Fond of country life, addicted to serious studies, sober in his tastes, and cheerful in his spirits, pious, and unaffectedly unambitious, he avoided the stream of the great world and lived retired. Community of interests brought him into close connection with the Cardinals Pole and Contarini, from whom he caught so much of the Reformation spirit as a philosophical Italian could assimilate; but it was not in his modest and quiet nature to raise the cry of revolt against authority.[1] The most distinguished wits and scholars of the age were among his intimate friends. Both his poems and his correspondence reflect an agreeable light upon the literary society of the late Renaissance. The Latin verses, with which we are at present occupied, breathe genuine piety, healthful simplicity, and moral purity, in strong contrast with the neopaganism of the Roman circle. These qualities suit the robust style, clear, terse, and nervous, he knew how to use. It is pleasant to close the series of Italian Latinists with one who combined the best art of his century with the temper of a republican and the spirit of a Christian.

The most prominent quality of Flaminio as a poet is love

---

[1] This epigram on Savonarola shows Flaminio's sympathy with the preachers of pure doctrine:—

> Dum fera flamma tuos, Hieronyme, pascitur artus,
>   Relligio, sacras dilaniata comas,
> Flevit, et o, dixit, crudeles parcite flammæ,
>   Parcite, sunt isto viscera nostra rogo.

of the country. Three little compositions describing his own farm are animated with the enthusiasm of genuine affection.[1] We feel that no mere reminiscence of Catullus makes him write—

> Jam vos revisam, jam juvabit arbores
>   Manu paternâ consitas
> Videre, jam libebit in cubiculo
>   Molles inire somnulos.[2]

Nor is it an idle prayer he addresses to the Muses in these lines:—

> At vos, o Heliconiæ puellæ,
> Queis fontes et amœna rura cordi,
> Si carâ mihi luce cariores
> Estis, jam miserescite obsecrantis,
> Meque, urbis strepitu tumultuosæ
> Ereptum, in placido locate agello.[3]

He is never tired of contrasting the pleasures of the country with the noise and weariness of Rome :—

> Ipse miser tumultuosâ
> Urbe detinear; tibi benignus
> Dedit Jupiter in remoto agello
> Latentem placidâ frui quiete,
> Inter Socraticos libros, et inter
> Nymphas et Satyros, nihil profani
> Curantem populi leves honores.[4]

Flaminio's thought of the country is always connected

---

[1] 'Ad Agellum suum.'—*Poemata Selecta*, pp. 155, 156, 177.

[2] 'Now shall I see you once again; now shall I have the joy of gazing on the trees my father planted, and falling into gentle slumber in his little room.'

[3] 'Maidens of Helicon, who love the fountains and the pleasant fields, as you are dearer to me than the dear light, have pity now upon your suppliant, take me from the tumult of the noisy town, and place me in my tranquil farm.'

[4] 'I, poor wretch, am prisoned in the noisy town. Kind Jupiter allows you, secluded in your distant farm, to take the joys of peace among Socratic books, among the nymphs and satyrs, unheeding the light honours of the vulgar crowd.'—'Ad Honoratum Fascitellum,' *Poemata Selecta*, p. 178.

with the thought of study. The picture of a tranquil scholar's
life among the fields, diversified by sport and simple pleasures
of the rustic folk, gives freshness to his hendecasyllables,
whether addressed to his patron Alessandro Farnese, or to his
friends Galeazzo Florimonte and Francesco Torriani : [1]—

> Inde ocellos
> Ut primum sopor incubans gravabit,
> Jucundissime amice, te sub antrum
> Ducam, quod croceis tegunt corymbis
> Serpentes hederæ, imminensque laurus
> Suaviter foliis susurrat : at tu
> Ne febrim metuas gravedinemve ;
> Est enim locus innocens : ubi ergo
> Hic satis requieveris, legentur
> Lusus Virgilii, et Syracusani
> Vatis, quo nihil est magis venustum,
> Nihil dulcius, ut mihi videtur.
> Cum se fregerit æstus, in virenti
> Convalle spatiabimur ; sequetur
> Brevis cœna ; redibis inde ad urbem. [2]

One of Flaminio's best poems is written from his friend
Stefano Sauli's villa near Genoa. [3] It describes how he
spends his time between the philosophy of Aristotle and the
verses of Catullus, while Sauli at his side devotes himself to
Cicero. The fall of evening lures them from their study to
the sea-beach : perched upon a water-girded rock, they angle
with long reeds for fishes, or watch the white sails on the
purple waves. The same theme is repeated in a copy of

---

[1] *Poemata Selecta*, pp. 153, 169, 173.

[2] 'Then, when sleep descends upon your eyes, best friend of mine,
I'll lead you to a cave o'ercurtained by the wandering ivy's yellow
bunches, whereby the sheltering laurel murmurs with her gently waving
leaves. Fear no fever or dull headache. The place is safe. So when
you are rested, we will read the rustic songs of Virgil or Theocritus ;
sweet and more charming verse I know not ; and after the day's heat is
past, we will stroll in some green valley. A light supper follows, and
then you shall return to town.'—*Ib.* p. 174.

[3] 'Ad Christophorum Longolium,' *Ib.*

hexameters addressed to Sauli.[1] Flaminio had fallen ill of
fever at Rome. To quit the city was his cure :—

> Scilicet ut Romæ corruptas fugimus auras,
> Et riguos patriæ montes saltusque salubres
> Venimus, effœtos venit quoque robur in artus :
> Diffugit macies, diffugit corpore pallor ;
> Et somnus vigiles irrepsit blandus ocellos,
> Quem neque desiliens crepitanti rivulus undâ,
> Nec Lethea mihi duxere papavera quondam.[2]

Sauli, for his part, is congratulated on having exchanged
the cares of Church and State for Ciceronian studies among
his laurel groves and gleaming orange gardens.

Flaminio's intimate relations with the ablest men of the
century, those especially who were engaged in grave and
Christian studies, add extrinsic interest to his fugitive pieces.
In one poem he alludes to the weak health of Cardinal Pole ;[3]
in another he compares Plato's description of the ideal
republic with Contarini's work upon the magistrates and
commonwealth of Venice :—

> Descripsit ille maximus quondam Plato
> Longis suorum ambagibus voluminum,
> Quis civitatis optimus foret status :
> Sed hunc ab ipsâ sæculorum origine
> Nec ulla vidit, nec videbit civitas.
> At Contarenus optimam rempublicam
> Parvi libelli disputationibus
> Illam probavit esse, plus millesima
> Quam cernit æstas Adriatico in mari
> Florere pace, litteris, pecuniâ.[4]

[1] *Poemata Selecta*, p. 163.

[2] 'No sooner had I left Rome's tainted air for the clear streams
and healthful forests of my native land, than strength returned into my
wasted limbs ; my body lost the pallor and emaciation of disease, and
sweet sleep crept upon my wakeful eyes, such as no waters falling with
a tinkling sound or Lethe's poppies had induced before.'

[3] *Poemata Selecta*, p. 162.

[4] 'Plato, the greatest of sages, once described in his long volumes
the best form of a State ; but this from the beginning of the world till

When Vittoria Colonna died, Flaminio wrote a lamentation on the loss he had sustained, and on the extinction of so great a light for Italy. These verses are remarkable for their sobriety and strength :—

> Cui mens candida, candidique mores,
> Virtus vivida, comitasque sancta,
> Cœleste ingenium, eruditioque
> Rara, nectare dulciora verba,
> Summa nobilitas, decora vultûs
> Majestas, opulenta sed bonorum
> Et res et domus usque aperta ad usus.[1]

The same firm and delicate touch in the delineation of character gives value to the lines written on his father's death :—

> Vixisti, genitor, bene ac beate,
> Nec pauper, neque dives, eruditus
> Satis, et satis eloquens, valente
> Semper corpore, mente sanâ, amicis
> Jucundus, pietate singulari.
> Nunc lustris bene sexdecim peractis
> Ad divûm proficisceris beatas
> Oras ; i, genitor, tuumque natum
> Olympi cito siste tecum in arce.[2]

At the risk of extending this notice of Flaminio's poetry beyond due limits, I must quote from a copy of verses sent to

now hath never yet been seen, nor will it afterwards be seen in any city. Contarini in his little book has proved that the best commonwealth is that which now for more than a thousand years has flourished in the Adriatic with peace, letters, and wealth.'—*Poemata Selecta*, p. 162.

[1] 'Ad Hieronymum Turrianum,' *ib.* p. 168. 'Her mind was pure, her manners pure; her virtue lively, her courtesy without a taint of earth ; her intellect was heavenly, her learning rare ; her words sweeter than nectar ; her nobility the highest; her features beautiful in their majesty ; her wealth liberally open to the use of good men.'

[2] 'Well and happily hast thou lived, my father; neither poor nor rich ; learned enough and eloquent enough ; of vigorous body and of healthy mind ; pleasant to thy friends, and in thy piety unrivalled. Now, after sixteen lustres finished, thou goest to the regions of the blest. Go, father, and soon greet thy son, to stay with thee in heaven's high seat.'—'Ad Patrem morientem,' *Poemata Selecta*, p. 157.

Alessandro Farnese, together with a volume containing the Latin *prolusiones* of the North Italian scholars:—

> Hos tibi lepidissimos poetas
> Dono, tempora quos tulere nostra,
> Fortunata nimis, nimis beata
> Nostra tempora, quæ suos Catullos,
> Tibullos, et Horatios, suosque
> Marones genuere. Quis putasset,
> Post tot sæcula tam tenebricosa,
> Et tot Ausoniæ graves ruinas,
> Tanta lumina tempore uno in una
> Tam brevi regione Transpadanâ
> Oriri potuisse ? quæ vel ipsa
> Sola barbarie queant fugatâ
> Suum reddere litteris Latinis
> Splendorem, veteremque dignitatem.[1]

There is the whole of humanism in this passage—the belief in the unity of Italian civilisation, the conviction that the Middle Ages were but an interruption of historic continuity, the confidence in the restoration of classic literature, and the firm hope that Latin would never cease to be the language of culture. Flaminio says nothing, unless parenthetically, about the real woes of his country. The tyranny of the Spaniard and the violence of the German are reckoned with the old wrongs of the Goth and the Vandal in one phrase—'*tot graves ruinas.*' He does not touch upon the

---

[1] *Poemata Selecta*, p. 166. ' These most graceful poets I give you, the offspring of our too, too happy times, which have produced their Catullus and their Horace, their Tibullus and their Maro. Who could have thought, after so many ages of such darkness, and all the ruin that has weighed on Italy, that so many lights could have arisen at one epoch in one little region of the land above the Po ? They alone are enough to put to flight the gloom of barbarism, and to restore its antique glory and own splendour to Latin literature.' After this he goes on to add that these poets will confer eternal lustre on Italy. Not only the northern nations of Europe, but America also has begun to study Latin ; and races in another hemisphere will take their culture from these pages. The Cardinal is finally reminded that immortality of fame awaits him in their praises.

dismemberment of Italy into mutually jealous and suspicious
States: for him the Italian nation, even in a dream, has no
existence. He is satisfied with a literary ideal. Too fortunate,
too blessed, are these days of ours, in spite of Florence extinguished, Rome sacked, Milan devastated, Venice curbed,
because, forsooth, Bembo and Fracastoro have made a pinch-
beck age of poetry. Here lay the incurable weakness of the
humanistic movement. The vanity of the scholar, determined
to seek the present in the past, building the walls of Troy
anew with borrowed music, and singing in falsetto while
Rome was burning—this blindness to the actual situation of
Italy was scarcely less pernicious, scarcely less a sign of
incapacity for civil life than the selfishness of the Despots
or the egotism of the Papacy. Italy was foredoomed to lose
her place among the nations at the very moment when she
was recovering culture for the modern world ; and when that
culture was recovered through her industry and genius, not
she, but the races of the North, began to profit by the acquisition—not her imitations of the Latin Muse, but the new
languages of Europe were destined to prevail and lead the age.

Another point for observation is that the centre of
humanistic studies has shifted.[1] Florence, disillusioned,
drained of strength, and sucked dry by the tyrants, holds
her tongue. The schools of Naples and of Rome are silent.
Lombardy is now the mother of poets, who draw their
inspiration no longer from Valdarno or the myrtle groves of
Posilippo, but from the blue waves of Garda.[2] The university
where science still flourishes is Padua. The best professors
of the classics, Celio Calcagnini and Lilius Gyraldus, teach
at Ferrara. Bembo, the dictator of letters for his century,
Navagero, the sweetest versifier, Contarini, the most sober

[1] ' Tam brevi regione Transpadanâ.'
[2] Cf. Bembo's *Benacus*, Bonfadio's *Gazani Vici Descriptio*, Fracastoro's *Ad Franciscum Turrianum Veronensem*, &c.

student, are Venetians.   Stefano Sauli, the author of a Ciceronian treatise on the Christian hero, is a patrician of Genoa. Sadoleto and Molsa are Modenese. Verona claims Fracastoro and the Torriani. Imola is the mother city of Flaminio. Castiglione and Capilupo are natives of Mantua ; Amalteo and Vida of Forli and Cremona ; Bonfadio and Archio of Lake Garda. If we seek the causes of this change, we find them partly in the circumstance that Venice at this period was free, while Ferrara still retained her independence under native princes ; partly also in the fact that Florence had already overtaxed her intellectual energies. Like a creeping paralysis, the extinction of liberty and spiritual force was gradually invading all the members of the Italian community. The Revival of Learning came to an end, as far as Italy was concerned, in these Transpadane poets.

To trace the history of philosophic thought, set in motion by the Renaissance and stamped out by the Counter-Reformation, and to describe the aftergrowth of art and literature encouraged by the Catholic reaction, must form the subject of a separate inquiry.

I hope, if I have time and strength, after the completion of my work on the Renaissance, to trace this sequel in a volume on 'Italy and the Council of Trent.' To this chapter of Italian history will also belong the philosophy of the sixteenth century, the poetry of Tasso, the painting of the Bolognese masters, and the new music of Palestrina.

CHAPTER IX

CONCLUSION

General Survey—The Part played in the Revival by the Chief Cities
—Preoccupation with Scholarship in spite of War and Conquest—
Place of the Humanists in Society—Distributors of Praise and
Blame—Flattery and Libels—Comparison with the Sophists—The
Form preferred to the Matter of Literature—Ideal of Culture as
an end in itself—Suspicion of Zealous Churchmen—Intrusion of
Humanism into the Church—Irreligion of the Humanists—Gyraldi's
' Progymnasma '—Ariosto — Bohemian Life — Personal Immorality
—Want of Fixed Principles—Professional Vanity—Literary Pride—
Estimate of Humanistic Literature—Study of Style—Influence of
Cicero—Valla's ' Elegantiæ '—Stylistic Puerilities—Value attached to
Rhetoric—' Oratore '—Moral Essays—Epistolography — Histories—
Critical and Antiquarian Studies—Large Appreciation of Antiquity
—Liberal Spirit—Poggio and Jerome of Prague—Humanistic Type
of Education—Its Diffusion through Europe—Future Prospects—
Decay of Learning in Italy.

In tracing the history of the Revival, we have seen how the
impulse, first communicated by Petrarch, was continued by
Boccaccio and his immediate successors. We have watched
the enthusiasm for antiquity strike root in Florence, spread
to Rome, and penetrate the Courts of Italy. One city after
another receives the light and hands it on, until the whole
cycle of study has been traversed and the vigour of the
nation is exhausted. Florence discovers manuscripts, founds
libraries, learns Greek, and leads the movement of the fifteenth century. Naples criticises; Rome translates; Mantua
and Ferrara form a system of education; Venice commits
the literature of the classics to the press. By the combined

and successive activity of the chief Italian centres, not only is the culture of antiquity regained ; it is also appropriated in all its various branches, discussed and illustrated, placed beyond the reach of accident, and delivered over in its integrity to Europe. The work thus performed by the Italians was begun in peace ; but it had to be continued under the pressure of wars and national disasters unparalleled in the history of any other modern people. Not for a single moment did the students relax their energy. In the midst of foreign armies, deafened by the roar of cannon and the tumult of sacked towns, exiled from their homes, robbed of their books, deprived of their subsistence, they advanced to their end with the irresistible obstinacy of insects. The drums and tramplings of successive conquests and invasions by four warlike nations—Frenchmen, Spaniards, Germans, Swiss—could not disturb them. Drop by drop, Italy was being drained of blood ; from the first the only question was which of her assailants should possess the beauty of her corpse. Yet the student, intent upon his manuscripts, paid but little heed. So non-existent was the sense of nationality in Italy that the Italians did not know they were being slowly murdered. When the agony was over, and the ruin was accomplished, they congratulated themselves on being still the depositaries of polite literature. Nations that are nations, seek to inspire fear, or at least respect. The Italians were contented with admiration, and looked confidently to the world for gratitude. The task of two toilsome, glorious centuries had been accomplished. The chasm between Rome and the Renaissance was bridged over, and a plain way was built for the progressive human spirit. Italy, downtrodden in the mire of blood and ruins, should still lead the van and teach the peoples. It was a sublime delusion, the last phase of an impulse so powerful in its origin that to prophesy an ending was impossible. Yet how delusive was the expectation is proved by the immediate history of Italy, enslaved and decadent, outstripped by the nations she had taught, and scorned by the world that owed her veneration.

The humanists, who were the organ of this intellectual movement, formed, as we have seen, a literary commonwealth, diffused through all the Courts and cities of Italy. As the secretaries of Popes and princes, as the chancellors of republics, as orators on all occasions of public and private ceremony, they occupied important posts of influence, and had the opportunity of leavening society with their opinions. Furthermore, we have learned to know them in their capacity of professors at the universities, of house-tutors in the service of noblemen, and of authors. Closely connected among themselves by their feuds no less than by their friendships, and working to one common end of scholarship, it was inevitable that these men, after the enthusiasm for antiquity had once become the fashion, should take the lead and mould the genius of the nation. Their epistles, invectives, treatises, and panegyrics, formed the study of an audience that embraced all cultivated minds in Italy. Thus the current literature of humanism played the same part in the fifteenth century as journalism in the nineteenth, and the humanists had the same kind of coherence in relation to the public as the *quatrième état* of modern times. The respect they inspired as the arbiters of praise and blame, was only equalled by their vast pretensions. Eugenius IV., living at the period of their highest influence, is reported to have said that they were as much to be feared for their malice as to be loved for their learning. While they claimed the power of conferring an immortality of honour or dishonour, no one dared to call their credit with posterity in question. Nothing seemed more dreadful than the fate reserved for Paul II. in the pages of Platina ; and even so robust a ruler as Francesco Sforza sought to buy the praises of Filelfo. Flattery in all its branches, fulsome and delicate, wholesale and allusive, was developed by them as an art whereby to gain their living. The official history of this period is rendered almost worthless by its sustained note of panegyrical laudation. Our ears are deafened with the eulogies of petty patrons transformed into Mæcenases, of carpet knights compared to Leonidas, of tyrants equalled with Augustus, and of generals who never looked on blood-shed tricked out as Hannibals or Scipios. As a pendant to panegyric, the art of abuse reached its climax in the invectives whereby the scholars sought to hand their comrades down to all time 'immortally immerded,' or to vilify the public enemies of their employers. As in the case of praise, so also in the case of blame, it is impossible to attach importance to the writings of the humanists. Their vaulting ambition to depreciate each other overleaped itself. All their literature of defamation serves now only to throw light on the general impurity of an age in which such monstrous charges carried weight. Unluckily, this double vice of humanism struck deep roots into Italian literature. Without the scholars of the fifteenth century, it is hardly possible that such a brigand as Pietro Aretino, who levied black mail from princes at the point of his venomous quill, or such an unprincipled biographer as Paolo Giovio, who boasted that he wrote with a golden or a silver pen, as pleased him best, could have existed. Bullying and fawning tainted the very source of history, and a false ideal of the writer's function was established by the practice of men like Poggio.

It is obvious and easy to compare the humanists of the Renaissance with the sophists of antiquity. Whether we think of the rivals of Socrates at Athens, or of the Greek rhetoricians of the Roman period,[1] the parallel is tolerably

---

[1] 'Græculi esurientes.' Lives written by Philostratus.

close. From certain points of view the Italian scholars remind us of the former class; from others, again, they recall
the latter. The essence of sophism is the substitution of
semblance for reality, indifference to truth provided a fair
show be made, combined with verbal ingenuity and practice
in the art of exposition. The sophist feels no need of forming
opinions on a sound basis, or of adhering to principles. Regarding thought as the subject-matter of literary treatment,
he is chiefly concerned with giving it a fair and plausible investiture in language. Instead of recognising that he must
live up to the standard he professes, he takes delight in
expressing with force the contrary of what he acts. The discord between his philosophy and his conduct awakes no shame
in him, because it is the highest triumph of his art to persuade
by eloquence and to dazzle by rhetoric. Phrases and sentences supply the place of feelings and convictions. Sonorous
cadences and harmonies of language are always ready to
conceal the want of substance in his matter or the flimsiness
of his argument. At the same time the sophist's enthusiasm
for a certain form of culture, and his belief in the sophistic
method, may be genuine.

The literature of the Revival is full of such sophism.
Men who lived loose lives, were never tired of repeating the
commonplaces of the Ciceronian ethics, praising simplicity
and self-control with the pen they used for reproducing the
scandals of Martial, mingling impudent demands for money
and flatteries of debauched despots with panegyrics of Pætus
Thrasea and eulogies of Cincinnatus. Conversely, students of
eminent sobriety, like Guarino da Verona, thought it no harm
to welcome Beccadelli's 'Hermaphroditus' with admiration;
while the excellent Nicholas V. spent nine days in perusing
the filthy satires of Filelfo. It was enough that the form
was elegant, according to their standards of taste, the Latinity
copious and sound:—the subject-matter raised no scruples.

This vice of regarding only the exterior of literature produced a fatal weakness in the dissertations of the age. If a humanist wanted to moralise the mutability of fortune or the disadvantages of matrimony, he did not take the trouble to think, or the pains to borrow illustrations from his own experience. He strung together quotations and classical instances, expending his labour on the polish of the style, and fancying he had proved something by piquancy displayed in handling old material. When he undertook history, the same fault was apparent. Instead of seeking to set forth the real conditions of his native city, to describe its political vicissitudes and constitutional development, or to paint the characters of its great men, he prepared imaginary speeches and avoided topics incapable of expression in pure Latin. The result was that whole libraries of ethical disquisitions and historical treatises, bequeathed with proud confidence by their authors to the admiration of posterity, are now reposing in unhonoured dust, ransacked at rare intervals by weary students with restless fingers in search of such meagre scraps of information as even a humanist could not succeed in excluding.

The humanists resembled the sophists again in their profession to teach wisdom for pay. What philosophy was for the early Greeks, classic culture was for Italy in the Renaissance ; and this the scholars sold. Antiquity lay before them like an open book. From their seat among the learned they doled out the new lore of life to eager pupils. And as the more sober-minded of the Athenians regarded the educational practice of the sophists with suspicion, so the humanists came to be dreaded as the corrupters of youth. The peculiar turn they gave to mental training, by diverting attention from patriotic duties to literary pleasures, by denationalising the interests of students, and by distracting serious thought from affairs of the present to interests of the past, tended to confirm the political debility of the Italians ; nor can it be doubted that the substitution of Pagan for Christian ideals intensified the demoralisation of the age. Many arguments used by Aristophanes and Xenophon might be repeated against these sophists of the Renaissance.[1]

On this point it is worth observing that, though humanism took the Papal Court by storm and installed itself in pomp and pride within the Vatican, the lower clergy and the leaders of religious revivals, in no mere spirit of blind prejudice, but with solid force of argument, denounced it. S. Bernardino and Savonarola were only two among many who preached against the humanists from the pulpit. And yet, while we admit that the influences of the Revival injured morality, and gave a cosmopolitan direction to energies that ought to have been concentrated on the preservation of national existence, we are unable to join with these ecclesiastical antagonists in their crusade. Humanism was a necessary moment in the evolution of the modern world; and whatever were its errors, however weakening it may have been to Italy, this phase had to be passed through, this nation had to suffer for the general good.

The intrusion of the humanists into the Papal Curia was a victory of the purely secular spirit. It is remarkable how very few scholars took orders except with a view of holding minor benefices. They remained virtual laymen, drawing the emoluments of their cures at a distance. If Filelfo, after the death of his second wife, proposed to enter the Church, he did so because in his enormous vanity he hoped to gain the scarlet hat, and thought this worth the sacrifice of independence. The only great monastic *litteratus* was Ambrogio, General of the Camaldolese Order. Maffeo Vegio is the single instance I can remember of a poet-philologer who assumed the cowl. These statements, it will be understood,

---

[1] Aristoph., *Clouds*, Speeches of Dikaios Logos; Xen., *On Hunting*, chap. xiii.

refer chiefly to the second or aggressive period of the Revival. Classic erudition was so common in the fourth that to be without a humanistic tincture was, even among churchmen, the exception rather than the rule. In the age of Leo, moreover, the humanists as a class had ceased to exist, merged in the general culture of the nation. Their successors were for the most part cardinals and bishops, elevated to high rank for literary merit. This change, however, really indicated the complete triumph of an ideal that for a moment had succeeded in paganising the Papacy, and substituting its own standard of excellence for ecclesiastical tradition.

This external separation between the humanists and the Church corresponded to their deep internal irreligiousness. If contemporary testimony be needed to support this assertion, I may quote freely from Lilius Gyraldus, Battista Mantovano, and Ariosto, not to mention the invectives that record so vast a mass of almost incredible licentiousness. A rhetorical treatise, addressed to Gian Francesco Pico by Lilius Gyraldus, himself an eminent professor at Ferrara, acquaints us with the opinion formed in Italy, after a century's experience, of the vices and discordant lives of scholars.[1] ' I call God and men to witness,' he writes, ' whether it be possible to find men more affected by immoderate disturbances of soul, by such emotions as the Greeks called $\pi \acute{a} \theta \eta$, or by such desires as they named $\acute{o}\rho\mu a\grave{\iota}$, more easily influenced, driven about, and drawn in all directions. No class of human beings are more subject to anger, more puffed up with vanity, more arrogant, more insolent, more proud, conceited, idle-minded, inconsequent, opinionated, changeable, obstinate ; some of them ready to believe the most incredible nonsense, others sceptical about notorious truths, some full of doubt and suspicion, others void of reasonable circumspection. None are of a less free spirit, and that for the very reason I have touched before,

[1] *Progymnasma adversus Literatos. Op. Omn.*, Basle, 1582, vol. ii.

because they think themselves so far more powerful. They
all of them, indeed, pretend to omniscience, fancy themselves
superior to everything, and rate themselves as gods, while we
unlearned little men are made of clay and mud, as they
maintain.' Having for some space discoursed concerning their
mad ways of life, Gyraldus proceeds to arraign the humanists
in detail for vicious passions, want of economy, impiety,
gluttony, intemperance, sloth, and incontinence.[1] This
invective reads like a paradoxical thesis supported for the sake
of novelty by a clever rhetorician ; and, indeed, it might pass
for such were it not for the confirmation it receives in Ariosto's
seventh satire addressed to Pietro Bembo.[2] The poet, anxious
to find a tutor for his son, dares not commit the young man
to the care of a humanist. His picture of their personal
immorality, impiety, pride, and gluttony acquires weight
from the well-known tolerance of the satirist, and from his
genial parsimony of expression. To cite further testimony
from the personal confessions of Pacificus Maximus would
hardly strengthen the argument, though students may be
referred to his poems for details.[3]

The alternations of fortune to which the humanists
were exposed—living at one time in the lap of luxury,
caressed and petted ; then cast forth to wander in almost
total indigence, neglected and derided—encouraged a
Bohemian recklessness injurious to good manners. Their
frequent change of place told upon their character in the
same way, by exposing them to fresh temptations and with-
drawing them from censure. They had no country but the
dreamland of antiquity, no laws beyond the law of taste and

[1] 'Pudet me, Pice, pigetque id de literatis afferre quod omnium
tamen est in ore, nullos esse cum omnium vitiorum etiam nefandissi-
morum genere inquinatos magis, tum iis præcipue, quæ præter naturam
dicuntur,' &c.—*Progymnasma adversus Literatos*, p. 431.

[2] Lines 22–129.

[3] *Quinque Illustrium Poetarum Lusus in Venerem*, Parisiis, 1791,
p. 107.

inclination. They acknowledged no authority superior to their own exalted judgment; they bowed to no tribunal but that of posterity and the past. Thus they lived within their own conceits, outside of custom and opinion; nor was the world, at any rate before the period of their downfall, scrupulous to count their errors or correct their vices.

Far more important, however, than these circumstances was their passion for a Pagan ideal. The study of the classics and the effort to assimilate the spirit of the ancients, undermined their Christianity without substituting the religion or the ethics of the old world. They ceased to fear God; but they did not acquire either the self-restraint of the Greek or the patriotic virtues of the Roman. Thus exposed without defence or safeguard, they adopted the perilous attitude of men whose regulative principle was literary taste, who had left the ground of faith and popular convention for the shoals and shallows of an irrecoverable past. On this sea they wandered, with no guidance but the promptings of undisciplined self. It is not, therefore, a marvel that, while professing Stoicism, they wallowed in sensuality, openly affected the worst habits of Pagan society, and devoted their ingenuity to the explanation of foulness that might have been passed by in silence. Licentiousness became a special branch of humanistic literature. Under the thin mask of humane refinement leered the untamed savage; and an age that boasted not unreasonably of its mental progress, was at the same time notorious for the vices that disgrace mankind. These disorders of the scholars, hidden for a time beneath a learned language, ended by contaminating the genius of the nation. The vernacular *Capitoli* of Florence say plainly what Beccadelli, Poggio, and Bembo piqued themselves on veiling.

Another notable defect of the humanists, equally inseparable from the position they assumed in Italy, was

their personal and professional vanity. Battista Mantovano,
writing on the calamities of the age in which he lived,
reckons them among the most eminent examples of pride
in his catalogue of the deadly sins. Regarding themselves
as resuscitators of a glorious past and founders of a new
civility, they were not satisfied with asserting their real
merits in the sphere of scholarship. They went further,
and claimed to ·rank as sages, political philosophers, writers
of deathless histories, and singers of immortal verse. The
most miserable poetasters got crowned with laurels. The
most trivial thinkers passed verdict upon statecraft. Mis-
taking mere cultivation for genius, they believed that,
because they had perused the authors of antiquity and could
imitate Ovid at a respectful distance, their fame would endure
for all ages. On the strength of this confidence they gave
themselves inconceivable airs, looking down from the height
of their attainment on the profane crowd. To understand
that, after all, antiquity was a school wherein to train the
modern intellect for genuine production, was not given to
this epoch of discovery. Posterity has sadly belied their
expectations. Of all their treatises and commentaries, poems
and translations, how few are now remembered ; how rarely
are their names upon the lips of even professed students !
The debt of gratitude we owe them is indeed great, and
should be amply paid by our respectful memory of all they
wrought for us with labour in the field of learning. Yet
Filelfo would turn with passionate disappointment in his
grave, if he could know that men of wider scope and
sounder erudition appreciate his writings solely as shed
leaves that fertilised the soil of literature.

Before turning, as is natural at this point, to form an
estimate of the humanists in their capacity of authors, it
will be right briefly to qualify the condemnation passed upon
their characters. Taken as a class, they deserve the hardest

words that have been said of them. Yet it must not be forgotten that they numbered in their ranks such men as Ambrogio Traversari, Tommaso da Sarzana, Guarino, Jacopo Antiquari, Vittorino da Feltre, Pomponius Lætus, Ficino, Pico, Fabio Calvi, and Aldus Manutius. The bare enumeration of these names will suffice for those who have read the preceding chapters. Piety, sobriety of morals, self-devotion to public interests, the purest literary enthusiasm, the most lofty aspirations, fairness of judgment, and generosity of feeling distinguish these men, and some others who might be mentioned, from the majority of their fellows. Nor, again, is it fair to charge the humanists alone with vices common to their age. The picture I ventured to draw of Papal and despotic manners in a previous volume, shows that a too strict standard cannot be applied to scholars, holding less responsible positions than their patrons, and professing a far looser code of conduct. Much, too, of their inordinate vanity may be ascribed to the infatuation of the people. Such scenes as the reception of the supposed author of 'Hermaphroditus' in Vicénza were enough to turn the heads of even stronger men.[1]

It is difficult to appraise humanistic literature at a just value, seeing that by far the larger mass of it, after serving a purpose of temporary utility, is now forgotten. Not itself, but its effect, is what we have to estimate; and the ultimate product of the whole movement was the creation of a new capacity for cultivation. To have restored to Europe the knowledge of the classics, and to have recovered the style of the ancients, so as to use Latin prose and verse with freedom at a time when Latin formed an universal medium of culture, is the first real merit of the humanists. Nothing can rob them of this glory; however much we may be forced to feel that their critical labours have been superseded, that their

[1] See above, p. 185, note 4.

dissertations are dull, that their poems at the worst fall far
below the level of an Oxford prize exercise, and at the best
supply a decent appendix to the ' Corpus Poetarum.'   Nor can
we defraud them of the fame of having striven to realise
Petrarch's ideal.[1]   That ideal, only partially attained at any
single point, developed in one direction by Milton, in another
by Goethe, still guides, and will long guide, the efforts of the
modern intellect.

The most salient characteristic of this literature was
study of style.   The beginners of the humanistic movement
were conscious that what separated them more than anything else from their Roman ancestors, was want of elegance
in diction.   They used the same language; but they used it
clumsily.   They could think the same thoughts, but they
had lost the art of expressing them with propriety.   To
restore style was therefore a prime object.   Exaggerating its
importance, they neglected the matter for the form, and
ended by producing a literature of imitation.   The ideal they
proposed in composition included limpidity of language,
simplicity in the structure of sentences however lengthy,
choiceness of phrase, and a copious vocabulary.   To be
intelligible was the first requisite; to be attractive the
second.   Having mastered elementary difficulties, they proceeded to fix the rules for decorative writing.   Cicero had
said that nothing was so ugly or so common but that
rhetoric could lend it charm.   This unfortunate dictum,
implying that style, as separate from matter, is valuable
in and for itself, led the Italians astray.   To form commonplace books of phrases culled from the ' Tusculans ' and the
' Orations,' to choose some trivial theme for treatment, and
to make it the occasion for verbal display, became their
business.   In the coteries of Rome and Florence scholars
measured one another by their ingenuity—in other words,

[1] See above, Chapter II.

by their aptness for producing Ciceronian and Virgilian centos. Few indeed, like Pico, raised their voices against such trifling, or protested that what a man thought and felt was at least as important as his power of clothing it in rhetoric.

The appearance of Valla's ' Elegantiæ ' marked an epoch in the evolution of this stylistic art. It reached its climax in the work of Bembo. What the humanists intended, they achieved. Purity and perspicuity of language were made conditions of all literature that claimed attention ; nor is it, perhaps, too much to say that Racine, Pascal, and Voltaire owe something of their magic to the training of these worn-out pedagogues. Yet the immediate effect in Italy, when Machiavelli's vigour had passed out of the nation, and the stylistic tradition survived, was deplorable. Nothing strikes a northern student of the post-Renaissance authors more than the empty smoothness of their writing, their faculty of saying nothing with a vast expenditure of phrase, their dread of homely details, and the triviality of the subjects they chose for illustration. When a man of wit like Annibale Caro could rise to praise the nose of the president before a learned academy in periods of this ineptitude—' Naso perfetto, naso principale, naso divino, naso che benedetto sia fra tutti i nasi ; e benedetta sia quella mamma che vi fece così nasuto, e benedette tutte quelle cose che voi annusate ! ' [1] —we trace no more than a burlesque of humanistic seeking after style. It must, however, be admitted that it is not easy for a less artistic nation to do the Italians justice in this respect. They derived an æsthetic pleasure from refinements of speech and subtle flavours of expression, while they remained no less conscious than we are that the workman-

[1] ' Perfect nose, imperial nose, divine nose, nose to be blessed among all noses; and blessed be the breasts that made you with a nose so lordly, and blessed be all those things you put your nose to ! ' The above is quoted from Cantù's Storia della Letteratura Italiana. I have not seen the actual address.

ship surpassed the matter. The proper analogue to their rhetoric may be found in the exquisite but too unmeaning arabesques in marble and in wood, which belong to Cinque Cento architecture. Viewed as the playthings of skilled artists, these are not without their value; and we are apt, perhaps, unduly to depreciate them, because we lack the sense for their particular form of beauty.

If the most marked feature of humanistic literature was the creation of a Latin style, the supreme dictators were Cicero in prose and Virgil in verse. That Cicero should have fascinated the Italians in an age when art was dominant, when richness of decoration, rhetorical fluency, and pomp of phrase appealed to the liveliest instincts of a splendour-loving, sensitive, declamatory race, is natural. The Renaissance found exactly what it wanted in the manner of the most obviously eloquent of Latin authors, himself a rhetorician among philosophers, an orator among statesmen, the weakness of whose character was akin to that which lay at the root of fifteenth-century society. To be the 'apes of Cicero,' in all the branches of literature he had cultivated, was regarded by the humanists as a religious duty.[1] Though they had no place in the senate, the pulpit, or the law court, they were fain to imitate his oratory. Therefore public addresses to ambassadors, to magistrates on assuming office, and to Popes on their election; epithalamial and funeral discourses; panegyrics and congratulations—sounded far and wide through Italy. The fifteenth century was the golden age of speechification. A man was measured by the amount of fluent Latinity he could pour forth; copiousness of quotations secured applause; and readiness to answer on the spur of the moment in smooth Ciceronian phrases, was reckoned among the qualities that led to posts of trust in

[1] The phrase is eulogistically used by F. Villani in his *Life of Coluccio Salutato.*

Church and State. On the other hand, a failure of words on any ceremonial occasion passed for one of the great calamities of life. The common name for an envoy, *oratore*, sufficiently indicates the public importance attached to rhetoric. It formed a necessary part of the parade which the Renaissance loved, and, more than that, a part of its diplomatic machinery. To compose orations that could never be recited was a fashionable exercise ; and since the ' Verrines ' and the ' Philippics ' existed, no occasion was lost for reproducing something of their spirit in the invectives whereof so much has been already said. The emptiness of all this oratory, separated from the solid concerns of life, and void of actual value, tended to increase the sophistic character of literature. Eloquence, which ought to owe its force to passionate emotion or to gravity of meaning, degenerated into a mere play of words ; and to such an extent was verbal cleverness over-estimated, that a scholar could ascribe the fame of Julius Cæsar to his ' Commentaries ' rather than his victories.[1] It does not seem to have occurred to him that Pompey would have been glad if Cæsar had always wielded his pen, and that Brutus would hardly have stabbed a friendly man of letters. When we read a genuine humanistic speech, we find that it is principally composed of trite tales and citations. To play upon the texts of antiquity, as a pianist upon the keys of his instrument, was no small part of eloquence ; and the music sounded pleasant in ears greedy of the very titles of old writings. Vespasiano mentions that Carlo Aretino owed his early fame at Florence to one lecture, introducing references to all the classic authors.

The style affected for moral dissertation was in like manner Ciceronian. The dialogue in particular became fashionable ; and since it was dangerous to introduce matter unsuited to Tully's phrases, these disquisitions are usually devoid of local

[1] See Muratori, vol. xx. 442, 453.

colouring and contemporary interest. Few have such value
as attaches to the opening of Poggio's essay on Fortune, to
Valeriano's treatise on the misfortunes of the learned, or to
Giraldi's attack upon the humanists.

Another important branch of literature, modelled upon
Ciceronian masterpieces, was letter-writing. The epistolography of the humanists might form a separate branch of
study, if we cared to trace its history through several stages,
and to sift the stores at our disposal. Petrarch, after discover-
ing the familiar letters of the Roman orator, first gave an
impulse to this kind of composition. In his old age he tells
how he was laughed at in his youth for assuming the Latin
style of *thou* together with the Roman form of superscription.[1]
I have already touched upon the currency it gained through
the practice of Coluccio Salutato and the teaching of Gasparino
da Barzizza.[2] In course of time books of formulæ and polite
letter-writers were compiled, enabling novices to adopt the
Ciceronian mannerism with safety.[3] The Papal Curia sanctioned a set of precedents for the guidance of its secretaries,
while the epistles of eminent chancellors served as models
for the despatches of republican governments.

The private letters of scholars were useful in keeping up
communication between the several centres of culture in
Italy. From these sources too we now derive much interesting
information respecting the social life of the humanists. They
seem to have avoided political, theological, and practical
topics, cultivating a style of urbane compliment, exchanging
opinions about books, asking small favours, acknowledging

---

[1] *Epist. Rer. Senil.* xv. 1. 'Styli hujus per Italiam non auctor
quidem, sed instaurator ipse mihi videor, quo cum uti inciperem, adolescens a coætaneis irridebar, qui in hoc ipso certatim me postea sunt
secuti.'

[2] See above, pp. 76–78.

[3] Gian Maria Filelfo, son of the celebrated professor, published an
Epistolarium of this kind.

obligations, recommending friends to favourable notice, occasionally describing their mode of life, discussing the qualities
of their patrons with cautious reserve, but seeking above all
things to display grace of diction and elegant humour rather
than erudition. The fact that these Latin epistles were invariably intended for circulation and ultimate publication,
renders it useless to seek for insight from them into strictly
private matters.[1] For the historian the most valuable collections of Renaissance letters are composed in Italian, and are
not usually the work of scholars, but of agents, spies, and
envoys. Compared with the reports of the Venetian ambassadors, the correspondence of the humanists is unimportant.
In addition to familiar letters, it not unfrequently happened,
however, that epistles upon topics of public interest were
indited by students. Intended by their diffusion to affect
opinion, and addressed to influential friends or patrons, these
compositions assumed the form of pamphlets. Of this kind
were the letters on the Eastern question sent by Filelfo to
Charles VII. of France, to the Emperor, to Matthias Corvinus,
to the Dukes of Burgundy and Urbino, and to the Doge of
Venice. The immortality expected by the humanists from
their epistles, has hardly fallen to their lot; though much of
Poliziano's, Pico's, Antiquari's, and Piccolomini's correspondence is still delightful and instructive reading. The masses
extant in MS. exceed what has been printed; while the
printed volumes, with some rare exceptions, among which

---

[1] Francesco Filelfo, quoted in Rosmini's Life, vol. ii. pp. 304, 282,
448, writes, 'Le cose che non voglio sieno copiate, le scrivo sempre
alla grossolana.' 'Hoc autem scribendi more utimur iis in rebus
quarum memoriam nolumus transferre ad posteros. Et ethrusca
quidem lingua vix toti Italiæ nota est, at latina oratio longe ac late
per universum orbem est diffusa.' ('Matters I do not wish to have
copied I always write off in the vulgar. This style I use for such
things as I do not care to transmit to posterity. Tuscan, to be sure, is
hardly known to all Italians, while Latin is spread far and wide through
the whole world.')

may be mentioned Poliziano's letter to Antiquari on the death of Lorenzo, are only used by students.[1]

Since Cicero had left no specimen of history, the humanists were driven to follow other masters in this branch of literature. Livy was the author of their predilection. Cæsar supplied them with a model for the composition of commentaries, and Sallust for concise monographs. Suetonius was followed in such minute studies of character as Decembrio's 'Life of Filippo Maria Visconti.' I do not find that Tacitus had any thoroughgoing imitators; the magniloquence of rhetoric, rather than the pungency of sarcasm, suited the taste of the age. The faults of the humanistic histories have been already pointed out.[2]

The services of the humanists, as commentators, translators, critics of texts, compilers of grammars and dictionaries of all kinds, collectors of miscellaneous information, and writers on antiquities, still remain to be remembered. Their industry in this field was quite different from the labour they devoted to the perfecting of style. Whatever we may think of them as men of letters, we are bound to give their erudition almost unqualified praise. Not, indeed, that their learning any more than their literature was final. It too has been superseded; but it formed the basis of a sounder method, and rendered the attainment of more certain knowledge possible. It is not too much to say that modern culture, so far as it is derived from antiquity, owes everything to the indefatigable energy of the humanists. Before the age of printing, scholars had to store their memories with encyclopædic information, while the very want of a critical method, by preventing them from exactly discerning the good and the bad, enabled them to take a broader and more comprehensive view of classical

---

[1] See Voigt, pp. 421, 422, for an account of Filelfo's, Traversari's, Barbaro's, and Bruni's letters.

[2] See Vol. I., *Age of the Despots*, pp. 216, 217, and above, p. 377.

literature than is now at any rate common. Antiquity as a whole—not the authors merely of the Attic age or the Augustan—claimed their admiration; and though they devoted special study to Cicero and Virgil for the purposes of style, they eagerly accepted every Greek or Latin composition from the earliest to the latest. To this omnivorous appetite of the elder scholars we are perhaps indebted for the preservation of many fragments which a more delicate taste would have rejected. Certainly we owe to them the conception of the classics in their totality, as forming the proper source of culture for the human race. The purism of Vida and Bembo, though it sprang from more refined perceptions, was in some respects a retrogression from the wide and liberal erudition of their predecessors. Discipleship under Virgil may make a versifier; but he who would fain comprehend the Latin genius must know the poets of Rome from Ennius to Claudian.

Finally we have to render the tribute due to the humanists for their diffusion of a liberal spirit. Sustained by the enthusiasm of antiquity, they first ventured to take a standpoint outside catholicity; and though they made but bad use of this spiritual freedom, inclining to levity and godlessness instead of fighting the battle of the reason, yet their large and human survey of the world was in itself invigorating. Poggic at the Council of Constance regarded Jerome of Prague not as a heretic, not as a fanatic, but as a Stoic. In other words, he was capable of divesting his mind of temporary associations and conventional prejudices, and of discerning the true character of the man who suffered heroically for his opinions. This instance illustrates the general tone and temper of the humanists. Their study of antiquity freed them from the scholastic pedantries of theologians, and from the professional conceits of jurists and physicians. There is nothing great and noble in human nature that might not, we fancy, have

grown and thriven under their direction, if the circumstances
of Italy had been more favourable to high aspirations. As it
was, the light was early quenched and clouded by base vapours
of a sensual, enslaved, and priest-corrupted society. The
vital force of the Revival passed into the Reformation; the
humanists, degraded and demoralised, were superseded. Still
it was they who created the new atmosphere of culture,
wherein whatever is luminous in art, literature, science,
criticism, and religion has since flourished. Though we may
perceive that they obeyed a false authority—that of the classics,
and worshipped a false idol—style, yet modern liberty must
render them the meed of thanks for this. When we consider
that before the sixteenth century had closed, they had imbued
the whole Italian nation with their views, forming a new
literature, directing every kind of mental activity, and producing a new social tone, and furthermore that Italy in the
sixteenth century impressed her spirit on the rest of Europe,
we have a right to hail the humanists as the schoolmasters of
modern civilisation.

As schoolmasters in a stricter sense of the term, it is not
easy to exaggerate the influence exercised by Italian students.
They first conceived and framed the education that has now
prevailed through Europe for four centuries, moulding the
youth of divers nations by one common discipline, and establishing an intellectual concord for all peoples. In spite of
changes in government and creed, in spite of differences caused
by race and language, we have maintained an uniformity of
culture through the simultaneous prosecution of classic studies
on the lines laid down for teachers by the scholars of the
fifteenth century. The system of our universities and public
schools is in truth no other than that devised by Vittorino
and Guarino. Thus humanism in modern Europe has continued the work performed during the Middle Ages by the
Church, uniting in one confederation of spiritual activity

nations widely separated by all that tends to keep the human
families apart.

Until quite recently in England, the *litteræ humaniores*
were accepted as the soundest training for careers in Church
and State, for the learned professions, and for the private
duties of gentlemen. If the old ideal is yielding at last to
theories of a wider education based on science and on modern
languages, that is due partly to the extension of useful knowledge, and partly to the absorption of classic literature into
the modern consciousness. The sum of what a cultivated
man should know, in order to maintain a place among the
pioneers of progress, is so vast, that learners, distracted by a
variety of subjects, resent the expenditure of precious time
on Greek and Latin. Teachers, on the other hand, through
long familiarity with humane studies, have fallen into the
languor of routine. Besides, as knowledge in each new
department increases, the necessity of specialising with a
view to adopting a professional career, makes itself continually felt with greater urgency. It may therefore be
plausibly argued that we have outgrown the conditions of
humanism, and that a new stage in the history of education
has been reached. Have not the ancients done as much for
us as they can do ? Are not our minds permeated with their
thoughts ? Do not the masterpieces of modern literature
hold in solution the best that can be got from them for future
uses ?

These questions can perhaps be met by the counter-ques-
tion whether the arts and letters of the Greeks and Romans
will not always hold their own, not only in the formation of
pure taste, but also in the discipline of character and the
training of the intelligence. Just as well might we cease to
study the sacred books of the Jews, because we have incorporated their ethics into our conscience, and possess their
religion in our liturgy. No transmission of a spirit at second

or third hand can be the same as its immediate contact ; nor can we afford, however full our mental life may be, to lose the vivid sense of what men were and what they wrought in ages far removed from us, especially when those men were our superiors in certain spheres. Again, it may be doubted whether we should understand the masterpieces of modern literature, when we came to be separated from the sources of their inspiration. If Olympus connoted less than Asgard, or Hercules were no more familiar to our minds than Rustem, or the horses of the Sun stood at the same distance from us as the cows of Indra—if, in fact, we abandoned Greek as much as we have abandoned Scandinavian, Persian, and Sanskrit mythology, would not some of the most brilliant images of our own poets fade into leaden greyness, like clouds that have lost the flush of living light upon them ?

It is therefore not improbable that for many years to come the higher culture of the race will still be grounded upon humanism : true though it be that the first enthusiasm for antiquity shall never be restored, nor the classics yield that vital nourishment they offered in the spring-time of the modern era. For average students, who have no special vocation for literature and no æsthetic tastes, it may well happen that new methods of teaching the classics will have to be invented. Why should they not be read in English versions, and the time expended upon Greek and Latin grammar be thus saved ? The practice of Greek and Latin versification has been virtually doomed already ; nor is there any reason why Latin prose should form a necessary part of education in an age that has ceased to publish its thoughts in a now completely dead language. Our actual relation to the ancients, again, justifies some change. We know far more about them now than in the period of the Renaissance ; but they are no longer all in all for civilised humanity, eager to reconstitute the realm of thought, and find its nobler self anew in the image of a glorious past, reconquered and inalien-able. The very culture created by the study of antiquity through the last four centuries stands between them and our apprehension, so that they seem at the same moment more distinct from us and more a part of our familiar selves.

When we seek the causes which produced the decay of learning in Italy about the middle of the sixteenth century, we are first led to observe that the type of scholarship in-augurated by Petrarch had been fully developed. Nothing new remained to be worked out upon the lines laid down by him. Meanwhile the forces of the nation, both creative and receptive, were exhausted in the old fields of humanism. The reading public had been glutted with epistles, invectives, poems, orations, histories of antiquities, and disquisitions of all kinds. The matter of the ancient literatures had been absorbed, if superficially, at least entirely, and their forms had been reproduced with wearisome reiteration. The Paganism that had so long ruled as a fashion, was now passing out of vogue, because of its inadequacy to meet the deeper wants and satisfy the aspirations of the modern world. The humanists, moreover, as a class, had fallen into disrepute through faults and vices whereof enough has been already said. Nothing short of the new impulse which a new genius, equal at least in power to Petrarch, might have communicated, could have given a fresh direction to the declining enthusiasm for antiquity. But for this display of energy the Italians were not prepared. As in the ascent of some high peak, the traveller, after surmounting pine woods and Alpine pastures, comes upon bare grassy slopes that form an intermediate region between the basements of the mountain and the snow-fields overhead, so the humanists had accomplished the first stage of learning. But it requires a fresh start and the employment of other faculties to scale the final heights ; and for this the force was wanting. Erasmus, at the opening of the century, had, indeed, initiated a second age of scholarship. The more exact methods of criticism and comparison were already about to be instituted by the French, the Germans, and the Dutch. It was too much, however, to expect that the Italians, who had expended their vigour in recovering the classics and reviving a passion for knowledge, should compete upon the ground of modern erudition with these fresh and untried races.

What they might have done, if circumstances had been less unfavourable, and if the way of progress had been free before them, cannot be conjectured. As it was, all things contributed to the decline of intellectual energy in Italy. The distracting wars of half a century told more heavily upon the literati, who depended for their very existence upon the liberality of patrons, than on any other section of the people. What miseries they endured in Lombardy may be gathered from the prefaces and epistles of Aldus Manutius; while the blow inflicted on them by the sack of Rome is vividly described by Valeriano.[1] When comparative peace was restored, liberty had been extinguished. Florence, the stronghold of liberal learning, was enslaved. Scholarship no less than art suffered from the loss of political independence. Rome, terror-stricken by the Reformation, turned with rage against the very studies she had helped to stimulate. The engines of the Inquisition, wielded with all the mercilessness of panic by men who had the sombre cruelty of Spain to back them up, destroyed the germs of life in science and philosophy.

To some extent, again, the Italian scholars had prepared their own suicide by tending more and more to subtleties of taste and affectations of refinement. The purism of the sixteenth century was itself a sort of etiolation, and the puerilities

---

[1] See above, p. 321.

of the academies distracted even able men from serious
studies. It was one of the inevitable drawbacks of humanism
that the new culture separated men of letters from the nation.
Dante and the wool-carders of the fourteenth century understood each other; there was then no thick veil of erudition
between the teacher and the taught. But neither Bembo
nor Pomponazzi had anything to say that could be comprehended by the common folk. Therefore scholarship was left
in mournful isolation; suspected, when it passed from trifles
to grave speculations, by the Church; viewed with indifference
by the peoplē; unsustained by any sympathy, and, what was
worse, without a programme or a watchword. The thinkers,
whose biography belongs to the history of the Counter-
Reformation in Italy, were all solitary men, voices crying in
the wilderness with none to listen, bound together by no
common bond, unnoticed by the nation, extinguished singly
on the scaffold by an ever-watchful league of tyrants spiritual
and political.

Before the end of the sixteenth century Greek had almost
ceased to be studied in Italy. This was the sign of intellectual death. All that was virile in humanism fled beyond the
Alps. This transference of intellectual supremacy from Italy
to Germany was speedily accomplished. 'When I was a boy,'
said Erasmus,[1] 'sound letters had begun to revive among the
Italians; but by reason of the printer's art being as yet undiscovered or known to few, no books had reached us, and in
the deep tranquillity of dulness there reigned a set of men
who taught in all our towns the most illiterate learning.
Rodolph Agricola was the first to bring to us from Italy some
breath of a superior culture.' Again, he says of Italy, 'In
that land, where even the very walls are both more learned
and more eloquent than men with us; so that what here

---

[1] See the passages quoted by Tiraboschi, vol. vi. lib. iii. cap. v. 71.

seems beautifully said, and elegant and full of charm, cannot
be held for aught but clumsy, stupid, and uncultivated there.'
Less than half a century after Erasmus had gained the right
to hold the balance thus between the nations of the North
and South—that is, in 1540 or thereabouts—Paolo Giovio,
at the close of his 'Elogia Literaria,' while speaking of the
Germans, felt obliged to confess that 'not only Latin letters,
to our disgrace, but Greek and Hebrew also have passed into
their territory by a fatal simultaneous migration.'

Thus Italy, after receiving the lamp of learning from the
dying hands of Hellas, in the days of her own freedom, now,
in the time of her adversity and ruin, gave it to the nations
of the North. Her work was ended. Three centuries of
increasing decrepitude, within our recent memory at length
most happily surmounted, were before her. Can history, we
wonder, furnish a spectacle more pathetic than that of the
protagonist of spiritual liberty falling uneasily asleep beneath
the footstool of the Spaniard and the churchman, while the
races who had trampled her to death went on rejoicing in the
light and culture she had won by centuries of toil ? This is
the tragic aspect of the subject which has occupied us through
the present volume. At the conclusion of the whole matter
it is, however, more profitable to remember, not the intellectual death of Italy, but what she wrought in that bright
period of her vigour. She was the divinely appointed birthplace of the modern spirit, the workshop of knowledge for
all Europe, our mistress in the arts and sciences, the Alma
Mater of our student years, the well-spring of mental freedom
and activity after ages of stagnation. If greater philosophers
have since been produced by Germany and France and England, greater scholars, greater men of science, greater poets
even, and greater pioneers of progress in the lands divined
by Christopher Columbus beyond the seas—this must not
blind us to the truth that at the very outset of the era in

which we live and play our parts, Italy embraced all philosophy, all scholarship, all science, all art, all discovery, alone.
Such is the Lampadephoria, or torch-race, of the nations.
Greece stretches forth her hand to Italy; Italy consigns the
sacred fire to Northern Europe; the people of the North pass
on the flame to America, to India, and the Australasian
isles.

NEW CAPRICORN BOOKS

15. *Anton Chekhov*, ST. PETER'S DAY AND OTHER TALES. For the first time in English, here is a hilarious collection of early Chekhov stories and sketches. Resembling Dickens, Gogol and the Keystone Kops in their comic method, these stories will undoubtedly consolidate Chekhov's growing reputation as a major comic writer. Translated by Frances H. Jones. *A Putnam Capricorn Original.* 224 pp. $1.25 (Hardcover, $2.50).

16. *Thomas Nashe*, THE UNFORTUNATE TRAVELLER, OR JACK WILTON. Edited, with an Introduction, by John Berryman. Illustrated by Michael Ayrton. "The first novel in English" is the claim that has been made for this wonderful book. Published in 1594, it displays Nashe's madly inventive prose style, which has been compared to the style of Joyce's FINNEGANS WAKE, and Nashe's uncanny ability to create marvellously alive personalities. Of the first importance in the history of the novel. *A Putnam Capricorn Original.* 128 pp. $1.15 (Hardcover $2.50).

17. *Simone Weil*, WAITING FOR GOD. With an Introduction by Leslie Fiedler. T. S. Eliot said of it, "This book, by the late Simone Weil, is almost too important to be included in one's list of preferred reading for one year only." Andre Gide said, "It is clear that Mlle. Weil is the most truly spiritual writer of this century." 240 pp. $1.25.

18. *Robert M. Coates*, THE EATER OF DARKNESS, by the author of THE HOUR BEFORE WESTERLY. It is difficult to describe this superb novel adequately, but it can be said that it is written in an experimental style resembling that of the early Dos Passos and the style of the Nighttown scene in ULYSSES. It was originally published in Paris more than thirty years ago, and it has been called every-

thing from "a great comic adventure" to "the first surrealist novel in English." Completely revised for this edition by Mr. Coates, it contains an introduction by him giving in detail the circumstances of its composition and his intentions in writing it. *A Putnam Capricorn Original.* 128 pp. $.95.

19a, and 19b. *James Viscount Bryce*, THE AMERICAN COMMONWEALTH. Completely edited, abridged and introduced by Louis Hacker, Professor of Economics, Columbia University, and former Dean of the School of General Studies. A completely new edition of this great work on the American system of government. Always mentioned in the same breath with De Tocqueville's earlier work, Lord Bryce's superb study of the American commonwealth has been edited for Capricorn by a distinguished American scholar and historian for the present age. *A Putnam Capricorn Original.* 2 vols. $1.35 each (Hardcover, 1 vol. $5.00).

20. *George Moore*, CONFESSIONS OF A YOUNG MAN, A famous book by a most unusual man, this memoir concerns Moore's life in the Paris of the Nineties, when he lived a rich and crowded existence in his apartment in the *Rue de la Tours des Dames* (an unusually appropriate name), "with all its charming adjuncts, palms and pastels, my cat, my python, my friends, blonde hair and dark." It also details Moore's friendships with the Decadent and Symbolist writers, and with Manet, Degas and Renoir. This account sums up the artistic life of the Nineteenth Century, and was a prime influence on Ezra Pound, T. S. Eliot and James Joyce. 288 pp. $1.25.

OTHER CAPRICORN BOOKS

1. *John Dewey*, ART AS EXPERIENCE. 384 pp. $1.35.

2. *Rainer Maria Rilke*, NOTEBOOKS OF MALTE LAURIDS BRIGGE. 256 pp. $1.15.

3. *Alfred Adler*, WHAT LIFE SHOULD MEAN TO YOU. 320 pp. $1.25.

4. *Clive Bell*, ART. 192 pp. $1.25.

5. *Alfred North Whitehead*, MODES OF THOUGHT. 256 pp. $1.15.

6. *Henry Adams*, DEGRADATION OF THE DEMOCRATIC DOGMA. With an Introduction by Brooks Adams. 320 pp. $1.25.

7. *Frederick Law Olmsted*, THE SLAVE STATES (BEFORE THE CIVIL WAR). Edited, with an Introduction, by Harvey Wish, author of SOCIETY AND THOUGHT IN AMERICA. 256 pp. $1.25 (Hardcover $2.50).

8. THE AUTOBIOGRAPHY OF THOMAS JEFFERSON. With an Introduction by Dumas Malone. 128. pp. $.95 (Hardcover $2.50).

9. NEWS AND RUMOUR IN RENAISSANCE EUROPE — THE FUGGER NEWSLETTERS. Edited by George T. Matthews. 256 pp. $1.25 (Hardcover $2.50).

10. *Graham Hough*, THE DARK SUN: A STUDY OF D. H. LAWRENCE. 272 pp. $1.25.

11. COLERIDGE'S WRITINGS ON SHAKESPEARE. Edited by Terence Hawkes. With an Introduction by Alfred Harbage. 256 pp. $1.35. (Hardcover $2.50).

12. *George Bernard Shaw*, THE ADVENTURES OF THE BLACK GIRL IN HER SEARCH FOR GOD. Illustrations by John Farleigh. 98 pp. $.95. (Hardcover $2.50).

13. *Alfred North Whitehead*, SYMBOLISM. 98 pp. $.95.

14. *William Golding*, LORD OF THE FLIES. With a biographical and critical note by E. L. Epstein. 256 pp. $1.25.

G. P. PUTNAM'S SONS

210 Madison Avenue • New York 16, N. Y.

E DUE

DEC 1 6 1977	
	PRINTED IN U.S.A.